The Origin of Ratha-yātrā

śrī śrī guru-gaurāṅgau jayataḥ

The Origin of Ratha-yātrā

a compilation of lectures by

ŚRĪ ŚRĪMAD BHAKTIVEDĀNTA NĀRĀYAṆA MAHĀRĀJA

Vṛndāvana, Uttar Pradesh, India

OTHER TITLES BY ŚRĪLA NĀRĀYAṆA MAHĀRĀJA:

The Nectar of Govinda-līlā
Going Beyond Vaikuṇṭha
Bhakti-rasāyana
Śrī Śikṣāṣṭaka
Veṇu-gīta
Śrī Prabandhāvalī
Śrī Bhakti-rasāmṛta-sindhu-bindu
Śrī Manaḥ-śikṣā
Bhakti-tattva-viveka
Pinnacle of Devotion
Śrī Upadeśāmṛta
Arcana-dīpikā
The Essence of All Advice
Śrī Gauḍīya Gīti-guccha
Dāmodara-līlā-madhurī
Śrīmad Bhagavad-gītā
Śrīmad Bhakti Prajñāna Keśava Gosvāmī – His Life and Teachings
Five Essential Essays
Śrī Harināma Mahā-mantra
Secret Truths of the Bhāgavata
Jaiva-dharma
Śrī Vraja-maṇḍala Parikramā
Śrī Bhajana-rahasya
Śrī Brahma-saṁhitā
Rays of the Harmonist (periodical)

For further information, please visit www.igvp.com or www.gaudiya.net

ISBN 81-86737-13-8

First printing – 5000 copies, June 2003

CONTENTS

	Preface	*i*
	Acknowledgements	*v*
	Introduction	*vii*
	Maṅgalācaraṇa	*xv*
CHAPTER 1:	The First History	*1*
CHAPTER 2:	The Second History	*17*
CHAPTER 3:	Guṇḍicā-mandira-mārjana	*41*
CHAPTER 4:	Mahāprabhu and King Pratāparudra	*71*
CHAPTER 5:	Reunion at Kurukṣetra	*99*
CHAPTER 6:	Kṛṣṇa meets the Gopīs at Kurukṣetra	*123*
CHAPTER 7:	Herā-pañcamī	*187*
CHAPTER 8:	The Third History	*225*
CHAPTER 9:	Just after the Festival	*241*
CHAPTER 10:	The Relationship between Jagannātha Purī and Navadvīpa	*259*
CHAPTER 11:	Closing Words	*287*
	Appendix	*305*
	Glossary	*315*
	Verse Index	*337*

PREFACE

Our most worshipable Śrī Śrīmad Bhaktivedānta Nārāyaṇa Mahārāja began to preach in the West in 1996. In July 1997, he began to observe the Ratha-yātrā Festival in the West along with his followers, at the same time that it was taking place in Jagannātha Purī. The festival was observed in Holland in 1997; in England in 1998; in France, England, and Holland in 1999; in Wales in 2000; and again in England in 2001 and 2002.

On one occasion, when Śrīla Mahārāja was addressing his international audience, he gave the following explanation for his traveling and holding these festivals: "Today is *pratipat*, one day before Ratha-yātrā. I remember when Śrīla Prabhupāda Bhaktivedānta Swāmī Mahārāja called for me in his last days. He was going to join his Rādhā and Kṛṣṇa in Goloka Vṛndāvana, and He requested me to help the many devotees whom he had brought from both Western and Eastern countries. In those last days he also requested me to place him into *samādhi*, which I did. There is no difference between *śikṣā-guru* and *dīkṣā-guru* if they are both qualified; and Śrīla Swāmī Mahārāja is my *śikṣā-guru*, so I must obey his order. That is why I am traveling around the world in my old age, by the combined mercy of my *dīkṣā-* and *śikṣā-gurus*, without any desire for worldly profit."

During each Ratha-yātrā Festival, Śrīla Mahārāja thanked and blessed the devotees for participating. In 1997, seeing the success of the festivities, he told his audience, "Previously, I observed Jagannātha Ratha-yātrā Festival in Mathurā every year. I am not there this year, but I am glad that you have helped me to make a festival here. You were all joining in the *kīrtanas*, and all of you were happy, so I think you'll have the grace of Jagannātha."

In each such week-long festival, Śrīla Mahārāja discussed the quintessence of *Śrīmad-Bhāgavatam* and *Śrī Caitanya-caritāmṛta*. He explained that entering into the deep meaning of Ratha-yātrā enables the devotee to realize the mission of Śrī Caitanya Mahāprabhu, the secret truths of the *tattva* (philosophical truths) and *līlā* (pastimes) of Rādhā-Kṛṣṇa, and the ultimate goal of serving Them. Toward the end of one of his Ratha-yātrā lectures, Śrīla Mahārāja told his audience, "You are lucky to hear all these topics; it is rare that one possesses the good fortune to hear all these truths. Try to take something from what you are hearing. If you take only a hundred-thousandth part of this teaching of Śrī Caitanya Mahāprabhu, you will be fully successful in life. I have come here only to give you inspiration, and all of you who have assembled here are certainly very fortunate."

It was in France, in 1999, that Śrīla Mahārāja first brought up the idea of publishing this book. After relating the first history of Lord Jagannātha's appearance, he told his audience, "I wanted to publish the history of Ratha-yātrā in *Bhāgavata Patrikā* and *Gauḍīya Patrikā*, our Hindi and Bengali monthly magazines. Now I am thinking that I should make an entire book on this subject, explaining the three reasons behind Jagannātha's appearance. It will be very interesting and helpful for all devotees."

Among the Ratha-yātrā Festivals mentioned above, the largest thus far was held in Birmingham on June 24, 2001. Here are some excerpts from a report on the festival, published on www.vnn.org:

> The cart procession proceeded to Victoria Square, where a large pavilion had been set up. The organizers of the event, the devotees of the Birmingham Gour-Govinda Gauḍīya Maṭha, also set up a mini-fair just in front of the pavilion, with stalls manned by the local devotees and their friends from many diverse groups. The fair was thus billed, "A Universal Interfaith Gathering," in honor of the Lord of the Universe, Lord Jagannātha.
>
> Birmingham dignitaries who attended the festival included the Council General of the Indian Consulate, the Deputy Mayor of Birmingham, and the president of the National Council of Hindu Temples and Vice Co-chairman of Interfaith Network U.K. Before Śrīla Nārāyaṇa Mahārāja gave his own talk, they gave speeches in the presence of Śrīla Mahārāja, his devotees, and the thousands of guests. They expressed appreciation for Śrīla Mahārāja's message and the importance of the devotees' efforts in bringing Lord Jagannātha to the people of Birmingham. Ms. Wood of Life Foundation Worldwide had brought the world peace flame, which had traveled around the world to five continents and had been presented to the Pope, Nelson Mandela, and others who were considered instrumental in bringing about world peace, and she presented it to Śrīla Mahārāja with honor.

The material that comprises this book was taken solely from public lectures that Śrīla Nārāyaṇa Mahārāja spoke in English on his world preaching tours during the years 1997–2002. Some of the chapters consist of entire lectures. Others are compilations of different lectures and parts of lectures, and they are divided by subtitles. In presenting this material, for the most part we have tried to follow the sequence of the events as they are presented

in *Śrī Caitanya-caritāmṛta, Madhya-līlā*, Chapters 12–15, which elaborately describe the Ratha-yātrā pastimes of Caitanya Mahāprabhu and His devotees.

Please forgive us fallen conditioned souls for any mistakes we may have made in presenting Śrīla Mahārāja's teachings in this book.

An aspirant for eternal service to the Vaiṣṇavas,

ŚYĀMARĀṆĪ DĀSĪ

Pāpa-mocanī Ekādaśī
March 28, 2003
Gopīnātha-bhavana, Śrī Vṛndāvana

ACKNOWLEDGEMENTS

Editorial advisors: Śrīpāda Bhaktivedānta Mādhava Mahārāja, Brajanātha dāsa
Editors: Śyāmarāṇī dāsī, Jñāna dāsa Vanacārī, Prema-vilāsa dāsa
Sanskrit Editors: Śrīpāda Bhaktivedānta Bhāgavata Mahārāja, Atula-kṛṣṇa dāsa
Proofreaders: Śānti dāsī, Lavaṅga-latā dāsī, Giridhārī dāsa Brahmacārī
Manuscript Coordinator: Sulatā dāsī
Layout and design: Kṛṣṇa-prema dāsa
Typesetting: Prema-vilāsa dāsa
Typists: Mana-mohana dāsa, Sulatā dāsī, Sāvitrī dāsī, Rādhikā dāsī, Premavatī dāsī, Anaṅga dāsī, Lalitā-kiśorī dāsī
Glossary: Śānti dāsī, Sulatā dāsī

Most of the Sanskrit and Bengali verses and their translations quoted from *Śrī Caitanya-caritāmṛta*, *Śrīmad-Bhāgavatam*, and other scriptures were taken from the Bhaktivedānta Vedabase folio. Special thanks to the Bhaktivedānta Book Trust for its kind permission to use these invaluable reference quotes.

The many other devotees who have helped with the production of *The Origin of Ratha-yātrā* are too numerous to name here, but Kṛṣṇa and His associates know who they are.

INTRODUCTION

In Birmingham, England, on July 22, 2001, the first day of his visit there and the first day of his series of classes on Ratha-yātrā, Śrīla Bhaktivedānta Nārāyaṇa Mahārāja gave a commencement address that heralded the arrival of the festival. He began his class by glorifying the many well-decorated deities that he saw on the altar.

Today I have become very happy. When I first sent the deity of Śrī Caitanya Mahāprabhu from Navadvīpa to England, I was very worried that He would be quite alone there. But now that I have come here, I see a great *utsava* (festival) surrounding Him. He is not at all alone here. He is in the Gambhīrā and He is absorbed in the Chariot Festival. Jagannātha, Baladeva, and Subhadrā are here, Nityānanda Prabhu and all his associates are here, and even Girirāja-Govardhana and all the associates of Vṛndāvana are here. Vasanta-ṛtu (springtime) is here, as the scene is full with yellow flowers, and Caitanya Mahāprabhu is very happy here, weeping, "O My Prāṇanātha, where are You? O Kṛṣṇa, where are You? Today I am meeting You after a long time; after a long separation."

sei ta parāṇa-nātha pāinu
yāhā lāgi' madana-dahane jhuri' genu

Śrī Caitanya-caritāmṛta (*Madhya-līlā* 13.113)

Now I have gained the Lord of My life, in whose absence I was being burned by Cupid and was withering away.

Today is the observance of *guṇḍicā-mandira-mārjana*; it is the day to cleanse our hearts. Caitanya Mahāprabhu wanted to make a seat for Jagannatha, Baladeva, and Subhadrā – especially for Vrajendra-nandana Muralīdhara Navakiśora Naṭavara. When He was in Jagannātha's temple He never saw Jagannātha, Baladeva, and Subhadrā. Rather, He always saw Vrajendra-nandana Śyāmasundara playing a flute and wearing peacock feathers in His turban.

Early this morning, Caitanya Mahāprabhu departed for the Guṇḍicā Mandira with His entire group of associates, headed by Nityānanda Prabhu, Advaita Ācārya, Gadādhara Paṇḍita, Svarūpa Dāmodara, Rāya Rāmānanda, Kāśī Miśra, and so many others. He took all the Gauḍīya *bhaktas* from Bengal, Oriyā *bhaktas* from Orissa, and all the others, and He requested Kāśī Miśra, "Tell the King that, together with My associates, I want to wash the whole temple and surrounding area. He should not send any of his own servants. We will do all the cleaning ourselves, and then we will observe a grand Ratha-yātrā Festival. The King can help from outside."

Mahāprabhu Himself took many brooms and clay pots. Starting from Gambhīrā, and performing *kīrtana*, He walked through Jagannātha Purī and finally reached the Guṇḍicā Mandira. We also went there many times with our *gurudeva*, Śrī Śrīmad Bhakti Prajñāna Keśava Gosvāmī, along with over 500 other devotees, and during Mahāprabhu's participation there were thousands of parties in that very big area, with hundreds of people in each party.

On this day you should try to clean your hearts, for there are so many dirty and unwanted things there. We must try to be careful to avoid the ten *nāma-aparādhas*, and also *vaiṣṇava-*

aparādha, *dhāma-aparādha*, *seva-aparādha*, and so on. After that, our many unwanted habits, especially lust and anger, should be driven from our hearts. *Bhakti* can never manifest if lust and anger are present, because *bhakti* is very soft, mild, and especially sweet.

What is the meaning of *kuṭīnāṭī*? You should at once try to give up *ku* (bad habits and activities), those things that are not favorable for *kṛṣṇa-bhakti*. You must give up even those activities, objects and persons that are very near and dear to you, if they are not favorable. *Nāṭī* means those things that are forbidden for *bhakti*, and they are discussed in the first and second verses of *Upadeśāmṛta*:

vāco vegaṁ manasaḥ krodha-vegaṁ
jihvā-vegam udaropastha-vegam
etān vegān yo viṣaheta dhīraḥ
sarvām apīmāṁ pṛthivīṁ sa śiṣyāt

A wise and self-composed person can instruct the entire world if he can subdue the impetus to speak, the agitation of the mind, the onset of anger, the vehemence of the tongue, the urge of the belly and the agitation of the genitals. In other words, everyone may become a disciple of such a self-composed person.

atyāhāraḥ prayāsaś ca
prajalpo niyamāgrahaḥ
jana-saṅgaś ca laulyaṁ ca
ṣaḍbhir bhaktir vinaśyati

Bhakti is destroyed by the following six faults: (1) eating too much, or collecting more than necessary; (2) endeavors that are opposed to *bhakti*; (3) useless mundane talks; (4) failure to adopt essential regulations, or fanatical adherence to regulations; (5) association with persons who are opposed to *bhakti*; and (6) greed, or the restlessness of the mind to adopt worthless opinions.

You will also have to give up all worship of demigods. As Caitanya Mahāprabhu instructed Rūpa Gosvāmī, this should be uprooted, along with all varieties of worldly desires.

You can even give up *nārāyaṇa-sevā*, service to Nārāyaṇa in Vaikuṇṭha, as well as *dvārakādhīśa-sevā*, service to Kṛṣṇa in Dvārakā. Offer *praṇama* to Dvārakādhīśa and say, "You are the same Kṛṣṇa, but do You have a flute or peacock feather? Can You accept Nanda as Your father and Yaśodā as Your mother?" If He cannot show all these qualifications, then our attitude toward Him will be, "I offer *daṇḍavat-praṇāma* unto You, but from far away."

Offer more *praṇāma* to Mathureśa-Kṛṣṇa, and still more to Yaśodā-nandana Kṛṣṇa. Offer *praṇāma* to Dāmodara-Kṛṣṇa. We want to serve Dāmodara, but which Dāmodara? We want to serve Rādhā-Dāmodara. We like Śrīdāmā, Subala, Madhumaṅgala, and all of Kṛṣṇa's friends. We like the fact that they are Kṛṣṇa's friends, but we don't want them to be our friends, because we do not want to be cowherd boys in our perfectional stage. Beyond that, we offer *praṇāma* to Kṛṣṇa as the beloved of the *aṣṭa-sakhīs*, but we actually want only one thing. We want to serve the mood of Śrī Rūpa Mañjarī. If you can have a taste for this service, and if you can make this your objective, then your life will be successful.

Śrīla Swāmī Mahārāja came to Western countries and introduced the Ratha-yātrā Festival, but after his departure many of his disciples began doing something wrong; they have chosen a wrong path, and they do not honor senior devotees. They have so much opulence, and their gatherings are quite large in number, but they have no mood of *rati*, transcendental love and affection. The actual mood of Ratha-yātrā was shown by Śrīla Bhaktivedānta Swāmī Mahārāja in his translation of *Śrī Caitanya-caritāmṛta*. In the mood of Śrīmatī Rādhikā meeting Kṛṣṇa at Kurukṣetra, Caitanya Mahāprabhu said:

sei ta parāṇa-nātha pāinu
yāhā lāgi' madana-dahane jhuri' genu

Śrī Caitanya-caritāmṛta (*Madhya-līlā* 13.113)

Now I have gained the Lord of My life, in whose absence I was being burned by Cupid and was withering away.

Mahāprabhu also sang this song:

yaḥ kaumāra-haraḥ sa eva hi varas tā eva caitra-kṣapās
te conmīlita-mālatī-surabhayaḥ prauḍhāḥ kadambānilāḥ
sā caivāsmi tathāpi tatra surata-vyāpāra-līlā-vidhau
revā-rodhasi vetasī-taru-tale cetaḥ samutkaṇṭhate

Śrī Caitanya-caritāmṛta (*Antya-līlā* 1.78)

That very personality who stole my heart during my youth is now again my master. These are the same moonlit nights of the month of Caitra. The same fragrance of *mālatī* flowers is there, and the same sweet breezes are blowing from the *kadamba* forest. In our intimate relationship, I am also the same lover, yet still my mind is not happy here. I am eager to go back to that place on the bank of the Revā under the Vetasī tree. That is my desire.

Mahāprabhu had taken this song from a Sanskrit book named *Sāhitya-darpaṇa.* Although it was a mundane love song, which appealed to lusty people, Mahāprabhu was singing it with His heart melting and tears in His eyes. Śrī Svarūpa Dāmodara understood His deep mood, and there was a boy named Rūpa, the Rūpa of Mahāprabhu, who also understood it. After watching Mahāprabhu, he at once wrote a poem in the same mood in which Mahāprabhu was singing, and that poem was very high-class:

priyaḥ so 'yaṁ kṛṣṇaḥ saha-cari kuru-kṣetra-militas
tathāhaṁ sā rādhā tad idam ubhayoḥ saṅgama-sukham
tathāpy antaḥ-khelan-madhura-muralī-pañcama-juṣe
mano me kālindī-pulina-vipināya spṛhayati

Śrī Caitanya-caritāmṛta (*Antya-līlā* 1.79)

My dear friend, now I have met My old and dear friend Kṛṣṇa on this field of Kurukṣetra. I am the same Rādhārāṇī, and now we are meeting together. It is very pleasant, but I would still like to go to the bank of the Yamunā beneath the trees of the forest there. I wish to hear the vibration of His sweet flute playing the fifth note within that forest of Vṛndāvana."

Rādhārāṇī told Kṛṣṇa, "Oh, My beloved is here, I am here Myself, and we are meeting here; but there is so much opulence here. I want to be by the bank of the Yamunā again, where the *kadamba* trees emanate a sweet fragrance and where the beautiful spring season is present. No one is there; it is a secluded place. My beloved and I are both there, and we are speaking about so many things. I want to be there again."

This parallel verse of Śrīla Rūpa Gosvāmī, so much greater than the verse in *Sāhitya-darpaṇa,* is the mood of the Ratha-yātrā Festival. If this Chariot Festival is performed under the guidance of a high-class devotee, then it is really Ratha-yātrā.

Prior to Caitanya Mahāprabhu, the Ratha-yātrā Festival had been taking place for many thousands of years, since ancient times. There was not so much *rasa* in it, however, for the King was observing it alone, with the help of so much money, and with only his own people. But now, by the presence of Mahāprabhu, the entire public was able to participate. Moreover, Mahāprabhu brought all the moods of Vṛndāvana, especially separation and meeting after separation, and He instructed us in so many ways.

Gradually, in seven days, I will try to explain all these truths so that you can develop greed to obtain this highest goal of life: service to Śrīmatī Rādhikā. Śrīla Swāmī Mahārāja wanted to give all this, but at that time the forest was full of so many unwanted thorn trees everywhere. In order to make the land fertile so that he could give this, he first had to cut the jungles of *māyāvāda*, *sahajiyā*, *sakhi-bhekī*, Buddhism, and all the other bogus philosophies.

He requested me to help him, and that is why I have come here. I promised to help, so I'm going everywhere to preach his mission, the mission of my *gurudeva*, of Śrīla Prabhupāda Bhaktisiddhānta Sarasvatī Ṭhākura, and especially of Śrīla Bhaktivinoda Ṭhākura. Bhaktivinoda Ṭhākura was the first person to preach to the entire world, and he inspired Śrīla Prabhupāda Bhaktisiddhānta Sarasvatī Ṭhākura, who sent so many disciples here and there, especially to England. At last, Śrīla Prabhupāda inspired Śrīla Bhaktivedānta Swāmī Mahārāja to serve as his own hands, and Śrīla Swāmī Mahārāja quickly spread Kṛṣṇa consciousness everywhere in the world.

I pray that by Śrīla Swāmī Mahārāja's mercy you can also preach everywhere in the world, and be of pure, high character. Distribute books – and read them yourselves as well – and try to have that greed which is essential for *rāgānuga-bhakti*. This is our mission.

A glorification of Śrīla Prabhupāda Bhaktivedānta Swāmī Mahārāja

Śrīla Nārāyaṇa Mahārāja profusely glorified Śrīla Prabhupāda Bhaktivedānta Swāmī Mahārāja at every Ratha-yātrā Festival, and this is how he began his Herā-pañcamī lecture when he held Ratha-yātrā in Wales in July 2000:

My humble obeisances unto the lotus feet of my spiritual master, *oṁ viṣṇupāda* Śrī Śrīmad Bhakti Prajñāna Keśava Gosvāmī Mahārāja, and the same unto the lotus feet of my *śikṣā-guru, oṁ viṣṇupāda* Śrī Śrīmad Bhaktivedānta Swāmī Mahārāja. It is only by the mercy of my *dīkṣā-guru* and *śikṣā-guru* that I am traveling throughout the world, even in this old age, and that so many devotees are coming. I want to give the water that Śrīla Swāmī Mahārāja has given me, to invigorate the devotees who have now become weak and who – like creepers, trees, and sprouts – need "watering" so that they may become stronger.

When Śrīla Swāmī Mahārāja was physically present, his disciples tried their level best to serve him. At that time, even very beautiful teenage girls were working hard here and there in airports, in seaports, and so on, with no care at all for their tender age. There were also many very energetic young teenage boys at that time, working so hard that Śrīla Swāmī Mahārāja's mission was spread everywhere in only a few years.

If anyone is coming to me, that is only the fruit of Śrīla Swāmī Mahārāja's preaching – his books, and so on – and therefore we beg for his mercy. Now he will be very happy that his followers are again becoming enthusiastic and inspired. Wherever I go, big crowds like this and even greater come to hear. They want to revive their Kṛṣṇa consciousness, and I want to help them as much as I can.

Śrīla Swāmī Mahārāja said that the right and the left hand of his preaching was book publishing and distribution, and *nagara-saṅkīrtana*, and we are doing this. *Nagara-saṅkīrtana* is going on again, and we have published thousands of books. The devotees want still more, and we are printing them, along with many magazines. From time to time try to do *nagara-saṅkīrtana* in any place or town nearby you, and never think that you are weak.

MAṄGALĀCARAṆA

oṁ ajñāna-timirāndhasya
jñānāñjana-śalākayā
cakṣur unmīlitaṁ yena
tasmai śrī gurave namaḥ

O Gurudeva, you are so merciful. I offer my humble obeisances unto you and I pray from the core of my heart that, with the torchlight of divine knowledge, you open my eyes that have been blinded by the darkness of ignorance.

vāñchā-kalpa-tarubhyaś ca
kṛpā-sindhubhya eva ca
patitānāṁ pāvanebhyo
vaiṣṇavebhyo namo namaḥ

I offer obeisances unto the Vaiṣṇavas, who are just like desire trees, who are an ocean of mercy, and who deliver the fallen, conditioned souls.

namo mahā-vadānyāya
kṛṣṇa-prema-pradāya te
kṛṣṇāya kṛṣṇa-caitanya-
nāmne gaura-tviṣe namaḥ

I offer my obeisances unto Śrī Kṛṣṇa Caitanya, who is Śrī Kṛṣṇa Himself. Having assumed the golden hue of Śrīmatī Rādhikā, He is munificently bestowing that rare gift of *kṛṣṇa-prema.*

gurave gauracandrāya
rādhikāyai tadālaye
kṛṣṇāya kṛṣṇa-bhaktāya
tad bhaktāya namo namaḥ

I offer my obeisances unto Śrī Gurudeva, Śrī Gauracandra, Śrīmatī Rādhikā and Her associates, Śrī Kṛṣṇa and His devotees, and to all Vaiṣṇavas.

jaya jaya śrī-caitanya jaya nityānanda
jayādvaita-candra jaya gaura-bhakta-vṛnda

Glory to Śrī Caitanya and Nityānanda! Glory to Advaitacandra! And glory to all the devotees of Śrī Gaura!

bhaktyā vihīnā aparādha-lakṣaiḥ
kṣiptāś ca kāmādi-taraṅga-madhye
kṛpāmayi! tvāṁ śaraṇaṁ prapannā
vṛnde! numas te caraṇāravindam

O merciful Vṛndā-devī! Devoid of devotion and guilty of unlimited offences, I am being tossed about in the ocean of material existence by the turbulent waves of lust, anger, greed, and other inauspicious qualities. Therefore, I take shelter of you and offer obeisances unto your lotus feet.

tavaivāsmi tavaivāsmi
na jīvāmi tvayā vinā
iti vijñāya devī tvaṁ
naya māṁ caraṇāntikam

I am Yours! I am Yours! I cannot live without You! O Devī (Rādhā), please understand this and bring me to Your lotus feet.

ŚRĪ ŚRĪMAD BHAKTIVEDĀNTA NĀRĀYAṆA MAHĀRĀJA

ŚRĪ ŚRĪMAD A.C. BHAKTIVEDĀNTA SWAMI PRABHUPĀDA

ŚRĪ ŚRĪMAD BHAKTI PRAJÑĀNA KEŚAVA GOSVĀMĪ

NIGHT VIEW OF THE JAGANNĀTHA TEMPLE IN PURĪ

ŚRĪ JAGANNĀTHA-DEVA DURING THE FESTIVAL

BAGPIPER

ŚRĪ CAITANYA MAHĀPRABHU AND RŪPA GOSVĀMĪ – SEE P. 76

CHAPTER ONE

THE FIRST HISTORY

The appearance of Lord Jagannātha

Today is the day of the Jagannātha Chariot Festival. What is the meaning behind this festival? Our heart is like a chariot, and we pray to Kṛṣṇa, "Please come and sit in my heart." This is how the *gopīs* prayed to Him at Kurukṣetra: "You should come and sit in our hearts. Our hearts are Vṛndāvana."

The first history of the appearance of Lord Jagannātha is given in the *Skanda Purāṇa*, as well as in the *Padma Purāṇa*, the *Puruṣottama-māhātmya*, and *The Diary of Jagannātha*. The particular version presented here is from the *Skanda Purāṇa* and the *Puruṣottama-māhātmya*. There are minor differences in the versions from the other scriptures, but the history is basically the same.

In Satya-yuga there lived a King named Indradyumna Mahārāja, and his wife was Guṇḍicā. That King reigned in the beginning of the first half of Lord Brahmā's day, when Brahmā first created the material world by the mercy of Kṛṣṇa and with the help of Mahāmāyā. He lived in middle-India, in the ancient city of Avanti Nagari in Ujjain, where Kṛṣṇa was taught by

Sāndīpani Muni. He and his queen were very religious and advanced devotees, and although they were royalty they were always engaged in the service of Bhagavān. That King wanted to see the Supreme Personality of Godhead with his own eyes, and he continually waited for an opportunity. He always prayed, "When will a day come that I will see my Lord?"

The King used to receive and host travelers from the various holy places of the world, especially those in India, in the compound of his palace. One day, some pilgrims came and spent the night there. They had just come from a very high class of holy place (*tīrtha*) and had taken *darśana* of the beautiful four-handed Nīla-mādhava; now they discussed among themselves the glories of that deity. A *brāhmaṇa* devotee overheard their conversation and informed the King's minister about it, and he in turn informed the King and made him aware of the deity's beauty. He told the King, "Anyone who receives Nīla-mādhava's *darśana* will not have to return to this world and will be liberated forever. He will attain a four-handed form and become an associate of Nārāyaṇa in Vaikuṇṭha. Even if someone simply vows, 'I will go to His temple to see Him tomorrow,' but dies that day without reaching the temple, he will still go to Vaikuṇṭha and attain a four-handed form."

The King wondered, "How can I obtain the *darśana* of Nīla-mādhava? Where is He located?" He wanted to ask the pilgrims, "Where can I find Him?" but they had departed during the night; so he became upset and decided to somehow search for the deity. He called Vidyāpati, the very intelligent son of his priest, as well as his officials and commanders, and ordered them all to search in different directions: "Some of you go to the east, others to the west, others south, and so on. You should all return within three months. I will give vast wealth and an important position to the one who informs me of the deity's whereabouts." In this way, all the officials enthusiastically set out in all directions from Madhya Pradesh. Vidyāpati, who was very young and handsome and who possessed all good qualities, went toward the east.

After three months they had all returned except Vidyāpati, and the King was worried because no one knew where he was. Vidyāpati had gone to the east coast of India, near the Indian Ocean, and there he traveled continually, searching and searching for Nīla-mādhava. One day, on the shore of the ocean, he saw a very beautiful village, where there was a mountain covered with flowers and trees and where the residents were very cultured. Evening was approaching and he decided to stay in that village, so he told some of the residents, "I would like to rest here tonight." They replied, "Viśvavasu is the prominent leader of this village. He is a *śabara* (a lower caste), but he is very qualified and religious-minded, and he is also intelligent, humble, and liberal. Whenever any traveler or guest comes, he visits Viśvavasu's house; so you must go there."

When Vidyāpati arrived, Viśvavasu was not at home. Only his very beautiful sixteen-year-old daughter, Lalitā, was there. She opened the door and said, "You can wait for my father, because he is not here. He has gone out, but when he returns home he will arrange everything. Kindly wait outside." After some time Viśvavasu arrived. A very sweet fragrance emanated from his body, and he was wearing very beautiful and aromatic *tilaka*. When he saw his guest, he became ashamed and told him, "Oh, excuse me for returning so late. Now you may come in." He and his daughter took their guest inside. Very happy to see that beautiful personality, Viśvavasu told him, "You can reside here for some days." Then he told his daughter, "Take care of this *brāhmaṇa*. Give him food and everything else he requires, and look after him in all respects. There should be no lack of anything."

Vidyāpati took his meal and rested there. He smelled a very beautiful fragrance in the house, especially when the master of the house was home, and he wondered, "Where does that beautiful fragrance come from? I have never smelled anything like it in my entire life. And that girl is so beautiful. I should wait here for a few days, and it may be that I can find Nīla-mādhava." He then began searching here and there for some days.

Lalitā was now regularly serving him, and gradually she became attached to him. Vidyāpati began to develop a close friendship with her, and after some time he fell in love with her. He was already married to someone else, but still he had great affection for Lalitā; so he requested her to ask her father to allow him to marry her. She asked her father, he agreed, and Vidyāpati became Viśvavasu's son-in-law.

Viśvavasu went out regularly every day, and returned in the evening very fresh and fragrant. One day Vidyāpati privately said to his wife, "My dear, now you are my wife, and I have great faith in you. Can you tell me where your father goes every day for worship, and where that fragrance comes from? Please tell me."

Lalitā replied, "I cannot say. My father ordered me, 'Do not tell anyone where I go. Keep it secret – very, very secret.'"

Vidyāpati said, "You cannot tell me? You are one with me, non-different from me. You must tell me, because I am your husband."

She replied, "Then you must promise that you will never tell anyone."

Vidyāpati then said, "A wife should not speak like this. I know you are a very chaste wife, so you must tell me." He then became silent.

Lalitā said, "I will tell you. He goes to worship a deity."

"Which deity?" Vidyāpati asked.

She replied, "I promised not to tell, but I will tell you because you are my husband. He goes to worship Nīla-mādhava."

Vidyāpati became very happy and thought, "After such a long time I have finally heard the name Nīla-mādhava. Nīla-mādhava must be somewhere nearby." He began to show so much love and affection to his wife that she revealed everything to him, and he then requested her, "Please ask your father to take his son-in-law with him."

She said, "Yes, I will help you."

After her father returned from worship in the evening and had taken *prasāda*, Lalitā approached him and sat on his lap. With much love and affection she told him, "My dear father, I want one benediction from you."

He replied, "Oh, very good. I desire to give you a benediction. What do you want?"

She told him, "I want something very special. I know that you will be hesitant to give this to me, but I want it."

He father asked, "What do you want?"

She replied, "O father, I desire that you take my husband with you to see Nīla-mādhava. He wants to take *darśana*."

Viśvavasu pondered whether or not to take him. Worried that if he brought anyone the deity might be taken or simply vanish, Viśvavasu was hesitant. When Lalitā saw that he was not very willing, she said, "If you do not show Nīla-mādhava to my husband, I will take poison and die right in front of you. Your objection means that you do not consider me your loving daughter." And she prepared herself to take poison.

These are the most powerful weapons of ladies: "I will die," "I will take poison," "I will commit suicide." What will a husband or father say then? Of course, he will say, "Oh, you can have whatever you want."

Viśvavasu was now in a dilemma and thought, "What shall I do? I must save my only daughter. I must give her this benediction."

He said, "I don't want you to die. I will take your husband with me and show him Nīla-mādhava, but there is one condition. I will tightly bind his eyes with a black cloth, and when we reach there I will remove it so he can take *darśana*. After that, I will put on the blindfold again. So he will have *darśana*, but he will not know where he is."

Lalitā then went to her husband and told him, "Father has agreed to take you. He will blindfold you during the journey there, but never mind." Vidyāpati was overjoyed and agreed to wear the blindfold. After that she told her father, "Yes, you can bind his eyes with a black cloth." Later, when they were seated on the bullock cart, Viśvavasu placed the black cloth over Vidyāpati's eyes. Lalitā, being very clever and intelligent, gave her husband some mustard seeds and said, "Keep these in your pocket. Now it is the rainy season. You can drop them one after another along the way. After some time, those mustard seeds will grow into plants producing bright yellow flowers. Then you will be able to follow the flowers and go there by yourself; you will not have to ask my father the way."

Viśvavasu then took Vidyāpati with him along a zigzag route on the bullock cart. Vidyāpati dropped the mustard seeds one by one on the ground without his father-in-law knowing. When they arrived at the foot of the mountain, they left the bullock cart there, and Viśvavasu took Vidyāpati by the hand and led him to the temple of Nīla-mādhava on the top of the mountain. When they entered the temple, Viśvavasu removed the blindfold so that Vidyāpati could see Nīla-mādhava. The deity was four-handed, and He carried the *śaṅkha* (conch), *cakra* (disc), *gadā* (club), and *padma* (lotus flower). He was very beautiful, but unlike Nanda-nandana Kṛṣṇa, He had no flute and no peacock feather – He was more like Nārāyaṇa. Nārāyaṇa is very beautiful, but Kṛṣṇa is the most beautiful of all.

Vidyāpati became very happy and began to weep, thinking, "I

have been searching for Him for such a long time – so many months – and now I am satisfied. My life is now successful." Viśvavasu then told him, "Wait here a while. I am going to the forest to bring some flowers and other paraphernalia to worship Him. Then I will offer *candana* and other articles, perform *arcana*, and then we will return home."

While Vidyāpati waited, he noticed a beautiful lake with lotus flowers, humming bees, and some sweetly-singing birds. The branches of a mango tree hung over the lake, and a black crow that was sleeping on one of the branches fell in. Immediately, his soul appeared with four hands. Then Garuḍa quickly came, took that very beautiful and glorious four-handed personality on his back, and flew to Vaikuṇṭha. Vidyāpati began to think, "Oh! With no practice in *bhakti* at all, he very quickly went to Vaikuṇṭha. He never did anything auspicious. He was impure – a crow – eating flesh and other abominable things. Yet, simply by falling into the pond he became four-handed and went to Vaikuṇṭha. Why should I remain here?" He wanted to climb the tree and jump into the lake as well, so that he could also attain a four-handed form and go to Vaikuṇṭha. "I should not wait another moment," he thought, and at once began to climb the tree. When he was about halfway up the tree, however, an aerial voice called to him, "Don't commit suicide just so that you can be liberated and go to Vaikuṇṭha. You will have to perform many important services for the benefit of the entire world, so don't die yet. Be patient. Everything will be accomplished. Return to Mahārāja Indradyumna at once and tell him that Nīla-mādhava is here."

In the meantime, Viśvavasu returned with many flowers and other paraphernalia and said to Vidyāpati, "Oh, come join me." He had no idea what had happened. Viśvavasu prepared *candana* and other ingredients, and throughout the whole day he performed worship, offered prayers, and engaged in many other devotional activities. All the residents of that village were known as *dayitās*, which means those who are very near and dear to Kṛṣṇa. Viśvavasu was known as *dayitā-pati*, the master of all those who are near and dear. He served in this way, although he was a *śabara*. He was fully surrendered and always called out, "Nīla-mādhava!" Now Vidyāpati was also very much charmed with the glories of the deity and, seeing the worship of Nīla-mādhava performed by his father-in-law, he became overjoyed.

When Viśvavasu had completed his services, he again covered Vidyāpati's eyes with the blindfold, and they departed. After some hours, traveling again in that zigzag way, they reached their home. Then Viśvavasu heard Nīla-mādhava telling him, "You have served Me for a long time. Now I want to take the royal service of a very high class of devotee named Indradyumna Mahārāja. Don't be afraid and don't worry." Viśvavasu, however, immediately became upset and thought, "Oh, Ṭhākurajī will go to Mahārāja Indradyumna? I cannot bear the thought of separation. This boy will return and tell the King, and the King will come and take Nīla-mādhava." He then practically arrested Vidyāpati and imprisoned him within one of the rooms of his house.

Vidyāpati could not go anywhere, so he told his wife, "Please help me. I want to return to Madhya Pradesh very soon. I have promised my King, who wants to come with his whole family to serve Nīla-mādhava. Please help me. You are my wife – my other half."

Lalitā agreed and said, "You can go. I will help you." She then told her father, "If you do not release him from this jail, I will commit suicide at once." She was ready to commit suicide, so her father's heart melted in compassion and he released Vidyāpati. Now free, Vidyāpati assured his wife, "I will return very soon. Don't worry." He then quickly left and proceeded towards Indradyumna's kingdom.

He walked continually until he finally arrived back in Avanti Nagari. He had been gone for over six months, and King Indradyumna became very happy when he heard from Vidyāpati, "I have discovered Nīla-mādhava. Please come with me." The King decided, "I shall go with my entire kingdom, my wealth, my wife, and my soldiers and commanders." He wanted to bring Nīla-mādhava to his kingdom, to worship Him for the rest of his life. Proceeding from Ujjain, he reached the place about a hundred miles south of Purī. But when he reached there, there were no mustard seed flowers. There was also no hill and no village, for by the desire of Nīla-mādhava, the entire village was covered with over a hundred feet of sand. Everything was covered, including the hill, and Nīla-mādhava was not there.

The King began to weep. He sat down on a straw mat facing the ocean and decided, "I will not take anything to eat until I have *darśana* of Nīla-mādhava; if I do not see Him, I will die. I came with my whole kingdom, all my wealth, my wife, and family, but I did not get the *darśana* of the Lord. Oh, I must give up my life." Then, as he began to chant, "Nīla-mādhava! Nīla-mādhava! Nīla-mādhava!" remembering the Lord, an aerial voice called to him, "I will not come, but do not worry. I will not come here to give you *darśana*, but you will be able to see Me. I am sending Brahmā. You should come with Brahmā to Vaikuṇṭha, and there you can take My *darśana*. In this world I will not give you *darśana* in the shape of Nīla-mādhava, but I will manifest in four forms: Jagannātha, Baladeva, Subhadrā, and Sudarśana *cakra*. Wait near the sea where Baṅki-muhana is located." This place is presently known as Cakra-tīrtha, and it is by the part of the ocean known as the Bay of Bengal, where the water moves towards West Bengal. "Go there and wait, and *dāru-brahma* (Bhagavān in the form of wood) will come. He will manifest in the form of a very large, fragrant, reddish log, and the signs of *śaṅkha*, *cakra*, *gadā*, and *padma* will be seen everywhere on that form. Go there. Take Me out and make four deities from that log. Then you will be able to worship Me."

Brahmā quickly came and took the King with him to Vaikuṇṭha, where he could freely gaze at Nīla-mādhava as He conversed with His associates. The King became even more attached and began to weep, and then Brahmā told him, "Let us go. He will not come to Earth in this form, but He will come as four forms. Let us now go to the place that He has designated, and wait for Him there."

In the meantime, while the King was gone, many years had passed and the entire world had now changed. Before going he had constructed a very large and beautiful, high temple, but now it was also covered by sand. The sand had been removed many times, but the temple had become old and dilapidated. A new King had come and repaired it, and he had declared, "I am the builder of this temple." Now that King Indradyumna returned, he told the new King, "This is not yours; I have built it, so I am the owner of this temple. You have only made repairs." There was a crow named Kākabhuśuṇḍi, who had been witness to the pastimes of Rāmacandra and also King Indradyumna's building the temple; and now he testified on the King's behalf. Brahmā also came forward and agreed, "This King has built the temple. You have only repaired it." In this way, King Indradyumna again became the master.

Somehow, by Kṛṣṇa's mercy, the King's wife was there. He had no child at all, so there was only he and his wife. The King and his new associates and army waited for the deity, and at last he saw the red tree-trunk, marked everywhere with *śaṅkha*, *cakra*, *gadā*, and *padma*. He approached that trunk with his soldiers and elephants and they tried very hard to take it out of the water, but they could not do so. Many elephants and strong men, and even his entire army, could not take the tree-trunk out of the water.

The aerial voice came again and told the King, "Bring My old servant Dayitā-pati Viśvavasu, and his daughter as well. Viśvavasu will carry Me from one side, and the *brāhmaṇa* Vidyāpati will take Me from the other side. And bring a golden chariot for Me. I will come out easily, and then you can arrange everything." By the power and will of Nīla-mādhava, Viśvavasu, Lalitā, and Vidyāpati were still alive and now they were brought on a chariot with honor. The King requested the three of them to enter the waters of the ocean and lift the log. Vidyāpati and his wife and father-in-law then began to lift and simultaneously pray to the log, "Jaya Jagannātha! Jaya Jagannātha! Nīla-mādhava! Nīla-mādhava! O please, please be merciful and come upon our chariot."

The log came out very easily, and it was brought on the golden chariot to the place near to where the Jagannātha Temple is now situated. The King kept the log there in a big hall, and he invited all the carpenters of Orissa, telling them, "I will give you vast wealth if you can make the *vigraha*." Very famous carpenters came there wanting to make the deity, but their instruments and tools broke as soon as they touched the iron-hard log. An old but beautiful *brāhmaṇa* then came forward. He had brought some tools, and he told them, "My name is Mahāraṇa. I am very expert, and I can make you the *vigraha*." That *brāhmaṇa* was actually Nīla-mādhava or Jagannātha Himself, in the form of an old *brāhmaṇa*. He continued, "I will complete the *vigraha* in twenty-one days, but you must promise that the door of this hall will remain closed. I will be alone there with my tools, and after twenty-one days I will open the door so that you can see the deity. At that time you can take Him into the temple and serve and worship Him." The King replied, "Yes, I will obey your instructions. I will not open the door."

The *brāhmaṇa* went inside with his tools, and locked the door from inside. For fourteen days there was no sound, and Indradyumna Mahārāja became very worried. He thought, "What can be the matter? The *brāhmaṇa* has not taken a drop of water or anything to eat this entire time. Perhaps he is dead." His Prime Minister then told him, "Don't open the door. There is some mystery behind this. Only open it after twenty-one days; not before." However, his wife pleaded with him, "If you don't open the door now, the *brāhmaṇa* may die and we will be guilty of *brahma-hatyā* (the sin of killing a *brāhmaṇa*). We must open the door. Please hurry." The King replied, "The *brāhmaṇa* told me not to open it before twenty-one days have elapsed. How can I open it?" She beseeched him again and again, and finally the King called for his carpenters to cut away the locks; he opened the doors forcibly and entered.

Inside the hall, the King was struck with wonder, for he could not see the *brāhmaṇa*. "Where is the *brāhmaṇa* Mahāraṇa?" he asked. The four deities – Jagannātha, Baladeva, Subhadrā, and Sudarśana *cakra* – were there, but they had not been fully completed. Their eyes and noses were only round shapes, their arms were not full-length, and their hands and feet were not completed – nothing was completed. The King began to weep. Opening up his heart to his Prime Minister, he said, "I have committed an offense by breaking my promise. Now what shall I do?" Weeping, he again wanted to commit suicide.

In another account, perhaps in another creation, when the King opened the door, the *brāhmaṇa* was present and at once told him, "Why have you come in the middle of my work? Now only fourteen days have passed. I wanted another seven days to make the *vigrahas* very beautiful. Why did you open the door? Now there are only round eyes. Well, I think it must be the wish of God Himself – Jagannātha. Otherwise I would have been able to complete the task, and you would not have interrupted me." Saying this, the carpenter disappeared, and at that time the King and his associates knew that he was not simply a *brāhmaṇa* carpenter – he was Kṛṣṇa Himself. They began to lament in separation.

The deity then ordered the King through His aerial voice, "Don't worry. There is a mystery behind this. I desired to manifest like this, and there is a very deep reason for it. Keep Me in the temple and begin to worship Me in the form of these deities." Jagannātha continued, "Please carry out My orders. Viśvavasu and his son-in-law Vidyāpati will worship Me, along with Vidyāpati's two wives. The sons of Vidyāpati's *brāhmaṇa* wife will take turns to worship Ṭhākurajī, and the sons of his *śabara* wife will cook many varieties of preparations. Many *dayitās* in the dynasty of Viśvavasu will serve Me for ten days during a Ratha-yātrā Festival. Only they will worship Me at that time; no one else will perform the worship. They alone will take Baladeva, Subhadrā, and Me on chariots, and they will bring us to Guṇḍicā Mandira. Make a festival for ten days beginning from today, and take these chariots to the Guṇḍicā Mandira."

It was due to the request of Queen Guṇḍicā that the events of this pastime unfolded as they did, which is why the *mandira* was named after her. Ṭhākurajī continued, "We will remain there for those days, and then you may take us back. You should perform many festivals, like Snāna-yātrā, Candana-yātrā, Herā-pañcamī, and so on."

During Candana-yātrā, Jagannātha's entire body is covered with *candana* for many days. At that time, the *vijaya-vigraha* deity known as Govinda[1] is placed on a very beautiful boat in

[1] When there is a need to take Jagannātha somewhere, this smaller *vijaya-vigraha* deity from the Jagannātha temple is taken because the body of Jagannātha is very heavy.

Narendra-sarovara, and His boat pastimes take place. Then, during Snāna-yātrā, the deity receives *abhiṣeka* from thousands of pitchers of water brought from all the holy places in India, and His bath is so long that he becomes sick. His stomach becomes upset and He falls ill. At that time, Lakṣmī takes Him to her palace and closes the door for fifteen days. Śrī Caitanya Mahāprabhu could not survive without the deity, and therefore He went to Ālālanātha and cried, "Where is Kṛṣṇa? Where is Kṛṣṇa?" He became mad, so much so that when He touched the stones at Ālālanātha they melted. Wherever He offered his *praṇāma* – wherever His hands, head, and other limbs were placed – their impressions became visible in that piece of stone.

Only the *dayitās*, the family of Viśvavasu Śabara, can serve Jagannātha at the time of Ratha-yātrā. Actually, there are two kinds of servants. One is coming from the dynasty of Vidyāpati's original *brāhmaṇa* wife, and these devotees do *arcana* and *sevā*. Those who descend from Lalitā are called *supakara* (excellent cooks), because Jagannātha has accepted them as His cooks even though they are of a low-class birth. They very quickly and easily cook not less than one hundred mounds of rice and dahl, and a variety of other preparations. They are expert in using many stoves, and they place at least twenty earthen pots on one stove.[2]

The King prayed, "O Ṭhākurajī, I want a boon so that I may serve You."

Ṭhākurajī replied, "What boon do you want?"

[2] The stove is an Indian *cullī*. It has five burners (one in the middle and one on each corner) and each burner has four pots on it, one on top of another, with only a small hole at the bottom of the three higher pots. Everything is evenly and perfectly cooked. It is understood that Lakṣmī herself is cooking and the servants (the descendants of the *śabara* wife of Vidyāpati) are only assisting her, and that is why the cooking can be done so magically.

The King said, "I desire that there should be neither sons nor daughters in my dynasty. I do not want any children. I know You will grant my desire."

Ṭhākurajī smiled and asked, "Why don't you want children?"

The King replied, "After I die, they will quarrel over money, and they will have no interest in serving You. So much money will come for Your service, and they will think, 'This property is mine' or 'Jagannātha is my property.' I don't want any of my family members to think, 'This temple is mine, Jagannātha, Baladeva, and Subhadrā are my property, and all the money coming as *praṇāmī* (donations) is therefore mine to enjoy.' If they think in that way, they will use everything for their own sense gratification and go to hell."

Nowadays we see this mentality all over India and everywhere else. These days, neophyte devotees approach people and say, "Give me some money to serve my *gurudeva.* I want to serve Ṭhākurajī – Jagannātha, Baladeva, and Subhadrā. I want to serve Rādhā and Kṛṣṇa, so donate something." Then, when they get that donation, they do not give a single cent to *gurudeva* or to Ṭhākurajī. They think, "Now I am the enjoyer!" They keep the money in their pocket, and then they enquire, "Where is the best bank for me to make a deposit?" Someone may reply, "You can go to Switzerland; it is the very best." Then they will say, "No, I want to keep my money in India so that I can live there. Can you tell me which is the safest bank in India to keep my money?" They forget that they collected that money for *gurudeva.* Would anyone have given the money if they thought it was for that disciple? And what will be the punishment? Kṛṣṇa is in anxiety that He has yet to create a hell that is appropriate for them.

In India, too, many *gosvāmīs* think they are the owners of their temples. They take the *praṇāmī* and engage in many bogus activities. You should be always careful about this; otherwise *bhakti* will not come to you. She will think, "This person is very selfish. He wants to be the master of his *gurudeva*, and also of Kṛṣṇa."

The King therefore requested, "There should be no one to take even a single *paisā*. You are the owner. You Yourself should depute those who will serve You. The managers should regularly be changed, and they should be servants, like trustees." A trustee is one who can be trusted to serve without any desire for self-gain. The King of Orissa is always the trustee, and someone else is selected after him. They are not actually kings, in the sense that they cannot take a farthing or a *paisā* for themselves. If they were to, they would be ruined.

Upon hearing the King's words, Jagannātha began to smile, and thus the Ratha-yātrā Festival began. There are so many relevant teachings found in this history.

CHAPTER TWO

THE SECOND HISTORY

The reason behind Lord Jagannātha's appearance

You have now heard the first history, but it does not fully explain why Jagannātha desired to manifest in a form that appeared to be incomplete. That explanation is contained in a somewhat different history, which was discovered by the Gosvāmīs in Śrī Caitanya Mahāprabhu's line. It is not written down anywhere in its entirety; it exists only in the hearts of pure devotees, especially those devotees who have received Śrī Caitanya Mahāprabhu's mercy. Actually, there are two histories like this, not just one, and they are both very beautiful. Śrīla Sanātana Gosvāmī has included part of the first of these histories, which is most interesting, in his *Bṛhad-bhāgavatāmṛta*.

Kṛṣṇa took birth in Gokula. He manifested Himself partially in Mathurā as well, but He Himself is fully the son of Mother Yaśodā and Nanda Bābā. In Mathurā He did not appear as a son – He appeared with four hands, and was sixteen years old. He was wearing golden ornaments, a golden crown, and very opulent clothing, and His wavy hair was very long. In Gokula, on the other hand, He emerged from the womb of Yaśodā as a baby, along with His younger sister. He was actually the son of Nanda and Yaśodā, not their adopted son. Sometimes it is written that He was the son of Vasudeva and Devakī, but the Vrajavāsīs do not accept that idea. They personally saw Him come from the womb of Yaśodā, so how could they believe that He took birth in Mathurā? There was no birth ceremony in Mathurā, but in Vraja, Nanda Bābā gave thousands of cows to the *brāhmaṇas* on Kṛṣṇa's birthday. He donated everything and kept nothing in his house, but his house still filled up with wealth again. It was such a good festival.

Kṛṣṇa was raised in Gokula, where Yaśodā bound Him to the grinding mortar by her love and affection, and where so many other sweet pastimes took place. When Kṛṣṇa became older, He went cowherding with His friends, playing sweetly on His flute. Over a period of time, He killed Tṛṇāvarta, Bakāsura, Aghāsura, and other demons. He performed the *rāsa-līlā* in Vṛndāvana, and He played at Vaṁśīvaṭa and Keṣī-ghāṭa. Then, after some time, Akrūra came to Vṛndāvana and told Kṛṣṇa, "Kaṁsa wants to kill Your father and mother, Vasudeva and Devakī." Kṛṣṇa replied, "My father is Nanda Bābā and My mother is Yaśodā-maiyā. But Vasudeva and Devakī are friends of My father and mother, so I should go and save them." He immediately went with Akrūra, killed Kaṁsa, enthroned Ugrasena as the king, and after some time He went to Dvārakā.

Śrī Sanātana Gosvāmī's *Bṛhad-bhāgavatāmṛta* relates the following pastime that took place while Kṛṣṇa was residing in Dvārakā. You have heard of Śrī Nārada Muni, who is very expert in performing many unfathomable pastimes to please Kṛṣṇa. He is very near and dear to Kṛṣṇa, and he always discovers new ways by which he can glorify Kṛṣṇa's various manifestations and pure devotees. It may be said that Nārada Muni is very "tricky," because no one can comprehend what he is doing, or why, or how, or where he is going. Kṛṣṇa is "tricky," and so are His *gopīs*, His mother, His Vraja, His Yamunā, and His devotees. Similarly, wherever Nārada goes, only for the purpose of serving Kṛṣṇa, he is always busy inventing unique ways to glorify his holy master Kṛṣṇa, along with Rādhikā, the *gopīs*, and the devotees.

Once Nārada went to Dvārakā in order to see the ever-increasingly new glories of Kṛṣṇa and the *gopīs*. No one would understand who are the greatest devotees if Nārada had not revealed this knowledge. He went to Dvārakā to discover a scheme to glorify them.

In the palace of Rukmiṇī, Nārada saw a big festival taking place. All the 16,108 queens were present, headed by the eight prominent queens, such as Rukmiṇī, Satyabhāmā, Jāmbavatī, Bhadrā, Mitravindā, and Nāgnajitī; and other Dvārakāvāsīs were also there. Nārada approached Rukmiṇī, Satyabhāmā, and the other queens and said in their assembly, "You are very fortunate to serve Kṛṣṇa. You are the best servants of Kṛṣṇa. You are His queens. You are the most glorious in this entire world. I pay my respects to you." What Nārada was really conveying to the queens was: "Kṛṣṇa does not love any of you. I know that He only and always remembers the *gopīs*. He does not really want to be with you – really He wants to return to Vṛndāvana and taste the love of the *gopīs*."

Rukmiṇī and Satyabhāmā became unhappy and informed Nārada, "You are glorifying us, but we are well aware that we have not been able to make Kṛṣṇa happy since the time He married us. Our love cannot control Him. There are so many of us, and we are very beautiful and qualified in all the arts, but still we cannot satisfy Him."

Rukmiṇī said, "When He sleeps in my room, on my bed, He cries continually. Sometimes when He dreams, He takes hold of my veil and pulls on it, crying, 'O Rādhikā! O Rādhikā! Where are You? I will die without You! O Lalitā, where are you? O Viśākhā, where are you?' Sometimes He weeps piteously and calls out, 'Mother Yaśodā, where are you? I want to eat bread and butter! I want to sit in your lap! I want to drink your breast milk! Where are you?' Sometimes He calls His friends, 'O Śrīdāmā! Subala! Madhumaṅgala! Kokila! Bhṛṅga! Where are you? Come on! Come on! I cannot maintain My life without you. Where are you? The cows are waiting and you aren't coming. Now it's time for cowherding. You must come.' And sometimes He even calls His cows, 'Śyāmalī, Dhavalī, Kālindī, Gaṅgā, Piśaṅgā! Where are you? Where are you?' He weeps like this throughout the night, and the entire bed becomes wet with His tears. And this did not happen on just one night – He is always like this. He never sees where we are or who we are. We are just 'there.'

"We are very sad. We are not near and dear to Him at all. If we're near and dear, why does He not call out, 'Rukmiṇī! Satyabhāmā!'? He never calls out our names."

Then Satyabhāmā said, "O *sakhī*, you speak the truth. Last night He wept bitterly and pulled my veil, calling out, 'O Rādhā! O Rādhā!' He fell unconscious, and I could not think of what to do. What is the history behind this? Why does Kṛṣṇa never look upon us, although we are married to Him? We are so sweet and beautiful, and we are so expert in all the arts, yet we cannot please Kṛṣṇa. We want to know how we can please Him."

Meanwhile, Kṛṣṇa was sitting in His assembly hall named Sudharmā. This hall was equipped with all kinds of facilities. Sometimes it was large, sometimes small, sometimes cool, sometimes warm, and sometimes it was air-conditioned. It would provide whatever one desired simply by the power of his mind. Sometimes one hundred people would be present there, and sometimes thousands. It expanded and contracted, like Kṛṣṇa

Himself. While the queens were talking, Kṛṣṇa's associates were sitting in the council chamber, discussing various problems and how to solve them. Ugrasena Mahārāja sat on the throne in the middle, and Akrūra, Kṛṣṇa, Baladeva, Uddhava, and others sat beside him.

Kṛṣṇa was not His normal self. He was somewhat upset, absorbed in worrying about something. In the *Padma Purāṇa* it is said:

nāhaṁ tiṣṭhāmi vaikuṇṭhe
yogināṁ hṛdayeṣu vā
tatra tiṣṭhāmi nārada
yatra gāyanti mad-bhaktāḥ

Kṛṣṇa once told Nārada, "I never live in Vaikuṇṭha, nor do I live in the hearts of the *yogīs.* I live in the hearts of pure devotees. I live wherever they remember me, and I take rest very comfortably there. I do not live anywhere else." It was for this reason that Kṛṣṇa was upset. Being the Supreme Personality of Godhead, He could understand the following pastime was taking place in Rukmiṇī's palace:

Mother Rohiṇī entered in the midst of the queens. She was Baladeva Prabhu's mother, had lived in Vṛndāvana with Yaśodā for many years, and had nourished and supported both Kṛṣṇa and Baladeva. As soon as she came in, all the queens present offered her *praṇāma* and gave her a good seat. Then, when she was comfortably seated, they all approached her and said, "O Mother, we know that you were in Vraja when Kṛṣṇa and Baladeva were babies, and you stayed there for eleven years. You know the history of all the *gopīs.* You know about the love and affection of the *gopīs,* of Mother Yaśodā, and of all the Vrajavāsīs. We want to know the importance of Vraja. We want to know what it is about the nature of the Vrajavāsīs' love that makes Kṛṣṇa unable to forget them. Many years have now passed. We have been serving Kṛṣṇa for more than fifty years, but still He is not controlled by our loving service. He never calls out, 'O Rukmiṇī! O Satyabhāmā!' Rather, He always calls, 'Rādhā! Rādhā! Lalitā! Viśākhā!' What is the reason for all this?

"Sometimes His heart melts so much that He calls out, 'Mother! Mother Yaśodā! Where are you? Give Me bread and butter. My cows are hungry. I must go out cowherding at once. The boys are calling Me – Dāmā, Sudāmā, Śrīdāmā, and others are calling Me. They are waiting for Me by the door, and all the cows are mooing very loudly. They are not giving milk to their calves, because they are all hankering for Me; so I must go at once.'

"He does not think, 'I am in Dvārakā with My beloved Rukmiṇī and Satyabhāmā.' Why? What is there in Vraja? They do not have any wealth, as we do here. The *gopīs* have no ornaments like us, and they are not as beautiful. They live in the forest, and they can only decorate themselves with flowers, not with gold and jewels as we do. Kṛṣṇa used to go cowherding there, and here He is like a king, so why does He always remember them? Why has He given His heart to them? We want to know. Do they know some magic? Do they know an enchanting *mantra*? They must know one, and that must be why Kṛṣṇa always remembers them and weeps for them.

"We are Kṛṣṇa's 16,108 queens. We are the most beautiful ladies in the entire world, and our qualities and expertise in everything is unique and unparalleled. Still, all of us together can never control Him. Mother, what is the reason that He never looks toward us? Why is it that we cannot satisfy one Kṛṣṇa although we are so many? We serve Him in innumerable ways and we love Him so much, but we cannot satisfy Him. He is only worried about the *gopīs* – and about calling out to them. What is the reason? We want to know everything."

When Rohiṇī-maiyā remembered her friend Yaśodā and all the *gopīs*, she began to weep, and then she began to explain the reason. She related all of Kṛṣṇa's pastimes, from boyhood up to His twelfth year. Meanwhile, Kaṁsa's mother came in their midst. Being more than a hundred years old, she was bent over with her head at an odd angle and walked with a stick. "This is very dangerous," she told them. "Why talk about the *gopīs* and *gopas*? They are very cruel, very cruel. Yaśodā could not nurture Kṛṣṇa and Baladeva properly. They are the sons of Devakī, but somehow they were sent to Gokula because their parents were afraid of Kaṁsa. Yaśodā never gave a drop of yogurt or butter to Kṛṣṇa and Baladeva, so they were forced to steal them from neighbors' houses. Then, when the neighbors complained to Yaśodā, she would immediately chastise Kṛṣṇa, and sometimes she would tie His hands and bind Him to a grinding mortar. Yaśodā and Nanda Bābā were so cruel and evil that they never gave Kṛṣṇa any shoes or sandals, although the forests were full of many thorns and hard pieces of stone. Don't talk about them.

"Kṛṣṇa used to herd the cows from morning to evening all over Vraja, with no pay and without shoes or an umbrella to shield Him from the afternoon sun. There are great quantities of butter there in Vraja, but He never got any of it. Anyone would give butter even to a servant, but they never gave Him any.

"Yaśodā once tied Kṛṣṇa up with ropes. He was weeping bitterly, but that lady had no mercy. She took a stick and wanted to beat Him, although He was crying, 'Mother! Mother! Please don't beat Me! I will never do it again!' He never did anything wrong, but still she wanted to beat Him. On the other hand, my husband, Ugrasena, is extremely merciful.

"I think Kṛṣṇa was there for twelve years, and during that entire time He only received a small quantity of milk from Mother Yaśodā. Between the ages of five and twelve years He and

Balarāma were merely given some bread and butter. So we should count how much Yaśodā and Nanda Bābā spent on Kṛṣṇa during those twelve years. We should also count how many days He herded the cows there, and we also have to consider that sometimes He went to others' houses and stole their goods. They should pay Kṛṣṇa and Baladeva some money for the cow-grazing they did. But on the other hand, Kṛṣṇa received at least some clothing from them. Anyway, we will count everything up and call Gargācārya, because he is an expert accountant, as well as an astrologer. He knows everything. When he writes the accounts, he will make a statement regarding the salary owed to Kṛṣṇa and Baladeva for cowherding, and what was actually already spent on them.

"We will not pay for Rohiṇī, because she is a member of the party of Nanda, Yaśodā, and the *gopīs.* We will never pay for her. We can only pay for Kṛṣṇa and Baladeva. There should be a report. When the accounts are written and balanced, if anything is owed to Yaśodā and Nanda, we will pay double."

Rohiṇī became more and more angry as Padmāvatī continued, "My husband is extremely broadminded, generous, and merciful. If anything is owed to Yaśodā and Nanda, we can pay double, and if something is owed for Kṛṣṇa and Baladeva's herding the cows, we will immediately be compassionate and say, 'We will not take anything.' So we are going to call Gargācārya."

Mother Rohiṇī then became extremely angry and said, "I know who you are!" Padmāvatī was the wife of Ugrasena, but Kaṁsa was not Ugrasena's son. Once, when Padmāvatī was very young, she was playing with her friends on the bank of the Yamunā in the evening. A demon named Drumila approached her in a lusty mood, and that is how Kaṁsa was conceived. Rohiṇī continued, "I know that you are not a chaste lady, and that is why you can't understand the glory of the Vrajavāsīs' love and affection."

Rohiṇī stopped speaking to Padmāvatī and now addressed the queens. One by one, she explained the moods of Nanda Bābā, Yaśodā, Subala, and Śrīdāmā; and at last she began to speak about the *gopīs*. She said, "The Vrajavāsīs love Kṛṣṇa so much that they cannot live without Him. When Kṛṣṇa and Baladeva were still very young, they wanted to take the cows out to graze, so they told Mother Yaśodā again and again, 'Mother, we want to go cowherding, because we are *gopas*. Please give us the order to go.' When they were not given permission, they began to weep. At last, Mother Yaśodā told them, 'You may go with the calves to a nearby forest in Vṛndāvana, but you must return home soon.' She brought them very beautiful shoes and umbrellas to shade them from the sun, but Kṛṣṇa told her, 'The cows are worshipable for us because they are like our mothers. If you want to give Me shoes, then bring shoes for all the 900,000 cows. You should bring 400,000 shoes for every 100,000 cows, because they each have four feet. Bring umbrellas for all of them, too, and then I will also take the shoes and umbrella; otherwise I won't. I don't want to be their master. I want to be a servant of the cows, because I am a *gopa*. *Gopa* means maintainer, supporter, and nourisher of the cows – as their servant.'

"Yaśodā once told Kṛṣṇa, 'My son, all the *gopīs* come to me and complain that You have been going to their houses and taking butter from their storerooms.' Kṛṣṇa said, 'Mother, why are you speaking like this? *Maiyā, maiṅ nahīṅ makkhana khāya* – Mother, why do you say that I have stolen butter? I have not stolen butter and eaten it. You sent Me cowherding in Madhuvana in the very early morning, so I went there, and I was always with the cows. Now it's evening, so I have come back with the cows, and after this I will go to bed. When did I have time to steal butter? If you think I've stolen it, then it must be because I'm not your son. Either you've borrowed Me, or else I took birth somewhere and My mother left Me, and that is why you think I'm a thief. I want to go to the Yamunā and jump in – I will not live with you anymore.'

"Yaśodā at once began to weep bitterly. She embraced Kṛṣṇa and said, 'O Kṛṣṇa, You have not taken butter. I have not said this.' Kṛṣṇa replied, 'Mother, I have taken butter: *Maiyā, maiṅ ne hī makkhana khāya*,' and Yaśodā replied to Him, 'No, no, You have not taken butter.' Then she began to caress Kṛṣṇa. She wept and bathed Him in her tears, and milk flowed spontaneously from her breasts. Yaśodā cried, 'I will never say such a thing again.'"

Rohiṇī-devī continued, "The Vrajavāsīs only know that Kṛṣṇa is their son, their beloved, or their friend. You sometimes think that Kṛṣṇa is the Supreme Personality of Godhead Himself, and you can see His four hands, but this idea is never present in Vraja. The Vrajavāsīs see Kṛṣṇa as an innocent boy. He is always dancing and playing on His flute, His turban is decorated with a peacock feather, and all the *gopīs* are His beloveds. He is Gopījana-vallabha, the beloved of all the *gopīs*.

"The *gopīs* do not require a formal relationship with Kṛṣṇa. Since childhood they have given their hearts and everything else to Him, and therefore He cannot repay them. Oh, listen attentively. The *gopīs* never want to gain anything from Kṛṣṇa. They always serve Him without any desire for self-gain. In Dvārakā, you, Rukmiṇī and Satyabhāmā, are Kṛṣṇa's wives, but not His beloveds. Do you know why? Because your love and affection is divided into many fractions. Besides your husband Kṛṣṇa, you each have ten sons and a daughter as well. Your one husband plus these eleven make twelve, so your love and affection is divided into twelve parts. The *gopīs'* love, on the other hand, is not divided. They have given up their husbands, they have no children, they do not take care of their houses, and they have no animals – they have nothing to look after. Their love and affection is *akhaṇḍa* – total, full, and undivided.

"In the relationship of a lover and beloved, a lady gives her entire time for her beloved, but her love and affection becomes divided if a child is born. She will give much more time to the baby than to her husband. If she has ten or eleven children, her love and affection will then be divided still further."

Rohiṇī explained that when the *gopīs* perform any duty, such as sweeping in their homes, they always keep Kṛṣṇa foremost in their minds and hearts. They sweep, and at the same time they chant, "Govinda Dāmodara Mādhaveti," and while cooking, they sing, "Govinda Dāmodara Mādhaveti." If a *gopī* is looking after her elders' small son and she wants him to sleep, she pats him and sings, "Govinda Dāmodara Mādhaveti." The *gopīs* do not tell the babies, "Go to sleep, go to sleep." Instead they sing, "Govinda Dāmodara Mādhaveti." If they are threshing corn, wheat, or rice, they sing, "Govinda Dāmodara Mādhaveti." There are some parrots in the *gopīs'* homes, and very early in the morning, at four a.m., they teach those parrots, "Repeat after me: 'Govinda Dāmodara Mādhaveti.'"

The minds and hearts of the *gopīs* are always absorbed in Kṛṣṇa. Their minds and hearts are like a chariot on which Kṛṣṇa is always sitting, and His mind and heart is like a chariot on which the *gopīs* ride. Kṛṣṇa always thinks of the *gopīs*, calling, "Rādhe, Rādhe, Rādhe, Jaya, Jaya, Jaya, Śrī Rādhe..." He always remembers, "Rādhā, Rādhā! Lalitā! Viśākhā! Mother Yaśodā!"

Kṛṣṇa's love and affection is divided into many parts. In the *Gītā* (4.11) He has promised, "*ye yathā māṁ prapadyante* – I will remember those who remember Me," and He is bound to keep His promise. He will go to that place where His devotee remembers Him and chants His name. He is very loving towards the Vrajavāsīs, but at the same time, He cannot give up the devotees of Mathurā, Dvārakā, or other parts of India or the rest of the world. If anyone chants, He will go to that person. He always remembers them, and He always feels great separation from them. Consequently, His love is divided; but the *gopīs'* love is not divided, and that is why He is so attached to them.

Mother Rohiṇī continued, "Kṛṣṇa used to wipe the faces of the *gopīs* when they became tired from dancing and singing during the *rāsa-līlā*. The *gopīs* can sing more sweetly than He can. He can sing, '*sā, re, gā, mā, pā*,' but the *gopīs* can do more than this. Kṛṣṇa will stop there, but they will sing, '*sā, re, gā, mā, pā, dā, ni, sā*.' When Kṛṣṇa heard them He became very happy and said, '*Sādhu, sādhu*! Very good! I cannot do as you have done.' He always used to praise them."

The *gopīs' rati*, their love and affection for Kṛṣṇa in *mahābhāva*, is called *samartha-rati*. The word *samartha* means capable, suitable, and complete; therefore *samartha-rati* means "capable of controlling Kṛṣṇa." The *rati* of the queens of Dvārakā is called *samañjasā*, which means that it is doubtful that their love can control Kṛṣṇa. They are not like the *gopīs*, whose love is capable of controlling Him. The *gopīs' prema* is so elevated that the queens' love can never even be compared with it. The queens' love reaches the stages of *prema*, *sneha*, *māna*, *praṇaya*, *rāga*, and *anurāga*. Sometimes they attain a shadow of *mahābhāva*, and sometimes they experience *divyonmāda* and *citra-jalpa*, but only to a very slight extent. Their *aṣṭa-sāttvika-bhāvas* cannot go up to *ujjvalita* (blazing) and *prajvalita* (inflamed). Their *bhāva* may go up to *dhūmāyita*, which is compared to a flame covered with smoke. Sometimes their *bhāva* is also without smoke, in other words more intense, but it is never as high as that of the *gopīs*. The "smokeless" flame of the *gopīs'* love goes up to the highest extent.

Mother Rohiṇī then began to glorify Śrīmatī Rādhikā's affection for Kṛṣṇa. She said, "Once Śrīmatī Rādhikā was sitting on Kṛṣṇa's lap. A bee came by, humming, thinking that Her feet were a very fragrant, sweet and tasteful lotus flower. It wanted to enter Her lotus feet and Rādhikā became frightened. She tried to chase the bee away, but it kept coming back. Meanwhile, Madhumaṅgala came and drove it away with his stick. When he returned, he boasted, 'Madhusūdana has gone. I have driven him away and he will not come back.' When Śrīmatī Rādhikā heard this, She forgot that She was sitting in Kṛṣṇa's lap and being caressed by Him, and She began to weep. Taking the word Madhusūdana to mean Kṛṣṇa Himself, She cried out, 'O Madhusūdana! Where have You gone? When will You come back? You must come, otherwise I will die.' Speaking in this way, She became unconscious in Her mood of separation. Astonished, Kṛṣṇa thought, 'What shall I do? How will I pacify Her?'"

Rohiṇī-maiyā continued, "Once Kṛṣṇa was going cowherding with Dāmā, Śrīdāmā, Madhumaṅgala, and all the other cowherd boys and His hundreds of thousands of cows. Some of the cows were black, some were golden, and some were white, and it looked as though the rivers Gaṅgā, Yamunā, and Sarasvatī were mixing together and separating again. All that could be seen for miles and miles were the heads and bodies of cows. Kṛṣṇa was just going to enter the forest, and Mother Yaśodā and Nanda Bābā were following Him. They could not leave Him easily, although Kṛṣṇa told them, 'It is My wish that you return home now.' Just then, Kṛṣṇa somehow saw Lalitā, Viśākhā, and all the other *gopīs* as they peered from their windows, groves, and doors here and there. Kṛṣṇa was at once attracted, and then He saw Śrīmatī Rādhikā."

veṇu-karān nipatitaḥ skhalitaṁ śikhaṇḍaṁ
bhraṣṭaṁ ca pīta-vasanaṁ vraja-rāja-sūnoḥ

In this verse (*Śrī-Rādhā-rasa-sudhā-nidhi* (39)), Prabodhānanda Sarasvatī Ṭhākura is explaining that Kṛṣṇa saw Śrīmatī Rādhikā performing *arcana* from the corners of Her eyes, and He very lovingly accepted Her glance. He began to tremble, His flute fell from His hands, and His yellow garment fell from His shoulders. He was just about to faint when Madhumaṅgala pushed Him and said, "Don't You see that Your father Nanda Bābā is here? What are You doing?"

Kṛṣṇa is controlled by this kind of love and affection. The *gopīs* have so much affection that they think that they have only a little.

dhanyāḥ sma mūḍha-gatayo 'py hariṇya etā
yā nanda-nandanam upātta-vicitra-veśam
akarṇya veṇu-raṇitaṁ saha kṛṣṇa-sārāḥ
pūjāṁ dadhur viracitāṁ praṇayāvalokaiḥ

Śrīmad-Bhāgavatam (10.21.11)

[The *gopīs* lamented:] The female deer are coming with their husbands. Their husbands are somewhat black in color, so they are called *kṛṣṇa-sāra*. Their husbands tell them, "You can happily go and see Kṛṣṇa. Don't fear – we are with you." Our husbands are just the opposite. If they see us talking with Kṛṣṇa or looking at Him, they come and chastise us. We want to die and take birth again as deer.

Sometimes Kṛṣṇa becomes upset because He lacks the moods enjoyed by Śrīmatī Rādhikā, Lalitā, and Viśākhā. Therefore He comes in the form of Śrī Caitanya Mahāprabhu to learn those moods. Mahāprabhu went to Godāvarī and met Śrī Rāya Rāmānanda, who is Viśākhā-devī in his *gopī-svarūpa*, and there He underwent training for many days. After that He went to the Gambhīrā, and only then was He able to taste something of Rādhikā's love. The moods of the *gopīs* are thus very high.

Kṛṣṇa is the ocean of *rasa*, the mellows exchanged in transcendental loving relationships. He Himself is *rasa*, and He is also *rasika*, the taster of *rasa*. At one and the same time, He is *eka-rasa* (one *rasa*) and *aneka-rasa* (many *rasas*). When He is *eka-rasa*, there is nothing in all the three worlds, even in Goloka Vṛndāvana, that is not in Him. He is *pūrṇatama*, most complete. He knows everything; nothing is unknown to Him. When He is *aneka-rasa*, however, there is a certain mixture of *rasas* that He both knows and does not know. Although He knows the *rasa* (the taste that He experiences) in Himself, He does not know the *rasa* in Śrīmatī Rādhikā. He knows what He can taste as the enjoyer, but He does not know what is tasted by the enjoyed. The pastimes of Caitanya Mahāprabhu, Śacīnandana Gaurahari, are a mixture of both *eka-rasa* and *aneka-rasa*. *Eka-rasa* is fully in Kṛṣṇa, but *aneka-rasa* is fully in Caitanya Mahāprabhu, because in Him Śrīmatī Rādhikā is present with Kṛṣṇa.

What are the moods in Rādhikā? They are of *mahābhāva*, and especially *adhirūḍha* and *mādana*.[1] Even if Śrīmatī Rādhikā is sitting on the lap of Kṛṣṇa, She may forget that She is with Him. She thinks, "Where am I? Where has Kṛṣṇa gone?" She feels such separation in meeting that Kṛṣṇa cannot imagine its depth. He thinks, "I am here, and She is on My lap. My hand is on Her shoulder, and yet She is searching for Me, crying, 'Where is He? Where is He?' Why is this so?"

To understand Rādhikā's mood, Kṛṣṇa assumed the form of Śrī Caitanya Mahāprabhu. Sometimes it is said that He stole it, and sometimes it is said that He begged for it. Rādhikā gave Him something of Her mood, and in the form of Śrī Gadādhara Paṇḍita, She was testing to see whether He was playing Her part well or not.

[1] Please refer to the Glossary for explanations of these terms.

In this way there is something that Kṛṣṇa never knows, and that is the mood of Rādhikā, the nature of Her love for Him, and the way in which She tastes the *mādhurīs* (sweet mellows) of His flute playing, His beautiful face, His form, His qualities, and His pastimes. Although those *mādhurīs* exist in Kṛṣṇa Himself, He does not fully know their sweetness – He cannot taste their sweetness fully. In *aneka-rasa*, therefore, Kṛṣṇa lacks something and He has to go to the school of the *gopīs*. There, Śrīmatī Rādhikā is like the principal, and Viśākhā and Lalitā are like departmental heads, and there He learns something about love and affection.

You should know that if one performs *bhajana* of Rādhā-Kṛṣṇa Yugala, and at the same time worships Dvārakādhīśa and Rukmiṇī or Satyabhāmā, Śrīmatī Rādhārāṇī will give him up. She will say, "Go to the queens in Dvārakā."

An incident occurred one hundred and fifty years ago, in a place in India called Raṇavāḍī, a village in Vraja-maṇḍala. A very advanced devotee lived there, and he always remembered Rādhikā and Kṛṣṇa and Their eternal pastimes throughout the eight *praharas* (periods) of the day. He was so absorbed that he almost forgot his body, senses, and everything else. One day, however, he had a desire to go to the places of pilgrimage. As he had never been to Dvārakā before, he especially desired to go there. In the meantime, a *brāhmaṇa* of his village came to him and said, "I am going to Dvārakā. If you want, you can come with me. I will pay the full fare and take care of everything." The devotee replied, "Yes, I want to go with you." So they traveled here and there together, and finally arrived in Dvārakā.

There is a rule in Dvārakā that if one wants to enter its territory he must be stamped with the hot firebrand of a *cakra*. The brand will remain throughout his life, but he will receive some medicine so that it will not be like a scar. That devotee from

Vṛndāvana was branded, and then he entered the city and had *darśana* of many places there. After that, he returned to his own place in Vṛndāvana and tried to resume his *bhajana*. However, something strange occurred when he wanted to remember all of Kṛṣṇa's pastimes: the pastimes no longer came in his memory, and instead he remembered incidents from Dvārakā and other places. He became very, very worried and disturbed because of not being able to chant and remember as he had done before. He wanted to know the cause of his misfortune, but he could not discern it. Although he practiced for many days, the *līlās* did not manifest as before.

This Bābājī Mahārāja had a very dear friend who lived at Rādhā-kuṇḍa. He was called Siddha Kṛṣṇadāsa Bābājī, and he was always absorbed in remembering Kṛṣṇa, and in chanting. Tears constantly fell from his eyes, and his heart was always melted. Bābājī Mahārāja went to visit his friend, but when Siddha Kṛṣṇadāsa saw him from a distance, he turned away and refused to converse with him. "Go away from here at once," he said, "otherwise Śrīmatī Rādhikā will be displeased with me as well. I know that you have gone to Dvārakā and you have accepted the firebrand there. Why have you come here? If Rādhikā knows that you have come to me, She will be displeased with me. Go at once. At once!"

That devotee became very upset and thought, "If the pastimes of Rādhikā and Kṛṣṇa do not come in my meditation, what is the use of my life?" He returned to his *bhajana-kuṭīra* and locked the door from inside in a mood of great separation from Śrīmatī Rādhikā. After three days a fire emanated from his heart, and he was totally consumed, so that only some ashes remained. The villagers could not understand why he had not come out for three days, and finally they broke open the door and saw that there were only the ashes remaining. "Perhaps Bābājī was in a mood of separation," they said. When they put some wooden sticks in those ashes, the sticks burned at once, and thus they realized, "Yes, Bābājī has left his body in separation." To this very day, the residents of that village celebrate his disappearance day.

Śrīmatī Rādhikā may give up a devotee if he worships Rādhikā and Kṛṣṇa of Vraja, but is simultaneously remembering Rukmiṇī and Satyabhāmā, and offering *praṇāma* and *arcana* to them. You should know all these truths. Śrīla Rūpa Gosvāmī and Śrīla Viśvanātha Cakravartī Ṭhākura have written that you should be one-pointed in your devotion to your *gurudeva* and your *iṣṭadeva.* You can honor everyone, including trees, creepers, animals, and devotees who are favorable to Kṛṣṇa, and even those who are not favorable. You can think that Kṛṣṇa is everywhere, and that all beings are His eternal servants in their constitutional spiritual forms. However, if one takes initiation in the *rūpānuga* line and is trying to be one-pointed, especially in trying to be a servant of Rādhikā, he cannot honor everyone in the same way. He cannot think that all are in the same category. Dvārakādhīśa-Kṛṣṇa and Vrajeśa-Kṛṣṇa are not the same. They are the same, but at the same time, They are different.

If one is just entering *bhakti,* there is no harm in worshiping Jagannātha, Rukmiṇī, Satyabhāmā, Rāmacandra, Nṛsiṁhadeva, Gaura-Nitāi, and also Rādhā-Kṛṣṇa. However, this is not for advanced *madhyama-adhikārīs* in Śrī Caitanya Mahāprabhu's line. One will have to be determined in one-pointed devotion; otherwise, Śrīmatī Rādhikā, the *gopīs,* and Yogamāyā will give him up. Though all incarnations and expansions are the same in *tattva-siddhānta,* there is some difference from the perspective of *rasa.* One cannot remain a neophyte devotee forever. He should gradually learn all these truths and try to become one-pointed.

There is no harm in worshiping Jagannātha if one sees Him as Vrajendra-nandana Śyāmasundara, which is how He appears in the eyes of Śrī Caitanya Mahāprabhu and Śrīla Rūpa Gosvāmī. Whenever Mahāprabhu went to the Jagannātha Temple, He did not see Baladeva Prabhu and Subhadrā. He simply thought, "O Vrajendra-nandana!" and He ran like a mad person to embrace Him. He never saw Jagannātha's large, round eyes, and He never saw Him without His peacock feather and flute. He thought, "Kṛṣṇa is there, playing on His flute, His eyes are very attractive, and He is wearing a large peacock feather."

Do you see that very Kṛṣṇa there in Jagannātha Purī? Do you see Rādhikā? At present you do not see Them, and therefore, in order to achieve this vision, you should be one-pointed to your *gurudeva*. There may be many *śikṣā-gurus*, but one *śikṣā-guru* should be prominent so that we can follow him and give him our hearts. Even the cloud, the mountain, the earth, and the python may be our *śikṣā-gurus*, but one *śikṣā-guru* should be prominent, and he is similar to our *dīkṣā-guru*. There is no difference between the two. Sometimes the *śikṣā-guru* may be superior to the *dīkṣā-guru*, sometimes the *dīkṣā-guru* may be superior, or they may be on the same level.

From the beginning, we should be one-pointed to Vrajendra-nandana Kṛṣṇa. That Kṛṣṇa should not simply be Gopī-kānta, the beloved of the *gopīs*, because if He is, then He may also be Candrāvalī-kānta, Padmā-kānta, and Śaibyā-kānta. We should be one-pointed to Rādhā-kānta and pray, *rādhā-kānta namo 'stu te*. This is a very deep and high *siddhānta*. During the Ratha-yātrā Festival, Caitanya Mahāprabhu engaged in many elevated dialogues with His intimate associate, Svarūpa Dāmodara, about the difference between the love of the *gopīs* and that of the queens of Dvārakā. If one has some taste and greed to follow the *gopīs*, and his aim and object is *samartha-rati*, then he can know something about these topics. This is the essence of the entire Chariot Festival.

Caitanya Mahāprabhu added to the meaning of the Ratha-yātrā Festival, turning it in a different way than previously performed. He made Guṇḍicā like Sundarācala, Vṛndāvana, while the Jagannātha Purī temple in Nilācala represented Dvārakā. All the *gopīs* were in a mood of great separation at their Guṇḍicā Mandira, just as they were in Vṛndāvana. That is why, after Jagannātha had been in the Purī temple for an entire year, He made an excuse to leave. He told His wife Lakṣmī, "I am so sick. I need to go somewhere else for ten days, for a change. I will go and then return very quickly." That is how He got permission from Lakṣmī to go.[2]

Jagannātha-deva took Baladeva with Him, because Baladeva had taken birth in Gokula as Rohiṇī-suta, the son of Rohiṇī. His sister Subhadrā is a manifestation of Yogamāyā, and she always used to associate with Rohiṇī, so she knew the glories of the *gopīs* and *gopas*. She requested Kṛṣṇa, "Brother, I want to go with You. Please take me." And He replied "Yes, you can come." Lakṣmī never knew where Kṛṣṇa desired to go. None of the queens ever knew. Vimalā-devī,[3] who represents the queens of Dvārakā, never knew, and that is why she allowed Him to go.

Kṛṣṇa was so engaged in playing in the groves with the *gopīs* that He forgot to return. On the fifth day, called Herā-pañcamī, Lakṣmī became very worried and wondered, "Where has my husband gone?" She searched here and there, but could not discover His whereabouts. Then, adorned with great opulence, she sat on a golden chariot and went to search further with many associates, who were holding sticks and other paraphernalia. When they arrived at the Guṇḍicā Mandira and saw Kṛṣṇa's chariot there, the

[2] This subject is more elaborately discussed in Chapter 7, Herā-pañcamī, wherein Śrī Caitanya Mahāprabhu and His associates enjoy seeing the enactment of this drama.

[3] More information on Vimalā-devī can be found in the Appendix.

associates of Lakṣmī picked up their sticks and began to beat the chariot. They captured all the associates of Jagannātha, who were all actually associates of Mahāprabhu and who represented the *gopīs.* When Kṛṣṇa entered a room and locked it from the inside, Lakṣmī told the *gopīs*, "You must return Him; otherwise I will come again and punish you, and Kṛṣṇa as well." After speaking like this, she returned.

rathera upare kare daṇḍera tāḍana
cora-prāya kare jagannāthera sevaka-gaṇa

saba bhṛtya-gaṇa kahe, – yoḍa kari' hāta
'kāli āni diba tomāra āge jagannātha'

tabe śānta hañā lakṣmī yāya nija ghara
āmāra lakṣmīra sampad – vākya-agocara

Śrī Caitanya-caritāmṛta (*Madhya-līlā* 14.211–13)

All the maidservants began to beat the chariot with sticks, and they treated the servants of Lord Jagannātha almost like thieves. Finally all of Lord Jagannātha's servants submitted to the goddess of fortune with folded hands, assuring her that they would bring Lord Jagannātha before her the very next day. Being thus pacified, the goddess of fortune returned to her apartment. Just see! My goddess of fortune is opulent beyond all description.

Mahāprabhu added this idea to the Ratha-yātrā Festival, that the *gopīs* brought Kṛṣṇa from the *mandira* in Nilācala – they brought Him from Dvārakā.

sei ta parāṇa-nātha pāinu
yāhā lāgi' madana-dahane jhuri' genu

Śrī Caitanya-caritāmṛta (*Madhya-līlā* 13.113)

[Śrīmatī Rādhikā said:] Now I have gained the Lord of My life, in the absence of whom I was being burned by Cupid and was withering away.

This singing of Rādhikā and the *gopīs* is the deep mood behind the Ratha-yātrā Festival. They were pulling the ropes of Jagannātha's chariot by their moods of separation, and He was coming with them to Vṛndāvana. Caitanya Mahāprabhu was in the mood of Rādhikā, and therefore, when He came in front of the *ratha*, it made a *haḍa haḍa, haḍa haḍa* (cracking) sound. It was coming – running – toward Guṇḍicā Mandira. In the mood of Rādhikā, Caitanya Mahāprabhu did not think, "I am Kṛṣṇa." Rather, He saw Kṛṣṇa in the deity of Jagannātha.

Rohiṇī-maiyā related many pastimes, and all the queens were listening eagerly. As Kṛṣṇa sat in His Sudharmā assembly hall, He was aware that Rohiṇī was speaking in Rukmiṇī's palace, and He could no longer remain where He was. He wanted to go to the place where Rohiṇī-maiyā was talking about Vṛndāvana, and at once He arrived at her door with Baladeva. Subhadrā was already standing guard at the door, and as she heard Rohiṇī's words she said, "Brother, You cannot go in. Maiyā Rohiṇī will rebuke me if I let You enter. She told me, 'Stay by the door, and make sure that no males come here – not even Kṛṣṇa and Baladeva. If they come, stop them.' So please remain here. You can go in when the discussion is finished."

Although Subhadrā stopped Kṛṣṇa and Baladeva from entering, they could hear through the door what Rohiṇī was telling the queens. Kṛṣṇa was standing at Subhadrā-devī's left, and Baladeva Prabhu at her right, and together they began to listen very carefully. As Rohiṇī-maiyā continued to speak, her heart began to melt, and all the queens were struck with wonder. As she described the glories of the love and affection of Vṛndāvana, Kṛṣṇa became so absorbed that His own heart began to melt, and His fingers also melted in that love and affection. As all three heard about the glories of the *gopīs* and how they love Kṛṣṇa, they all began to melt. They wept, and as they wept, their hands melted, their feet melted, their mouths melted, and only the shapes of the Jagannātha deities remained. At that time Rohiṇī-maiyā could not continue her description. She could no longer speak, for she had fainted from her bitter weeping.

Gradually, Kṛṣṇa began to return to external consciousness, and His former shape began to come back, little by little. When His form had fully returned to its normal features, Kṛṣṇa entered the palace room and saw that Mother Rohiṇī had fainted. Then He saw Nārada, who was looking very guilty, thinking, "I am responsible for all these incidents. I said something to Rukmiṇī and Satyabhāmā, and then they called Mother Rohiṇī and she began to speak about all these topics. So I am guilty." As he was thinking like this, Kṛṣṇa told him, "I think all this has happened only because of you – you are the main cause. Perhaps you said something to the queens to worry them, and that is why they began questioning Mother Rohiṇī. You are the root cause of these events. I am very happy – very happy. You reminded Me of Vraja, and I heard its glories. I want to give you a boon. You may ask Me for anything."

Nārada then became very happy as well, and he told Kṛṣṇa, "I want this boon: all three of you melted when you heard about your pastimes, and the glories of the *gopīs* and Vrajavāsīs. My desire is that you will remain in those forms somewhere in this world, and that the whole world will see you. In that form, you will be *patita-pāvana*, the savior of the fallen, and the entire world will be liberated by your *darśana*. That is what I want. Your hands and feet shrank and you melted completely. Everything was melted, and at that time you were absorbed in love and affection. I want the deities of you three to be manifest in this world and worshiped everywhere. People throughout the world will see you, they will learn this history, and they will develop pure love and affection for you."

Kṛṣṇa replied, "Yes. *Tato 'stu* – it will be. I will manifest these three deities and Sudarśana *cakra* in Jagannātha Purī, on the bank of the ocean. We will always remain there. There is a mountain called Nīlādri there, and that mountain is in the shape of a tortoise or a conchshell. I will always be there, and everyone will be able to see us."

It is because of this incident that the deity of Jagannātha smiled when speaking to King Indradyumna. Jagannātha-deva had been remembering this pastime of Rohiṇī-maiyā speaking to the queens, and also His promise to Nārada Ṛṣi.

Why did Kṛṣṇa mention Sudarśana *cakra* here? *Su* means "very good" and *darśana* means "vision." If Sudarśana does not give you eyes, if he does not help you by purifying you and giving you transcendental vision, you cannot actually see Jagannātha, Baladeva, and Subhadrā. You will think they are made of wood, and not very beautiful. But if Sudarśana gives you this light, this vision, then you can realize, "He is Vrajendra-nandana Śyāmasundara." This history of the appearance of Jagannātha is very lovely, and you are fortunate to hear it.

CHAPTER THREE

GUṆḌICĀ-MANDIRA-MĀRJANA

We should know that the Supreme Personality of Godhead is one without a second. He is the same God for the Christians, Muslims, Hindus, and all others. There are not different Gods – He is the same God, the same Allah, the same Christ. Just as there is one sun and one moon for the entire world, similarly, there are not different Gods for different people. How can God be divided? There cannot be more than one God; otherwise all the gods will quarrel over territory and position. There is only one God, but He appears according to the vision of the devotee.

An analogy can be given in relation to the moon. It appears that there are fifteen different moons. For fifteen days the moon gradually increases in size, eventually becoming a full moon. After that it decreases in size again, becoming a new moon on the last day of the month. The "moons" are not different; it is the names of the moon that are different: full moon, new moon, quarter moon, and so on. Similarly, there is only one God, but He appears to be many because people have seemingly divided Him up by their different languages and understandings.

Kṛṣṇa is the Supreme Personality of Godhead. He has many manifestations such as Rāma, Nṛsiṁha, Jagannātha, Baladeva, and Nārāyaṇa, and they are all the same. Even the person Christians call "God" is the same, for He is also one of Kṛṣṇa's manifestations, as are Allah and Jehovah. These are all names of God's manifestations. Some of these manifestations are more complete and have more power, and some have less power. The full moon, the new moon, and the stages in between all belong to the same moon, but we see differences according to our angle of vision. Actually, the moon is always full, but we consider that it is waxing or waning when it is covered to varying degrees.

In the same way, Kṛṣṇa is one without a second. He has innumerable manifestations, but they are all Kṛṣṇa. We are also parts and parcels of Kṛṣṇa. We are not Kṛṣṇa, but at the same time, we are non-different from Him. Both principles are there: difference and non-difference. We can use the analogies of the sun and its rays, and the fire and its heat; they are also different and non-different. This is an astonishing truth, which Caitanya Mahāprabhu has explained thoroughly.

The Supreme Personality of Godhead is one without a second. Sometimes He manifests in this world personally, and sometimes He sends His associates to give pure knowledge. All the souls here in this world are eternal servants of that Supreme Personality of Godhead. This is the true conception, whether we accept it or not. We have forgotten Him from the beginning of the creation of this world, so He sometimes descends and performs very sweet and powerful pastimes so that all conditioned souls will be attracted to Him and engage in His service. He sometimes descends as Kṛṣṇa, sometimes as Rāma, and sometimes as Jagannātha, Baladeva, and Subhadrā.

We cannot realize Kṛṣṇa if our hearts are full of lust, worldly desires, and unwanted habits. He cannot come into our hearts under these circumstances; so these impurities must first be given up. There is no place for doubt in devotion. No one has any confusion or doubt about whether the sun exists, so why should there be any doubt about the existence of the creator of millions of suns? He can create millions and millions of worlds in a moment, and He can also destroy them. Sometimes He comes here, only to save us and to engage us all in His service. Other than serving Him, there is no way to be happy in this world or in any other world. There is only one God, and ignoring Him is the cause of our unhappiness.

We can be happy if we engage in Kṛṣṇa's service. Don't be afraid that serving Him will be like serving someone in this world. There is immense happiness in serving Him, more so than in serving your wife, husband, children, father, and so on. There is very, very relishable love and affection in His service. There is so much love and affection in Kṛṣṇa's transcendental abode – oceans of love and affection. In this world the master gains and the servant has to lose something, but it is not like that there.

First we should know that we are Kṛṣṇa's eternal servants, but we have forgotten Him, and that is the cause of all our suffering and sorrow, birth and death. We should have very firm faith in this. Don't have any doubt that we are spirit souls, parts and parcels of Godhead, that we are His eternal servants, and that it is due to forgetting Him that we are suffering now. We can realize His mercy if we chant His name and surrender to Him, giving up all doubts as Arjuna did.

Jagannātha-deva, Baladeva Prabhu, and Subhadrā have descended to this world from their transcendental abode. We will gradually try to explain the true identity (*svarūpa*) of Jagannātha, Baladeva, and Subhadrā – who they are and how they came to this world.

Today is the day of *guṇḍicā-mandira-mārjana*, the cleansing of the Guṇḍicā Temple. *Śrī Caitanya-caritāmṛta* states that the temple of Jagannātha represents Dvārakā, while the temple at Guṇḍicā is called Sundarācala and represents Vṛndāvana. All the *gopīs*, such as Lalitā, Viśākhā, and Śrīmatī Rādhikā, are there in Vṛndāvana, and so are Nanda Bābā, Yaśodā, and all the other Vrajavāsīs. Vasudeva, Devakī, Baladeva, Subhadrā, and all the other Dvārakāvāsīs reside in Dvārakā. While Kṛṣṇa resides in Dvārakā, He always remembers the Vrajavāsīs – His father Nanda Bābā, His mother Yaśodā, His cows, calves, friends, and especially His beloved *gopīs*. He sometimes becomes so distraught in separation from them that He arranges to go to Vṛndāvana to meet them.

One day before the Ratha-yātrā Festival, Mahāprabhu leads all the devotees to the Guṇḍicā Mandira to clean it. On the next day, Jagannātha goes to Guṇḍicā Mandira along with Baladeva, Subhadrā, and His devotees for ten days, after which they all return. Just as Jagannātha goes to Guṇḍicā Mandira after it is cleaned, so He may come into your heart if you make it very pure and clean.

This festival of *guṇḍicā-mārjana* has been performed every year since Satya-yuga. In *Śrī Caitanya-caritāmṛta* we see that previously, before the participation of Śrī Caitanya Mahāprabhu, the servants of the King used to clean that temple, but they would not clean it properly because they were being paid to do it. They could not give Jagannātha much pleasure because they had no devotion. Śrī Caitanya Mahāprabhu therefore told the King through his priest Kāśī Miśra, "I would like the service of cleaning the temple and the surrounding area to be given to us." He told Kāśī Miśra, Sārvabhauma Bhaṭṭācārya, and others, "Please get permission from the King so that this year I Myself will serve the Guṇḍicā Mandira along with My associates. We will sweep and clean it ourselves. There is no need to send any servants of the King; no need at all. We only need some brooms and pitchers."

Hundreds and thousands of pitchers and brooms were obtained, and Caitanya Mahāprabhu's associates arrived. Thousands of Bengali devotees and many thousands of Orissan devotees accompanied Caitanya Mahāprabhu with dancing and *kīrtana*. They had about fifteen *mṛdaṅgas* and many *karatālas.* Caitanya Mahāprabhu personally gave them all garlands and *candana*, and then, dancing in line formation, they all began to sing. They all went to Guṇḍicā Mandira, singing and dancing, and holding their brooms and pitchers.

The King became very happy. He wanted to meet Caitanya Mahāprabhu and serve Him, but although he was a very high-class devotee, he had the name and position of a king. He had great wealth and reputation and was always surrounded by armies, commanders, and so on. Following the regulations of the *sannyāsa* order, Caitanya Mahāprabhu never wanted a sense enjoyer (*viṣayī*) such as a king to come to Him. He considered that it would be a disturbance, because He would be bound to hear mundane talk (*viṣayi-kathā*). We will be alarmed and fearful if a snake comes near us, even if its poison has been removed. Similarly, a devotee fears association with a sense enjoyer because it will disturb his *sādhana-bhajana.* Now, however, we ourselves are like sense enjoyers, because we are hankering for wealth, reputation, and position.

Caitanya Mahāprabhu is Svayam Bhagavān Himself. He is non-different from Jagannātha, but He was playing the role of a devotee, which is why He had sent a representative to tell the King, "I want to go personally and clean the entire temple." The King had then requested Kāśī Miśra, who was his superintendent, minister, priest, and spiritual master, "His devotees can take whatever utensils and other paraphernalia He wants."

Mahāprabhu had thus called His associates, such as Svarūpa Dāmodara, Rāya Rāmānanda, Gadādhara Paṇḍita, and others.

Advaita Ācārya and Nityānanda Prabhu were also there, along with all the Gauḍīya *bhaktas*. There were thousands and thousands of devotees, and on the evening before the festival, Mahāprabhu had told them all, "You should each bring a big broom made of coconut tree fibers, and each of you should also bring a clay pitcher."

Now, on the next day, at about seven in the morning, devotees assembled from all over India and all over the world – not only one or two hundred thousand, but about one million. First Caitanya Mahāprabhu accepted flower garlands and *candana* Himself, and then He gave them to all the devotees. They all wanted to offer *praṇāma* to Him, but instead He very humbly offered *praṇāma* to all of them. Nityānanda Prabhu wanted to touch His feet, but He very humbly touched Nityānanda's feet. He had no false ego, thinking, "I am a *guru*; everyone should respect me. Why should I respect others?" Actually, people who think like that are not pure devotees. A *guru* is one who respects others. His symptoms are:

tṛṇād api sunīcena
taror api sahiṣṇunā
amāninā mānadena
kīrtanīyaḥ sadā hariḥ

Śikṣāṣṭaka (3)

He is very humble, even more so than a blade of grass, and he is also very tolerant, more so than a tree. Even if a tree is dry, it will never request, "Water! Water! Water!" If someone cuts the branches of a tree, it will not protest, "Oh, spare me! Don't cut me!" It will never speak like that. Mango trees give very sweet mangoes, even if one throws stones at the tree in an attempt to make the mangoes fall. The bark, seeds, fruits, leaves, and sap of trees are always for others, not for themselves. Kṛṣṇa tells us that we should be like the trees. In other words, our lives should be for others, not for ourselves, and our lives should be especially for Kṛṣṇa. If one lives only for himself, he is lower in consciousness than the trees.

The devotees with Mahāprabhu were touching each other's feet and at the same time performing *kīrtana*. Each holding a broom and a pitcher, they performed *nagara-saṅkīrtana* the entire distance from the Jagannātha Temple to Guṇḍicā. The hundreds of thousands of devotees began to bring water from the very large pond known as Indradyumna-sarovara, and as they did so, they said, "Kṛṣṇa! Kṛṣṇa!" to each other as they gave and received the clay pitchers. They were filling their clay pots with water, carrying the pots on their heads or in other ways, and giving them to others, saying, "Hare Kṛṣṇa!" to others on the way. Then, taking back the empty pots, they again said, "Hare Kṛṣṇa!" In this way they were running back and forth very quickly. Similarly, while the devotees were sweeping, they were saying, "Kṛṣṇa! Kṛṣṇa!" Everything was going on only with the chanting of the names, "Kṛṣṇa! Kṛṣṇa!" and no other sound could be heard. If a clay pot was broken due to the haste, there would be sounds of, "O Kṛṣṇa! Kṛṣṇa!" and new clay pots were brought from a shop at once.

In this way, everyone was engaged in cleaning the courtyard of the Guṇḍicā Mandira. Water was thrown everywhere, and all the areas were cleared so that torrents of water flowed from the drain like the current of a river. Mahāprabhu cleaned everywhere, high and low, throwing water here and there, and thus everything became as clean as His own heart. This is known as *guṇḍicā-mandira-mārjana.*

Your heart is like a throne (*siṁhāsana*), and you will have to clean it if you want to keep Kṛṣṇa and Rādhikā there. First clean it, and then They will come. Who will clean it? Nityānanda Prabhu may do so and *gurudeva* may do so, but you will also have to do something. *Guru* will help you; he has the power to do so, and he is very merciful, but you will also have to do something. You must follow his orders. Be like Arjuna, who told Kṛṣṇa in *Bhagavad-gītā* (2.7): "*śiṣyas te 'haṁ śādhi māṁ tvāṁ prapannam* – I have offered myself at Your lotus feet. I will follow Your order and obey all Your instructions." Kṛṣṇa then ordered him to fight, and he was successful.

Similarly, *guru* can help you if you follow and obey him, but if you disobey, that is an offense and your desire to serve Kṛṣṇa will disappear. Try to obey. For example, *gurudeva* says, "You should chant every day. You should chant not less than sixteen rounds, and chant your *guru-gāyatrī* and all other *gāyatrī-mantras* daily." A disciple may say, "Gurudeva, I'm very weak, I cannot chant *gāyatrī-mantra.* When I chant, I get a headache. I become sick and my mind becomes upset. What should I do?" *Gurudeva* will reply, "You should continue to chant, and your headache, sickness, and all other disturbances will go away. But you will have to do it." Then, if you do not obey, what can he do?

Although Caitanya Mahāprabhu is Kṛṣṇa Himself, the Supreme Personality of Godhead, He was cleaning the temple. Merely sweeping with a broom will not do, for a broom can never touch our hearts. In order to demonstrate this, Mahāprabhu told His associates, "We should chant and remember, performing *kīrtana* along with the sweeping. Then it will have some effect." If you are cleaning your house in your householder life, while you sweep you can sing, "Govinda Dāmodara Mādhaveti, Govinda Dāmodara Mādhaveti." Whatever job you do, chant these names with your heart, and then your heart will be "swept." It will become pure and clear, neat and clean.

Caitanya Mahāprabhu and all His associates began to perform *kīrtana* with many *mṛdaṅgas*, *kholas*, and *karatālas*. The temple compound was so large that over two million devotees were able to fit there, and they swept and cleaned everywhere. Mahāprabhu personally took His *uttarīya-veśa* (*sannyāsa* upper cloth), and He cleaned the spots that were very stubborn. *Śrī Caitanya-caritāmṛta* (*Madhya-līlā* 12.1, 99, 104) has stated:

śrī-guṇḍicā-mandiram ātma-vṛndaiḥ
sammārjayan kṣālanataḥ sa gauraḥ
sva-citta-vac chītalam ujjvalaṁ ca
kṛṣṇopaveśaupayikaṁ cakāra

Śrī Caitanya Mahāprabhu washed and cleansed the Guṇḍicā Temple with His devotees and associates. In this way He made it as cool and bright as His own heart, and thus He made the temple a befitting place for Śrī Kṛṣṇa to sit.

śrī-haste kareṇa siṁhāsanera mārjana
prabhu āge jala āni' deya bhakta-gaṇa

Then Śrī Caitanya Mahāprabhu began to wash the sitting place of Lord Jagannātha with His own hands, and all the devotees began to bring water to the Lord.

nija-vastre kaila prabhu gṛha sammārjana
mahāprabhu nija-vastre mājila siṁhāsana

Thc Lord mopped the rooms with His own clothes, and He polished the throne with them also.

We should give up all our worldly positions and ego that dictates, "I am so intelligent; I have so much power; I am the superintendent; I am the monarch of all; I am *guru*." Advaita Ācārya was Mahā-Viṣṇu Himself, but he was very humble and polite, and he also cleaned the temple.

All the devotees were sweeping, as was Caitanya Mahāprabhu Himself. First they swept away very big stones, stone chips, and pieces of grass. If you want to make a seat in your heart for Rādhā and Kṛṣṇa, your heart must be like Vṛndāvana, and if you do not make your heart very pure and transcendental like Vṛndāvana, Kṛṣṇa cannot come. If you have any worldly desires, they will be like thorns pricking Kṛṣṇa's body. These thorns are lust, anger, greed, envy, attachment for worldly things, quarreling, and criticizing. If you want *bhakti*, don't criticize anyone. Be tolerant and follow this verse:

tṛṇād api sunīcena
taror api sahiṣṇunā
amāninā mānadena
kīrtanīyaḥ sadā hariḥ

Śikṣāṣṭaka (3)

One who thinks himself lower than the grass, who is more tolerant than a tree, and who does not expect personal honor, yet is always prepared to give all respect to others, can very easily always chant the holy name of the Lord.

If you do not have these four qualities, you will never be able to chant, because the holy name is transcendental. You cannot chant with your tongue, and you cannot see Kṛṣṇa with your eyes.

ataḥ śrī-kṛṣṇa-nāmādi
na bhaved grāhyam indriyaiḥ
sevonmukhe hi jihvādau
svayam eva sphuraty adaḥ

Bhakti-rasāmṛta-sindhu (1.2.234)

Material senses cannot appreciate Kṛṣṇa's holy name, form, qualities, and pastimes. When a conditioned soul is awakened to Kṛṣṇa consciousness and renders service by using his tongue to chant the Lord's holy name and taste the remnants of the Lord's food, the tongue is purified, and one gradually comes to understand who Kṛṣṇa really is.

You should think, "I am serving Kṛṣṇa by chanting – this is my service. O Kṛṣṇa, please purify me." If you surrender and offer yourself unto the lotus feet of Kṛṣṇa, He will mercifully come and dance on your tongue.

There are three stages of chanting: *nāma-aparādha*, *nāma-ābhāsa*, and *śuddha-nāma*. When you practice by your tongue and by your endeavor, this is *nāma-aparādha*. When you chant with some *śraddhā* (faith), then it will be *nāma-ābhāsa*, and if your chanting is pure, then Kṛṣṇa Himself will dance on your tongue. We should try to pray to Kṛṣṇa, "I offer myself unto Your lotus feet, giving up all worldly desires. I have no beloved except You. You are mine." Be like the *gopīs*, and then Kṛṣṇa may come.

When the stones were cleared away, the thousands of devotees, along with Śrī Caitanya Mahāprabhu, Śrī Nityānanda Prabhu, Śrī Advaita Ācārya, and Śrī Svarūpa Dāmodara, swept again. Mahāprabhu told them, "I want to see who has swept up the biggest pile of dust. Everyone should collect their pile in their cloths, and I will examine them; otherwise some may cheat the others by only pretending to sweep, but not really doing so." In the end, everyone saw that Mahāprabhu had swept up much more than all the others combined. Sometimes Mahāprabhu would give a very sweet lesson to those who were only pretending, instead of actually sweeping. He would say to them, "Oh, you have done so much. You should teach others." Hearing these joking words, all the devotees would laugh.

The devotees swept three times, and there is a deep meaning behind this. We have committed so many offenses, we are in so much ignorance, and we have so many unwanted habits. We should very boldly and strongly give up activities that are not favorable for *kṛṣṇa-bhakti*, and we should very boldly reject things and people that are not favorable to *bhakti*. We should totally reject any wish, any desire, or any result that is not favorable for pleasing Kṛṣṇa or a pure devotee and *guru*.

You should reject anyone who criticizes high-class devotees. You can defeat his arguments, and if you are like Hanumān, you can burn all of Laṅkā and also cut out his tongue. If you are not of Hanumān's caliber, then you should block your ears and simply leave that place where criticism is going on. Always try to accept only the things, the society, and the association that are favorable for *bhakti*. Do not desire or expect praise for yourself. Never have any wish to be honored by others, but always give honor to all devotees according to their standard of *bhakti*.

The heart of a devotee who is chanting and remembering Kṛṣṇa should be pure. Why should a *brahmacārī* or *sannyāsī* who has been worshiping, chanting, and serving his *gurudeva* for twenty years have the desire to marry and amass wealth? And why does he leave aside his *sannyāsa* or *brahmacārī* saffron cloth, and get a girlfriend or even a boyfriend? This is not advancement towards Kṛṣṇa. It may be that he has neglected pure devotees and has no faith in his *gurudeva's* words, and it may also be that his *gurudeva* is fallen.

A devotee who is chanting the holy name purely from the beginning will be like Śrīla Raghunātha dāsa Gosvāmī. Dāsa Gosvāmī left everything and never again accepted worldly enjoyment. Śrīla Bhaktivedānta Swāmī Mahārāja left worldly life and his wife and children, and he never returned to them again. If *brahmacārīs* and *sannyāsīs* accept worldly life again, it means they have no faith in Kṛṣṇa's name. Kṛṣṇa has invested His whole power, His whole mercy, opulence, and so forth in His name. Brahmā can create the world only by the mercy of this name – by his chanting of this name. Śaṅkara, too, can only perform any task by chanting Kṛṣṇa's name. Neither of them can do anything without the help of the holy name.

We have no faith that Kṛṣṇa's name can maintain our lives. From the beginning, we have no taste and have committed so many offenses. Śrī Caitanya Mahāprabhu is therefore telling us, "You must purify your hearts, if you want to be devotees and realize Kṛṣṇa, and if you want Kṛṣṇa to be seated in your hearts." But you have no power to do it. You cannot purify your hearts, so who will purify them? You can do it if you are under the guidance of Mahāprabhu, Śrī Nityānanda Prabhu, Śrī Advaita Ācārya, Śrī Gadādhara Paṇḍita, Śrī Svarūpa Dāmodara, and Śrī Rāya Rāmānanda. Otherwise, your doubts will never go away, you will commit offenses, and you will remain attached to unwanted habits. So many desires to taste worldly enjoyment will come to you, and you will not be able to check them.

Caitanya Mahāprabhu is therefore instructing us. He Himself was sweeping, along with His devotees, in order to teach us. That is why His devotees swept a first time, then a second time, and then a third time. The first time they swept, they removed big stones, chips, and grasses; the second time, they removed very fine dust; and the third time still finer dust.

When all the dust was taken out, there still remained spots of black tar, which cannot be removed simply by sweeping. For this you will have to try much harder. You will have to use a very sharp instrument, and then you will have to wash off the spots with a cleaner like kerosene or alcohol. These spots are our offenses, and they will not disappear by sweeping alone. These spots are deceit (*kuṭīnāṭī*) and desires for profit (*lābha*), adoration (*pūjā*), and fame (*pratiṣṭhā*). *Śrī Caitanya-caritāmṛta* (*Madhya-līlā* 19.159) has explained this, and Śrīla Swāmī Mahārāja has given the translation:

niṣiddhācāra kuṭīnāṭī jīva-hiṁsana
lābha-pūjā-pratiṣṭhādi yata upaśākhā-gaṇa

Some unnecessary creepers growing with the *bhakti* creeper are the creepers of behavior unacceptable for those trying to attain perfection: diplomatic behavior, animal killing, mundane profiteering, mundane adoration, and mundane importance. All these are unwanted creepers.

Nowadays, many persons have no proper respect for Vaiṣṇavas. They tell them, "Oh, you cannot enter our temple." Juniors are not giving proper respect to seniors, and seniors are not giving proper respect, love, and affection to juniors. This is the problem, and the root of it is offenses to the holy name. Many devotees have no regard for the holy name. They have no strong faith in chanting, and that is why so many senior devotees are going away and junior devotees are coming, becoming senior, and then also going away. These are the problems nowadays. You can easily give up your children, your wives, your husbands, your relatives, and even your wealth. But it is very hard to give up the desire for praise, and it is hard to follow this verse (*Śikṣāṣṭaka* (3)):

tṛṇād api sunīcena
taror api sahiṣṇunā
amāninā mānadena
kīrtanīyaḥ sadā hariḥ

Thinking oneself to be even lower and more worthless than insignificant grass that is trampled beneath everyone's feet, being more tolerant than a tree, being prideless, and offering respect to all others according to their respective positions, one should continuously chant the holy name of Śrī Hari.

This is the meaning of "sweeping the heart," and Śrī Caitanya Mahāprabhu wanted this. At this stage you will honor even a creeper and a tree, what to speak of devotees. You will see Kṛṣṇa in everyone and everywhere, and then you will be able to honor everyone properly. We should try to sweep in our hearts today, on this sacred day of *guṇḍicā-mandira-mārjana.*

We should try to understand what are *niṣiddhācāra*, prohibited activities. For example, if you are a *brahmacārī* or *sannyāsī*, be far away from lust.

asat-saṅga-tyāga, – ei vaiṣṇava-ācāra
'strī-saṅgī' – eka asādhu, 'kṛṣṇābhakta' āra

Śrī Caitanya-caritāmṛta (*Madhya-līlā* 22.87)

A Vaiṣṇava should always avoid the association of ordinary people. Common people are very much materially attached, especially to the opposite sex. Vaiṣṇavas should also avoid the company of those who are not devotees of Lord Kṛṣṇa.

Try to follow this, whether you are a family man or in the renounced order. Do not associate with Māyāvādīs who do not believe in the personal form of Kṛṣṇa or Godhead. To such persons, everything is God, which means that everything is zero. Also, do not associate with those who are lusty – one should remain very far away from such people. Do not tell lies, do not be duplicitous, do not be politicians, and do not be hypocrites. These are basic principles.

Kuṭīnāṭī: *ku* means "evil," *ṭī* means "the," *nā* means "no" or "that which is prohibited," and *ṭī* means "particular." *Kuṭīnāṭī* means activities that are like those of Pūtanā. The word *pūtanā* means impure, and she was the first demon killed by Kṛṣṇa; He killed impurity first of all. First be pure by body, mind, and soul, by chanting and remembering, and by always serving Vaiṣṇavas and giving them proper respect.

Jīva-hiṁsana: don't kill anything, even a creeper. This is also a basic principle. *Jīva-hiṁsana* means violence, but in this connection violence does not only mean killing by the hands or by a weapon. It also means killing by the tongue, mind, or heart. Do not be envious. If you want to be pure devotees, remove envy from your hearts and don't criticize any Vaiṣṇava, for this is also *hiṁsā*.

These spots will not be removed merely by sweeping, nor will they disappear simply by washing them with water. Rather, they will only become stronger and more prominent. In other words, these spots are not very easy to remove. They manifest as offenses at the lotus feet of Vaiṣṇavas and *guru*, and also as neglect of *guru*. Among the ten kinds of *nāma-aparādha*, the first is the offense to pure devotees. The aspiring devotee must remove all these spots quickly, and Caitanya Mahāprabhu therefore took His own outer garment and washed everything – up, down, here, there, and everywhere. He did not leave even one corner unclean.

Thousands and thousands of devotees continually took water from Indradyumna Sarovara, and placed the water-pots in the hands of Śrī Svarūpa Dāmodara, Śrī Rāya Rāmānanda, Śrī Gadādhara Paṇḍita, Śrī Nityānanda Prabhu, Śrī Advaita Ācārya, and Śrīman Mahāprabhu Himself. Nowadays, those who consider themselves *gurus* will give orders to others and do nothing themselves. They think that they should only taste delicious *mahā-prasāda* and enjoy opulent surroundings; they may even have chairs made of gold. Such false *gurus* do not remain; rather, they go to hell.

In this way, Śrī Caitanya Mahāprabhu was clearing away all unwanted mentalities and behaviors. In the first and second verses of his *Upadeśāmṛta*, Śrīla Rūpa Gosvāmī also discusses the unwanted habits to be swept away. Without such sweeping, pure *bhakti* cannot be attained even in millions of births. In the first verse Rūpa Gosvāmī states:

vāco vegaṁ manasaḥ krodha-vegaṁ
jihvā-vegam udaropastha-vegam
etān vegān yo viṣaheta dhīraḥ
sarvām apīmāṁ pṛthivīṁ sa śiṣyāt

A sober person who can tolerate the urge to speak, the mind's demands, the actions of anger and the urges of the tongue, belly, and genitals is qualified to make disciples all over the world.

There are six kinds of *vegas* (urges), and the root is the tongue, which has no backbone. If you cannot control the tongue, all the other five urges will control you; and if you do control it, everything else is controlled. The tongue has two functions, the first of which is speaking. If this function is not controlled, you may say something wrong to another person and that may create a very big problem for you – you may even be ruined forever.

Draupadī, the wife of the Pāṇḍavas, once said something that was actually correct, but the circumstance in which she said it was inappropriate. She told Duryodhana, "Your father is blind, and you are also blind. Like father, like son." Duryodhana was offended, and as a result the great Mahābhārata War was fought and millions of people were killed. Similarly, the Rāmāyaṇa War was fought only because of Sītā's tongue. She chastised Lakṣmaṇa, and this ultimately led to a war in which so many were killed. You should therefore try to control your tongue; do not speak what should not be spoken.

The second function of the tongue is eating. If you eat meat, fish, and other prohibited items, or if you take drugs, they will also harm you, and you will not be able to control your mind or your heart. On the other hand, everything will be controlled if you take only *mahā-prasāda* and chant Hare Kṛṣṇa, Hare Kṛṣṇa....

In the second verse of *Upadeśāmṛta*, Śrīla Rūpa Gosvāmī states:

atyāhāraḥ prayāsaś ca
prajalpo niyamāgrahaḥ
jana-saṅgaś ca laulyaṁ ca
ṣaḍbhir bhaktir vinaśyati

One's devotional service is spoiled when he becomes too entangled in the following six activities: (1) eating more than necessary or collecting more funds than required, (2) over-endeavoring for mundane things that are very difficult to attain, (3) talking unnecessarily about mundane subject matters, (4) practicing the scriptural rules and regulations only for the sake of following them and not for the sake of spiritual advancement, or rejecting the rules and regulations of the scriptures and working independently or whimsically, (5) associating with worldly-minded persons who are not interested in Kṛṣṇa consciousness, and (6) being greedy for mundane achievements.

Both Śrīla Bhaktisiddhānta Sarasvatī Ṭhākura and Śrīla Bhaktivedānta Swāmī Mahārāja have written commentaries on how to be free from these habits, and we can clean our hearts by reading these commentaries. It is stated in Śrīla Swāmī Mahārāja's purport (*Śrī Caitanya-caritāmṛta* (*Madhya-līlā* 12.135)):

Śrīla Bhaktisiddhānta Sarasvatī Ṭhākura explains that even though one may become free from the desire for fruitive activity, sometimes the subtle desire for fruitive activity again comes into being within the heart. One often thinks of conducting business to improve devotional activity. However, the contamination is so strong that it may later develop into misunderstanding, described as *kuṭīnāṭī* (faultfinding) and *pratiṣṭhāśā* (the desire for name and fame and for high position), *jīva-hiṁsā* (envy of other living entities), *niṣiddhācāra* (accepting things forbidden in the *śāstra*), *kāma* (desire for material gain), and *pūjā* (hankering for popularity). The word *kuṭīnāṭī* means "duplicity." As an example of *pratiṣṭhāśā*, one may attempt to imitate Śrīla Haridāsa Ṭhākura by living in a solitary place.

Some Western devotees once went to Purī. They were not allowed to take *darśana* of Jagannātha, Baladeva, and Subhadrā in the temple, but they were able to go to the Ṭoṭā Gopīnātha Temple, Śrīla Haridāsa Ṭhākura's *samādhi*, and Siddha-bakula. One of those devotees gave over a thousand dollars to an Indian *pūjārī* at Siddha-bakula and said, "Give me the *mālā* kept here, the beads on which Haridāsa Ṭhākura was chanting." The man took the thousand dollars, stole the *mālā*, and gave it to that "devotee" who then thought, "Oh, when I chant on this *mālā*, I will be liberated and I will have *bhakti*." Imitation will not do, however. That person was offensive. Nowadays many people want to have large *mālā* weighing not less than five kilos. They cannot chant properly, but still they collect big *tulasī* neckbeads with "Rādhe, Rādhe" written on them. This will not do; rather, false ego will increase by this. Try to chant and remember purely, and associate with devotees. It is stated in the same purport:

> One's real desire may be for name and fame. In other words, one thinks that fools will accept one to be as good as Haridāsa Ṭhākura just because one lives in a holy place. These are all material desires. A neophyte devotee is certain to be attacked by other material desires as well, namely desires for women and money. In this way the heart is again filled with dirty things and becomes harder and harder, like that of a materialist. Gradually one desires to become a reputed devotee or an *avatāra* (incarnation).

Nowadays there are so many "incarnations" like this. They have no belief in God, but they want to be *guru*, and after some days they fall down. This disease of false *gurus* and gods is spreading like the plague, and now there are so many "gods," both in India and the West. We have been duplicitous since our birth; but now we must become very simple, and we should always honor devotees.

Also, be free from *lobha*, the greed for worldly things. Be free from thinking, "I must have this thing," or "My relatives and neighbors have very good cars, but I don't." Be simple like Śrīla Raghunātha dāsa Gosvāmī, who followed the instructions given to him by Caitanya Mahāprabhu:

grāmya-kathā nā śunibe, grāmya-vārtā nā kahibe
bhāla nā khāibe āra bhāla nā paribe

amānī mānada hañā kṛṣṇa-nāma sadā la'be
vraje rādhā-kṛṣṇa-sevā mānase karibe

Śrī Caitanya-caritāmṛta (*Madhya-līlā* 6.236–7)

Do not talk like people in general or hear what they say. You should not eat very palatable food, nor should you dress very nicely. Do not expect honor, but offer all respect to others. Always chant the holy name of Lord Kṛṣṇa, and within your mind render service to Rādhā and Kṛṣṇa in Vṛndāvana.

Follow Śrīla Raghunātha dāsa Gosvāmī, Śrīla Jīva Gosvāmī, and others like them. Be simple like Caitanya Mahāprabhu and His associates. Mahāprabhu personally removed all the spots from the *siṁhāsana* on which Jagannātha, Baladeva, and Subhadrā would sit – He did not leave it to anyone else to do. This means that we should try to make our hearts like a *siṁhāsana* where Jagannātha, Baladeva, and Subhadrā will sit, where Rādhā and Kṛṣṇa will sit, and where Mahāprabhu will sit.

This opportunity will not come if there are dirty thoughts and aspirations in our hearts. They will never come. Take your ears in your hands[1] and promise, "From today I will practice properly." Kṛṣṇa will provide for you if you are always chanting and remembering. He will look after you, and sometimes He may come to you as a servant, bringing paraphernalia for you on His head. There are many examples as evidence of this, so do not worry about how to maintain yourselves. The only problem should be how to purify yourselves, and how to attain love and affection for Kṛṣṇa.

While Caitanya Mahāprabhu was cleaning, a very young Gauḍīya *bhakta* took a pitcher of water, poured the water on Mahāprabhu's feet, and drank some of it. Mahāprabhu then appeared very angry and said, "What are you doing? Nonsense! Jagannātha is coming here. Jagannātha is the Supreme Personality of Godhead Himself, and we are cleaning here, preparing for Him to come. I am an ordinary person, a man, and yet this person is washing My feet and taking that water to drink. This offense is very bad for Me, and for him."

If you wash the feet of an ordinary person in Kṛṣṇa's temple, it is a very big offense. Of course, Caitanya Mahāprabhu is Jagannātha Himself, but He is giving instruction to others. A bona fide *guru* will never proudly think, "Very good! My disciple comes and places flowers on my feet, pours water on them, washes them, sprinkles that water on others, and then drinks it." A pure Vaiṣṇava or *guru* never considers, "I am an advanced devotee." Even Śrī Caitanya Mahāprabhu, in the mood of Śrīmatī Rādhikā, has said:

[1] This is an Indian expression. In India when one is expressing regret due to a sense of guilt, he holds his earlobes as he apologizes.

na prema-gandho 'sti darāpi me harau
krandāmi saubhāgya-bharaṁ prakāśitum
vaṁśī-vilāsy-ānana-lokanaṁ vinā
bibharmi yat prāṇa-pataṅgakān vṛthā

Śrī Caitanya-caritāmṛta (*Madhya-līlā* 2.45)

My dear friends, I have not the slightest tinge of love of Godhead within My heart. When you see Me crying in separation, I am just falsely exhibiting a demonstration of My great fortune. Indeed, not seeing the beautiful face of Kṛṣṇa playing His flute, I continue to live My life like an insect, without purpose.

"I have not even a scent of *bhakti* to Kṛṣṇa. I am more wretched than anyone." Rādhikā Herself is saying, "Oh, the forest deer are superior to me. They can go near to Kṛṣṇa and beg His love and affection as a beloved, but we cannot go there. The rivers are also so much more fortunate than us *gopīs.* Kṛṣṇa goes to the Yamunā to bathe and she can embrace Kṛṣṇa; she can give Him a lotus flower from her hand-like waves. She can give her whole heart to Kṛṣṇa and tell Him, 'O my beloved.' When Kṛṣṇa plays on His flute, she becomes stunned and stops flowing. She is much greater than us, for we cannot do as she does.

"And what is the condition of the calves and cows? The cows are grazing, but when they hear the sweet sound of Kṛṣṇa's flute, they raise their ears to hear and to drink in the sweet nectar of that flute. Their calves also drink the nectar of Kṛṣṇa's flute through their ears. While they drink the milk from their mothers' udders, they hear the flute, and at that time they forget the milk altogether; they neither swallow it nor spit it out, and it simply remains in their mouths. Oh, we are not like this."

Mahāprabhu similarly laments, "The fish are superior to me. If they are taken from water, they will die at once; but I am not dying although I have no *darśana* of Kṛṣṇa. How wretched I am!"

Nowadays many devotees think, "Gurudeva simply gave us chanting beads, and by this we became more than God and we began to control the whole world." The next day, however, we see that nothing is there – no *tulasī* beads, no chanting beads; nothing. And now they have again become mice.[2]

Mahāprabhu performed this pastime in order to teach us devotional principles, so He called Svarūpa Dāmodara and told him, "Svarūpa Dāmodara Prabhu! Just see the behavior of your Gauḍīya *bhakta*. He is insulting Me in front of Ṭhākurajī. You have not instructed him how to be a pure devotee. See how he is behaving! He is in the temple of Jagannātha, who is the Supreme Personality of Godhead, and although I am an ordinary person, he is pouring water on My feet and drinking it. This is very offensive to Jagannātha, Baladeva, and Subhadrā, and I am very upset about this."

Svarūpa Dāmodara then slapped the young devotee and dragged him outside – as a gesture. Actually, he was very happy with him. Outside the temple, when he was beyond Caitanya Mahāprabhu's view, he told that devotee, "You have done very well. Caitanya Mahāprabhu is Jagannātha Himself, but He wants to teach others that we should not behave like this towards ordinary persons. You have not done anything wrong. You have done the right thing. Wait here, and I will call for you again." Then, when he was called, that Bengali devotee told

[2] There is an instructive story called "Punar Mūṣīka Bhava – Again Become a Mouse." A mouse was very much harassed by a cat, and therefore he approached a saintly person to request to become a cat. When the mouse became a cat, he was harassed by a dog, and then, being blessed by the *sādhu*, when he became a dog, he was harassed by a tiger. When by the grace of the saint he became a tiger, he stared at the saintly person, who then asked him, "What do you want?" The tiger replied, "I want to eat you." Then the saintly person cursed him, saying, "May you again become a mouse."

Mahāprabhu, "I have done wrong." He begged for forgiveness, and Mahāprabhu forgot the matter.

No one should tell anyone else to worship him. One should not love anyone or weep for anyone in front of the deity. You can only do *praṇāma* to your pure *gurudeva*, not to anyone else. Wherever the deities are present, we should not try to control anyone; that will be an offense. We can learn all the rules and regulations of deity worship by reading the book *Arcana-dīpikā*.

Nowadays, *gurus* are coming like kan-gurus. All are *gurus* but none are *gurus*. They are everywhere, like the germs of a plague. They are cheaters, not *gurus*. They are not Bhagavān. In India you can very easily find so many "Gods," so many "Supreme Personalities of Godheads." One thinks that he is Śaṅkara, another thinks that he is Gaṇeśa, and someone else thinks he is Sarasvatī. Caitanya Mahāprabhu knew this day would come.

Try to enter the real process of *bhakti*. Hear from the proper person, take his words into your heart and try to follow him. Then you can sweep your heart and also become a pure devotee. First you will enter the stage of *kaniṣṭha-adhikāra*, then *madhyama-adhikāra*, and then you will be a devotee. Otherwise, you are like a shadow devotee – fallen. Kṛṣṇa has given you good intelligence. You should realize whether someone is a pure devotee or not, and if he is, then you can hear from him. A *sādhu* is a very elevated devotee who embodies the verse:

anyābhilāṣitā-śūnyaṁ
jñāna-karmādy-anāvṛtam
ānukūlyena kṛṣṇānu-
śīlanaṁ bhaktir uttamā

Bhakti-rasāmṛta-sindhu (1.1.11)

The cultivation of activities that are meant exclusively for the pleasure of Śrī Kṛṣṇa, or in other words the uninterrupted flow of service to Śrī Kṛṣṇa, performed through all endeavors of the body, mind, and speech, and through the expression of various spiritual sentiments (*bhāvas*), which is not covered by *jñāna* (knowledge aimed at impersonal liberation) and *karma* (reward-seeking activity) and which is devoid of all desires other than the aspiration to bring happiness to Śrī Kṛṣṇa, is called *uttama-bhakti*, pure devotional service.

Such a *sādhu* or *guru* has no worldly desires. His devotion is always like a stream of sweet honey, which flows like an unbroken current when it is poured.

Similarly, you should see whether your own activities – by body, by words, by mind, and by heart or mood – are to please Kṛṣṇa or not. Suppose you are taking *mahā-prasāda*. Why are you taking it? Is it to please Kṛṣṇa or not? If you are not taking it to please Kṛṣṇa, then it is like *karma*. If you go to sleep for yourself, it is *karma*, not *bhakti*. However, if you go to sleep thinking, "I will take some rest, and from early morning I will serve Kṛṣṇa. I will be always chanting, remembering, worshiping, and serving here and there," then even your sleeping is for Kṛṣṇa.

yat karoṣi yad aśnāsi
yaj juhoṣi dadāsi yat
yat tapasyasi kaunteya
tat kuruṣva mad-arpaṇam

Bhagavad-gītā (9.27)

Whatever you do, whatever you eat, whatever you offer or give away, and whatever austerities you perform – do that, O son of Kuntī, as an offering to Me.

After some time, whatever you do will be to please Kṛṣṇa and your pure *gurudeva*. If someone follows this principle and always acts to please Kṛṣṇa, you can accept him as your *guru*; otherwise don't. If, when you were ignorant, you selected as *guru* someone who does not perform all his activities to please Kṛṣṇa, Guru, and Vaiṣṇavas, then reject that person. Reject him totally. Choose another *guru* very carefully and take initiation; otherwise you cannot have pure devotion and love for Kṛṣṇa.

If you were initiated by a *guru* who was sincere at one time, but who fell down later on, reject him at once. Then you may enter the proper line and accept the self-realized devotees who are actually following *anyābhilāṣitā-śūnyaṁ jñāna-karmādy-anāvṛtam ānukūlyena kṛṣṇānuśīlanam.* Whatever they do, they do to please Kṛṣṇa, Guru, and Vaiṣṇavas. They will be in the line of Śrīla Rūpa Gosvāmī, Śrīla Sanātana Gosvāmī, and Śrīla Raghunātha dāsa Gosvāmī. If a person professing to be a *guru* is not actually in that line, he should be rejected at once. Bali Mahārāja rejected his *gurudeva*, Śukrācārya. Bharata Mahārāja rejected his mother, Prahlāda Mahārāja rejected his father, the *gopīs* rejected their husbands, and Vibhīṣaṇa rejected his brother Rāvaṇa. There are abundant examples of this.

If the *guru* is chanting and is somewhat in this line but he cannot give you *prema-bhakti*, then request him, "Please permit me to associate with a self-realized devotee." If he does not give permission for you to do so, he is not a pure Vaiṣṇava and he also should be rejected. However, if he gives the order, "You should go, and I will also go," then he is a Vaiṣṇava. You should respect him, and also go to take the association of that high-class devotee. This is the proper process, and it was followed by Śrī Śyāmānanda Gosvāmī, Śrī Narottama dāsa Ṭhākura, Śrī Śrīnivāsa Ācārya, Śrīla Haridāsa Ṭhākura, and so many others. If you follow *śāstra* and your superiors, you will come to the stage of *madhyama-adhikāra*. This is actually the meaning of *guṇḍicā-mandira-mārjana*.

It is better to honor real Vaiṣṇavas than to only worship the deities. Worship the deity, but serve the Vaiṣṇavas at the same time. Gradually try to come from the stage of *kaniṣṭha* to the stage of *madhyama*. We are entering *kaniṣṭha*, but we are not even *kaniṣṭha* yet, because we do not have full faith in the deity. When we realize *siddhānta*, the established truths of Vaiṣṇava philosophy, in the association of pure Vaiṣṇavas, we will gradually become *madhyama-adhikārī*. This is the object of today's function. By this, the seed of the *bhakti*-creeper that your *gurudeva* has given to you will sprout, and it will then develop into the shape of a creeper that will ultimately lead you to Goloka Vṛndāvana. This is the real process.

When all the spots are removed, your status will be of the nature of pure devotion. Whatever we do, we should do as a service to Kṛṣṇa, for His pleasure, but this is not sufficient by itself. There should be no worldly desire at all in that service. If one takes initiation from a bona fide *guru*, and he is chanting, remembering, and reading books, but he thinks, "I want to be wealthy, I want to have a very well-qualified son, and a very beautiful home and wife," his *bhakti* will not be pure. Rather, it will be completely ruined. Even the desire for liberation is not pure *bhakti*. It is *bhakti*, but not pure *uttama-bhakti*. It is called *āropa-siddha-bhakti*, or sometimes *saṅga-siddha-bhakti*. His *bhakti* will be mixed with *karma*, *jñāna*, *yoga*, or anything else.

More than ninety-five percent of those who call themselves *bhaktas* don't actually follow *uttama-bhakti* or pure *bhakti*. They follow only *āropa-siddha-bhakti* and *saṅga-siddha-bhakti*. What is *āropa-siddha-bhakti*? Making a garden or establishing *gurukulas* and *gośālās* is not really *bhakti*, but it may create impressions (*saṁskāras*) in the heart if the fruits are given to Kṛṣṇa. If there is a *gurukula*, there is an opportunity that the boys will be given impressions from childhood for later development in *bhakti*. We see, however, that the students very rarely get these impressions. Many are ruined and are without character, they do not obey their fathers and mothers, they are not humble, and they do not honor devotees. Many are desperate. If that impression of *bhakti* had come, it would have been very good for them. It is only to give this impression that high-class devotees or *gurus* establish such institutions.

If we make a garden, we can take the fruits to the deities and to pure devotees, but if the fruit is not given to them, the result will be very bad. Actual *bhakti* is that activity in which there is chanting and remembering only to please Kṛṣṇa. In the past, many devotees collected vast wealth for their temples. They collected vast amounts of money in a few days, but what became of them? They left Kṛṣṇa consciousness. Śrīla Bhaktivedānta Swāmī Mahārāja wanted them to become qualified devotees.

It is not sufficient merely to sweep, or merely to wash off all the varieties of unwanted habits such as *aparādhas*. Something affirmative should be there – a strong taste for *harināma* and for hearing *hari-kathā*. It is not enough just to clean your heart. What will remain if you simply do that? Nothing. There should be something positive. There is no harm if you have no taste for chanting *harināma*, but you should have a taste for hearing *hari-kathā*. If you do not, then hear again and again, and give proper respect to the pure devotees from whom you are hearing.

satāṁ prasaṅgān mama vīrya-saṁvido
bhavanti hṛt-karṇa-rasāyanāḥ kathāḥ
taj-joṣaṇād āśv apavarga-vartmani
śraddhā ratir bhaktir anukramiṣyati

Śrīmad-Bhāgavatam (3.25.25)

In the association of pure devotees, discussion of the pastimes and activities of the Supreme Personality of Godhead is very pleasing and satisfying to the ear and the heart. By cultivating such knowledge one gradually becomes advanced on the path of liberation, and thereafter he is freed, and his attraction becomes fixed. Then real devotion and devotional service begin.

The speaker should be *satām*, a pure devotee. Do not maintain your own false idea that an ordinary person or devotee is a *mahā-bhāgavata.* Who has the qualification to realize who is a *mahā-bhāgavata*? Śrīla Vaṁśī dāsa Bābājī Mahārāja, a disciple of Śrīla Gaura-kiśora dāsa Bābājī Mahārāja, was an exalted *uttama-mahā-bhāgavata,* but he used to pretend he was smoking marijuana. He sometimes put dry fish bones here and there around his hut so people would think that he ate fish. He considered, "Those who are materially inclined should remain far away from me so I can be alone to chant Kṛṣṇa's name and remember Him."

Śrīla Gaura-kiśora dāsa Bābājī Mahārāja was on friendly terms with Śrīla Vaṁśī dāsa Bābājī Mahārāja, and Śrīla Prabhupāda Bhaktisiddhānta Sarasvatī Ṭhākura honored him so much. Our Guru Mahārāja, Śrīla Bhakti Prajñāna Keśava Mahārāja, used to take his *darśana,* and at that time Bābājī Mahārāja gave him many deep teachings. Guru Mahārāja told us, "Sometimes he spoke such high philosophy that I could not understand him." If a devotee is ignorant and not even a *kaniṣṭha* Vaiṣṇava, how can he know who is actually a *mahā-bhāgavata*? He will choose an unqualified person as a "*mahā-bhāgavata,*" and the next day he will see how that person has fallen down.

You should see what is your superior's idea regarding who is a *madhyama-adhikārī* or who is an *uttama-adhikārī,* and you can also realize this if you follow Kṛṣṇa consciousness and establish yourself on the platform of the advanced stage of *madhyama-adhikāra.* It is an offense at the lotus feet of the real *mahā-bhāgavata* if you do not give him proper respect, and instead give great respect to a third-class, bogus person, calling him "*mahā-bhāgavata.*"

CHAPTER FOUR

MAHĀPRABHU AND KING PRATĀPARUDRA

The Chariot Festival is performed every year in Jagannātha Purī, a very beautiful place near the shore of the Indian Ocean. I have explained that Śrī Caitanya Mahāprabhu Himself made the Guṇḍicā Temple neat and clean on the previous day, using His own garments, and after that Jagannātha went there. I have also related two histories explaining how Jagannātha, Subhadrā, and Baladeva Prabhu manifested their forms.

Śrī Caitanya Mahāprabhu brought new meaning and light to the Ratha-yātrā Festival, but only a very few, rare souls will understand these topics, even if they are explained completely. Yet, one day you will have to understand the truths within these topics.

Come with me

You can all come with me to the shore of the ocean at Nīlācala, to the Bay of Bengal at Purī, where more than four million devotees have assembled. These devotees are pulling the chariots and shouting, "Jagannātha-deva *kī jaya*, Baladeva Prabhu *kī jaya*, Śrī

Subhadrā-devī *kī jaya*, Śacīnandana Gaurahari *kī jaya*," and Caitanya Mahāprabhu is dancing here and there.

Sometimes the chariot does not reach the Guṇḍicā Temple even after an entire day; it may take two or three days. Sometimes it will not even move an inch, although crowds of devotees try to pull it. The devotees want to pull it, but it cannot move unless Jagannātha desires. When He wants it to move, it does so very quickly and easily.

Mahāprabhu refuses the King

At the time of Mahāprabhu, Pratāparudra Mahārāja was the King of Orissa. Although he was the supreme ruler of that kingdom and a very powerful emperor, he served Jagannātha by sweeping. He used an ordinary broom made from the sticks of a coconut tree, with a golden handle, and he himself swept during the procession. Mahāprabhu became very happy to see him working and serving like an ordinary sweeper, and He wanted to meet him. There was a wall between Mahāprabhu and King Pratāparudra, however, and that wall was the word "king." This is a very dangerous word, because "king" generally refers to one who has great opulence and wealth, and who is full of material desires.

Mahāprabhu wanted to be merciful to King Pratāparudra, but that wall was there, and it could only be dissolved by love and affection. There would be no other process. Although the King was a very high-class devotee, he was still a king. He had a kingdom, a very beautiful wife and children, and he possessed great wealth and power. A very dangerous, poisonous snake is still a snake, even if its poison has somehow been taken out and its fangs removed; if anyone comes close to it, it will hiss and attack. It was for this reason that, prior to the festival, Caitanya

Mahāprabhu had refused to meet King Pratāparudra, although he was an advanced devotee.

At that time, when the King heard that Mahāprabhu had refused to meet him, he said, "Caitanya Mahāprabhu has promised to liberate the entire world and give everyone *kṛṣṇa-prema*. I am the only exception. If He is determined not to see me, then I am determined to give up my life. If I do not see Him, if He does not give me His mercy, I will give up my kingdom, my wife, children, and everything else. I do not need my wealth, reputation, or position anymore. I will give them all up."

Sārvabhauma Bhaṭṭācārya pacified the King by saying, "Don't do anything in a hurry – wait. The right time will come and you will be able to serve Him. There is one means by which you can see Him directly. On the day of the Chariot Festival, Śrī Caitanya Mahāprabhu will dance before the deity in great ecstatic love. After dancing before Jagannātha, He will enter the Guṇḍicā garden, absorbed in a deep mood. At that time you can go there alone, without your royal dress, and you can approach Him as a mendicant – a street beggar. You can recite *Gopī-gīta* and the other chapters of *Śrīmad-Bhāgavatam* concerning Lord Kṛṣṇa's dancing with the *gopīs*, and in this way you will be able to catch hold of the Lord's lotus feet."

Mahāprabhu's dancing

Jagannātha-deva, Baladeva Prabhu, and Subhadrā were riding on very large, newly built chariots. Baladeva's chariot was in front, followed by Subhadrā's chariot, and Kṛṣṇa's chariot came last. As the chariot stood still, Śrī Caitanya Mahāprabhu gathered all His devotees, and with His own hand decorated them with flower garlands and *tilaka* made with sandalwood pulp. He then divided all His close associates into four *kīrtana* parties. Each party had eight chanters, and He gave two *mṛdaṅgas* to each party and ordered them to begin *kīrtana*. Śrī Nityānanda Prabhu danced in one party, Advaita Ācārya danced in the second, Haridāsa Ṭhākura in the third, and Vakreśvara Paṇḍita danced beautifully in the fourth. All of them were very good dancers, and they could all dance throughout the entire day and night. Svarūpa Dāmodara, Śrīvāsa Paṇḍita, Mukunda, and Govinda Ghoṣa were the main singers in each of the four respective groups.

Mahāprabhu then created three more parties. One was made up of Bengali householder devotees from the village of Kulīnagrāma, the second party came from Śāntipura, and the third party was from Śrīkhaṇḍa. Thus, four parties chanted and danced in front of Jagannātha-deva, one more party on each side of Him, and another party behind Him. In this way there were seven parties, and each party was followed by thousands and thousands of devotees.

After dividing the devotees into *kīrtana* parties, Śrī Caitanya Mahāprabhu began to dance, sometimes in all the parties at the same time. Caitanya Mahāprabhu is one, but He manifested seven forms, and He thus began to dance and sing in each *kīrtana* party at the same time. Tears shot from His eyes as if from a syringe, and He danced very quickly, as Kṛṣṇa had danced in His *līlā*. At that time King Pratāparudra saw Him in the form of Kṛṣṇa and thought, "Oh, He is Kṛṣṇa Himself!"

Although Mahāprabhu was in seven groups at one and the same time, the devotees in each group were thinking, "Mahāprabhu is only with us," and they sang and danced very happily. This incident was like the pastime that took place when Kṛṣṇa was taking His meal with His *sakhās* at Bhāṇḍīravaṭa, when there were many thousands of circles of *sakhās*. Some of the cowherd boys were behind Kṛṣṇa, some were by His side, and some were very far away; yet all of them thought, "I'm in front of Kṛṣṇa. I'm taking *prasāda* with Him, I'm putting my *prasāda* in His mouth and He is putting His in mine." All of them – whether they were behind Kṛṣṇa, in front of Him, beside Him, or anywhere here and there – were thinking that Kṛṣṇa was always with them. Similarly, at the time of *rāsa-līlā*, Kṛṣṇa appeared to be thousands and thousands of Kṛṣṇas, as many Kṛṣṇas as there were *gopīs*, and there was one Kṛṣṇa with each *gopī*. There was one Kṛṣṇa in between each pair of *gopīs*, and one *gopī* in between each pair of Kṛṣṇas. Śrī Caitanya Mahāprabhu now performed the same miracle.

Except for three people – Pratāparudra Mahārāja, Kāśī Miśra, and Sārvabhauma Bhaṭṭācārya – everyone saw Caitanya Mahāprabhu only in their own group. By Mahāprabhu's mercy, the King saw that He was dancing in the seven *kīrtana* parties at the same time. His tears were falling in showers, and sometimes He fell down and rolled on the earth and the devotees lifted Him up. The King asked the others, "What am I seeing? Am I wrong? No, I see Him. He is here, and He is there at the same time. He is dancing in all seven parties." Kāśī Miśra and Sārvabhauma Bhaṭṭācārya replied, "You are very fortunate. You have received Śrī Caitanya Mahāprabhu's mercy. Only a select few people are seeing this scene as you are."

Just to prevent the crowds from coming too near the Lord, the devotees formed three circles, keeping Mahāprabhu in the middle. Nityānanda Prabhu led the first circle; devotees headed by Kāśīśvara and Govinda linked hands and formed a second circle; and a third circle was formed around the two inner circles by King Pratāparudra and his personal assistants, as well as by his police and soldiers. Pratāparudra's general, Haricandana, was with the King, wearing many medals and guarding him very carefully as hundreds of thousands of people watched Mahāprabhu dance. So he could see Lord Caitanya Mahāprabhu dancing, King Pratāparudra lifted himself by putting his hands on Haricandana's shoulders, and he felt great ecstasy.

Śrīvāsa Paṇḍita, who is Nārada Ṛṣi in *kṛṣṇa-līlā*, also wanted to watch Mahāprabhu's beautiful dance. The King was standing behind Śrīvāsa Ṭhākura, and he wanted to see Mahāprabhu without interference; but as Śrīvāsa Paṇḍita was absorbed in watching Mahāprabhu, he was moving from side to side in such a way that the King could not see properly. The King's general warned Śrīvāsa Ṭhākura, "Don't do that. The King wants to see. Stay here on one side." Śrīvāsa Paṇḍita was so absorbed that he did not take any notice of the warning at first; but after Haricandana had told him twice, Śrīvāsa Paṇḍita became angry and slapped him.

The commander-in-chief was very tall, strong, and stout, and he wanted to retaliate by arresting Śrīvāsa Paṇḍita. All the guards also became angry and they wanted to arrest him as well, but King Pratāparudra immediately told Haricandana, "Don't do anything. These are Caitanya Mahāprabhu's associates, and Mahāprabhu is Kṛṣṇa Himself. You are so fortunate to be slapped by this very elevated devotee. You are very fortunate, so be silent." And the general did as he was told.

Caitanya Mahāprabhu was reciting a *śloka* while He danced, but no one could understand or explain its meaning – no one, that is, except a boy named Rūpa. Mahāprabhu's mood entered Śrī Rūpa Gosvāmī's heart, and he thus wrote a similar *śloka*, which Mahāprabhu later took from the roof of Haridāsa Ṭhākura's *bhajana-kuṭīra*, where Rūpa Gosvāmī was also residing. "How did you know My mood?" Mahāprabhu asked Rūpa Gosvāmī. Svarūpa Dāmodara, Rāya Rāmānanda, and all of Mahāprabhu's other associates then glorified Rūpa Gosvāmī, and they told Mahāprabhu, "You have inspired him. How could he have known without Your inspiration? No one can know this without

Your mercy." Only someone on the level of Svarūpa Dāmodara could know; no one else.

Mahāprabhu meets the King

King Pratāparudra was an exalted devotee, and he wanted to take *darśana* of Caitanya Mahāprabhu's lotus feet; but Mahāprabhu told His associates, "I cannot give him *darśana*. He is a king, so he is like a black serpent."

Mahāprabhu has also said that a wooden statue of a lady can attract even a *muni*: *dāravī prakṛti hareta muner api mana*. *Munis* such as Viśvāmitra and Nārada are renounced and realized, but just to set an example for us and to teach us how careful we must be, they both performed pastimes in which they appeared to be under the spell of illusion. We should be very cautious in the association of the opposite sex because men and women are like Kāmadeva (Cupid) for one another; they cannot control their senses or hearts when they are together. I therefore request my disciples and friends to be very careful. You are independent, but you should always remember these principles.

Mahāprabhu was very strict, so He did not give the King His association, even though the King was a very advanced devotee. Moreover, when Nityānanda Prabhu, Advaita Ācārya, Rāya Rāmānanda, and Sārvabhauma Bhaṭṭācārya requested Mahāprabhu to see the King, He told them, "I will leave Purī and go to Ālālanātha or somewhere else. I will not remain here; you can stay here with him."

Since Śrī Caitanya Mahāprabhu would not agree to see the King, Sārvabhauma Bhaṭṭācārya, Rāya Rāmānanda, and other associates told the King, "When your beautiful son went to Mahāprabhu, the Lord embraced him and said, 'Come and meet with Me daily.' In this way, somehow or other you have 'half' taken His *darśana*, and He has shown His compassion to you. Mahāprabhu is very satisfied and pleased with you, and He has given you so much mercy, especially because you are a very simple person and have engaged in the service of the Lord as a sweeper. So now, if you want to have His *darśana* directly, dress very simply and go secretly to meet Him when He becomes tired from dancing in seven parties. He will be lamenting continually in Śrīmatī Rādhikā's mood, and at that time you can approach Him and sing the sweet *Gopī-gīta*."

jayati te 'dhikaṁ janmanā vrajaḥ
śrayata indirā śaśvad atra hi
dayita dṛśyatāṁ dikṣu tāvakās
tvayi dhṛtāsavas tvāṁ vicinvate

[The *gopīs* said:] O beloved, Your birth in the land of Vraja has made it exceedingly glorious, and thus Indirā, the goddess of fortune, always resides here. We cannot live without You, and only maintain our lives for Your sake. We have been searching everywhere for You, so please show Yourself to us.

tava kathāmṛtaṁ tapta-jīvanaṁ
kavibhir īḍitaṁ kalmaṣāpaham
śravaṇa-maṅgalaṁ śrīmad ātataṁ
bhuvi gṛṇanti te bhūri-dā janāḥ

The nectar of Your words and the descriptions of Your activities are the life and soul of those who are suffering in this material world. When these narrations are transmitted by learned sages, they eradicate one's sinful reactions and bestow good fortune upon whoever hears them. They are broadcast all over the world, and they are filled with spiritual power. Certainly those who spread the message of Godhead are most munificent.

Śrīmad-Bhāgavatam (10.31.1, 9)

These verses are some of the most valuable diamonds in the *Śrīmad-Bhāgavatam*. First comes *pūrva-rāga*[1] in *Veṇu-gīta*, then this *Gopī-gīta*, and then *Yugala-gīta*, *Bhramara-gīta*, and *Praṇaya-gīta*. These most precious jewels are called *pañca-prāṇa-vāyu*, the five life airs, and our main objective is to enter the deep truths of these *gītas*. Your life will be successful if you can realize these topics, especially with the commentaries by Śrī Sanātana Gosvāmī and Śrī Jīva Gosvāmī, and above all with that of Śrīla Viśvanātha Cakravartī Ṭhākura, who has explained these *ślokas* in an especially marvelous way. There are more than one thousand commentaries on *Śrīmad-Bhāgavatam*, but it is the commentaries of our Gosvāmīs that express the moods of Śrī Caitanya Mahāprabhu.

As mentioned, Caitanya Mahāprabhu had become pleased and satisfied to see the King sweeping the road. Consequently, by the influence of His *yogamāyā-śakti*, the King was able to see His miracle of dancing in seven groups at the same time. "What am I seeing?" the King had said to Sārvabhauma Bhaṭṭācārya. "This is very wonderful. There is one Caitanya Mahāprabhu dancing in each party." Sārvabhauma replied, "This is His mercy. You swept the road like a street beggar, and now He is pleased with you. Not everyone sees as you do. Others think, 'He is only in our party.' You have already received His mercy, so what else remains? Just dress as a very simple devotee and wait until He takes rest in the garden."

Śrī Caitanya Mahāprabhu will also sprinkle His mercy upon you if you give up all your opulence and the conception that you are intelligent and qualified. This will happen if you become like

[1] *Pūrva-rāga* is described in *Ujjvala-nīlamaṇi* as follows: "When attachment produced in the lover and beloved before their meeting by seeing, hearing, and so on becomes very palatable by the mixture of four ingredients, such as *vibhāva* and *anubhāva*, it is called *pūrva-rāga*."

King Pratāparudra, whose heart was as hollow as a flute for Caitanya Mahāprabhu to play on, and if you serve your *gurudeva* and Rādhā-Kṛṣṇa in this way. By Mahāprabhu's mercy you can know His opulence, and everything about His love and affection as well.

Caitanya Mahāprabhu and the Ratha-yātrā chariot stopped midway between the Jagannātha Temple and Guṇḍicā. There were hundreds of thousands of devotees there, offering many coconuts from wherever they stood, and He accepted the essence of their offerings with His eyes. They also offered many sweet and tasty preparations, including jackfruits, mangoes, and other fruits, some from as much as a mile or two away, and He ate those by His glance as well.

jagannāthera choṭa-baḍa yata bhakta-gaṇa
nija nija uttama-bhoga kare samarpaṇa

Śrī Caitanya-caritāmṛta (*Madhya-līlā* 13.197)

All kinds of devotees of Lord Jagannātha – from neophytes to the most advanced – offered their best cooked food to the Lord.

āge pāche, dui pārśve puṣpodyāna-vane
yei yāhā pāya, lāgāya – nāhika niyame

Śrī Caitanya-caritāmṛta (*Madhya-līlā* 13.200)

The devotees offered their food everywhere – in front of the car and behind it, on both sides and within the flower garden. They made their offering to the Lord wherever possible, for there were no hard and fast rules.

bhogera samaya lokera mahā bhiḍa haila
nṛtya chāḍi' mahāprabhu upavane gela

Śrī Caitanya-caritāmṛta (*Madhya-līlā* 13.201)

A large crowd of people gathered while the food was being offered, and at that time Śrī Caitanya Mahāprabhu stopped His dancing and went to a nearby garden.

Caitanya Mahāprabhu had been dancing for some time, and now He became somewhat tired.

yata bhakta kīrtanīyā āsiyā ārāme
prati-vṛkṣa-tale sabe karena viśrāme

Śrī Caitanya-caritāmṛta (*Madhya-līlā* 13.204)

All the devotees who had been performing *saṅkīrtana* came there and took rest under each and every tree.

Mahāprabhu was thinking, "I am Rādhikā. Kṛṣṇa has left Me and gone to Mathurā." His eyes were full of tears and He wept, not knowing where He was, or what He was doing. He did not know anything – only, "Kṛṣṇa, Kṛṣṇa!" He wanted to take some rest along with Nityānanda Prabhu, Advaita Ācārya, Svarūpa Dāmodara, Vakreśvara Paṇḍita, Puṇḍarīka Vidyānidhi, Paramānanda Purī, and other exalted associates. Accordingly, He went into the Jagannātha-vallabha Garden at Āiṭoṭa in a mood of great separation, with His heart melting and tears flowing from His eyes. He laid His head on the root of a tree and cried, "Where is My *prāṇanātha*? Where is My Kṛṣṇa?"

The King had been trying to meet Mahāprabhu for many years, but Caitanya Mahāprabhu had given the instruction, "I don't want to meet with a king; he should not come to Me." King Pratāparudra had invited Caitanya Mahāprabhu to his palace, but He had refused to come. He never met a king or any other royal person, or anyone who was very wealthy. Beside that, He never touched any woman, even if she was a young girl.

Now Caitanya Mahāprabhu was lying down and weeping, lamenting as Śrīmatī Rādhikā had done in separation from Kṛṣṇa.

The King approached Rāya Rāmānanda, Sārvabhauma Bhaṭṭācārya, Advaita Ācārya, and Nityānanda Prabhu. He offered *praṇāma* to them all and said, "I am going to Caitanya Mahāprabhu. Please bless me." He then took off his royal dress and ornaments, and put on very simple clothes. Wearing only a *dhotī* and looking like an ordinary person, he approached Mahāprabhu, took His lotus feet in his hands, and began to massage them very gently and expertly. As he did so, he sang:

jayati te 'dhikaṁ janmanā vrajaḥ
śrayata indirā śaśvad atra hi
dayita dṛśyatāṁ dikṣu tāvakās
tvayi dhṛtāsavas tvāṁ vicinvate

Śrīmad-Bhāgavatam (10.31.1)

He sang *ślokas* like this in a melody so full of feeling that Caitanya Mahāprabhu wept more and more, and His heart melted still further. He had been unconscious, but now He sat up and cried, "Who is pouring such sweet nectar in My ears? Go on, go on. Keep on giving Me this nectar."

The King continued:

tava kathāmṛtaṁ tapta-jīvanaṁ
kavibhir īḍitaṁ kalmaṣāpaham
śravaṇa-maṅgalaṁ śrīmad ātataṁ
bhuvi gṛṇanti te bhūri-dā janāḥ

Śrīmad-Bhāgavatam (10.31.9)

Mahāprabhu could not control Himself. He embraced the King and asked, "Who are you? Who are you?" King Pratāparudra told Him, "I am the servant of the servant of the servant of Your servant." Mahāprabhu was satisfied and said, "I am a street beggar, a *niṣkiñcana-sannyāsī*. I have no pockets at all, so I have nothing to give you. I shall therefore give you My embrace, which is My only wealth." Mahāprabhu then embraced the King heart to heart. Both their hearts mixed, and Mahāprabhu transferred some of His moods to the King's heart, empowering and satisfying him.

All the verses of *Gopī-gīta* have beautiful and esoteric meanings. They are all connected with each other, and a *rasika* devotee can explain the meaning of each *śloka* for a month or more. These verses reveal a very pathetic scene. All the *gopīs* are feeling separation and begging, "O Kṛṣṇa, come and meet with us; otherwise we will die." *Janmanā vrajaḥ* means, "You took birth in Gokula-Vṛndāvana, in Vraja, and that is why Mahā-Lakṣmī sweeps and serves here, making Vṛndāvana beautiful. It is the best place for Your sweet pastimes."

There are many hundreds of meanings for the verse beginning with the words *tava kathāmṛtaṁ tapta-jīvanam*, but I will tell you two meanings in brief. The first is general, and the second is somewhat deeper. The *gopīs* tell Kṛṣṇa: "*tava kathāmṛtam* – Your sweet pastimes are the life and soul of those who face great difficulties, sorrows, and sufferings in the endless chain of birth and death in this world. Your pastimes are like nectar for them, and if they hear those pastimes, You Yourself enter their hearts in the form of *hari-kathā*."

śṛṇvatāṁ sva-kathāḥ kṛṣṇaḥ
puṇya-śravaṇa-kīrtanaḥ
hṛdy antaḥ-stho hy abhadrāṇi
vidhunoti suhṛt satām

Śrīmad-Bhāgavatam (1.2.17)

Śrī Kṛṣṇa, the Personality of Godhead, who is the Supersoul in everyone's heart and the benefactor of the truthful devotee, cleanses the desire for material enjoyment from the heart of the devotee who has developed the urge to hear His messages, which are in themselves virtuous when properly heard and chanted.

Kṛṣṇa Himself enters the ears and hearts of those who hear these pastimes very carefully. He comes as a dear and intimate friend, and clears away their lust, anger, worldly desires, and problems. He quickly sweeps all these impediments from their hearts, and when He has made those hearts clear, He comes to live there. One who is always unhappy due to being tossed on the ocean of problems will become happy upon hearing *hari-kathā*.

Parīkṣit Mahārāja was due to die after seven days from the bite of a poisonous snake, and no one in this world was competent to save him. He therefore gave up eating, drinking, and sleeping altogether, and remained on the bank of the Gaṅgā for those seven days, hearing from Śukadeva Gosvāmī.

nivṛtta-tarṣair upagīyamānād
bhavauṣadhāc chrotra-mano-'bhirāmāt
ka uttamaśloka-guṇānuvādāt
pumān virajyeta vinā paśu-ghnāt

Śrīmad-Bhāgavatam (10.1.4)

Glorification of the Supreme Personality of Godhead is conveyed from spiritual master to disciple in the *paramparā* system. Such glorification is relished by those who are no longer interested in the false, temporary glorification of this cosmic manifestation. Descriptions of the Lord are the right medicine for the conditioned soul who is undergoing repeated birth and death. Who, therefore, will refrain from hearing such glorification of the Lord, except for a butcher, or one who is killing his own self?

Śukadeva Gosvāmī had no worldly desires at all. The *hari-kathā* spoken by a *rasika-tattvajña*[2] devotee like him is the greatest medicine for you, for it will cure you of all diseases and problems. Snakebites and other calamities will disappear very quickly, along with lust, anger, and all worldly desires. Do not have any doubt about this.

Tava kathāmṛtaṁ tapta-jīvanam. The *hari-kathā* of a self-realized devotee who explains the sweet pastimes of Kṛṣṇa will pacify you; you will become calm and quiet, and you will have a new life. *Tapta-jīvanam.* When those who are suffering hear these glories, they will become happy forever – in this life, and in all their lives to come. After liberation they will go to Vṛndāvana, and they will be happy forever. Nityānanda Prabhu assures us, "I guarantee this. If you are not happy, then chant and remember Kṛṣṇa. If you do not feel happy as a result of this, it will be my responsibility."

Kavibhir īḍitam. Kavis (poets and writers) such as Brahmā, Śukadeva Gosvāmī, Vālmīki, and Kṛṣṇa-dvaipāyana Vyāsadeva, who is the highest type of *kavi*, have all said *kalmaṣa-apaham*: all kinds of sins and past fruitive *karmas* will disappear very soon. *Śravaṇa-maṅgalam*: all kinds of auspiciousness will come to you if you do nothing but hear *hari-kathā*. *Śrīmad ātatam*: this will cause the glories of your *śrī* – your opulence, wealth, beauty, and fortune – to spread all over the world.

One who gives *hari-kathā* purely will be famous throughout the world. For example, Śrīla Bhaktivedānta Swāmī Mahārāja was not a very popular speaker before he took *sannyāsa* and came to the West. He was very learned, but not many people came to

[2] *Rasika* means one who is able to fully appreciate and explain the transcendental mellows of pure devotional service, and *tattvajña* means one who fully understands the various truths described in the scriptures, such as *bhagavat-tattva*, *śakti-tattva*, *jīva-tattva*, and *māyā-tattva*.

hear him, and his wife and children rejected him. However, a miracle occurred after he took the renounced order and reached America. Within a very short time he established many centers all over the world, and he made hundreds of thousands of devotees. So many people became his servants and disciples that we cannot count them; this was a miracle. And I am also now experiencing something similar to this, although I am like a dry piece of straw.

The greatest donors in this world are those who explain sweet *hari-kathā* under the guidance of Śrīla Śukadeva Gosvāmī, Śrīla Rūpa Gosvāmī, Śrīla Bhaktivinoda Ṭhākura, Śrīla Prabhupāda Bhaktisiddhānta Sarasvatī Ṭhākura, my *gurudeva*, and Śrīla Swāmī Mahārāja. *Bhuvi gṛṇanti te bhūri-dā janāḥ* – they glorify Kṛṣṇa and thereby benefit the whole world. There are so many benefactors who can donate thousands and thousands of dollars or pounds. A king may give his entire kingdom and a wealthy man may give the opulence and wealth of even the entire world, but still they would not be *bhūri-dāḥ*. The greatest benefactors are those who describe Kṛṣṇa's sweet pastimes to others.

This is a general understanding of the *tava kathāmṛtam* verse, which clearly glorifies Kṛṣṇa. Perhaps this is Candrāvalī's mood when she is speaking and praying. Śrīmatī Rādhikā, on the contrary, is in an angry mood, and She says: "*tava kathāmṛtam* – Your *kathā* is not *amṛtam* (nectar); it is poison. What type of poison? Deadly (*mṛtam*) poison. One should certainly avoid drinking this poison; in fact, one should keep very far away from it. If a person merely smells it he will die, and no one will be able to save him. Those who hear Your pastimes must die like flapping fish. First they will flap, and then they will die."

Tapta-jīvanam. Gopīs like Rādhikā say, "We are the proof of this. We were perfectly happy in our family life, but then Kṛṣṇa came and created so many problems, and now we are helpless.

He made us street beggars; we have no place to stay and now we are on the verge of death. Anyone who wants to be happy with his family should never hear Kṛṣṇa's pastimes.

"*Kavibhir īḍitam.* Poets will glorify even a paper horse. They will say, 'It is very strong, and it runs faster than the wind and the mind,' but there is no substance in their words. Similarly, such *kavis* have said, 'Hearing *hari-kathā* will make you very happy,' but this idea is not true; it is bogus. Kṛṣṇa cheated us and His *hari-kathā* also cheated us. But now we are intelligent; we don't believe in hearing these pastimes anymore, and we warn everyone else to never hear them. If a lady hears these pastimes, she will forget her husband and children. She will become like a bird without a nest, and she will weep all the time.

"Those who want to be happy with their families, wives, children, and husbands should not hear the glories of that black Kṛṣṇa. If anyone hears them, he will cut off the relationship with his family. Fathers and sons, and husbands and wives will be separated from each other. Everyone who hears this *hari-kathā* will forget their husbands, wives, children, and everyone else. They will become mad, always calling, 'Kṛṣṇa! Kṛṣṇa! Kṛṣṇa!' We also became mad, and now we roam here and there, always weeping and weeping. So Kṛṣṇa's glories are like poison.

"Anyone who doesn't want to be like this must not hear Kṛṣṇa's pastimes, especially from the mouths of cheaters. They will come with a book under their arms and say, 'Come here! Come here! I will relate Kṛṣṇa's sweet and beautiful pastimes to you, and I won't charge you anything at all. Don't worry about giving a donation. There is no cost. Simply hear.' Such *kavis* will sing with a beautiful tune like a *śuka*, male parrot. They will charm a person, and then kill him at once with a very sharp knife. They are *bhūri-dā janāḥ*, greatly cutting: they will take away all one's worldly happiness, create trouble for him, and make him like a beggar. So no one should hear from them.

"Those who give *hari-kathā* are very cruel, even if they do it as charity, giving classes on *Bhāgavatam* without taking any money in return. Instead of listening to them, he should simply give them a donation and say, 'Go away from here. We don't want to hear from you, because we will forget our wives, our husbands, and all our relatives. We will lose our wealth and everything else. We will become beggars and weep forever.' Nowadays we are very careful to avoid hearing the glories of Kṛṣṇa.

"But what can we do?" Rādhikā and Her associates continue, "We cannot give up chanting about Kṛṣṇa and remembering Him, and we cannot give up hearing His glories. So what can we do? Those who distribute these glories are like hunters."

There are two ways of saying something: a negative way and a positive way. The negative way has the same meaning as the positive; it only appears to be negative. For example, the *gopīs* once complained to Kṛṣṇa, "We cannot maintain our lives without You." Kṛṣṇa replied, "Then why are you still alive? I am separated from you, but I see that you have not died yet." The *gopīs* replied, "Do You know why we are still alive? You and Your friend Brahmā, the Creator, are very cruel. You both want to give suffering to others; you become very happy when you see others suffering. How will You be able to make others suffer if we die? Because of You, we are the best candidates for suffering, and You will never find anyone like us. We tolerate so much. To whom will You give this much suffering if we die? How will You be happy? Your cruel creator-friend is also like You, and he also wants to see us suffer. That is why he put our lives in You, and that is why we don't die. Our souls are not here within us. They are in You, and it was Brahmā who created us like this. If our souls were with us, we would already have died long ago.

mṛgayur iva kapīndraṁ vivyadhe lubdha-dharmā
striyam akṛta-virūpāṁ strī-jitaḥ kāma-yānām
balim api balim attvāveṣṭayad dhvāṅkṣa-vad yas
tad alam asita-sakhyair dustyajas tat-kathārthaḥ

Śrīmad-Bhāgavatam (10.47.17)

[The *gopīs* said:] Like a hunter, He cruelly shot the king of the monkeys with arrows. He was conquered by a woman, so He disfigured another woman who came to Him with lusty desires. And even after consuming the gifts of Bali Mahārāja, He bound him up with ropes as if he were a crow. So let us give up all friendship with this dark-complexioned boy, even if we can't give up talking about Him.

The *gopīs* lament and weep, "Why do we remember You, hear so much about You, and chant Your name? We don't want to have any love and affection for You, but what can we do about it? We cannot do anything. We want to forget You, but Your pastimes always come into our memory."

The *gopīs* are *anupamā*, incomparable; no one in this world can compare with them. If you hear their pastimes and try to remember them, they will give you so much energy and strength that all your unwanted bad habits (*anarthas*) will disappear very soon. It is better to forget your jobs and everything else. There will be no harm in that, and Yogamāyā will arrange everything for your maintenance. Kṛṣṇa has given an order to Yogamāyā, and I myself will also manage everything for you. Don't worry that you will have to go to work and perform many other duties. I have no job, so who is managing all my affairs? I have thousands and thousands of servants who always help me. They worry about me and think, "I should give something to Mahārāja." Who is behind this? It is Kṛṣṇa Himself. Have strong faith in Kṛṣṇa. Do not worry about your maintenance. Chant and remember Kṛṣṇa more and more.

Don't worry and wonder, "Who will look after me? What will become of me after Mahārāja leaves this world? This is a very big problem." Actually there is no problem at all. Chant and remember Kṛṣṇa. By Kṛṣṇa's order, Yogamāyā will always help you, and Kṛṣṇa's *cakra* will always save you from danger; do not be worried. Keep this valuable jewel – the message of the Festival of the Chariots – in your hearts.

These are not my teachings; they are the teachings of Śrī Caitanya Mahāprabhu, Śrīla Rūpa Gosvāmī, Śrīla Bhaktivinoda Ṭhākura, and all the other *ācāryas.* I have brought their message to you as a postman. Take it and be happy. Try to help each other and thus be happy.

The previous king of Orissa

At the commencement of the Chariot Festival, Pratāparudra Mahārāja, the Emperor of Orissa, began sweeping the road. Although he was the King, he wore the dress of a devotee and looked very simple, like a beggar. He swept using a broom with a golden handle and, so that the dust on the road would not rise up, with his own hands he watered the ground with fragrant substances like rose water. This was the job of a sweeper.

The tradition of the King of Orissa sweeping the road at the beginning of the Ratha-yātrā Festival is an old one. Many years before, the previous King, Mahārāja Puruṣottama Jānā, had also swept the road every year for Jagannātha-deva. Puruṣottama Jānā was very influential and powerful, but he would take a golden broom in his hand and sweep in front of Jagannātha's chariot, sprinkling the ground with rose water and other aromatic substances. Like Mahārāja Pratāparudra, he also dressed himself like a common person, without shoes and without royal dress.

When Puruṣottama Jānā (also known as Puruṣottama-deva) was about 24 years old, he was very beautiful and strong, and he had an agreement with the King of Vidyānagara in South India that he would marry the King's daughter. He had been communicating with the King of Vidyānagara through messengers and the King informed him that he would come to meet him in person, but he did not specify when. Later, the King went unannounced to see with his own eyes how beautiful, wealthy, and qualified Puruṣottama Jānā actually was. He went along with his whole family, to see if they would agree with the marriage proposal.

At that time, fortunately or unfortunately, it was the first day of the Chariot Festival, and King Puruṣottama Jānā was dressed as a sweeper, sweeping the road before Jagannātha-deva. Seeing this, the King of Vidyānagara became quite upset and felt some disgust toward him. He appreciated that Puruṣottama Jānā was very youthful and beautiful, but he considered him to be a mere sweeper. He thought, "He is supposed to be so wealthy and qualified, but he is sweeping? I wanted to give my daughter to him, but now I see that he is not qualified. He is sweeping like a street-cleaner. I cannot give my daughter to this sweeper." Thinking like this, he returned home and canceled the marriage.

A few days after the festival was over, Puruṣottama Jānā remembered the agreement and wondered what had happened. He asked his counselors, "That king wanted to give his daughter to me in marriage, but there has been no recent indication at all. Why not?" The counselors informed him, "He saw you sweeping on the day of the Ratha-yātrā Festival and thought you were a mere sweeper. He doesn't want to give his daughter to a common sweeper." When Puruṣottama Jānā heard this, he became angry and said, "I must invade his kingdom!" In his mind, he told that king, "You don't know the glory of my Jagannātha-deva!" He collected all his soldiers and generals, declared war on that king, and a ferocious battle took place in the state of that other king.

The King of Vidyānagara worshiped the demigod Gaṇeśa, who was therefore somewhat favorable towards him. Gaṇeśa fought against Puruṣottama Jānā's party and defeated them. Thus, extremely disturbed, they returned to Purī empty-handed. Weeping, Puruṣottama Jānā went to the temple and told Lord Jagannātha, "O Lord, I am your servant. That very mighty King told me, 'You are only a sweeper of Jagannātha,' and he refused to give me his daughter in marriage. Please help me. I was sweeping for You. I thought You would help me at all times, but he defeated me. I'm serving You, and yet You didn't help me. I was defeated because Gaṇeśa helped him. I remembered You, but You did not help me. Now everyone in the world will think, 'Jagannātha has no power, and that is why His devotee has no power. Jagannātha is very weak and insignificant.' This is so shameful; I will die here. I will not eat or drink anything, and I will die here in front of You, in Your temple."

Later that night, King Puruṣottama Jānā had a dream in which Jagannātha-deva told him, "Try again. Last time you went straight to war without calling Me and therefore I did not help you. But now I will help you. March again with all your soldiers and generals. Don't be afraid, and don't worry. Go and invade that king's territory again. Baladeva and I will go there personally, and somehow you will be aware of this. You will defeat that king, along with Gaṇeśa, and everyone else on his side." Puruṣottama Jānā became very happy and made arrangements to again invade the kingdom. The next day he called for more soldiers and generals, and they started on their way and marched quickly towards Vidyānagara.

Meanwhile, Jagannātha and Baladeva got up on very strong and beautiful horses. Baladeva's horse was white, and Kṛṣṇa Himself rode a red one. They were both sixteen years of age, one blackish and the other white, and both were very powerful, strong, and beautiful. They wanted Puruṣottma Jānā to have faith that they were going to fight for him, so they went some miles ahead of him. Many miles from Purī, they reached a village near Chilka, Ālālanātha, near a very large and beautiful lake. There, Kṛṣṇa and Baladeva came upon an old village *gvālinī* (milk-lady) carrying a large pot of buttermilk on her head. It was a hot summer day, and Jagannātha and Baladeva said to her, "Mother, can you give us some buttermilk? We are very thirsty."

"Can you pay me?" the *gvālinī* asked them. "I will give you some buttermilk if you pay me." Kṛṣṇa and Baladeva replied, "We cannot pay you. We are soldiers of the King, and we are on the way to battle. Our King is coming and he will pay you when he reaches here. You can tell him, 'Your two soldiers were going this way. One was blackish and the other white. They were riding on their horses with their swords and other weapons.'" She asked, "How will he be able to recognize that you are his soldiers? How will he know that it is his own soldiers who have taken this buttermilk?" They replied, "We will give you some proof to show the King, and then he will pay you."

The village lady gave them her whole pot of buttermilk, and they drank it all and felt satisfied. Then they gave her their very beautiful rings and told her, "Give these rings to the King and tell him, 'The owners of these rings have gone before you, and they said that you will pay for their buttermilk.'" The boys then went happily onwards.

The milk seller waited and waited, and finally the King arrived there with his entire army of hundreds of thousands of soldiers. When the army arrived, the old lady began to search for him, asking, "Where is the King? Where is the King?" The soldiers told her, "The King is there," and she walked up to him and said, "Your two soldiers have gone ahead. They were both young, beautiful, and very energetic, and they were riding on horses. They drank my entire pot of buttermilk, and they told me, 'Our King will pay.' So you should pay for my buttermilk."

The King told the old lady, "None of my soldiers have gone before us." She replied, "Yes, they have. I've seen them and I've given them my buttermilk." The King told her, "How can I believe they are my soldiers? All my soldiers are with me. No one has gone ahead. We are the first to come." Then he asked her, "Do you have any proof?" "Yes," she said, "I have proof."

The milk-lady showed the two rings to the King, and on the rings he saw the names Jagannātha Siṁha and Baladeva Siṁha (Siṁha means "lion"). He became happy and inspired, and he thought, "These are the two rings I had made by the goldsmith. They are the same rings that I presented to Jagannātha and Baladeva! Jagannātha and Baladeva have done this for me so that I would know they are with me. This time I will surely conquer that King." He then donated some of his kingdom to that old village woman. He offered her a large estate, telling her, "Take this land and nourish many generations of your family with it." That lady's family is living on the same estate to this very day.

Puruṣottama Jānā then invaded his enemy's kingdom and defeated his entire army. He forcibly took away the King's daughter and imprisoned her, and all the King's counselors as well. He also took the King's golden throne, and the deity of Bhaṇḍa (cheater) Gaṇeśa. Bhaṇḍa Gaṇeśa had been fighting on the side of the King of Vidyānagara, so Kṛṣṇa and Baladeva captured him and bound him up, saying, "He is Bhaṇḍa Gaṇeśa." Gaṇeśa knows well that Kṛṣṇa is the Supreme Personality of Godhead and the all-in-all, yet he took the wrong side. That is why Kṛṣṇa and Balarāma called him "Cheater Gaṇeśa." Puruṣottama Jānā arrested the King, and then mercifully released him, saying, "I shall not kill you." Then, having conquered Vidyānagara, he took permission of the deity Sākṣi-gopāla, the witness of the young *brāhmaṇa*, and brought that deity to Kaṭaka. He also took the very large and beautiful deities of Rādhā-kānta, who are still in the Śrī Rādhā-kānta Maṭha in Jagannātha Purī, where Caitanya Mahāprabhu used to live in the Gambhīrā. He also took Bhaṇḍa Gaṇeśa, bringing all these deities to Purī.

In this regard, *Śrī Caitanya-caritāmṛta* (*Madhya-līlā* 5.120–4) states:

utkalera rājā puruṣottama-deva nāma
sei deśa jini' nila kariyā saṅgrāma

Later there was a fight, and this country was conquered by King Puruṣottama-deva of Orissa.

sei rājā jini' nila tāṅra siṁhāsana
'māṇikya-siṁhāsana' nāma aneka ratana

That King was victorious over the King of Vidyānagara, and he took possession of his throne, the Māṇikya *siṁhāsana*, which was bedecked with many jewels.

puruṣottama-deva sei baḍa bhakta ārya
gopāla-caraṇe māge, cala mora rājya'

King Puruṣottama-deva was a great devotee and was advanced in the civilization of the Āryans. He begged at the lotus feet of Gopāla, "Please come to my kingdom."

tāṅra bhakti-vaśe gopāla tāṅre ājñā dila
gopāla la-iyā sei kaṭake āila

When the King begged Him to come to his kingdom, Gopāla, who was already obliged for his devotional service, accepted his prayer. Thus the King took the Gopāla deity and went back to Kaṭaka.

jagannāthe āni' dila māṇikya-siṁhāsana
kaṭake gopāla-sevā karila sthāpana

After winning the Māṇikya throne, King Puruṣottama-deva took it to Jagannātha Purī and presented it to Lord Jagannātha. In the meantime, he also established regular worship of the Gopāla deity at Kaṭaka.

Puruṣottama Jānā also brought the King's daughter to Purī, but he decided, "I will not marry her; I will give her to my sweeper." Later, when he was ready to give her away, all of his ministers, who were very kind, saw her crying and lamenting, "He will give me to a sweeper." They pacified her and also told the King, "Don't worry. At the right time, during the next Chariot Festival, you can give this girl to your sweeper." The next year, when the Chariot Festival took place again, Mahārāja Puruṣottama Jānā again swept the road. At that time all his ministers inspired the beautiful princess to go to him and say, "I will marry this very sweeper, not any other." She boldly told him, "You are the sweeper of Jagannātha-deva. I only want to marry His sweeper; I cannot marry any other sweeper." The King's advisers then approached him and said, "Yes, yes, this is very good. We agree with this proposal. You are a sweeper, and this girl will be the wife of a sweeper. Why don't you accept her? You must accept her." The girl began to weep, and the King was bound to accept her as his wife. Puruṣottama Jānā's son became a very beautiful prince, and that prince later became King Pratāparudra, the associate of Caitanya Mahāprabhu.

The most merciful Jagannātha is surely *patita-pāvana*, the savior of the fallen, and He is also *bhakta-vatsala* – He always wants to please His devotees.

CHAPTER FIVE

REUNION AT KURUKṢETRA

Mahāprabhu's mood at Ratha-yātrā

At the beginning of the Ratha-yātrā Festival, Śrī Caitanya Mahāprabhu offers a prayer to Jagannātha-deva, not to His form as Lord Jagannātha or Vāsudeva-Kṛṣṇa, but to His form as Vrajendra-nandana Śrī Kṛṣṇa:

jayati jana-nivāso devakī-janma-vādo
yadu-vara-pariṣat svair dorbhir asyann adharmam
sthira-cara-vṛjina-ghnaḥ su-smita-śrī-mukhena
vraja-pura-vanitānāṁ vardhayan kāma-devam

Śrīmad-Bhāgavatam (10.90.48)

Śrī Kṛṣṇa is He who is known as *jana-nivāsa*, the ultimate resort of all living entities, and who is also known as Devakī-nandana or Yaśodā-nandana, the son of Devakī and Yaśodā. He is the guide of the Yadu dynasty, and with His mighty arms He kills everything inauspicious, as well as every man who is impious. By His presence He destroys all things inauspicious for all living entities, moving and inert. His blissful smiling face always increases the lusty desires of the *gopīs* of Vṛndāvana. May He be all-glorious and happy.

Caitanya Mahāprabhu is praying in the mood of Śrīmatī Rādhikā meeting Kṛṣṇa at Kurukṣetra. There, by their mood, the *gopīs* bring Kṛṣṇa to Vṛndāvana and decorate Him with flowers. By their mood they forcibly give Him the flute He left in Vṛndāvana with Mother Yaśodā, along with His peacock feather, and they whisper in His ear, "Don't say that Your father and mother are Vasudeva and Devakī. Don't say that You are from the Yadu dynasty and that You are a Yādava. Say only that You are a *gopa*." Kṛṣṇa replies, "Yes, I will follow your instructions."

Śrī Caitanya Mahāprabhu prays, *jayati jana-nivāso devakī-janma-vādo*. This *śloka*, which Śrī Sanātana Gosvāmī has quoted in his *Bṛhad-bhāgavatāmṛta*, has many profound meanings. If Caitanya Mahāprabhu or Śrīla Sanātana Gosvāmī were to explain it, they would do so with a hundred different meanings, each deeper and more unfathomable than the previous one. It contains the entire *Śrīmad-Bhāgavatam* from beginning to end.

The general meaning of *jana-nivāsa* is, "You are always in the hearts of all as Paramātmā." However, Kṛṣṇa cannot live as Paramātmā in the hearts of the Vrajavāsīs; He can only be present there in the form of Vrajendra-nandana Śyāmasundara. *Jana* also means *nija-jana* (near and dear), and therefore it means Kṛṣṇa's personal associates. All the Vrajavāsīs are Kṛṣṇa's *nija-jana*, for He is the *jīvana* (life-air) of Nanda, Yaśodā, all His friends, and especially of the *gopīs*. He is also *rādhikā-jīvanera jīvana*, the very life of Rādhikā's life, and He always resides in Her heart. This relationship is reciprocal; the Vrajavāsīs are His life, just as much as He is theirs.

Devakī-janma-vādo. Only Mathurāvāsīs and worldly people can say that Kṛṣṇa took birth from the womb of Mother Devakī. General people say this, but actually He is the son of Mother Yaśodā; she is His real mother.

Yadu-vara-pariṣat svair dorbhir. The members of the Yadu dynasty are the *nija-jana* of Dvārakādhīśa-Kṛṣṇa, for they are His associates. It seems that this *śloka* refers to Vāsudeva-Kṛṣṇa, and describes Arjuna, Bhīma, and His other associates as His arms. Vāsudeva-Kṛṣṇa fought in the Mahābhārata War and in various other battles, and He fought with Pauṇḍraka Vāsudeva and other demons. Thc *śloka* seems to describe *dvārakā-līlā*, but actually, in its deeper meaning, it glorifies Vrajendra-nandana Kṛṣṇa. In Vṛndāvana, Kṛṣṇa killed Pūtanā and other demons with his own arms. Moreover, in Vṛndāvana He killed the greatest demon – the feelings of separation felt by Śrīmatī Rādhikā and the *gopīs*.

Sthira-cara-vṛjina-ghnaḥ su-smita-śrī-mukhena vraja-pura-vanitānām. In Vṛndāvana, Kṛṣṇa always took away all kinds of problems and suffering, simply with His smiling face and His flute. What was the suffering of the Vrajavāsīs? It was only their mood of separation from Him. They had no other problems at all.

This verse includes the pastimes of Gokula, Vṛndāvana, Rādhā-kuṇḍa, Śyāma-kuṇḍa, *rāsa-līlā*, and all the other Vraja pastimes as well. *Vardhayan kāmadevam.* In this connection, Kāmadeva does not mean lust, but *prema*. What kind of *prema*? *Sneha, māna, praṇaya, rāga, anurāga, bhāva,* and *mahābhāva*. The *gopīs* tell Kṛṣṇa, "You are that person – that Kāmadeva." In this way, Śrī Caitanya Mahāprabhu is offering *praṇāma* and praying, putting the whole of *Śrīmad-Bhāgavatam*, and all of Kṛṣṇa's pastimes as well, into this one *śloka*.

The meaning of gopī-bhartuḥ

As I have explained before, Mahāprabhu very rarely sees Jagannātha, Baladeva, and Subhadrā. When He does, He at once enters a mood of very intense separation and prays, "After a long time I am meeting with My most beloved, for whom I was burning in the fire of separation." He addresses Jagannātha as *gopī-bhartuḥ* and prays, "*Pada-kamalayor dāsa-dāsānudāsaḥ.*" The word *gopī-bhartuḥ* reveals Kṛṣṇa's relationship with the *gopīs*, for it means "the *gopīs'* most beloved," or "He who is always controlled by the *gopīs.*" Mahāprabhu concludes, "I want to be the servant of the servant of the servant of that Kṛṣṇa."

nāhaṁ vipro na ca nara-patir nāpi vaiśyo na śūdro
nāhaṁ varṇī na ca gṛha-patir no vanastho yatir vā
kintu prodyan-nikhila-paramānanda-pūrṇāmṛtābdher
gopī-bhartuḥ pada-kamalayor dāsa-dāsānudāsaḥ

Śrī Caitanya-caritāmṛta (*Madhya-līlā* 13.80)

I am not a *brāhmaṇa*, a *kṣatriya*, a *vaiśya*, or a *śūdra*. Nor am I a *brahmacārī*, a *gṛhastha*, a *vānaprastha*, or a *sannyāsī*. I identify Myself only as the servant of the servant of the servant of the lotus feet of Śrī Kṛṣṇa, the maintainer of the *gopīs*. He is like an ocean of nectar, and He is the cause of universal transcendental bliss. He is always existing in full brilliance.

Śrī Caitanya Mahāprabhu prays not only for Himself, but for everyone. He is the Supreme Personality of Godhead, *gopī-bhartuḥ* Himself, and He offers prayers in order to teach us how to pray. He is teaching us our actual identity; we are not Indian or American, nor are we from Great Britain or anywhere else. We are not *brāhmaṇas*, administrative *kṣatriyas*, mercantile *vaiśyas* or *śūdra* laborers, nor are we *brahmacārī* students, *gṛhastha* householders, retired *vānaprasthas*, or *sannyāsīs* in the renounced order. We are eternally servants of Kṛṣṇa.

Śrī Caitanya Mahāprabhu uses the name *gopī-bhartuḥ* for further clarification, and by this He is indicating, "We are not servants of that Kṛṣṇa who lived here and there in Dvārakā without His flute. Others may be, but as for My associates and Myself, we are only *gopī-bhartuḥ pada-kamalayor dāsa-dāsānudāsaḥ*, the servants of the servants of the servants of the lotus feet of Śrī Kṛṣṇa, the beloved of the *gopīs*."

Who is *gopī-bhartuḥ*? He is Rādhā-kānta, Rādhā-ramaṇa, and Gopīnātha. The *gopīs* must be there as the *ārādhya* (worshipable deities) of Kṛṣṇa. He must be their worshiper, and then we are His servants; otherwise not. We are not Kṛṣṇa's servants if Rukmiṇī and Satyabhāmā are there, or if He is four-handed and holding His Sudarśana *cakra*. Kṛṣṇa must be with the *gopīs*, He must be controlled by their prominence, and especially by Rādhā. We are servants of that Kṛṣṇa.

We are all transcendental, and our intrinsic, constitutional nature is to serve Kṛṣṇa; but we are not servants of all His manifestations. There are very big differences in these manifestations, and to be the servant of *gopī-bhartuḥ* is very, very rare. We can consider that those who have come in the line of Mahāprabhu are *rādhā-dāsīs*, as *gopī-bhartuḥ pada-kamalayor dāsa-dāsānudāsaḥ* only applies to the maidservants of Rādhikā. Caitanya Mahāprabhu's statement therefore refers to those who are coming in His disciplic line, those who are coming in the line of Śrīla Rūpa Gosvāmī, Śrīla Raghunātha dāsa Gosvāmī, and our entire *guru-paramparā*. One day, if our creeper of *bhakti* blossoms and the fruits and flowers of *prema-bhakti* manifest, we will be able to realize this. This is the aim and object of our life.

Leading up to the meeting: Kṛṣṇa sends Uddhava to Vraja

Mahāprabhu was so absorbed that He could not utter Jagannātha's name. He could only chant, "Jaja gaga! Jaja gaga!" Tears fell from His eyes, and His heart melted. One can realize this state only if he is a devotee of the highest standard. What was the cause of Mahāprabhu's bitter weeping? What was the reason behind it? Mahāprabhu told Svarūpa Dāmodara to sing a song that suited His mood, and Svarūpa Dāmodara began to sing:

sei ta parāṇa-nātha pāinu
yāhā lāgi' madana-dahane jhuri' genu

Śrī Caitanya-caritāmṛta (*Madhya-līlā* 13.113)

Now I have gained the Lord of My life, in whose absence I was being burned by Cupid and was withering away.

You will have to consult *Śrīmad-Bhāgavatam* to understand the meaning of this verse, because the history of Ratha-yātrā has been indicated there. Kṛṣṇa left Vraja at the age of eleven[1] and went first to Mathurā, and then after some time He went to Dvārakā. While He was in Mathurā, He sent Uddhava to console the *gopīs*, and later He also sent Baladeva Prabhu from Dvārakā to console them. The *gopīs* had now been feeling separation for a long time. Everyone in Vṛndāvana was feeling separation from Him, and even the cows and calves were upset. The *gopas* and *gopīs* were weeping continuously, and everyone, including the entire forest of Vṛndāvana, was drying up.

When Kṛṣṇa was sending Uddhava from Mathurā, He told him, "Uddhava, go to Vṛndāvana and pacify My father and mother, Nanda and Yaśodā, and especially pacify the *gopīs* who have given Me their life and soul and everything they possess. The *gopīs* always remember Me, and they do nothing else. They never decorate themselves and they have even given up taking their meals. They don't bathe and they don't even sleep."

[1] Kṛṣṇa is exactly ten years and eight months old when He leaves for Mathurā, but His transcendental body is like that of a full-grown *kaiśora* of fourteen or fifteen years.

mac-cittā mad-gata-prāṇā
bodhayantaḥ parasparam
kathayantaś ca māṁ nityaṁ
tuṣyanti ca ramanti ca

Bhagavad-gītā (10.9)

The thoughts of My pure devotees dwell in Me, their lives are fully devoted to serving Me, and they derive great satisfaction and bliss from always enlightening one another and conversing about Me.

The *gopīs'* only relief from their feelings of separation came when they sometimes fainted and sometimes slept. However, even these two friends – fainting and sleeping – abandoned the *gopīs* when Kṛṣṇa took them with Him to Mathurā.

In this way Kṛṣṇa sent Uddhava to Vraja, and there Uddhava related His message, word by word, letter by letter. However, this only made the *gopīs* more unhappy. Previously they had thought, "Kṛṣṇa has promised that He will come;" but after hearing the message, they thought, "Kṛṣṇa will never come," and they felt even more separation. Śrīmatī Rādhārāṇī began to weep:

he nātha he ramā-nātha
vraja-nāthārti-nāśana
magnam uddhara govinda
gokulaṁ vṛjinārṇavāt

Śrīmad-Bhāgavatam (10.47.52)

O master of My life, O master of the goddess of fortune, O master of Vraja! O destroyer of all suffering, Govinda, please lift Your Gokula out of the ocean of distress in which it is drowning!

Śrīmatī Rādhikā said, "I am dying without Kṛṣṇa. My dear *sakhīs,* if Kṛṣṇa does not come, I will die; I will surely die. Take My body, place it at the base of a *tamāla* tree, and place My arms around that tree so that I may feel connected to Kṛṣṇa. I pray that the water in My body will mix with Pāvana-sarovara where Kṛṣṇa bathes, so that I may touch Him. Let the air in this body go to Nanda Bābā's courtyard and touch Kṛṣṇa when He is fanned. May the fire in this body become rays of sunshine in Nanda Bābā's courtyard, and then My soul will be happy. Now I cannot see Kṛṣṇa, or touch Him." She was in a very pitiful condition, always in a mood of deep separation.

Kṛṣṇa was also feeling unbearable separation, but no one knew that. The *gopīs* could share their suffering with each other, but Kṛṣṇa could not share His feelings with anyone. He wept alone. This is why He sent Uddhava to Vṛndāvana; He wanted Uddhava to be admitted into the school of the *gopīs*, so that he would learn the meaning of the two-and-a-half letters in the word *prema.*[1] Kṛṣṇa considered, "When Uddhava understands the love of the *gopīs*, he will be qualified to realize My feelings of separation."

When Uddhava returned from Vraja, he told Kṛṣṇa about the glories of the *gopīs* and their one-pointed love. He said, "It is so very high that I could not touch it. I only saw that mountain of love from a great distance, but still it was so high that my hat fell off the back of my head as I looked up at it. I cannot imagine how glorious the *gopīs* are. I wanted to take the dust of their lotus feet, but now I am hopeless. I am not qualified to touch their foot-dust, so I simply offer *praṇāma* to it from very far away. Uddhava then uttered the following prayer in glorification of the *gopīs*:

[1] Unlike English, which has only full letters, Sanskrit words can contain both full and half letters.

vande nanda-vraja-strīṇāṁ
pāda-reṇum abhīkṣṇaśaḥ
yāsāṁ hari-kathodgītaṁ
punāti bhuvana-trayam

Śrīmad-Bhāgavatam (10.47.63)

I repeatedly offer my respects to the dust from the feet of the women of Nanda Mahārāja's cowherd village. When these *gopīs* loudly chant the glories of Śrī Kṛṣṇa, the vibration purifies the three worlds.

Instead of becoming pacified by Uddhava's explanation, Kṛṣṇa felt more and more separation. He wanted to go to Vraja, but for some reason He could not.

What Kṛṣṇa never told before

Kṛṣṇa had told Uddhava, "My father and mother are weeping bitterly. They have become blind, and they are hardly more than skeletons. Perhaps they will only live for one or two days more; in fact, they may die at any moment. Please go and pacify them. And go also to the *gopīs*. I know that My father and mother are weeping bitterly, that they are blind, and may die... but I don't know what is the condition of the *gopīs*. They are feeling the topmost separation for Me. I don't know whether they are alive, or if they have already died; so go at once, quickly. They always remember Me, keeping Me on the chariots of their minds, without any selfish motive. They know that nobody in Mathurā knows My heart."

The *gopīs* know that Kṛṣṇa is very shy, and cannot ask anyone for something to eat when He feels hungry. Yaśodā-maiyā is not present in His palace; so who will pacify Him, and who will serve Him? This is why the *gopīs* feel so much separation.

Kṛṣṇa had told Uddhava, "The *gopīs* are *mat-prāṇa*, My life and soul." He had not said this about His father and mother, only about the *gopīs*. He continued, "They have left everything for Me. For My sake, they have stopped caring for their bodies and have forgotten all their bodily duties. I am their only beloved, and they are My most beloved; indeed, they are My life and soul. They have left their shyness and their worldly responsibilities, and they have also abandoned all social etiquette for Me. For My sake, they have disobeyed their parents and left their source of maintenance. I must somehow save them and maintain them. Now they are far away, thinking, 'Kṛṣṇa will surely come tomorrow. If we die now, He will also die when He finds out.' This is the reason they somehow maintain their lives without dying.

"The *gopīs* think, 'Kṛṣṇa has promised, and He cannot break His promise. He must come. He will come tomorrow.' That is why they maintain their lives. Actually, I think that they are not maintaining their own lives. Their lives rest in Me, and I am maintaining them, otherwise they would have been finished. Go at once and see whether they have died or not; and if not, please pacify them."

Kṛṣṇa had only spoken like this about the *gopīs*; never about anyone else, including Arjuna and the Pāṇḍavas, or His queens, Satyabhāmā and Rukmiṇī. The *gopīs* are unique in their boundless and causeless love and affection for Kṛṣṇa. Our highest aim and object is the love for Kṛṣṇa that is in the *gopīs*, and especially in Rādhikā.

When Rādhikā was feeling separation, *gopīs* like Lalitā, Viśākhā, Citrā, Campakalatā, and Rūpa Mañjarī were serving Her and trying to pacify Her; but who could actually pacify Her? She was totally mad, with no external sense at all. The others were trying to pacify Her because their consciousness was still somewhat functional. Their love is very high, millions of times greater than that of Uddhava, Satyabhāmā, and Rukmiṇī, and higher even than that of the other *sakhīs* of Vṛndāvana; but it is not as high as Rādhikā's love.

Rādhikā was totally mad, as Uddhava saw when he witnessed Her talking to the bumblebee. Actually, Kṛṣṇa Himself had gone to Vraja in the form of that bumblebee, and He also saw that Rādhikā was totally mad. She was lying on a bed of rose petals, which had become dried up by the touch of Her body, and all the *candana* that had been put on Her body to cool Her was also completely dried. At first, Uddhava could not understand whether She was dead or alive.

Then, he saw that Rādhikā was very angry with Kṛṣṇa, criticizing and abusing Him, and calling Him an ungrateful cheater. No one else could have spoken to Kṛṣṇa in this way, including Satyabhāmā and the other queens, and even Mother Yaśodā and Nanda Bābā. Rādhikā told Him, "You are ungrateful, and You are like a six-legged bumblebee. Human beings have two legs and animals have four; but bumblebees have six legs, so they are more ignorant than any animal. We don't want to have any relationship with that black person whose heart is as black as a bumblebee. Rāma was also black, and he cheated Śūrpaṇakhā and cut off her nose and ears."

Śrīmad-Bhāgavatam is actually an explanation of the glory of Rādhikā's love. Her love is supreme, and it is the goal of all living beings. We can never grasp its breadth, but we can taste a drop of it, and even that one drop can drown the entire universe. Śrī Caitanya Mahāprabhu gave Śrīla Rūpa Gosvāmī that drop of the endless ocean of nectar, *bhakti-rasa.* If we can serve the *gopīs*, and especially Rādhikā, we can also have love and affection for Kṛṣṇa, and then we can feel separation. Otherwise, it will never be possible. Caitanya Mahāprabhu, the Six Gosvāmīs, *Śrīmad-Bhāgavatam*, and Śukadeva Gosvāmī have proclaimed this conclusion: our goal is *kṛṣṇa-prema*, the *prema* that the *gopīs* have for Kṛṣṇa.

Previously, Uddhava had heard about how much love and affection the *gopīs* have for Kṛṣṇa, but he had no experience of it. He had heard that the *gopīs* are Kṛṣṇa's most beloved, and that Kṛṣṇa is their most beloved, but even knowing this, he could not know the intensity and the ways of their love.

Uddhava also loves Kṛṣṇa, and thinks, "Kṛṣṇa is my master, He is also like my brother, and we have so many other relationships." However, Kṛṣṇa did not say anything about Uddhava's love. Rather, He told him to go to Vraja and learn there: "Go and realize the nature of *prema.*" He said, "There is no one in Mathurā like these *gopīs.*"

Śrī Caitanya Mahāprabhu has mercifully sprinkled a drop of that love on the world (*Śrī Caitanya-caritāmṛta* (*Ādi-līlā* 1.4)):

anarpita-carīṁ cirāt karuṇayāvatīrṇaḥ kalau
samarpayitum unnatojjvala-rasāṁ sva-bhakti-śriyam
hariḥ puraṭa-sundara-dyuti-kadamba-sandīpitaḥ
sadā hṛdaya-kandare sphuratu vaḥ śacī-nandanaḥ

May the Supreme Lord who is known as the son of Śrīmatī Śacīdevī be transcendentally situated in the innermost chambers of your heart. Resplendent with the radiance of molten gold, He has appeared in the age of Kali by His causeless mercy to bestow what no incarnation has ever offered before: the most sublime and radiant mellow of devotional service, the mellow of amorous love.

Uddhava failed the entrance exam

Uddhava had great love and affection for Kṛṣṇa, but when he arrived in Vraja, he realized that *vraja-prema* was totally new to him. He saw Kṛṣṇa playing with all His *sakhās.* Millions and millions of cows were hankering after Him, and milk was flowing from their bulging udders because of their spontaneous love. The very beautiful black and white calves were jumping here and there, and Nanda Bābā's big bulls were fighting with each other.

As Uddhava saw that scene, beautiful ghee lamps flickered in the *gopīs'* rooms, and the light from these lamps was soft and fragrant – not like the dead light from electric bulbs. Varieties of flowers spread their sweet aroma in all directions, and the songs of the humming bumblebees were like the blowing of Cupid's conchshell. Cuckoos and other birds were singing everywhere, and peacocks were dancing about and calling, "Ke kaw! Ke kaw!"

All the *gopīs* were churning yogurt and singing, "Govinda Dāmodara Mādhaveti." They were all very beautiful, and Mother Yaśodā was the most beautiful of all. How else could Kṛṣṇa have become so beautiful? He would only have been black otherwise; it was because of her that His beauty was like the luster of pearls.

Uddhava saw all this, but in a moment the scene changed completely, and now he saw that all the residents of Vṛndāvana were weeping for Kṛṣṇa: "O Kṛṣṇa, where are You? Where are You?" Cows were not going out to graze. They simply wept, keeping their heads and eyes toward Mathurā, and the calves were not drinking the milk from the udders of their mothers. The peacocks were not dancing; rather, they looked as if they were blind. Every person and creature was mad in separation from Kṛṣṇa.

It was now evening, and Uddhava found himself in Kṛṣṇa's home, where he became dumbstruck to see the love and affection of Mother Yaśodā and Nanda Bābā. He could never have imagined that such high-class love could exist, but now he was able to realize something of its elevated nature.

Early the next morning, Uddhava went to Kadamba-kyārī, where, by Kṛṣṇa's mercy, he was able to see the *gopīs*, who were all mad in separation and just about to die. This is why Kṛṣṇa had sent him to Vṛndāvana: to try to be admitted into the school of the *gopīs*. Kṛṣṇa had told him, "Be admitted into the school in which I studied. Then, when you return, we will be able to have some discussion about love and affection. First, go and become qualified."

However, Uddhava was not qualified for admittance into the school of the *gopīs*. His entrance examination score was about 25 percent, but the *gopīs* demanded more than 85 percent. Still, although they rejected him, he was able to enter the school and see the very high-class students there. He saw professors like Viśākhā and Lalitā, and he saw the principal, Rādhikā Herself. Now he knew something of the glories of the *gopīs*, and he realized a little of their love for Kṛṣṇa. He had never seen anything like this before, and now he felt, "If I want to love Kṛṣṇa, I must be admitted into this school. But I am not qualified." He therefore requested the *gopīs*, "If you do not admit me, can you at least take me on as a servant, to bring water and clean the school?" The *gopīs* rejected even that request, however, and they told him, "You should go back to Mathurā. First become qualified, and then you can sweep our *kuñjas*; you cannot sweep here at the moment."

Uddhava then prayed:

vande nanda-vraja-strīṇāṁ
pāda-reṇum abhīkṣṇaśaḥ
yāsāṁ hari-kathodgītaṁ
punāti bhuvana-trayam

Śrīmad-Bhāgavatam (10.47.63)

Nanda-vraja-strīṇām means the beloved *gopīs* of Kṛṣṇa. Uddhava prayed to them, "I want to offer myself unto the dust of your lotus feet. I want to keep even one particle of your foot-dust on my head, and if I can only get one particle of dust, it must be Śrīmatī Rādhikā's." Neither Brahmā nor Śaṅkara, nor even Satyabhāmā and the other Dvārakā queens, can attain this.

Kṛṣṇa had sent Uddhava to see the glories of the *gopīs*, and now he saw Mount Everest, the highest peak of the Himālayas of the *gopīs'* love. He could not become like them, however, so he had to return to Kṛṣṇa empty-handed. "I went there and saw something very mysterious and wonderful, which I cannot explain," he told Kṛṣṇa. "You told me about the *gopīs*, and what I saw was even more wonderful than what You told me. But I had to return without realizing anything."

Yāsāṁ hari-kathodgītaṁ, punāti bhuvana-trayam. The songs of the *gopīs*, such as *Bhramara-gīta* and *Gopī-gīta*, purify the whole universe, and if one recites them, or even remembers them, he will actually be purified. So try to recite all these songs (*gītas*) and know them. The meanings are very deep, and Śrīla Bhaktivedānta Swāmī Mahārāja wanted to teach that the very wonderful moods therein are our aim and object. He wanted to teach this and he did discuss it in his books, but how could he actually plant it in barren lands and deserts? First he had to cultivate the lands to make them fertile. He wanted to give this highest goal, but in the meantime his Svāminī, Śrīmatī Rādhikā, called to him, "Come at once! We need your service."

This is our goal – the dust of the lotus feet of Śrīmatī Rādhikā.

āsām aho caraṇa-reṇu-juṣam ahaṁ syāṁ
vṛndāvane kim api gulma-latauṣadhīnām
yā dustyajaṁ sva-janam ārya-pathaṁ ca hitvā
bhejur mukunda-padavīṁ śrutibhir vimṛgyām

Śrīmad-Bhāgavatam (10.47.61)

The *gopīs* of Vṛndāvana have abandoned the association of their husbands, sons, and other family members who are very difficult to give up, and they have forsaken the path of chastity to take shelter of the lotus feet of Mukunda, Kṛṣṇa, which one should search for by Vedic knowledge. Oh, let me be fortunate enough to be one of the bushes, creepers, or herbs in Vṛndāvana, because the *gopīs* trample them and bless them with the dust of their lotus feet.

Uddhava prayed, "If I cannot attain Rādhikā's lotus feet, then I will be satisfied with the dust particles from the feet of any of Her *sakhīs.* I don't want the dust of Kṛṣṇa's lotus feet, because I will have to take a particle of the *gopīs'* moods if I want to please Kṛṣṇa."

We must engage in the process given by Śrīla Rūpa Gosvāmī, Śrīla Bhaktivinoda Ṭhākura, Śrīla Viśvanātha Cakravartī Ṭhākura, and Śrīla Narottama dāsa Ṭhākura. The teaching of our present *ācāryas* is the same wine in new bottles. The bottles are different colors, but the wine is the same. If you drink that wine, you will certainly become mad, but this madness is actually desirable.

Kṛṣṇa meets His parents at Kurukṣetra

Years later there was to be a solar eclipse and Kṛṣṇa planned to go to Kurukṣetra with all His commanders, His army, and all His 16,108 queens. He did not invite Nanda Bābā directly, but He thought, "Father will know, and he will not be able to remain in Vraja. He will come at once; he must come."

In Vṛndāvana, Nanda Bābā somehow came to know about the religious function to be held at Kurukṣetra. Thus, all the *gopas, gopīs,* and young people prepared their bullock carts and proceeded toward Kurukṣetra, leaving Upananda and some other elders in Vraja to look after everything. They took with them many personal items for Kṛṣṇa, such as butter and other things that He liked, and on the way they constantly remembered: "Kṛṣṇa, Kṛṣṇa, Kṛṣṇa."

By then, the *gopīs* had been lamenting for perhaps fifty, sixty, or seventy years. Kṛṣṇa also felt separation for that long, but even after all those years, He was still youthful (*kiśora*), and the *gopīs* remained young as well.

In the meantime, the sun was covered by a shadow and the whole world became dark. According to Vedic culture, during a solar eclipse one should take bath three times: when it is just beginning, when the sun is fully covered, and when it is again fully visible. At that time, one should bathe and give donations in charity. It is written in Indian history and in the Vedas and Upaniṣads that many kings used to donate their entire wealth to the *brāhmaṇas* and needy persons. Every golden pot and utensil was given in charity. Having given away their own clothing, keeping only a loincloth for themselves, the kings themselves would become penniless. Those charitable persons were giving so much charity that there was no longer anyone to take it. Those who had accepted charity began to give charity to others. They gave their charity in charity, and therefore there was no one left to think, "I want charity." All were giving and all were satisfied – because Kṛṣṇa was there. Even recently in India, many people would donate all these things. Now, however, although giving in charity is for the betterment of the donors, this culture is gradually reducing.

Everyone bathed there at Kurukṣetra, made their donations, and after that they came to Kṛṣṇa's tent to take His *darśana*. Thousands and thousands of *ṛṣis*, *maharṣis*, *brahmavādīs*, realized souls like Nārada, Bhīṣma Pitāmaha (the grandfather of the Kauravas and Pāṇḍavas), Vyāsadeva, Gautama, Yājñavalkya, Duryodhana and all his brothers, Droṇācārya, Karṇa, and all the Kauravas came from all over India, and from all over the world. *Ṛṣis* and *maharṣis* from the Caspian sea, like Kaśyapa, also came, and from Mongolia, sages like Maṅgala Ṛṣi came with all his sons and daughters. Almost all the kings of the world had assembled there to bathe in the very pious lake there, and the crowd consisted of more than ten million people. All were there to bathe in that lake, and all were residing there in separate camps.

Now, everyone assembled in the camp of Vasudeva and Devakī to take *darśana* of Kṛṣṇa, and they began to enter His tent. His tent was so large that thousands of people could sit inside. Although there was no arrangement for a loudspeaker, everyone could easily hear Him speak, and in fact everyone thought, "Kṛṣṇa is sitting near me. I'm joking with Him, I'm telling Him something, and He is very happy to hear it."

The Pāṇḍavas – Yudhiṣṭhira, Arjuna, Bhīma, Nakula, Sahadeva, and Draupadī – had also joined the assembly, and their mother, Kuntī, was also there. Kuntī met with her brother Vasudeva, and pitifully weeping with tears falling profusely from her eyes, she told him, "Brother, you did not remember me when my sons were given poison, when they were about to burn in a fire, or when all their wealth, kingdom, and everything else was taken and we were begging here and there. Like a demon, Duryodhana cheated my sons. He drove them from their kingdom, and he and Duḥśāsana also tried to strip Draupadī in the big council where Dhṛtarāṣṭra, Bhīṣma Pitāmaha, and other elders were present. You are my brother. You should have remembered me." Weeping loudly, she put her arms around Vasudeva's neck, and Vasudeva Mahārāja also began to weep. Kuntī continued, "Perhaps, my brother, you forgot me."

Vasudeva replied, "O elder sister, please do not lament. This was all caused by the time factor of Śrī Bhagavān. At that time my wife and I were imprisoned in the jail of Kaṁsa, and we were suffering so grievously. Kaṁsa was always abusing and insulting us. His men bound me in iron chains and they were kicking me with their boots. How could I do anything? Moreover, our six sons were killed right in front of us, snatched from my lap and put to death. Luckily, Baladeva and Kṛṣṇa are saved. I was in unbearable distress, and that is why I could not help you. Nevertheless, despite everything, somehow I always remembered you, and when I came out of jail I sent my first message to you.

"Everything depends on the mercy of God. Sometimes we meet and sometimes we are separated from each other. Sometimes there is suffering and sorrow, and sometimes we are very prosperous. Nothing depends on any soul. Don't worry anymore. Now it is over." In this way Vasudeva was consoling Kuntī.

In the meantime, Nanda Bābā and the Vrajavāsīs were coming on many bullock carts. Mother Yaśodā, Nanda Bābā, all the *gopīs* like Śrīmatī Rādhikā, Lalitā, and Viśākhā, and all Kṛṣṇa's cowherd friends like Dāmā, Śrīdāmā, Sudāmā, Vasudāma, Stoka-kṛṣṇa, Madhumaṅgala, and all others were on their way. Thousands of *gopas* and *gopīs* were on their way to Kṛṣṇa.

While everyone else was meeting with Kṛṣṇa, someone came and told Him and Baladeva, "Oh, Your father and mother are coming in a bullock cart." When Kṛṣṇa heard this, He immediately left all the members of the assembly. Although there were many thousands upon thousands of devotees, like Kaśyapa, Kavi, Havi, Antarikṣa, Nārada, Vasiṣṭha, Āgastya, and Vālmīki, Kṛṣṇa left them all and began to run at once towards Yaśodā and Nanda – weeping with tears in His eyes. In one second His heart had melted, and now He called out, "Oh, Mother is coming? Father is coming?" Upset, He cried out, "Mother, Mother, where are you?"

The bullock cart had now stopped. Baladeva Prabhu was following Kṛṣṇa, and they both exclaimed, "Oh, the bullock cart is here." Nanda Bābā and Yaśodā-maiyā came down from the cart, and when they saw Kṛṣṇa they became overwhelmed and began to weep, "O my son, my son! Kṛṣṇa, Kṛṣṇa!"

Standing at a distance, all the *gopas* and *gopīs*, including Rādhā, Lalitā, and Viśākhā, were also weeping. Somehow they had been tolerating their separation from Kṛṣṇa while traveling from Vraja, and in Vraja they were also somewhat tolerating. Now, however, as they came nearer and nearer, their tolerance began to disappear and they began to cry like babies.

Kṛṣṇa at once sat on the lap of Yaśodā-maiyā, and Baladeva Prabhu fell at the feet of Nanda Bābā. Seeing Kṛṣṇa, whom she had lost for years and years, all Yaśodā-maiyā's separation mood, in the form of tears, began to flow out. She wept loudly, "My dear son! My dear son!" She covered Kṛṣṇa's face as she had done when He was a baby, and milk flowed automatically from her breasts. She covered Him as though He was a helpless, small baby and she wept bitterly – so bitterly.

In Vṛndāvana she had never wept as much as she did now. There she was like a statue, and her heart was dried up in separation. Kṛṣṇa had also been like dry wood, or like a stone, but now He also wept aloud. Nanda Bābā took Baladeva in his lap and he also began to weep, and it was a very piteous scene. Kṛṣṇa cried out, "Mother! Mother!" Baladeva Prabhu, sitting on the lap of Nanda Bābā, was crying out, "Father! Father!" and Nanda Bābā caressed him.

Having followed Kṛṣṇa, Vasudeva, Devakī, and Mother Rohiṇī arrived there, and Rohiṇī thought, "Oh, how very wonderful this situation is!" Kṛṣṇa had always been somewhat shy in front of Devakī. If He was hungry, He would tell Mother Rohiṇī – not Devakī – and now Devakī saw Him weep uncontrollably.

Devakī thought, "Kṛṣṇa never sat on my lap. He has never called me, 'Mother, Mother.' But now He is in the arms of Yaśodā crying, 'Mother, Mother, Mother.' Yaśodā thinks, 'Kṛṣṇa is my own son,' and Kṛṣṇa also thinks, 'My mother is only Yaśodā – not Devakī.' Yaśodā will surely take Kṛṣṇa and return to Vraja. Kṛṣṇa will go forever and He will never return to Dvārakā!"

She wanted to tell Yaśodā, "O Yaśodā, Kṛṣṇa is not your son. He is my son, but now He is forgetting me and accepting you as His real mother." She also wanted to tell Kṛṣṇa, "You are not the son of Yaśodā. You are my son." She could not say all this in the assembly of so many persons, however, and therefore she spoke her mind in a roundabout way.

Being very intelligent, she said, "O dear friend Yaśodā, you are wonderful and merciful. When we were in the prison of Kaṁsa, we could not support Kṛṣṇa. Then, in a hidden way, we sent our son to Gokula – to you. Although He is my son, you have kept and supported Him. You have nourished Him better than anyone could nourish her own son. Although you knew that Kṛṣṇa is my son, you nourished Him as though He was yours. As the eyelids protect the most important part of the eyes – the pupils – you protected Kṛṣṇa. You never thought, 'He is the son of Devakī.' You saw Him only as your son. I see, therefore, that there is no one as merciful as you in the entire world. You are very humble and broadminded, and you have served Him up to now. Because of this, He never remembers me. He always thinks that you are His mother."

Rohiṇī saw that Devakī was trying to do something wrong – she was trying to come between Yaśodā and Kṛṣṇa. Rohiṇī wanted her not to disturb them. To trick her, therefore, she quickly said, "Oh, Mother Kuntī and so many more persons are waiting for you. We should go there." She cleverly sent her away to welcome all the guests, and she also sent Vasudeva Mahārāja.

After some time Yaśodā-maiyā became relieved, but she could not say anything. She was not in a state to say anything, and Kṛṣṇa was also in that condition. There was now only an exchange of moods – from heart to heart. Yaśodā then thought, "Outside, nearby, all the *gopīs* like Lalitā, Viśākhā, and Śrīmatī

Rādhikā are waiting. They cannot meet Kṛṣṇa if I am here – and Nanda Bābā and Baladeva are also here."

Up until now the *gopīs* were checking their moods of separation and their lives remained in their bodies. Once they reached Kṛṣṇa, however, they could no longer tolerate a moment's separation. They were about to die. Being very kind and generous, Mother Yaśodā thought, "They will die if I do not give a chance to them at once. I must take everyone away from here, by trick, and then the *gopīs* will come. If I delay, they will all die. They cannot tolerate the separation any longer."

I remember an example from my boyhood, when I was fifteen. My father was a farmer. I went with him to a place far from my house, and there I picked a bundle of very delicious, beautiful green chickpeas. At first I thought the bundle was very light, when I reached the midway point it became heavy, and as my village became nearer I could not bear the weight. When I came into the village I should have instantly fallen down, but somehow I persevered. When I reached the door of my house, however, I could not take the load inside. I dropped it outside.

This was also the case with the *gopīs*. When they were in Vraja they were somehow tolerating separation, and as they traveled to Kṛṣṇa their separation-feeling increased. Then, when they saw Kṛṣṇa but had no chance to meet Him because Yaśodā, Nanda Bābā, and others were with Him, they could not endure the separation at all. Yaśodā realized this fact, and she at once took the hand of Baladeva Prabhu. She put his fingers in her hand and, looking towards Nanda Bābā, she told him, "Let us meet with the others." Being very intelligent, Baladeva Prabhu also considered, "If I am here, the *gopīs* will not come," and he hurriedly left with his parents.

Yaśodā thus went to Devakī and embraced her, and some dialogue ensued. Nanda Bābā met with Vasudeva and others, and they also engaged in conversation.

CHAPTER SIX

KṚṢṆA MEETS THE GOPĪS AT KURUKṢETRA

That time has passed

As Śrī Caitanya Mahāprabhu dances at the Ratha-yātrā Festival, He remembers a poem from a mundane Sanskrit literature called *Sāhitya-darpaṇa*. He raises His arms and recites that poem in a loud voice:

yaḥ kaumāra-haraḥ sa eva hi varas tā eva caitra-kṣapās
te conmīlita-mālatī-surabhayaḥ prauḍhāḥ kadambānilāḥ
sā caivāsmi tathāpi tatra surata-vyāpāra-līlā-vidhau
revā-rodhasi vetasī-taru-tale cetaḥ samutkaṇṭhate

Śrī Caitanya-caritāmṛta (*Madhya-līlā* 13.121)

That very personality who stole away my heart during my youth is now again my master. These are the same moonlit nights of the month of Caitra. The same fragrance of *mālatī* flowers is there, and the same sweet breezes are blowing from the *kadamba* forest. In our intimate relationship, I am also the same lover, yet still my mind is not happy here. I am eager to go back to that place on the bank of the Revā under the Vetasī tree. That is my desire.

Mahāprabhu sings, "In our teenage years, when we were twelve or fourteen, we used to meet on the bank of the Revā river, where there were so many fragrant *kadamba* trees and *vetasī* canes." Cane cannot be uprooted, even if there is a strong wind. It will bend according to the direction in which the wind blows, and even a flood cannot uproot it. It will simply bend this way and that. Devotees should be like this *vetasī* cane in their practice of *bhakti*.

Mahāprabhu continues, "Although there are thorns in the groves of *vetasī* cane, we never cared for them when we were meeting. We never cared about any problems. We engaged in very sweet talks on the river bank, opening our hearts to one another in love and affection, and there was no one to create any walls or problems. But some time has passed, and now we are married. You are my husband and I am your wife, but I am not happy. I was happy then, but I am not happy now. We are meeting here, and there is no obstruction. We can live in our home together without any shame, because we have permission. We can meet now, because we have a 'passport' to meet. No one will criticize us now, but we don't have the love and affection that we had at our first meeting. How glorious, how beautiful, how sweet and pleasing was that love! I want you to come to those very groves on the banks of the Revā river, and I want our love and affection to be renewed. I want it to be the same as it was before."

Mahāprabhu remembers this scene, and He is dancing and weeping, and reciting this verse at the same time: "*yaḥ kaumāra-haraḥ* – He who stole our youth and teenage years, and played with us, has now become our husband. Our *kaumāra* age has been stolen away by marriage."

A girlfriend and boyfriend meet together without being married. They meet very secretly here and there, and enjoy themselves.

Then, if after some time they get married, there is no longer any restriction at all, and they can meet freely. Mahāprabhu's mood is like this, though not exactly the same. In other words, in the mood of the *gopīs*, and especially in Rādhārāṇī's mood, He is actually saying, "All Your relatives are here at Kurukṣetra. I cannot meet You in the forest, where we used to meet. There were many good *kadamba* trees with beautiful flowers, all with an abundance of fragrance. There was no one there to disturb us. There were only the two of us sitting on the bank of the river, talking throughout the day without ever stopping. We talked continually while we were meeting each other and pleasing each other. I remember this. I do not want a royal palace or vast wealth. I want to be in that place where we used to meet together and sit and talk."

Giving this example, Śrī Caitanya Mahāprabhu is thinking, "We were meeting there in Vṛndāvana, at Rādhā-kuṇḍa, in Nandagaon, Saṅkeṭa, Ṭera-kadamba, Kadamba-kyārī, and elsewhere." The air was so fragrant in the beautiful groves of *kadamba*, and Rādhā and Kṛṣṇa used to meet each other and perform so many pleasant pastimes there. Sometimes They played on swings and sometimes They gambled. When Śrīmatī Rādhikā used to defeat Kṛṣṇa, everyone on the *gopīs'* side clapped, and Kṛṣṇa became very happy even though He was defeated. Sometimes the *gopīs* stole Kṛṣṇa's flute, and He would look for it here and there. He would say, "Oh, I will die if you keep My flute. Why are you keeping it? I will have to search everywhere to see where you have kept it."

The *gopīs* remember these pastimes and they tell Kṛṣṇa at Kurukṣetra, "If You come to Vṛndāvana, we will meet freely there once again. We cannot meet You here, because there are thousands and thousands of horses, elephants, and soldiers. Grandfather Bhīṣma, Droṇācārya, and many kings are here;

Vasudeva and Devakī are here; and especially, all Your queens are here."

Kṛṣṇa asks the *gopīs*, "What shall I do?" They reply, "We want You to come with us to Vṛndāvana. We are feeling some happiness in our meeting here, but not full happiness. We cannot talk with You here in front of the others, and there is so much opulence here. We remember Vṛndāvana, when we were *kiśora* and *kiśorī*. You were *kiśora* at that time, entering Your teenage years, and You were more beautiful than in Your childhood. There was no restriction at all at that time. We met freely in the shade of the *kadamba* trees, where the fragrance of the *belī*, *cāmelī*, and *jūhī* flowers mixed together. We talked with each other happily, and there was no need of a mediator."

This is the hidden meaning of the poem of the mundane poet, which Śrī Rūpa Gosvāmī transformed into his own poem. Rūpa Gosvāmī heard this *śloka* from Mahāprabhu, and he at once wrote another *śloka* that explained it: "I am that same Rādhā, and You are that same Kṛṣṇa. We used to be lover and beloved. There was no mediator then, and we met freely. So many cuckoos were singing, and peacocks were dancing there. Now we are meeting here, but there is not as much pleasure as when we met freely in Vṛndāvana. We want You to come with us to Vṛndāvana, to play with all the *gopas* and *gopīs*. You should make Your friends happy, and we will also become happy by dancing and singing with You there – freely."

Rādhikā is like that lover and Kṛṣṇa is like Her beloved. They were meeting in Vṛndāvana outside of marriage – dancing in *rāsa-līlā*, and meeting each other and pleasing each other. Sometimes Kṛṣṇa massaged Rādhikā's feet and sometimes He applied red lac to Her feet. Sometimes Rādhikā placed Her foot on Kṛṣṇa's head, and Her footprint became like a stamp on it because the red lac was fresh and moist. That stamp stated: "Now You are Mine."

Now Kṛṣṇa becomes ready. A chariot is there, and that chariot is the *gopīs'* hearts. They have made their hearts like a chariot, and now they tell Kṛṣṇa to sit there. They say, "You should sit on this chariot of our hearts and come to Vṛndāvana. We will never give You up. You will always remain there." All the *gopīs* become very happy as they take Kṛṣṇa to Vṛndāvana on the chariots of their hearts, and Caitanya Mahāprabhu is bringing this same mood to Purī.

To bring Kṛṣṇa to His chariot

During the Ratha-yātrā Festival, bringing Kṛṣṇa (in the form of Jagannātha) to His chariot is a very difficult and dangerous task. Many strong, tall, and beautiful *dayitās* wrap their chaddars around themselves as wrestlers would, and then, imitating the mood of the *gopīs*, they tie Jagannātha-deva with ropes. They "abuse" Him in so many ways, addressing Him, "Sālā, Sālā!" *Sālā* means "brother-in-law," but in India the word is also used to abuse others. The *dayitās* are telling Kṛṣṇa, "We don't know where You took birth, or who Your mother and father are. Perhaps You are fatherless and motherless." This is like an abuse.

It is not certain who Kṛṣṇa's father is – Vasudeva or Nanda Mahārāja. Neither is it certain who is actually His mother; in fact, no one is actually His mother. The *gopīs* hurl so much abuse at Kṛṣṇa as they pull Him on the chariot of their hearts, and during the festival attended by Mahāprabhu, Jagannātha-deva is pulled by hundreds and hundreds of big wrestlers who jostle Him back and forth to make Him move forward. He is well decorated with jewels and many garlands, and He wears very large peacock feathers on His head.

Then, there is a very big problem when Jagannātha-deva approaches His chariot to get up on it. Sometimes He slips from above. Sometimes He does not reach His throne on the chariot, even after two, three, four, or five hours, and sometimes even for the whole day. There are always many parties continually performing *kīrtana* and chanting, "Jaya Jagannātha! Jaya Jagannātha! Jaya Jagannātha, Subhadrā, and Baladeva!", "Hare Kṛṣṇa, Hare Kṛṣṇa, Kṛṣṇa Kṛṣṇa, Hare Hare," and "*sei ta parāṇa-nātha pāinu.*"

In this way there were many *kīrtanas*, and millions of people were pulling the chariots.

sei ta parāṇa-nātha pāinu
yāhā lāgi' madana-dahane jhuri' genu'

Śrī Caitanya-caritāmṛta (*Madhya-līlā* 13.113)

Now I have gained the Lord of My life, in whose absence I was being burned by Cupid and was withering away.

Śrī Caitanya Mahāprabhu becomes completely immersed in this mood, and Jagannātha is totally absorbed in Mahāprabhu's dancing and singing. His chariot makes the sound, "*haḍa haḍa, haḍa haḍa.*"

gaura yadi pāche cale, śyāma haya sthire
gaura āge cale, śyāma cale dhīre-dhīre

Śrī Caitanya-caritāmṛta (*Madhya-līlā* 13.118)

When Caitanya Mahāprabhu was dramatically enacting the song, He would sometimes fall behind in the procession. At such times, Lord Jagannātha would come to a standstill. When Caitanya Mahāprabhu went forward again, Lord Jagannātha's car would slowly start again.

These are very pleasing pastimes. Who made it so? Śrī Caitanya Mahāprabhu Himself. The Ratha-yātrā Festival was not like this at first. Before Caitanya Mahāprabhu's time, there was only one *ratha.* It carried Jagannātha, Subhadrā, and Baladeva and was pulled by their servants and elephants, but there was no *kīrtana* and no special moods. Mahāprabhu introduced these moods by His dancing and singing when He joined along with His associates such as Vakreśvara Paṇḍita and others in His *kīrtana* party. Hundreds of thousands of devotees also began to join from Bengal, Orissa, and other places, and all in all there were not less than four million devotees.

Sometimes Caitanya Mahāprabhu wanted to test Jagannātha.[1] He thought, "Will Kṛṣṇa go forward or not, if I do not come?" He therefore went behind Jagannātha's chariot, and then the chariot stopped. Thousands of elephants pulled, and millions of people were chanting, "Jaya Jagannātha-deva! Jaya Jagannātha-deva!" but Jagannātha became "deaf" at that time, and did not hear them. Instead, He stood in one place for hours and hours, until Mahāprabhu came forward and began to sing. Then Mahāprabhu said, "Everyone else can stop trying. I will do it alone." He put His head against the chariot and pushed it, and it began moving in a good way. The chariot stopped when Mahāprabhu was behind it, and moved when He proceeded in front, dancing and singing. In this way Jagannātha watched the dancing and singing of Caitanya Mahāprabhu, and it took two or three days to reach the Guṇḍicā Mandira.

Mahāprabhu sang:

sei ta parāṇa-nātha pāinu
yāhā lāgi' madana-dahane jhuri' genu'

[1] Mahāprabhu "tested" Jagannātha by going behind the chariot to see if Jagannātha would continue onward without Him. Here Mahāprabhu is in the mood of Śrīmatī Rādhikā, so She is testing Kṛṣṇa to see if He is willing to go and be in Vṛndāvana with the other *gopīs* if She is not there. Jagannātha's stopping the chariot until Mahāprabhu pushed it very easily with His own head shows the superiority of Rādhikā over the other *gopīs*.

We should feel some separation for Kṛṣṇa. We begin by feeling separation from *gurudeva* and devotees, and gradually develop that feeling for Rādhā and Kṛṣṇa. This is our objective, and it has been explained very beautifully and sweetly in *Śrī Caitanya-caritāmṛta.*

The *gopīs* are weeping and half-dead when they first reach Kṛṣṇa. Then, when they meet Him, their whole mood pours from their hearts and they begin to weep even more bitterly. In their entire lives, they have never wept as they do on this day. They have become almost senseless and are about to die, but now they finally have the chance to come and meet Kṛṣṇa.

gopyaś ca kṛṣṇam upalabhya cirād abhīṣṭaṁ
yat-prekṣaṇe dṛśiṣu pakṣma-kṛtaṁ śapanti
dṛgbhir hṛdīkṛtam alaṁ parirabhya sarvās
tad-bhāvam āpur api nitya-yujāṁ durāpam

Śrīmad-Bhāgavatam (10.82.39)

[Śukadeva Gosvāmī said:] While the young *gopīs* used to gaze at their beloved Kṛṣṇa, they condemned the creator of their eyelids (which would momentarily block their vision of Him). Now, seeing Kṛṣṇa again after such a long separation, by their eyes they took Him into their hearts, and there they embraced Him to their full satisfaction. In this way they became totally absorbed in ecstatic meditation on Him, although those who constantly practice mystic *yoga* find it difficult to achieve such absorption.

Now, when Kṛṣṇa sees the *gopīs*, He also begins to weep more loudly than before.

Śrī Vyāsadeva and Śrī Śukadeva Gosvāmī explain the way in which they meet. A person becomes like this if he dies and then by good fortune is restored back to life. The *gopīs* are all as if dead, but they come to life again when they see Kṛṣṇa. Here Śukadeva Gosvāmī says: "*kṛṣṇam upalabhya cirād abhīṣṭam*

– they are meeting Kṛṣṇa after a long time." Through their eyes they take Him into their hearts, and there they embrace Him very tightly. It is there that they become as one, and this is especially true for Śrīmatī Rādhikā.

Lakṣmī, who resides on Nārāyaṇa's chest as a curl of golden-white hair, always remembers Kṛṣṇa in her heart, and the *ṛṣis* and *munis* who have purified their hearts do so as well. Still, Kṛṣṇa's lotus feet never actually manifest in their hearts. They try and try, but no such event ever occurs. On the other hand, these *gopīs*, who are weeping and feeling profound separation, take Kṛṣṇa into their hearts and embrace Him there.

They cannot speak. They want to speak, but they cannot; so Kṛṣṇa Himself says, "O *gopīs*, My friends! You are the life of My life. I know that you were feeling terrible separation, thinking that I was very cruel-hearted. You gave up everything for Me – your husbands, homes, wealth, reputation, and everything else. You even gave up your Vedic religious principles of chastity for My sake, but I left you. Please forgive Me for this. You must be thinking that I am a very ungrateful creature, but I am not ungrateful to you. I always remember you."

After some time, when their weeping subsides, Kṛṣṇa tells them:

ahaṁ hi sarva-bhūtānām
ādir anto 'ntaraṁ bahiḥ
bhautikānāṁ yathā khaṁ vār
bhūr vāyur jyotir aṅganāḥ

Śrīmad-Bhāgavatam (10.82.45)

Dear ladies, I am the beginning and end of all created beings. I exist both within them and outside them, just as the elements ether, water, earth, air, and fire are the beginning and end of all material objects.

"My dear *gopīs*, I want to tell you a secret. Have you heard that I am the Supreme Personality of Godhead? Really I am. You should know that I am Viṣṇu. I am everywhere, in everyone's heart, and I am even in the hearts of animals, grass, and particles of water and air. I am in your hearts as well. I am everywhere, and therefore you are never separate from Me.

"An earthen vessel cannot be separated from the earth from which it is made. You are My parts, so you are like My body. You are made of Me, and I am everywhere. I am inside and outside, and up and down. I am in you, so why do you feel separated? You should go into trance. Meditate on Me, and then you will realize that I am everywhere. You should think that your body, your mind – your everything – is made of My love and affection. Think about Me and remember Me, and do not be upset. I am always with you."

When the *gopīs* hear this, their feelings of separation increase more and more, and their mood changes to one of anger. They tell Kṛṣṇa, not by words, but by mood, "O big cheater, You are black inside and outside. You always want to cheat us. We know that You are not Bhagavān; You are not the Supreme Personality of Godhead. We know You from the beginning. We know that You came from Mother Yaśodā's womb. You were always weeping for her milk, and always wandering here and there, telling lies. You put earth in Your mouth, and then You told Your mother, 'I have not eaten earth!' You were always stealing butter and milk in the houses of the elderly *gopīs* and telling them, 'I have never stolen anything.' Bhagavān cannot be like this. Bhagavān cannot steal the garments of young girls and make them naked. Can He do that? Why would He do that? The Supreme Personality of Godhead would do that?

"We know that You are very passionate. You used to call us by the melody of Your flute: 'Rādhā! Rādhā! Lalitā! Viśākhā!' You called all the *gopīs* by playing '*klīṁ*' on Your flute, and then we came and danced with You. Why would the Supreme Personality of Godhead come and dance with us? We also know that You kept Your sweet *vaṁśī* and Your head at Rādhikā's lotus feet, and You begged for Her forgiveness. Would the Supreme Personality of Godhead behave like this? Never. You are cheating. We know that You are not Bhagavān."

āhuś ca te nalina-nābha-padāravindaṁ
yogeśvarair hṛdi vicintyam agādha-bodhaiḥ
saṁsāra-kūpa-patitottaraṇāvalambaṁ
gehaṁ juṣām api manasy udiyāt sadā naḥ

Śrīmad-Bhāgavatam (10.82.48)

[The *gopīs* spoke thus:] Dear Lord, whose navel is just like a lotus flower, Your lotus feet are the only shelter for those who have fallen into the deep well of material existence. Your feet are worshiped and meditated upon by great mystic *yogīs* and highly learned philosophers. We wish that these lotus feet may also be awakened within our hearts, although we are only ordinary persons engaged in household affairs.

The *gopīs* speak the words of this *śloka* externally, but their real mood is hidden. Internally they are saying, "You Yourself are drowning in the well of separation from our love and affection. We know this, and only we can save You. You cannot save us. We are powerful, and we can give You life by our love and affection. When You tell us, 'You should meditate,' it is like a joke; this is a laughing matter for us. You tell us, 'You should meditate on Me' but don't You remember that we were playing with You from the beginning of our lives? Brahmā, Śaṅkara, Śukadeva Gosvāmī, and others can meditate on Your lotus feet – and nothing but Your lotus feet – in their hearts, but it may be that these feet will still not come into their hearts. On the other hand, we have kept those same feet directly on our breasts. Why? To please You and to give You satisfaction, because You become happy when we keep Your feet there.

"Brahmā was born from the lotus-navel of Padmanābha Viṣṇu, so he is like that lotus flower. His intelligence is quite dull, because he has come from the stem of an inert lotus. How can demigods like Brahmā know anything? They can pray to You and believe that You are the Supreme Lord. They can believe that You can create this entire universe in a second and then destroy it. They can glorify You like this, but we have known You from the beginning of Your birth, and we know You at this very moment. These demigods and *yogīs* may pray to You for salvation, or they can pray to You that Your lotus feet may appear in their hearts. They should do so, because they are as foolish as anything.

"We are not like them, for we are very clever and intelligent. We know who You really are: You are only a black cheater. You can cheat anyone, and You can even easily take our hearts. Brahmā says – and others say so, too – that if anyone in this world is drowning in the well of birth and death, and suffering greatly from old age and all kinds of troubles and problems, he can chant Your name and escape from that well. But we are not in any well like that.

"We are not like Brahmā, that we will meditate on You. We are hankering for Your satisfaction, not for our own. We know that You will die without us, and that is why we have mercifully come to You. Don't think that we have come to enjoy our own happiness; we want You to be happy. We have come here because we want You to remain alive. We are not weeping for ourselves. We are weeping for You, because You are helpless. No one can satisfy You except us, and especially our *sakhī* Rādhikā. She is Your life and soul.

"If You want to be happy forever, then please come onto the chariot of our hearts. We will take You where our minds and hearts reside, and we will satisfy You there – not here. We don't want to meet You here, because we cannot satisfy You here. Here You have thousands of wives, so many children, so many generals, a great army, and so many friends, *ṛṣis*, and *maharṣis*. But we remember Vṛndāvana."

The gopīs remember Vṛndāvana

Kṛṣṇa tells the *gopīs*, "You should remember Me and see Me in trance. I am always there with you. I cannot give you up." Now He personally tells them what He explained in *Bhagavad-gītā*, what He had requested Uddhava to tell them, and what He had asked Baladeva Prabhu to tell them: "You should always remember Me as Paramātmā, as the *yogīs* do."

Somewhat angry, the *gopīs* continue their reply with this *śloka*:

anyera hṛdaya mana, mora mana vṛndāvana,
'mane' 'vane' eka kari' jāni
tāhāṅ tomāra pada-dvaya, karāha yadi udaya,
tabe tomāra pūrṇa kṛpā māni

Śrī Caitanya-caritāmṛta (*Madhya-līlā* 13.137)

[Speaking in the mood of Śrīmatī Rādhārāṇī, Caitanya Mahāprabhu said:] For most people, the mind and heart are one, but I consider My mind and Vṛndāvana to be one, because My mind is never separated from Vṛndāvana. My mind is already Vṛndāvana, and since You like Vṛndāvana, will You please place Your lotus feet there? I would deem that Your full mercy.

Mahāprabhu is remembering Kurukṣetra and thinking, "I am Rādhikā, and all my friends, the *gopīs*, are in Kurukṣetra with

Nanda Bābā and Yaśodā." From there, the *gopīs* carry Kṛṣṇa on their *mano-ratha*, the chariot of their hearts. They always carry Him in that way.

In Rādhikā's mood, Mahāprabhu tells Jagannātha-deva, "Our hearts and minds are the same, and especially, our hearts are Vṛndāvana. Others' hearts are not." We try to make our hearts and minds one, and we try to make them both like Vṛndāvana. We want to be in Vṛndāvana, but our hearts are not there because our minds and hearts are made of material things. The *gopīs* are quite different, and they tell Kṛṣṇa, "Our hearts are Vṛndāvana. You have said, 'You should remember Me in trance,' but we are not *yogīs*. We are ordinary people, and we were with You from the beginning of our lives; from birth."

Yogīs can meditate in trance, and sometimes they can see the lotus feet of Paramātmā, but not of Kṛṣṇa. Paramātmā is not *aṁśī*, the origin. The origin of Paramātmā is Garbhodakaśāyī Viṣṇu, and His origin is Kāraṇodakaśāyī Viṣṇu. His origin is Mahā-Saṅkarṣaṇa, His origin is Mūla-Saṅkarṣaṇa, His origin is Baladeva Prabhu, and His origin is Kṛṣṇa.

The *gopīs* continue, "We always kept Your feet on our breasts and upon our laps. We played with those feet. And what to speak of Your feet – You used to massage our feet with Your hands. We played with You as friends from the beginning, from our childhood. You could not be separated from us at that time. You were always with us, playing here and there in the groves of Govardhana, and we used to dance with You at Vaṁśīvaṭa. We are not like *yogīs*. In their trance, they may think, 'I pray that the lotus feet of Paramātmā should appear in my heart,' but those feet never come; they may come, but very seldom; very rarely. As far as we are concerned, we want to forget You – to forget You. The root of all our problems is remembering You and Your pastimes – especially remembering You – so we want to forget You.

If You can forget us, why can we not forget You? But this is the problem: we cannot forget You. We want to give You up, but we cannot. We can give You up in the sense that You can leave Vṛndāvana, as You have done – no harm. But we cannot give up remembering Your pastimes."

Previously, when Kṛṣṇa resided in Vṛndāvana, the *gopīs* used to say, "Don't have any relation with that black person, that cheater. Stay far away from Him and don't utter His name. He is the biggest cheater. If anyone remembers Him, or hears His pastimes, or chants His name, that person will become bewildered, like a mad person. If you want to live with your husbands, sisters, brothers, fathers, and other family members, and if you want to remain very happy with them, then don't remember this boy, or have any relationship with Him. We have seen that those who remember Him become like birds. Birds have no homes to live in, and no fields where they can grow flowers or wheat or anything else. They have nothing. Similarly, if anyone hears, chants, and remembers Kṛṣṇa's glories, they become like street beggars."

Now, at Kurukṣetra, they tell Kṛṣṇa, "We can give You up, as You have given us up. In other words, You are living in a place very distant from us, and we can also live far away from You. But we cannot give up remembering You. You instruct us to remember You, but we wonder why You are giving us such instructions. We have always remembered You since our childhood, and yet You say, 'You should remember Me.' We want to forget You forever, and not remember anything about You. We laugh at Your words. You are telling very learned Ph.D. scholars, 'Oh, you should go to primary school and learn A-B-C-D.'"

The *gopīs* begin to weep loudly, and at that time Kṛṣṇa tells them:

mayi bhaktir hi bhūtānām
amṛtatvāya kalpate
diṣṭyā yad āsīn mat-sneho
bhavatīnāṁ mad-āpanaḥ

Śrīmad-Bhāgavatam (10.82.44)

Devotional service that the living beings render to Me revives their eternal life. O My dear damsels of Vraja, your affection for Me is your good fortune, for it is the only means by which you have obtained My favor.

Kṛṣṇa is "tricky"

As you know, only Vedic Hindus can enter Lord Jagannātha's temple in Purī; no Western or Eastern devotees are allowed in. The temple administrators are very strict. Those who are not actually Hindu by birth cannot enter, even if they were born in India. Indira Gandhi, the former Prime Minister of India, was born of a *brāhmaṇa* family, but she left her brahminical religion and married a Muslim. She was a powerful and wealthy person, but still the *pāṇḍās* of Purī never allowed her or her son Rajiv Gandhi to enter the temple. They told them, "You can come to Purī, but you cannot enter the temple." There are so many police guards everywhere, at all the four doors of the temple. Not even a bird from a Western or Eastern country can enter; even Western air cannot get in there.

The guards once checked me at the gate. They said, "Your eyes are not like the Hindus' eyes, and you have a rather fair complexion." I am not really so fair, but still they checked me. My *paṇḍā* was there and he told them, "O bogus people, he is my client." And he took me inside.

The guards are very strict, but Kṛṣṇa is very funny and "tricky." They may make these rules, but Kṛṣṇa does not. Kṛṣṇa – that is,

Jagannātha, Baladeva, Subhadrā, and Sudarśana *cakra* – come out on the road, and they do not move quickly at all. They are not in a hurry. Sometimes they stand at the same place for a day, two days, or even three days, abundantly giving Their *darśana* to all. Jagannātha comes with Subhadrā and Baladeva, by a "trick," as Patita-pāvana, the deliverer of the most fallen. He is Patita-pāvana and He belongs to everyone. He does not make any distinction between an Indian devotee, a *brāhmaṇa*, a *kṣatriya*, or a Western devotee, and that is why He plays a trick. He thinks, "I will remain in the temple for the entire year, but for these nine or ten days I will be Patita-pāvana. I will go on the street, and then everyone can receive My *darśana* and be liberated."

Kṛṣṇa is very merciful, and His devotees are more merciful still. You could not have called *parama-pūjyapāda* Śrīla Bhaktivedānta Swāmī Mahārāja to preach in the West, and you have not called me. Our *guru-varga* (disciplic succession) has sent me, and Śrīla Swāmī Mahārāja came because his *gurudeva* mercifully ordered him to preach throughout Western countries. Śrīla Swāmī Mahārāja also came through his own compassion and mercy. He came on a ship belonging to Scindia Navigation, and, in his human-like pastimes, he almost died of a heart attack on the way. He thought, "Will I die? What will happen?" But Kṛṣṇa's mercy was with him. Kṛṣṇa wanted him to come, so he came; and he preached with immediate effect.

Kṛṣṇa also played a trick with Arjuna during the Mahābhārata battle. He told him:

sarva-dharmān parityajya
mām ekaṁ śaraṇaṁ vraja
ahaṁ tvāṁ sarva-pāpebhyo
mokṣayiṣyāmi mā śucaḥ

Bhagavad-gītā (18.66)

Abandon all varieties of material religion and just surrender to Me. I shall deliver you from all sinful reactions. Do not fear.

This is the best instruction to Arjuna in *Bhagavad-gītā*, but Mahāprabhu still rejected it. When He met Rāmānanda Rāya at Godāvarī, He told him, "These are external things. Say something more." Why did He reject this statement? Arjuna felt great pain when Kṛṣṇa gave him this instruction. He thought, "How 'funny' Kṛṣṇa is. He is telling me to be *śaraṇāgata*, surrendered. But He has been my bosom friend for so many years. He has even slept with me on the same bed."

Sometimes Arjuna used to place his feet on Kṛṣṇa's chest when they both lay down together, and Rukmiṇī and Satyabhāmā fanned them with *cāmaras*. At the same time, Kṛṣṇa's feet lay upon Arjuna's chest, and Draupadī and Subhadrā fanned at the other end of the bed. Kṛṣṇa was very happy to lie on the same bed as Arjuna, and also to take *prasāda* remnants with him.

Arjuna therefore thought, "Friends are far superior to *śaraṇāgatas*, and yet He is telling me to surrender. Haven't I surrendered? Why is this tricky person telling me this?" Arjuna was not satisfied, just as the *gopīs* were not satisfied, so Kṛṣṇa told him, "Don't worry. I am not giving this instruction for you. I am giving it to others through you."

Now, at Kurukṣetra, the *gopīs* also complain to Kṛṣṇa.

The gopīs are more "tricky" than Kṛṣṇa

Mādhurya (sweetness) and *aiśvarya* (opulence) can never exist together. There is immense opulence in Dvārakā. There Kṛṣṇa cannot say, "I am the son of Nanda Bābā and Yaśodā;" He is bound to say, "I am a *kṣatriya*, and I am the son of Vasudeva and Devakī." He cannot wear a peacock feather and He cannot play His flute. In Dvārakā He is surrounded by many thousands of *rāja-maharṣis*, queens, horses, and so on, so the *gopīs* request Him, "We want You to come to Vṛndāvana."

The *gopīs* seem to be very selfish. Why did they request Kṛṣṇa, "You should give up all the thousands of devotees in Mathurā and Dvārakā, and come to Vṛndāvana"? I am giving a very simple answer. All the Vrajavāsīs, and especially the *gopīs*, know Kṛṣṇa's heart. In Vraja, Kṛṣṇa is not like the Supreme Personality of Godhead. The Vrajavāsīs cannot think of Him in that way, even in dreams. They can only think that He is the son of Nanda Bābā and Yaśodā, the beloved of all the *gopīs*, and the friend of Śrīdāmā and Subala Sakhā.

All the Vrajavāsīs want Kṛṣṇa to be happy in every way, and they also know that He is always very shy. Therefore Nanda Bābā, Yaśodā, and all the *gopīs* and friends have to be very tricky with Him. They know that He will be shy to eat butter when Yaśodā offers it to Him, so she plays many tricks to induce Him to eat. Once she told Him, "Oh Kṛṣṇa, You are so weak, but still You don't want to take any bread and butter and other *prasāda*. How will Your *śikhā* become thick like Baladeva's? You see? Baladeva is very strong, and his *śikhā* is very thick and long. But You are so weak. We cannot compare You with Him." Kṛṣṇa replied, "Mother, I want to defeat Baladeva. Please give Me bread and butter." This is how Yaśodā and others trick Kṛṣṇa to make Him eat.

Yaśodā had previously thought, "Kṛṣṇa is going to become weak, because He doesn't want to eat anything." She therefore called Śrīmatī Rādhikā from Yāvaṭa by a trick, by regularly sending Rādhikā's in-laws in Yāvaṭa vast wealth in the form of many jewels, ornaments, and garments. Why did Yaśodā call Śrīmatī Rādhikā? She considered, "Kṛṣṇa doesn't eat very much, because He becomes shy and cannot admit His hunger. But He will become very strong if He eats what Rādhikā cooks.[2] If I send these gifts to Her in-laws, they will surely send Her to cook." As a result of Yaśodā's trick, Śrīmatī Rādhikā comes and prepares *manohara-laḍḍu*, *amṛta-keli*, and so many other dishes.

There is no one in Mathurā or Dvārakā who can give Kṛṣṇa delicious food like Yaśodā-maiyā, and Kṛṣṇa can never address other elderly relatives, "Mother! Mother!" Yaśodā-maiyā cooked a great variety of preparations through Rohiṇī, Rādhikā, Lalitā, and Viśākhā. She would call them all to her kitchen, and they would quickly prepare many delicious dishes. Then, if Kṛṣṇa was not eating, Mother Yaśodā would come over and tell Him, "Oh, I have made a vow to Nārāyaṇa that You will eat this. If You don't eat, Nārāyaṇa will be disappointed with You, and that will be very inauspicious for You." She would request Him again, and then He would take His meal. Neither Devakī nor anyone else in Dvārakā knew all these tricks. Kṛṣṇa may have felt hungry there, but He was too shy to ask for anything to eat.

All the *gopīs* know how Yaśodā-maiyā used to trick Kṛṣṇa into taking those preparations, so they think, "He will always be neglected in Dvārakā. He cannot say, 'Mother, give me bread and butter.'" The *gopīs* remember Kṛṣṇa's shy nature. Sometimes He would want something from them, and He would play on His flute to call them all. But then, when they came to Him, He would tell them, "You should return home now." In His heart He thought, "I want to dance with the *gopīs*," and the *gopīs* thought, "We want to satisfy Kṛṣṇa." But because Kṛṣṇa was tricky, He would tell them, "You should all return home." The *gopīs* are also tricky, however, and they knew how to satisfy Him. They would tell Him, "Oh, You are our *guru*, and we are all Your disciples.

[2] Rādhikā had received a boon from Durvāsā Ṛṣi that whoever will eat her cooking will be very powerful, long-lived, and able to defeat all enemies.

Disciples should worship their *guru*, and after that they can worship their husbands or even Nārāyaṇa. If someone is not worshiping his *guru*, he cannot satisfy the Supreme Personality of Godhead, Nārāyaṇa. Therefore, You will be an offender of the Vedas if You do not accept this worship."

ye yathā māṁ prapadyante
tāṁs tathaiva bhajāmy aham
mama vartmānuvartante
manuṣyāḥ pārtha sarvaśaḥ

Bhagavad-gītā (4.11)

I reward everyone according to their surrender unto Me. Everyone follows My path in all respects, O son of Pṛthā.

The *gopīs* would thus defeat Kṛṣṇa by clever words so that He could engage in the *rāsa* dance with them. Kṛṣṇa desired to touch their bodies, but they would tell Him, "Oh, You cannot touch us. You should remain far away." They were always able to satisfy Kṛṣṇa by continually increasing His greed.

Kṛṣṇa can only be satisfied by these tricks, which are not known in Dvārakā or Mathurā, or in any other place in the world. Thus, the *gopīs* are selfless. There is no blemish in their hearts, and they have no desire other than to please Kṛṣṇa. They serve Kṛṣṇa totally with all their senses, with their minds, and with their souls, and He is always indebted to them.

Now Kṛṣṇa assures them, "Those who are engaged in the process of attaining My love and affection – beginning with *śraddhā*, *niṣṭhā*, *ruci*, and so on – are all fortunate. But even more fortunate are those who already have *prema*, *sneha*, *praṇaya*, and beyond that. You have these qualities, and they attract Me to come to Vṛndāvana very soon. Don't worry. I must come to you, because you have that *sneha*, *māna*, *praṇaya*, *rāga*, *anurāga*, *bhāva*, and *mahābhāva*. Your qualities charm and attract Me, and they will also compel Me to return with you to Vṛndāvana."

The *gopīs* tell Kṛṣṇa, "You should come on our chariot." Their chariot is their minds and hearts, which are the same as Vṛndāvana. "You should come to Vṛndāvana, and then we will think that You are entering our trance. This is 'trance' – that You should come to Vṛndāvana."

Śrīmatī Rādhikā is reminding Kṛṣṇa – that is, Śrī Caitanya Mahāprabhu is reminding Kṛṣṇa as Jagannātha: "We are those unmarried teenage girls. We used to meet in Vṛndāvana with love and affection under the *kadamba* trees."

The meaning of prema

Try to understand the meaning of *prema*. In English, there is no exact word for *prema*; there are only words such as "love" and "affection." In Sanskrit, however, each word has a special meaning. All the stages of *prema*, such as *āsakti*, *bhāva*, *prema*, *sneha*, *māna*, *praṇaya*, *rāga*, *anurāga*, and so on, have specific meanings.

What kind of love does Rādhikā have for Kṛṣṇa? Her love increases more and more, even if there are circumstances that should make it diminish. This is the meaning of *prema*.

Kṛṣṇa left Rādhikā, the *gopīs*, and the other Vrajavāsīs and went to Mathurā, where He took *upanayana-saṁskāra* (brahminical initiation), became a *kṣatriya*, and declared, "I am the son of Devakī and Vasudeva. I am a Yādava." After that He went to Dvārakā, where He married eight very beautiful princesses, and then 16,100 more, and then He begot so many children. This should be enough to break anyone's love and affection, but here you can see the nature of the love and affection that Rādhikā has toward Kṛṣṇa. You can see the nature of the love of Mother Yaśodā and Nanda Bābā, the love of Kṛṣṇa's friends, and the love of all the Vrajavāsīs, including the cows and other animals. They did not give up their love and affection, although they were actually dying of separation.

Here in this world, if a husband divorces his wife and marries again, the ex-wife will go to court and file a suit, and he will be bound to sign an agreement to pay her maintenance. She will forcibly take that money, and she may also marry another man. She cannot tolerate the thought that he has given her up, but she will herself remarry two, three, four, or five times. Thus, here in this world, love and affection stops when there is an obstacle. But there, Rādhikā's love for Kṛṣṇa and His love for Her did not stop, even though He had so many wives and children, and even though He changed His name. If you want to realize that transcendental love, then try to be like the Vrajavāsīs. Love in this world is not actually love, it is merely sense gratification and lust. We simply kick away and divorce our spouse upon the slightest provocation.

Rādhikā knows that Kṛṣṇa has many wives and many children. Now He is like a king, and He has changed into a Yādava – but still Her love increases. This is called transcendental *prema*. Read these topics, and then go deeply into what you have read. Try to forget yourself, where you are, and what you are doing. Forget everything else, go deep, become totally absorbed in meditation upon these topics, and then you will be able to realize something of this love. It is because you cannot do this that you become weak in your spiritual life. So try to hear all these topics in elevated association.

The *gopīs* have forgotten everything other than Kṛṣṇa. They are feeling great separation for Him, and consequently they have become more than *yogīs*. Through the window of their eyes, they take Him in their hearts, and there they embrace Him so intensely that they lose external consciousness.

I have already described how Kṛṣṇa tried to pacify Rādhārāṇī and the *gopīs* by saying, "O *gopīs*, why are you feeling so much separation? I am not away from you for even a moment. There is no separation between clay and a clay statue or *mūrti*, because the clay is everywhere in the *mūrti*. In just the same way, this physical body is made of five elements – earth, water, fire, air, and ether – so one's body cannot be separated from them. As one cannot differentiate between the body and these elements, similarly, You are made of My mood."

Kṛṣṇa is *sac-cid-ānanda-vigraha*, the complete form of eternity, knowledge, and bliss, and Śrīmatī Rādhikā's constitutional position is *mahābhāva*. Because She is the embodiment of *mahābhāva*, She is called *hlādinī-śakti*. She and Kṛṣṇa are always combined as the essence of *hlādinī* and *saṁvit*. *Saṁvit* and *hlādinī* are the same as *cit* and *ānanda*, and that is why Kṛṣṇa told Her, "I am always with You. I am *sac-cid-ānanda*, so how can I be separated from You? I am always in Your body and Your heart."

I have already explained that the *gopīs* became very sulky and angry when they heard Kṛṣṇa's words, and they began to chastise Him, not by words but by mood: "Why are You telling us these things? We don't accept this theory of Yours. We are not *yogīs*. *Yogīs* worship You and meditate upon You, but they cannot purify their hearts, or even their minds, in thousands and thousands of births. We, on the other hand, want to forget You forever. We were so happy in the homes of our fathers and mothers in Vraja, but You have upset and destroyed everything. We gave You our whole love, one hundred percent, or one hundred and ten percent. We left our fathers, mothers, husbands, children, and everything else. Our relation was very deep when You were in Vraja, and it is the same even today. So we want to forget You forever.

"If You can forget us and all of Your Vṛndāvana – Gokula, Govardhana, and all Your cows, Your calves, Your peacocks, Your deer, and even Your own mother from whom You took birth – then why can we not forget You? This is the problem: we cannot forget You. From the beginning, whenever we were engaged in any household task, we sang, 'Govinda Dāmodara Mādhaveti, Govinda Dāmodara Mādhaveti.' Even when we were cleaning our houses, sweeping, or churning yogurt, tears came from our melting hearts as we remembered Your pastimes and sang, 'Govinda Dāmodara Mādhaveti,' 'Rādhā-ramaṇa hari bol,' and 'Govinda jaya jaya.'"

In Vraja, the *gopīs* had always been weeping and lamenting, "O Kṛṣṇa, where are You? Where are You?" Words cannot explain how they were behaving internally and externally. Now at Kurukṣetra, they say, "We want to drive You away from our hearts, but You come inside automatically. You tell us, 'Give up *saṁsāra-kūpa*, the deep, dark well of family life,' and, 'Meditate upon Me as the *yogīs* do.' But where is our family life? We have no *saṁsāra-kūpa*."

The *gopīs* had forgotten their homes, duties, husbands, fathers, and mothers, and they had even forgotten to eat anything or to see anything. They appeared to look at things just as we do, but they did not see anything. They only contemplated, "Where is my beloved Kṛṣṇa?" Only this. It is we who are in the well of family attachments. Still, although the *gopīs* were not attached to their families as we are, Kṛṣṇa advised them, "Come out of that well and meditate upon Me."

The *gopīs* now reply:

āhuś ca te nalina-nābha padāravindaṁ
yogeśvarair hṛdi vicintyam agādha-bodhaiḥ
saṁsāra-kūpa-patitottaraṇāvalambaṁ
gehaṁ juṣām api manasy udiyāt sadā naḥ

This *śloka* has two meanings. The meaning for general persons and for those who are not very advanced devotees is that the *gopīs* are requesting Kṛṣṇa, "You are the Supreme Personality of Godhead. O Kamala-nayana, You whose eyes are like reddish lotus petals, You are very, very merciful. We have now fallen into the well of family life, and we want to remember Your lotus feet as the *yogīs* do. We want to meditate, so please be merciful to us."

This meaning is external. Sometimes, when juniors try to instruct superiors, the superiors may reply, "I am very foolish, and you are so intelligent. I want to obey your instructions. Please instruct me how to act properly." In reality, the senior is angry at heart, and he is actually speaking sarcastically. His real meaning is, "I'm so many years older than you, and I am so much more intelligent than you. You're instructing me, even though you're so junior to me?" Similarly, the *gopīs* are in an angry mood, and their deeper meaning is, "O Kṛṣṇa, don't try to cheat us. We have known You from the beginning, and we know that You are a great cheater. You have been deceiving us for a long time, but now we have become somewhat clever. You can cheat Lakṣmī-devī, You can cheat Your wives in Dvārakā, and You can cheat everyone else; but as for us, we will not enter Your trap."

The heart cannot consider

anyera hṛdaya mana, mora mana vṛndāvana,
'mane' 'vane' eka kari' jāni
tāhāṅ tomāra pada-dvaya, karāha yadi udaya,
tabe tomāra pūrṇa kṛpā māni

Śrī Caitanya-caritāmṛta (*Madhya-līlā* 13.137)

[Caitanya Mahāprabhu, in the mood of Śrīmatī Rādhārāṇī, said:] Most people's minds are one with their heart, but I consider My mind to be one with Vṛndāvana, because My mind is never separated from Vṛndāvana. My mind is already Vṛndāvana, and since You like Vṛndāvana, will You please place Your lotus feet there? I would deem that Your full mercy.

The *gopīs* tell Kṛṣṇa, "We know, and You should also know, that there is so much difference between the heart and the mind of a worldly person. The heart is always full of love, whereas the mind calculates, 'What is better for me? What is good? What is bad? This is better; this is not so good.' The mind can do all this, but the heart can never consider whether a person is beautiful or not, or whether or not he is very intelligent or qualified."

Rukmiṇī had heard abundant glorification of Kṛṣṇa's mercy, beauty, and all His other qualities. Because of this, she did not accept the proposal of her friends, parents, and others to give her in marriage to Śiśupāla. They told her, "Kṛṣṇa is not a king; He is only the son of a landlord – and not even that. He is not as qualified as Śiśupāla. Śiśupāla is the King of kings. He is a very beautiful young emperor and he has a golden complexion, whereas this other person is black and unqualified. When Kṛṣṇa was younger, He always used to tell lies and steal from others' houses. You should give up that black fellow and marry Śiśupāla.

Try to obey your father, mother, and brother." Rukmiṇī replied, "Once I have given my heart to someone, I can never, ever reclaim it." Without the consent of her father, mother, and brother, she then sent a *brāhmaṇa* to Kṛṣṇa with a message: "I don't want to marry this jackal. I have given my heart to a lion. How can a jackal come and take me away in the presence of the lion? Everything depends on the lion. I have given myself solely to You, for You are that lion, and I will not go with that jackal. If that lion is not qualified and powerful enough to save me from the jackal, then I will take poison and die."

Before Umā was married to Śaṅkara, Nārada came and revealed Śaṅkara's glories to her. After that, Śaṅkara told someone, "Go and test that girl," so his messenger went to Umā and told her, "Śiva is an unintelligent, bogus man. He is always naked, he wears garlands of skulls and ornaments of snakes, he smears dust from the ashes of corpses all over his body, he wears *rudrākṣa* beads, he always carries a trident, and he sits on a bull like a mad person. Why have you chosen him to be your husband?"

Her father also told her, "O my dear darling daughter, change your mood. I will marry you to an exalted personality like Viṣṇu, or someone else who is very beautiful. Why have you chosen Śaṅkara?"

Umā told her father, "It may be that Śaṅkara wanders naked, plays with ghosts and witches, ornaments himself with serpents, and sometimes swallows poison. But even if this is true, I will marry him and no one else. I have chosen him for all time, even though he does nothing. I don't want to give him up. I will marry him." So many other suitors came, and even Śaṅkara came in disguise to test her, but she did not change her mind.

For worldly persons, for all of you, the mind and heart are different, but these examples confirm that the hearts of elevated personalities never consider whether someone is beautiful or not, or what he has done or not done. The decision to love is "forever." *Anyera hṛdaya mana.* For most people the mind always gives problems. Sometimes it accepts something, and at other times it rejects the same thing; this is called *saṅkalpa-vikalpa.* But "*mora mana vṛndāvana* – My mind is Vṛndāvana." The mind and heart of the *gopīs* are one.

The *gopīs* continue, "You have told us, 'Meditate upon Me,' but from where does meditation come? It comes from the mind. Understanding comes from the mind. But *mora mana vṛndāvana.* Let others meditate. You are instructing us, 'You should meditate, and My lotus feet will come in Your meditation.' Therefore, we will be satisfied if Your lotus feet walk to Vṛndāvana; otherwise, we can never be satisfied."

Try to make your heart and mind Vṛndāvana, under the guidance of the *gopīs.* It does not matter whether you are male or female. Śrī Caitanya Mahāprabhu has said that all *jīvas* – both male and female – are a transformation of *taṭastha-śakti,* Kṛṣṇa's marginal potency. We are *prakṛti* (the potency – feminine gender), not *puruṣa* (the possessor of the potency – male gender). Try to realize this. If you think very deeply, these meanings will come in your heart, and your heart will be greatly developed. There is no need to do anything else.

If Nārada Ṛṣi comes before the *gopīs,* however, they will offer him *praṇāma,* and it may be that they will take the dust of his lotus feet. Nārada Ṛṣi will then think, "I should not upset these *gopīs.* Kṛṣṇa is my worshipable Lord, and these *gopīs* are His worshipable deities, so I should not disturb their mood." Then, after the *gopīs* leave, he will take their foot-dust and rub it all over his body.

Even Nārada is not qualified to be the foot-dust of the *gopīs.* He prays for this perfection, but he cannot achieve it. Such perfection is very rarely achieved for anyone, even Brahmā. Śrī

Prabodhānanda Sarasvatī has written, "I always remember the dust of Rādhikā's lotus feet. Even Brahmā, Nārada, Śuka, Śaṅkara, Bhīṣma, and other devotees like them meditate on Kṛṣṇa's lotus feet so that His lotus feet may enter their hearts. On the other hand, when Kṛṣṇa calls to the maidservants of the *gopīs*, 'Come on! Come on!' they reply, 'We will not come. We know that You are a cheater.' Instead of their following Kṛṣṇa, He follows them."

yat-kiṅkarīṣu bahuśaḥ khalu kāku-vāṇī
nityaṁ parasya puruṣasya śikhaṇḍa-mauleḥ
tasyāḥ kadā rasa-nidher vṛṣabhānu-jāyās
tat-keli-kuñja-bhavanāṅgana-mārjanī syām

Rādhā-rasa-sudhā-nidhi (8)

O daughter of Vṛṣabhānu Mahārāja, O ocean of *rasa*! The Supreme Bhagavān, the source of all incarnations who wears a peacock feather in His hair, falls at the feet of Your maidservants and propitiates them with many humble and griefstricken words to be allowed entrance into Your *kuñja* where You engage in playful, amorous pastimes. I would consider my life a success if I could become one stick in the broom used by Your maidservants to clean Your delightful grove.

Kṛṣṇa knocks at the door of the *gopīs' kuñja*, and Śrī Rūpa Mañjarī and Śrī Rati Mañjarī stand there in a somewhat angry mood. They tell Kṛṣṇa, "Go back at once, You cheater. Go back! You cannot come and meet Śrīmatī Rādhikā. She is angry with You now, and She has told us, 'Be aware that this cheater may come in a disguise. Although disguised as a *gopī* or someone else, He will be that same Kṛṣṇa, the friend of Subala. I don't want to see anything black. Not even a black bumblebee should enter My *kuñja*. You should even remove your black *kajjala* before you come here.'"

Kṛṣṇa then offers His head at the lotus feet of Rūpa Mañjarī and her *sakhīs*, and begs them, "Please allow me to go there, just for a moment." They reply, "Never!" How can we imagine the greatness of Rādhikā's position? Śrī Prabodhānanda Sarasvatī concludes, "I want to be a broom – and not even a whole broom, just one straw of a broom – that is used for sweeping Rādhikā's *kuñja*." How glorious She is!

More mysterious meaning

After citing the *Śrīmad-Bhāgavatam* verse beginning *ahuś ca te nalina-nābha pādāravindaṁ*, Śrīla Kṛṣṇadāsa Kavirāja Gosvāmī quotes the *gopīs* (*Śrī Caitanya-caritāmṛta* (*Madhya-līlā* 1.82)):

tomāra caraṇa mora vraja-pura-ghare
udaya karaye yadi, tabe vāñchā pūre

[The *gopīs* thought:] If Your lotus feet again come to our home in Vṛndāvana, our desires will be fulfilled.

The *gopīs* tell Kṛṣṇa, "O Prāṇanātha! Vraja is our life and soul. We are telling You the truth: Vraja is our home. If You do not come and meet us in Vṛndāvana, we will not be able to remain alive. We will die at once. Fish become restless the moment they are taken out of water, and the next moment they are dead. We are in an even worse condition than that. Fish may have a moment to live, but we will not be able to live even that long."

Śrīla Kṛṣṇadāsa Kavirāja Gosvāmī then quotes Rūpa Gosvāmī's deep explanation of that same *Śrīmad-Bhāgavatam* verse:

yā te līlā-rasa-parimalodgāri-vanyāparītā
dhanyā kṣauṇī vilasati vṛtā māthurī mādhurībhiḥ
tatrāsmābhiś caṭula-paśupī-bhāva-mugdhāntarābhiḥ
saṁvītas tvaṁ kalaya vadanollāsi-veṇur vihāram

Śrī Caitanya-caritāmṛta (*Madhya-līlā* 1.84)

[The *gopīs* said:] Dear Kṛṣṇa, the fragrance of the mellows of Your pastimes is spread throughout the forests of the glorious land of Vṛndāvana, which is surrounded by the sweetness of the district of Mathurā. In the congenial atmosphere of that wonderful land, You may enjoy Your pastimes, with Your flute dancing on Your lips, and surrounded by us, the *gopīs*, whose hearts are always enchanted by unpredictable ecstatic emotions.

The *gopīs* are sad and feel separation when they see Kṛṣṇa in the royal dress of a prince of Dvārakā. Similarly, in their mood, Śrī Caitanya Mahāprabhu felt separation when He sometimes saw Baladeva and Subhadrā along with Jagannātha. Usually He saw only Jagannātha – as Vrajendra-nandana – but when He saw the three deities there, He immediately remembered the *gopīs'* pastimes at Kurukṣetra.

ei-mata mahāprabhu dekhi' jagannāthe
subhadrā-sahita dekhe, vaṁśī nāhi hāte

Śrī Caitanya-caritāmṛta (*Madhya-līlā* 1.85)

In this way, when Śrī Caitanya Mahāprabhu saw Jagannātha, He saw that the Lord was with His sister Subhadrā and was not holding a flute in His hand.

tri-bhaṅga-sundara vraje vrajendra-nandana
kāhāṅ pāba, ei vāñchā bāḍe anukṣaṇa

Śrī Caitanya-caritāmṛta (*Madhya-līlā* 1.86)

Absorbed in the ecstasy of the *gopīs,* Śrī Caitanya Mahāprabhu wished to see Lord Jagannātha in His original form as Kṛṣṇa, the son of Nanda Mahārāja, standing in Vṛndāvana and appearing very beautiful, His body curved in three places. His desire to see that form was always increasing.

The *gopīs* are actually telling Kṛṣṇa, not by their words but by their mood, "Kṛṣṇa, You cheater, You should know that our mind and heart are the same. Our heart is Vṛndāvana. *Tāhāṅ tomāra pada-dvaya karāha yadi udaya tabe tomāra pūrṇa kṛpā māni* (*Śrī Caitanya-caritāmṛta* (*Madhya-līlā* 13.137)): If you come to Vṛndāvana with us, You can meet us there with Your flute. Don't forget Your flute and peacock feather. And You should change Your dress. You will have to be the son of Nanda and Yaśodā. Be Gopī-kānta and Rādhā-kānta, and then You can enter Vṛndāvana. Otherwise don't come. We will not allow You to enter."

The gopīs' accusations

The moods of Lord Jagannātha's Chariot Festival are very, very mysterious. It seems from an external point of view that Kṛṣṇa simply instructed Śrīmatī Rādhikā and the *gopīs,* "You should chant, remember, and meditate on Me. Then you can realize My lotus feet in your heart, and by that meditation you will come out of the well of worldly attachment." It also seems that the *gopīs* appreciated this instruction and simply replied, "You have given us good instruction. From now on we will meditate on You and remember You, and then we will be able to come out of the well of worldly life and give up all kinds of attachments."

However, as I have already explained, the actual mood of the *gopīs* is quite different. Externally their words seem to have a particular meaning, but Śrīla Kṛṣṇadāsa Kavirāja has revealed their inner purport. He heard this meaning from Śrīla Raghunātha dāsa Gosvāmī, who had understood everything from Śrīla Svarūpa Dāmodara and Śrīla Rūpa Gosvāmī, and had noted it all down. Kṛṣṇadāsa Kavirāja Gosvāmī's explanation therefore follows the words of Svarūpa Dāmodara, and especially those of Rūpa Gosvāmī.

Although the *gopīs* are not satisfied at all by Kṛṣṇa's instruction, their anger is also a tie of love and affection – a crooked tie. The *gopīs* are actually saying, "You've just told us to meditate, and You previously sent Uddhava and Baladeva Prabhu, who also delivered Your message: 'Meditate on Me.' You must be joking! Where is our attachment to this world? Where is our family attachment? We've never had any. 'Who am I?' 'Where am I?' We have forgotten these things. We have completely forgotten everything, including all of our senses. Where has our attachment gone? To You! We are always remembering You when You were in Vṛndāvana. We remember how we sometimes played together at Rādhā-kuṇḍa and Śyāma-kuṇḍa, and sometimes under Bhāṇḍīravaṭa, or in Nandagaon, and how we sometimes used to meet together at Ṭera-kadamba as well. How glorious it was!"

In those days, Śrīmatī Rādhikā used to go from Yāvaṭa to Yaśodā-bhavana with all Her *sakhīs*, headed by Lalitā and Viśākhā, to cook for Kṛṣṇa. Meanwhile, Kṛṣṇa was milking His cows midway, at Ṭera-kadamba. As Rādhikā walked with Her *sakhīs*, Lalitā said, "We should change our direction and go by that other path. This cheater has blocked our way. He's only milking His cows here because He knows that we will come this way. Better that we change paths." Rādhikā replied, "Oh, why fear? We will not change our course. Let us see what happens." As She continued walking, Kṛṣṇa began milking a cow in such a way that Her whole face was splashed with milk, and everyone began to laugh. The *gopīs* always remembered all these pastimes. There were so many pastimes that Kṛṣṇa Himself would not be able to describe them all, even if He were to have thousands and thousands of mouths.

Now the *gopīs* say, "We only remember those pastimes! We already feel so much separation from You, and now You are telling us, 'You should meditate on My lotus feet.' We're not happy with this instruction. We're not like the four Kumāras. Grandfather Bhīṣma and Nārada can meditate on You, but we want to forget You altogether! We don't want to think about You, because You are very cruel and ungrateful."

Kṛṣṇa wanted to hear all this. He held His head down in shame and enjoyed thinking, "All the *gopīs* are blaming Me."

The *gopīs* continue, "Previously, when we were in Vṛndāvana, You told us, 'I am coming back tomorrow. If not, then surely I will come the day after tomorrow.' But You never came! You never returned! You told Uddhava, 'Tell them that I am coming right away. I am coming after only four days.' After that Baladeva came to Vraja, and He said on Your behalf, 'Oh, don't be worried. Kṛṣṇa is coming very soon.' But You never came."

nahe gopī yogeśvara, pada-kamala tomāra,
dhyāna kari' pāibe santoṣa
tomāra vākya-paripāṭī, tāra madhye kuṭināṭī,
śuni' gopīra āro bāḍhe roṣa

Śrī Caitanya-caritāmṛta (*Madhya-līlā* 13.141)

[In the mood of Śrīmatī Rādhikā, Śrī Caitanya Mahāprabhu said:] The *gopīs* are not like the mystic *yogīs*. They will never be satisfied simply by meditating on Your lotus feet and imitating the so-called *yogīs*. Teaching the *gopīs* about meditation is another kind of duplicity. When they are instructed to undergo mystic *yoga* practice, they are not at all satisfied. On the contrary, they become more and more angry with You.

"We don't like Your mode of expression. *Tāra madhye kuṭīnāṭī.* There are so many things that are not good about it. *Kuṭīnāṭī. Ku-ṭī-nā-ṭī.* You are telling so many *kuṭī*, things that are not good, and *nāṭī*, things that are not favorable. You say, 'You should try to meditate on Me and remember Me.' But You know that since our childhood we were never able to forget You for even a moment."

This is pure love, without desire for any gain. The *gopīs* continue, "You speak to us as if we are unintelligent, and that makes us angry."

deha-smṛti nāhi yāra, saṁsāra-kūpa kāhāṅ tāra,
tāhā haite nā cāhe uddhāra
viraha-samudra-jale, kāma-timiṅgile gile,
gopī-gaṇe neha' tāra pāra

Śrī Caitanya-caritāmṛta (*Madhya-līlā* 13.142)

[Śrī Caitanya Mahāprabhu continued:] The *gopīs* have fallen in the great ocean of separation, and they are being devoured by the *timiṅgila* fish, which represent the ambition to serve You. The *gopīs* are to be delivered from the mouths of these *timiṅgila* fish, for they are pure devotees. Since they have no material conception of life, why should they aspire for liberation? The *gopīs* do not want that liberation desired by *yogīs* and *jñānīs*, for they are already liberated from the ocean of material existence.

The *gopīs* continue, "You speak about a well of material life (*saṁsāra-kūpa*), but where are we? We are in an endless, bottomless ocean of separation. And what is going on in that ocean? There are whales, and there are also fish called *timiṅgila* fish, which are so huge that they can even swallow those whales."

vṛndāvana, govardhana, yamunā-pulina, vana,
sei kuñje rāsādika līlā
sei vrajera vraja-jana, mātā, pitā, bandhu-gaṇa,
baḍa citra, kemane pāsarilā

Śrī Caitanya-caritāmṛta (*Madhya-līlā* 13.143)

It is amazing that You have forgotten the land of Vṛndāvana. And how is it that You have forgotten Your father, mother, and friends? How have You forgotten Govardhana Hill, the bank of the Yamunā, and the forest where You enjoyed the *rāsa* dance?

vidagdha, mṛdu, sad-guṇa, suśīla, snigdha, karuṇa,
tumi, tomāra nāhi doṣābhāsa
tabe ye tomāra mana, nāhi smare vraja-jana,
se āmāra durdaiva-vilāsa

Śrī Caitanya-caritāmṛta (*Madhya-līlā* 13.144)

Kṛṣṇa, You are certainly a refined gentleman with all good qualities. You are well-behaved, soft-hearted, and merciful. I know that there is not even a tinge of fault to be found in You, yet Your mind does not even remember the inhabitants of Vṛndāvana. This is only My misfortune, and nothing else.

The *gopīs*, and especially Śrīmatī Rādhārāṇī, continue to voice their apparent complaints, "Do you remember Vṛndāvana for even a moment? Do you remember Govardhana? In Vṛndāvana, we *gopīs* were all assembled in *rāsa-līlā*. At that time, when we were tired and perspiring, You used to wipe our bodies with Your *pītāmbara* (upper yellow garment)."

Śrīmatī Rādhārāṇī tells Kṛṣṇa, "You would ask me, 'Are you tired?' and then I would keep My hand on Your shoulder." She used to stand in a "crooked" way and look at Kṛṣṇa with "crooked" sidelong glances. She leaned on Him with all Her weight, as if He were a pillar, and She looked at Him from the corners of Her eyes. When She leaned on Him in this way, He used to think, "Today, due to this pose of Rādhikā, My life is successful!"

"Do You remember this?" the *gopīs* continue. "Do You remember that we defeated You in dice games? And Rādhikā used to defeat You in debate. Do You remember that we used to meet with You in each and every grove of Girirāja-Govardhana? Do you remember that we served You in so many ways at Rādhā-kuṇḍa and Yamunā-pulina (the bank of the Yamunā)?"

Do you know the meaning of Yamunā-pulina? In his song *Yaśomatī-nandana*, Śrīla Bhaktivinoda Ṭhākura has written *yamunā-taṭa-cara gopī-vasana-hara, rasa-rasika-kṛpamaya*. Kṛṣṇa would always come to the bank of the Yamunā, because He was very eager to meet the *gopīs*, and He would think, "If I go there, surely the *gopīs* will come to take water from the Yamunā with their very big pots. Why will they come? Because they have promised, and I have also promised." That place on the bank of the Yamunā is called *panaghaṭa*, the place where Kṛṣṇa could easily meet with the *gopīs*.[3] Because all the *gopīs* came there, Kṛṣṇa also came. Everyone else thought that the *gopīs* were going to fetch water, but when they dipped their pots into the Yamunā, they never noticed whether the pots were filled with water or not. They only knew that their pots were filled with love and affection for Kṛṣṇa. They used to tell Him, "We cannot put these pots on our heads. Can You help us?" It was only for that kind of exchange that Kṛṣṇa would go there. He would lift their pots and proudly think, "I am helping them."

[3] *Panaghaṭa* has two meanings. *Pan* is an abbreviation for *pāni*, water. This *ghāṭa* was originally called *pāni-ghāṭa*, and later on it became known as *panaghaṭa*. *Pan* also means promise, and it is called *panaghaṭa* because Kṛṣṇa and the *gopīs* promised to meet each other there.

Śrīmatī Rādhikā now asks Kṛṣṇa, "Do You remember all these pastimes on the banks of the Yamunā? Do You remember what kind of pastimes we used to perform at Mānasi-gaṅgā? We always remember this! Do You remember Saṅketa-kuñja?" Saṅketa is halfway between Varṣāṇā and Nandagaon. "Do You remember Saṅketa? When I was on the swing with You, You pushed the swing so high that our garments flew here and there. I was afraid, and I embraced You and called out, 'Save me! Save me!' And You were easily satisfied by that. Do you remember?" As Kṛṣṇa heard all this, He was ashamed and held His head down.

By mood, the *gopīs* tell Kṛṣṇa, "It is very tragic. How could You have forgotten all Your *sakhās* like Dāmā, Śrīdāmā, Subala, Madhumaṅgala, Kokila, Kiṅkiṇi, Vasanta, and all others? How could You forget Your father and mother and all Your friends? It is quite astonishing that You could forget them all. You are very ungrateful, and Your heart is harder than a thunderbolt!"

While Śrīmatī Rādhikā and the *gopīs* were thinking this, they were in a particular type of very angry mood, but now their mood suddenly changes. Their various moods are called *bhāva-udaya*, *bhāva-sandhi*, *bhāva-śābalya*, and *bhāva-śānti.*[4] Anyone who has not studied *Bhakti-rasāmṛta-sindhu*, and what to speak of *Ujjvala-nīlamaṇi*, will not be able to taste these moods in thousands of lifetimes. One cannot know all these truths if he has not taken the *saṅga* of Śrī Caitanya Mahāprabhu's associates. He is bound to remain in the chain of birth and death, sorrow and suffering. I have come to give this message of Caitanya Mahāprabhu, Śrīla Rūpa Gosvāmī, and our entire *guru-paramparā*.

The *gopīs* continue to accuse Kṛṣṇa in various angry and mixed moods. Suppose there is an ugly person who is very black

[4] Please refer to the Glossary for explanations of these terms.

and unqualified, and his teeth stick out of his mouth. Someone may say to him, "How handsome you are! Your teeth are more beautiful than if they were made of gold, and the whole world is charmed by your smile! You are so qualified!" What is this? It is sarcasm or *parihāsa*, a joke. Similarly, the *gopīs'* words appear to mean, "You are very *rasika* – very, very *rasika*! You are also very sweet, and not at all cruel. You have all good qualities. Your tongue never speaks any lies; it can never do so. And Your hands are always controlled; they cannot do anything wrong." But what do the *gopīs* really mean? They are actually taunting Kṛṣṇa, and telling Him, "Your tongue is always controlled. How is it controlled? It has kissed millions of *gopīs*, and now perhaps it is satisfied. Your hands and feet are always going towards the *gopīs*, searching for them. You have touched the *gopīs*, and that is why Your tongue has become pure, You Yourself have become pure, and everything about You has become pure."

The *gopīs* continue with words that cover their actual mood, and they tell Kṛṣṇa, "You are very sweet and You have such a good character! You are very soft and mild, and You are also very merciful. All of these qualities are in You. But we are very unfortunate. Even though You are so qualified, sweet, soft, and merciful, You have left us, and this is our misfortune. We must have done something wrong, either in our past lives or in this life, and that is why You have left us."

Nanda Bābā has also spoken in this way. When he returned home after leaving Kṛṣṇa and Balarāma in Mathurā, he was weeping bitterly. "There was only one true father," he said, "and that was Daśaratha Mahārāja. He could not survive in separation from Rāma. He called out, '*Hā* Rāma! *Hā* Rā...!' and left his body. I cannot do this! My heart is very cruel, and it is harder than a thunderbolt. Why could I not die? I wanted to die, but I could not. Kṛṣṇa is very qualified in every way. He is sweet and mild, and He has all good qualities. He must have decided, 'My mother and father, Yaśodā and Nanda Bābā, are not qualified, and neither are all the other Vrajavāsīs. They cannot give Me the love and affection I want,' and that is why He left us and went where He would receive more love and affection." Speaking thus, Nanda Bābā fainted.

In the same way, the *gopīs* are telling Kṛṣṇa, "We are most unfortunate because You don't remember any of us. We know that we have no familial relationship with You, because we are not married to You. That is why a man can give up a lady, even if there is some love between them. On the other hand, if they are married, he will give his whole mood of love to her. We were not married, and that is why You could give us up so easily.

"But how could You give up Your mother and father, and especially Your mother? Your body is made of Your mother, so how could You forget her? Even if You can give her up, Your body will always tell You, 'I am the son of Mother Yaśodā' because You are made from her blood and everything else. It is very strange that You have left everyone.

"Do You know that because of You the birds are no longer singing? The cuckoo birds have stopped singing and now they only weep. The peacocks do not dance now; they are very sad. The calves do not drink their mothers' milk, and the cows are about to die. They no longer eat grass or anything else, and Mother Yaśodā never cooks."

Hearing this, Kṛṣṇa began to weep very loudly, and He was about to fall unconscious. There is a poem describing this, and it is very heart-rending.

tuhuṅ se rahila madhupura
vrajakula ākula, dukūla kalarava,
kānu kānu kari jhura (1)

yaśomati-nanda, andha sama baiṭhaī,
sāhase uṭhai nā pāra
sakhā-gaṇa dhenu, veṇu-rava nā śuniye,
vichurala nagara bājāra (2)

kusuma tyajiyā ali, kṣiti-tale luṭata,
taru-gaṇa malina samāna
mayurī nā nācata, kapotī nā bolata,
kokilā nā karatahi gāna (3)

virahiṇī rāī, viraha-jvare jare jare,
caudike viraha hutāśa
sahaje yamunā jala, āgi samāna bhela,
kahatahi govinda dāsa (4)

In this *kīrtana*, the Vaiṣṇava poet Govinda dāsa is singing in Rādhārāṇī's mood, "O Kṛṣṇacandra, now You live very far away in Madhupurī – in Mathurā. But what is the condition of Vṛndāvana? All the Vrajavāsīs are feeling extreme pain and distress in separation from You. They call out, 'Kānu, Kānu!' But there is no answer, and only an echo is heard." Kānu is a nickname of Kṛṣṇa. "Kānu, Kānu! O Kānu, where are You? Even the birds are calling, 'Where are You? O Kānu, where are You?' Everyone is weeping. O Yaśomatī-nandana, Yaśodā-maiyā and Nanda Bābā are crying bitterly. It is as if they have become blind; they cannot see anymore, and they only sit and cry. They have no strength, and they are hardly more than skeletons. They are about to die because they no longer cook anything. For whom will they cook? They do not even have enough strength in their bodies to stand up.

"And what is the condition of all Your cows and friends? They cannot hear You calling them with Your flute, so the marketplaces and the roads are all deserted. No one is there; no one at all. Not only that; previously, the bumblebees were very busy collecting honey, but now they are so upset that they have left the flowers, and even they are crying and rolling on the ground in the pain of separation.

"All the trees look drab and distressed. The peacocks no longer dance, and the pigeons no longer sing. The cuckoos are silent; they no longer call, 'Kuhu, kuhu.' All are feeling great pain in separation from You.

"*Virahiṇī rāī, viraha-jvare jare jare.* Śrīmatī Rādhārāṇī is burning and burning in the fever of separation. Everywhere, in all directions, everyone is sinking in the ocean of separation from You. Even the Yamunā does not flow anymore. This is the condition of Vṛndāvana! The water that is seen in the Yamunā is actually the tears that have fallen from the eyes of all the *gopīs. Tuhuṅ se rahila madhupura.* Why are you staying so far away in Mathurā, when everyone in Vṛndāvana is on the verge of death?"

There is another song by Caṇḍīdāsa, also written in the mood of Śrīmatī Rādhikā. The words of this song are heart-breaking, and it is unparalleled in any language of the world. You cannot hear these topics anywhere else:

sukhera lāgiyā, ei ghara bāṅdhinu, āgune puḍiyā gela
amiyā sāgare, sināna karite, sakali garala bhela (1)

sakhi! ki mora kapāle lekhi
śītala baliyā, cāṅda sevinu, bhānura kiraṇa dekhi (2)

ucala baliyā, acale caḍinu, paḍinu agādha-jale
lachamī cāhite, dāridrya beḍhala, māṇika hārānu hele (3)

nagara basālāma, sāgara bāṅdhilāma, māṇika pābāra āśe
sāgara śukāla, māṇika lukāla, abhāgī-karama-doṣe (4)

piyāsa lāgiyā, jalada sevinu, bajara paḍiyā gela
kahe caṇḍidāsa, śyāmera pirīti, marame rahala śela (5)

"I built a house in order to be very happy there, but that house was suddenly burned in a fire. I wanted to take bath in the ocean of nectar in order to make My heart very cool, but instead it was crushed and burned. I wanted to go to the ocean to bathe and to make My heart soft, but I saw that all the water was gone. There was no water left at all. Then I looked toward the moon so that some of its cooling rays would come upon Me, but it turned out that those were not the cool rays of the moon; instead, the blazing hot rays of the sun came and scorched Me.

"I thought I was in a very high place where there was no water, but instead I see that I've fallen into an endless ocean of water. I wanted wealth, but I became penniless. A very valuable jewel came into My hand, and then suddenly it was gone.

"I built a city near the ocean, so that I could get a valuable jewel from that ocean. Then I made a dam, and I moved the ocean from one side of the dam to the other. However, when the ocean was finally drained, the jewel was nowhere to be seen. It was hidden somewhere, due to My misfortune. I looked towards the clouds to quench My thirst, but instead of rain, a thunderbolt came on My head.

"I loved Kṛṣṇa in order to be happy, and I gave Him My body, mind, heart, soul, and everything, but He left Me. The fire of separation enveloped Me and I was burned. Kṛṣṇa's love is endless like the ocean, and I wanted to take bath in that ocean; but what happened? The water dried up and in its place was a great conflagration. Everything burned in separation. What should I do?" Kṛṣṇa would not be able to survive if He were to hear all these heart-breaking words.

These feelings of Śrīmatī Rādhikā are the mood at Ratha-yātrā, and this is Caitanya Mahāprabhu's mood at that time. He experiences all the sentiments of Rādhikā, and no one can explain Her moods without the help of His *bhāvas*. His moods have been passed on through Śrī Svarūpa Dāmodara to Śrīla Rūpa Gosvāmī and Śrīla Raghunātha dāsa Gosvāmī, who have expressed them in their own writings. Try to realize all these truths.

Who went to Kurukṣetra?

This subject matter is very extraordinary. It is not less in depth and significance than *Rāmānanda-saṁvāda* (Mahāprabhu's conversation with Rāya Rāmānanda as found in *Śrī Caitanya-caritāmṛta*); in fact, it is even deeper. Kṛṣṇa has promised, "I will never, never give up Vṛndāvana; I will always be there." Rādhikā has also promised, "Kṛṣṇa may go, but I cannot leave Vṛndāvana." Then who went to Kurukṣetra? There are innumerable manifestations of Kṛṣṇa, and so many of Rādhikā as well, and this is very wondrous. Kṛṣṇa can be thousands and thousands of Kṛṣṇas at the same time. Yet, there can be millions more manifestations of Rādhikā than there are of Kṛṣṇa (as She displayed during *rāsa-līlā*). She is very expert.

Rādhikā and Kṛṣṇa eternally play with Their *gopī* associates in Vṛndāvana, where Rādhikā is called Vṛṣabhānu-nandinī Rādhikā. She never leaves Vṛndāvana, and She hardly ever laments. So who was lamenting in Nandagaon when Uddhava went there? Rādhikā is always with Kṛṣṇa, so how did this separation come about?

Who went to Mathurā and Dvārakā? Kṛṣṇa's manifestations went. Similarly, who was weeping bitterly with all Her *sakhīs* in Nandagaon? It was Viyoginī-Rādhā. She was the one whom Uddhava met, who was feeling intense separation, and who recited *Bhramara-gīta*, which is one of the jewels of *Śrīmad-Bhāgavatam.*

Who went to Kurukṣetra? It was Vṛṣabhānu-nandinī Rādhikā, but in Her manifestation as Saṁyoginī-Rādhikā. She is the same Rādhā, but as a manifestation. She went to Kurukṣetra, and there She attracted Kṛṣṇa to return to Vṛndāvana.

Even Kṛṣṇa cannot know

Tad viddhi praṇipātena paripraśnena sevayā (*Bhagavad-gītā* (4.34)). Everything is reconciled when you approach a realized spiritual master, inquire from him submissively, and serve him. This process will enable you to realize everything automatically. Your mental speculation alone will not suffice. You may be a learned person, but your learning will not help you; instead, it will betray you.

I have been explaining the moods of the *gopīs* at Kurukṣetra, and Kṛṣṇa's statements to them. You can also study this subject matter yourselves, but only a rare person can go into it very deeply. It is stated in *Rādhā-rasa-sudhā-nidhi* (4):

yo brahma-rudra-śuka-nārada-bhīṣma-mukhyair
ālakṣito na sahasā puruṣasya tasya
sadyo vaśī-karaṇa-cūrṇam ananta-śaktiṁ
taṁ rādhikā-caraṇa-renum anusmarāmi

Brahmā, Rudra (Śaṅkara), Bhīṣma, Nārada, and others like them are very advanced *jñānī-bhaktas*. They are all *ātmārāma* and *āptakāma* (fully satisfied internally and externally, respectively), yet even they can only rarely have *darśana* of Kṛṣṇa, and what to speak of having *darśana* of Rādhikā. The demigods came during Kṛṣṇa's *rāsa-līlā*, but they only saw Kṛṣṇa dancing and singing; they did not see the *gopīs*. On the other hand, their wives saw Kṛṣṇa with the *gopīs* and fainted. The author of this prayer, Śrī Prabodhānanda Sarasvatī, says that if Kṛṣṇa knows that someone has on his head a minute dust-particle from Śrīmatī Rādhikā's lotus feet, He will wholly and solely give Himself to that devotee.

Devotees like Brahmā, Rudra, Śuka, Nārada, Bhīṣma, and the four Kumāras – Sanaka, Sanandana, Sanātana, and Sanatkumāra – are all very elevated, and they are prominent among the twelve *mahājanas*. Yet they cannot control Kṛṣṇa. On the other hand, *cūrṇam ananta-śaktim*: the dust of Rādhikā's lotus feet is so powerful that it can control Kṛṣṇa very easily. Kṛṣṇa may be happy and satisfied with the love and affection He receives from these other devotees, but in comparison to the *gopīs*, they cannot control Him in the slightest degree.

If one wants to control Kṛṣṇa, he must search for Śrīmatī Rādhikā's foot-dust – even a single particle of that foot-dust – and try to collect it. In other words, he must accept the guidance of Śrī Rūpa Gosvāmī, Śrī Sanātana Gosvāmī, and Śrī Raghunātha dāsa Gosvāmī, who are Rūpa Mañjarī, Lavaṅga Mañjarī, and Rati Mañjarī in Rādhā and Kṛṣṇa's pastimes. Kṛṣṇa will be controlled at once if He knows, "These are the maidservants of Rādhikā," but no one can control Him otherwise. Try to become a particle of dust of Rādhikā's lotus feet.

When Brahmā went to Vṛndāvana and saw Kṛṣṇa's pastimes, he personally prayed:

naumīḍya te 'bhra-vapuṣe taḍid-ambarāya
guñjāvataṁsa-paripiccha-lasan-mukhāya
vanya-sraje kavala-vetra-viṣāṇa-veṇu-
lakṣma-śriye mṛdu-pade paśupāṅgajāya

Śrīmad-Bhāgavatam (10.14.1)

My dear Lord, You are the only worshipable Lord, the Supreme Personality of Godhead, and therefore I offer my humble obeisances and prayers just to please You. O son of the King of the cowherds, Your transcendental body is dark blue like a fresh cloud, Your garment is brilliant like lightning, and the beauty of Your face is enhanced by Your *guñjā* earrings and the peacock feather on Your head. Wearing garlands of various forest flowers and leaves, and equipped with a herding stick, a buffalo horn, and a flute, You stand beautifully with a morsel of food in Your hand.

Śrī Śukadeva Gosvāmī is also an extremely elevated devotee, and in Rādhā-Kṛṣṇa's pastimes he is a special parrot belonging to Śrīmatī Rādhikā. He always sits on Her hand, and She caresses him, feeds him pomegranate seeds, and teaches him to chant, "Kṛṣṇa, Kṛṣṇa," "Govinda," "Vrajanātha," and "Prāṇanātha." Śuka always remains in the association of Rādhā and Kṛṣṇa, and he may even be there to awaken Them during Their pre-dawn pastimes of *niśānta-līlā*. That Śuka became Śukadeva Gosvāmī, and yet Śrī Prabodhānanda Sarasvatī says that even Śukadeva Gosvāmī cannot control Kṛṣṇa. He can serve Kṛṣṇa, but only the members of Śrīmatī Rādhikā's party can fully control Him.

Śrī Nārada Ṛṣi went to Gokula in Vṛndāvana and thought, "Kṛṣṇa has just descended to this world, so Rādhikā must also be present somewhere." He went to Rāval and discovered Her there. After that, he performed severe austerities at Nārada-kuṇḍa and became Nāradī-gopī, but even Nāradī-gopī cannot control Kṛṣṇa.

Kṛṣṇa Himself became a bumblebee and went to Nandagaon. There He took *darśana* of Rādhikā when She was in *mahābhāva-divyonmāda*, but He was still unable to understand the depth of Her mood. Three desires then manifested in His heart. He became intensely eager to relish the exalted state of Her *praṇaya* (loving mood), Her appreciation of His sweetness, and the rapture in Her heart at that time. Kṛṣṇa could never go deep enough to fully understand Rādhikā's moods of *mādana-* and *modana-mahābhāva*. Her highest mood of love, *sva-saṁvedya-daśā*,[5] never comes in Him, for He is the *viṣaya*, the object of love. It only comes in the *āśraya*, the reservoir of love. That is why Kṛṣṇa – in the form of Śrī Caitanya Mahāprabhu – went to the bank of

[5] This refers to the most elevated state of *kṛṣṇa-prema*, which is experienced only by Śrīmatī Rādhikā and which is comprehensible only to that person who directly experiences it.

Godāvarī and was admitted into the school of Rādhikā's personal secretary, Viśākhā, who was there in the form of Rāmānanda Rāya. Mahāprabhu heard many instructions there. He learned about Rādhā's moods, and then He went to Purī and realized those moods and relished them.

Śrīmatī Rādhikā's *sakhīs*, who are Her party members, can understand and realize Her moods to some extent – more so than Kṛṣṇa. Kṛṣṇa is *akhila-rasāmṛta-sindhu*, the object of love, but He is not the container of love. The container or reservoir is the *āśraya-bhakta*.

It has been explained in the above verse from *Rādhā-rasa-sudhā-nidhi* (*yo brahma-rudra-śuka-nārada*) that neither the four Kumāras, nor Nārada as a *gopī*, nor even Śukadeva Gosvāmī as Rādhikā's parrot can fully control Kṛṣṇa. Even Uddhava could not realize the moods of the *gopīs*, although he went to Vṛndāvana and had their association there. That is why he prayed:

vande nanda-vraja-strīṇāṁ
pāda-reṇum abhīkṣṇaśaḥ
yāsāṁ hari-kathodgītaṁ
punāti bhuvana-trayam

Śrīmad-Bhāgavatam (10.47.63)

I repeatedly offer my respects to the dust from the feet of the women of Nanda Mahārāja's cowherd village. When these *gopīs* loudly chant the glories of Śrī Kṛṣṇa, the vibration purifies the three worlds.

Be very humble, and hollow like a flute, and then go to *Śrīmad-Bhāgavatam* and *Śrī Caitanya-caritāmṛta* and pray. Then you will very easily realize something. You will realize that the *gopīs'* moods are the most elevated.

caitanya-gosāñira līlā – ananta, apāra
'sahasra-vadana' yāra nāhi pāya pāra

Śrī Caitanya-caritāmṛta (*Madhya-līlā* 14.256)

The pastimes of Caitanya Mahāprabhu are unlimited and endless. Even Sahasra-vadana, Lord Śeṣa, cannot reach the limits of His pastimes.

Kṛṣṇadāsa Kavirāja Gosvāmī has explained here that Caitanya Mahāprabhu's pastimes are unlimited, endless, and unfathomable, and even Ananta-śeṣa Baladeva Prabhu cannot explain them all with His unlimited mouths, even in unlimited time. How deep these pastimes are! Even Kṛṣṇa cannot know their depth, although He is an ocean of *rasa*. Yet, one can easily know something of their depth by taking shelter at the feet of Śrīla Rūpa Gosvāmī and Śrīla Raghunātha dāsa Gosvāmī.

śrī-rūpa-raghunātha-pade yāra āśa
caitanya-caritāmṛta kahe kṛṣṇadāsa

Śrī Caitanya-caritāmṛta (*Madhya-līlā* 14.257)

Praying at the lotus feet of Śrī Rūpa and Śrī Raghunātha, always desiring their mercy, I, Kṛṣṇadāsa, narrate *Śrī Caitanya-caritāmṛta*, following in their footsteps.

Kṛṣṇa's reply

You will be successful in your spiritual life if you develop positive understanding and moods. It will not be enough just to think, "Not this, not this, not this." Absorption in the positive must be accompanied by negation of the negative; otherwise you cannot advance. This is true; but still, absorption in negation will not help you very much. If one wants to advance in *bhakti*, he should try to understand these topics.

The *gopīs* tell Kṛṣṇa, "We cannot live without You. We cannot maintain our lives without You. It will be better if You come to Vṛndāvana, and that Vṛndāvana is non-different from our hearts. If You don't come, You will see Vṛndāvana become completely lifeless. Everyone and everything there will die."

śuniyā rādhikā-vāṇī, vraja-prema mane āni,
bhāve vyakulita deha-mana
vraja-lokera prema śuni', āpanāke 'ṛṇī' māni',
kare kṛṣṇa tāṅre āśvāsana

Śrī Caitanya-caritāmṛta (*Madhya-līlā* 13.148)

After Lord Kṛṣṇa heard Śrīmatī Rādhārāṇī's statements, His love for the inhabitants of Vṛndāvana increased, and His body and mind became very perturbed. After hearing of the Vrajavāsīs' love for Him, He immediately considered Himself to be always indebted to them. He began to pacify Śrīmatī Rādhārāṇī as follows:

prāṇa-priye, śuna, mora e-satya-vacana
tomā-sabāra smaraṇe, jhuroṅ muñi rātri-dine,
mora duḥkha nā jāne kona jana

Śrī Caitanya-caritāmṛta (*Madhya-līlā* 13.149)

My dearest Śrīmatī Rādhārāṇī, please hear Me. I am speaking the truth. I cry day and night simply upon remembering all you inhabitants of Vṛndāvana. No one knows how unhappy this makes Me.

When Kṛṣṇa heard the *gopīs'* desperate words, and especially when He heard from Rādhikā, He became restless and could not control Himself. He thought, "I cannot repay the Vrajavāsīs," and He began to pacify all the *gopīs*, especially Rādhikā. He began to weep as He replied: "*Prāṇa-priye, śuna, mora e-satya-vacana* – My most beloved, I am telling you the truth with My pure heart. *Tomā-sabāra smaraṇe, jhuroṅ muñi rātri-dine, mora duḥkha nā jāne kona jana* – My body is there in Dvārakā, but My heart is with You in Vṛndāvana. I am always restless, day and night, and I feel unbearable separation. There is no one in Mathurā to whom I can reveal My heart. I sent Uddhava to Vraja to be admitted into the school of *gopīs* so that he could learn something about the meaning of *prema*. I thought that if he were to become expert, then when he would return I could describe to him the extent of My separation and he would realize My heart. But I see that I cannot share My heart even with Uddhava, nor with Rukmiṇī or Satyabhāmā. I thus lament continually."

vraja-vāsī yata jana, mātā, pitā, sakhā-gaṇa,
sabe haya mora prāṇa-sama
tāṅra madhye gopī-gaṇa, sākṣāt mora jīvana,
tumi mora jīvanera jīvana

Śrī Caitanya-caritāmṛta (*Madhya-līlā* 13.150)

[Śrī Kṛṣṇa continued:] All the inhabitants of Vṛndāvana-dhāma – My mother, father, cowherd boyfriends, and everyone else – are the same as My life. Amongst all the inhabitants of Vṛndāvana, the *gopīs* are directly My life and soul. And You, Śrīmatī Rādhārāṇī, are the chief among the *gopīs*; so You are the very life of My life.

tomā-sabāra prema-rase, āmāke karila vaśe,
āmi tomāra adhīna kevala
tomā-sabā chāḍāñā, āmā dūra-deśe lañā,
rākhiyāche durdaiva prabala

Śrī Caitanya-caritāmṛta (*Madhya-līlā* 13.151)

My dear Śrīmatī Rādhārāṇī, I am always subservient to the love and affection that you all have for Me. I am under your control only. The creator is very cruel, for he has separated Me from You and made Me reside in distant places.

We are all helpless when it comes to stopping death. Actually, we are helpless in every way. Similarly, Kṛṣṇa is saying, "Now I am helpless, and You are also helpless. The creator has forcibly taken Me very far away from You and from My birthplace in Gokula. This is My misfortune."

priyā priya-saṅga-hīnā, priya priyā-saṅga vinā,
nāhi jīye, e satya pramāṇa
mora daśā śone yabe, tāṅra ei daśā habe,
ei bhaye duṅhe rākhe prāṇa

Śrī Caitanya-caritāmṛta (*Madhya-līlā* 13.152)

When a woman is separated from her lover, or a man from his beloved, neither of them can live. It is a fact that they only live for each other, for if one dies and the other hears of it, he or she will die also.

Kṛṣṇa continues, "It is true that a woman cannot maintain her life without her beloved. And that beloved can also not maintain his life without his dear one. *Mora daśā śone yabe, tāṅra ei daśā habe, ei bhaye duṅhe rākhe praṇa.* Why does a woman not die when she is separated from her lover? She remains alive only by thinking, 'If I die, my beloved will weep bitterly, and he may also die. So I should not die. I don't want to give him any suffering.' Her lover also thinks, 'If I die, she will suffer grievously, and then she may die of separation.' For this reason, neither want to die."

sei satī premavatī, premavān sei pati,
viyoge ye vāñche priya-hite
nā gaṇe āpana-duḥkha, vāñche priyajana-sukha,
sei dui mile acirāte

Śrī Caitanya-caritāmṛta (*Madhya-līlā* 13.153)

> Such a loving chaste wife and loving husband desire all welfare for each other in separation and do not care for personal happiness. Such a loving couple only desire each other's well-being, and they certainly meet again without delay.

This is an important point. The only chaste lady is one who has such overwhelming love and affection for her beloved that she always thinks of his welfare, even in separation. Rāma told Sītā, "I must abandon you for the rest of my life." He sent her to the forest, and she wept bitterly in deep separation. She might have died in separation, but she was pregnant at that time, and her two sons Lava and Kuśa took birth soon afterwards. Although she suffered on account of her husband, she would say, "I don't consider whether he has done right or wrong. I only want him to be happy, wherever he is."

At that time, Rāma was in his grand royal palace, but he gave up his pillows, his bed, and every other convenience. He became austere and renounced there, and he slept on a mat on the ground, just as Sītā-devī did. Instead of eating delicious food, he only took some fruits to maintain his life. He always felt the piercing pain of her separation, and it was because he could not survive without her that he performed fire sacrifices and made statues of her.

The chaste lady who has love and affection for her beloved husband always thinks of his welfare, and even if he does something wrong, she doesn't mind. And the man also thinks in the same way about his wife or his beloved. *Nā gaṇe āpana-duḥkha, vāñche priyajana-sukha, sei dui mile acirāte.* Neither of them cares for their own happiness or suffering. They always think of the happiness and suffering of their loved one.

You should try to understand the instruction given here, and follow it. If you want to enter that transcendental realm, then you should begin these dealings with your *gurudeva*. If *gurudeva* is a very high-class devotee, if he has love and affection for you, and if he is taking you more and more toward Kṛṣṇa consciousness, then place your whole concentration on him. Don't think about your own suffering and happiness. Rather you should think, "How can I please my *gurudeva*?" If this mood is not present in a disciple, he is bound to give up the line of devotion. It is stated in *Śrīmad-Bhāgavatam*:

śravaṇaṁ kīrtanaṁ viṣṇoḥ
smaraṇaṁ pāda-sevanam
arcanaṁ vandanaṁ dāsyaṁ
sakhyam ātma-nivedanam

iti puṁsārpitā viṣṇau
bhaktiś cen nava-lakṣaṇā
kriyeta bhagavaty addhā
tan manye 'dhītam uttamam

Śrīmad-Bhāgavatam (7.5.23–4)

[Prahlāda Mahārāja said:] The following nine processes are accepted as pure devotional service: hearing and chanting about the transcendental holy name, form, qualities, paraphernalia, and pastimes of Lord Viṣṇu; remembering them; serving the lotus feet of the Lord; offering Him respectful worship with sixteen types of paraphernalia; offering Him prayers; becoming His servant; considering Him one's best friend; and surrendering everything unto Him (in other words, serving Him with the body, mind, and words.) One who has dedicated his life to the service of Kṛṣṇa through these nine methods should be understood to be the most learned person, for he has acquired complete knowledge.

In this verse, Śrī Prahlāda Mahārāja uses the word *puṁsārpitā* to advise us that one must first offer himself unto the lotus feet of Kṛṣṇa. To understand this instruction, we must know that there are two Kṛṣṇas. The first is *guru-bhagavān*, and the second is *kṛṣṇa-bhagavān*. The first is *āśraya* (the abode of service), and the second is *viṣaya* (the object of service). The qualifications of a *mahā-bhāgavata guru* are explained in *Śrīmad-Bhāgavatam* and the Upaniṣads. You should have strong faith in such a *guru* and try to please him. He is very powerful, and by his own power he will transfer your sentiments to Rādhā-Kṛṣṇa and Mahāprabhu.

Prahlāda Mahārāja is instructing us that one should not only surrender, he should always engage his heart, mind, and all his senses to please that *sad-guru*. The disciple can please him if he is always chanting and remembering, glorifying *bhakti*, Kṛṣṇa, and Mahāprabhu, and preaching and practicing *bhakti-yoga*. Then he will be happy.

Śrīla Narottama dāsa Ṭhākura has explained how Rūpa Gosvāmī pleased his *guru*:

śrī-caitanya-mano-'bhīṣṭaṁ
sthāpitaṁ yena bhū-tale
svayaṁ rūpaḥ kadā mahyaṁ
dadāti sva-padāntikam

Śrīla Rūpa Gosvāmī Prabhupāda has established within the material world the mission to fulfill the desire of Lord Caitanya. When will he give me shelter at his lotus feet?

There are so many devotees who have pleased their *gurus*, but the author of this *śloka* has given the example of Rūpa Gosvāmī. Rūpa Gosvāmī knew what Caitanya Mahāprabhu wanted, and why He descended to this world. This is why he wrote books such as *Bhakti-rasāmṛta-sindhu* and *Ujjvala-nīlamaṇi*. He established the message of Caitanya Mahāprabhu and the method to please Him.

Kṛṣṇa continues: "*Nā gaṇe āpana-duḥkha, vāñche priyajana-sukha, sei dui mile acirāte* – if the lover and beloved engage in this way, they will be able to meet again." Here, Kṛṣṇa is consoling the *gopīs*, assuring them that they will certainly meet again.

rākhite tomāra jīvana, sevi āmi nārāyaṇa,
tāṅra śaktye āsi niti-niti
tomā-sane krīḍā kari', niti yāi yadu-purī,
tāhā tumi mānaha mora sphūrti

Śrī Caitanya-caritāmṛta (*Madhya-līlā* 13.154)

[Kṛṣṇa said to Śrīmatī Rādhikā:] You are My most dearly beloved, and I know that You cannot live for a moment in My absence. I worship Lord Nārāyaṇa just to keep You alive. By his merciful potency, I come to Vṛndāvana every day to enjoy pastimes with You, and then I return to Dvārakā-dhāma. That is why You can always feel My presence in Vṛndāvana.

We should try to realize Kṛṣṇa's statements. Do you have *madīya-bhāva*, this sense of possessiveness, toward *gurudeva* and the pure devotees? If not, then all your endeavors in spiritual life are zero, and you will not be able to accomplish anything. You should think, "Gurudeva is mine. I have left my father, mother, sister, and family for Kṛṣṇa, and my *gurudeva* can give me Kṛṣṇa. Now he is my everything." Such attachment for *gurudeva* will come by cultivation. If we are not attached to *gurudeva* and very much attached to everyone else, there is something wrong. There are two conceptions in relation to service to *gurudeva*. The first conception is, "I will serve all the devotees to please my *gurudeva*." The other conception is, "I will please all the devotees to serve my *gurudeva*." Our motive should be, "I want to please my *gurudeva*," not to please everybody else. Whatever we do should be to please *gurudeva*, not to please everybody else. You can never please everyone.

yasya prasādād bhagavat-prasādo
yasyāprasādān na gatiḥ kuto 'pi
dhyāyan stuvaṁs tasya yaśas tri-sandhyaṁ
vande guroḥ śrī-caraṇāravindam

Śrī Gurvāṣṭakam (8)

One receives Kṛṣṇa's benedictions by the mercy of the spiritual master, and one cannot make any advancement without his grace. Therefore, I should always remember and praise him. At the three junctions of the day – morning, noon, and evening – I should offer my respectful obeisances unto the lotus feet of my spiritual master.

Everyone will be pleased if *gurudeva* is pleased, and even if others are not pleased there is no harm, as long as he is pleased. If Kṛṣṇa is somewhat angry with me, no harm; *gurudeva* will save me. But if *gurudeva* is unhappy, even Kṛṣṇa cannot save me. He will say, "You should go to your *gurudeva*." We should know this fact. When Durvāsā Ṛṣi tried to kill Ambarīṣa Mahārāja, Kṛṣṇa saved Ambarīṣa Mahārāja and began to chase Durvāsā Ṛṣi with His Sudarśana *cakra*. Durvāsā ran throughout the universe, and finally reached the Vaikuṇṭha planet within this universe, where he begged Bhagavān to protect him. However, Bhagavān told him, "I cannot do anything to save you. You should go to Ambarīṣa Mahārāja."

Kṛṣṇa continues, "I worship Nārāyaṇa to please You, so that You will not die of separation from Me. By His merciful potency I go to Vraja to meet You. I wipe the tears from Your face with My *pītāmbara*, and I embrace You; and You think, 'Kṛṣṇa is in Dvārakā, so how can He come here? Prehaps I was dreaming, or perhaps I saw a *sphūrti* (momentary vision).' On the other hand, as soon as You see a *tamāla* tree, You think, 'Kṛṣṇa has come.' When I really come to You, You think, 'Kṛṣṇa has not come. It was just a *sphūrti*,' but this is not true. I always come to You, and

I meet and embrace You. I sport with You, and then I return to Dvārakā. Then, when Your condition is one of extreme separation again, I come to You again. I always do this."

mora bhāgya mo-viṣaye, tomāra ye prema haye,
sei prema parama prabala
lukāñā āma āne, saṅga karāya tomā-sane,
prakaṭeha ānibe satvara

Śrī Caitanya-caritāmṛta (*Madhya-līlā* 13.155)

Our love affair is more powerful because of My good fortune in receiving Nārāyaṇa's grace. This allows Me to come there unseen by others. I hope that very soon I will be visible to everyone.

"I think that Your unprecedented love and affection will very soon make Me come in such a way that everyone will see Me. I have killed so many kings and powerful demons who were fighting for Kaṁsa, but there are still some left."

yādavera vipakṣa, yata duṣṭa kaṁsa-pakṣa,
tāhā āmi kailuṅ saba kṣaya
āche dui-cāri jana, tāhā māri' vṛndāvana,
āilāma āmi, jāniha niścaya

Śrī Caitanya-caritāmṛta (*Madhya-līlā* 13.156)

I have already killed all the mischievous demons who are enemies of the Yadu dynasty, and I have also killed Kaṁsa and his allies, but there are two or four demons still alive. I want to kill them, and when I have done so, I shall return to Vṛndāvana very soon. Please know this for certain.

"You may say, 'Come immediately,'" Kṛṣṇa tells Rādhikā and the *gopīs*, "but if I am in Vraja, the demons will decide, 'Kṛṣṇa is there in Vṛndāvana with His father and mother, Nanda and Yaśodā, and all His friends. We should try to kill them all. He has no fort, no army, and nothing with which to fight.' That is why I purposely remain here in the fort of Dvārakā, surrounded by water on every side, and protected by many armies. If I were in Vṛndāvana and the opposition party came to know of it, I would not be able to save You. That is why I do not come right away. I must first kill the remaining demons."

sei śatru-gaṇa haite, vraja-jana rākhite,
rahi rājye udāsīna hañā
yebā strī-putra-dhane, kari rājya āvaraṇe,
yadu-gaṇera santoṣa lāgiyā

Śrī Caitanya-caritāmṛta (*Madhya-līlā* 13.157)

I remain in My kingdom because I wish to protect the inhabitants of Vṛndāvana from the attacks of My enemies; otherwise I am indifferent to My royal position. Whatever wives, sons, and wealth I maintain in the kingdom are only for the satisfaction of the Yadus.

Kṛṣṇa continues, "My only consideration is that the Vrajavāsīs should not suffer or be disturbed. I live in Dvārakā, but I am indifferent to My kingdom and associates there, to My many queens, and to My numerous sons and daughters. I have no attachment for them. Rather, I am suffering due to deep separation from the Vrajavāsīs. *Yebā strī-putra-dhane, kari rājya āvaraṇe.* It is only to satisfy the Yadus that I have married so many princesses and live like a king in Dvārakā. They are my father's friends. My father is Nanda Bābā, and everyone in the Yadu dynasty, such as Vasudeva and the others, are friends of Nanda Bābā. That is why I remain in Dvārakā; otherwise I would have already gone to Vṛndāvana."

tomāra ye prema-guṇa, kare āmā ākarṣaṇa,
ānibe āmā dina daśa biśe
punaḥ āsi' vṛndāvane, vraja-vadhū tomā-sane,
vilasiba rajanī-divase

Śrī Caitanya-caritāmṛta (*Madhya-līlā* 13.158)

Your loving qualities always attract Me to Vṛndāvana. Indeed, they will bring Me back within ten or twenty days, and when I return I shall enjoy both day and night with You and all the damsels of Vraja-bhūmi.

"I will kill the rest of the demons very quickly, within ten days. Then I will come back very soon. In fact, You can consider that I have already come."

eta tāṅre kahi kṛṣṇa, vraje yāite satṛṣṇa,
eka śloka paḍi' śunāila
sei śloka śuni' rādhā, khāṇḍila sakala bādhā,
kṛṣṇa-prāptye pratīti ha-ila

Śrī Caitanya-caritāmṛta (*Madhya-līlā* 13.159)

While Kṛṣṇa was speaking to Śrīmatī Rādhārāṇī, He became very anxious to return to Vṛndāvana. He made Her listen to a verse that banished all Her difficulties, and which assured Her that She would attain Kṛṣṇa again.

mayi bhaktir hi bhūtānām
amṛtatvāya kalpate
diṣṭyā yad āsīn mat-sneho
bhavatīnāṁ mad-āpanaḥ

Śrīmad-Bhāgavatam (10.82.44)

Any living being becomes qualified for eternal life by rendering devotional service to Me. But by Your good fortune, You have developed a special loving attitude toward Me, by which You have obtained Me.

"*Mayi bhaktir hi bhūtānām amṛtatvāya kalpate. Sādhana-bhakti*, devotional activities performed to attain Me, is like nectar, but Your *bhakti* is far superior to *sādhana-bhakti*. You have no *anarthas*, and You already have more than *niṣṭhā*, *ruci*, *āsakti*, *bhāva*, *prema*, and *sneha*." There are two kinds of *sneha*: *ghṛta-sneha* and *madhu-sneha*. *Māna* follows *sneha*, and there are two kinds of *māna*. There are also two kinds of *praṇaya*, and after *praṇaya* comes *rāga*, *anurāga*, *bhāva*, and finally *mahābhāva*. Kṛṣṇa tells the *gopīs*, "You have everything. *Sādhana-bhakti* is very rare in this world, but what you have is not in this world. Your *sneha*, *māna*, *praṇaya*, *rāga*, and *anurāga* are only found in Goloka Vṛndāvana. This is the reason that I cannot control Myself, and I am always bound to follow you; there will be no delay in My coming to you."

That love and how to attain it

When Śrīmatī Rādhikā was in Kadamba-kyārī, She remembered Kṛṣṇa deeply, with great love and affection. Weeping, She asked a bumblebee, "Kṛṣṇa is coming? When is He coming? Is He on the way here? Can you tell Me? How is He? Does He remember His friends in Vraja-bhūmi? Does He remember His father and mother? Does He remember us? Does He remember Me? Does He at least say to any of His queens, 'Rādhā is not as intelligent as you.' Or, does He perhaps tell one of them, 'That garland is not as good as the one that the *gopīs* used to make'?" While Rādhikā was speaking like this, She became unconscious.

This is the *gopīs'* love and affection for Kṛṣṇa, and to attain it we should try to take up *bhakti* from the beginning stages – starting from initial faith, associating with pure devotees, accepting initiation from a bona fide *guru*, and engaging in services under his direction.

Don't look here and there, otherwise *māyā* will attract you. We should try to be like Kṛṣṇa's flute; there is nothing inside it. We should try to accept the "air vibration" that *gurudeva* breathes into "that flute," because he has taken the moods of pure *bhakti* from his *guru-paramparā*, from Śrī Rādhā-Kṛṣṇa, and from Caitanya Mahāprabhu. Your speculation will not do. You may be a learned person in the material sense, but that will not help you in spiritual life. Your intelligence will betray you. You should know this truth, and then you will realize everything. Everything will come automatically.

CHAPTER SEVEN

HERĀ-PAÑCAMĪ

The difference between Vṛndāvana and Dvārakā

The meaning of Herā-pañcamī is as follows. On the fifth day of the Chariot Festival, Lakṣmī-devī becomes very worried and thinks, "Where has my husband gone? He told me, 'I am going for a change of environment for some days, and I will return very soon.' It has been five days now, and still He has not come back." Unable to tolerate this, she becomes very angry and gives orders to all her associates as though they had to fight with the enemy: "Take up your weapons!" Then she becomes the commander-in-chief of her "army," and goes to "attack" her husband.

During the Ratha-yātrā Festival, Śrī Caitanya Mahāprabhu wanted to taste the mellows of Herā-pañcamī. In early morning He went to Sundarācala along with His associates and took *darśana* of Jagannātha, Baladeva, and Subhadrā in the Guṇḍicā Mandira. Whenever He went to Jagannātha's temple, He used to see Jagannātha as Kṛṣṇa, Vrajendra-nandana Śyāmasundara, with a peacock feather in His crown, a flute in His hands, with very beautiful lotus eyes, and with all the other attributes of Kṛṣṇa when He is with the *gopīs* in Vṛndāvana. Mahāprabhu never saw

Baladeva, Subhadrā, or Sudarśana *cakra*, because Kṛṣṇa never carries Sudarśana in Vṛndāvana. Mahāprabhu never prayed to Baladeva or to Subhadrā in the temple. He saw them both during the Chariot Festival, but otherwise He saw only Jagannātha. This was all very wonderful.

Jagannātha had gone to Sundarācala (which represents Vṛndāvana) from His temple in Nīlācala (which represents Dvārakā) and, on the evening of the fifth day, Lakṣmī arrived at Sundarācala with all her associates.[1] She was decorated with many precious ornaments made of gold and jewels, and she wore very beautiful and opulent garments. The previous day, Kāśī Miśra, who was the *guru* of King Pratāparudra, had advised the King, "Bring Lakṣmī-devī very valuable gold and jeweled ornaments, and decorate her with them. Make such a beautiful festival for her that everyone will be struck with wonder. They should think they have never seen anything like this before. Caitanya Mahāprabhu wants to taste all the mellows of this festival." Accordingly, Lakṣmī was decorated with gold and jeweled ornaments, opulent garments, and other paraphernalia.

At the Siṁha-dvāra (lion gate) in front of the Jagannātha Temple, Kāśī Miśra gave very beautiful seats to Mahāprabhu and His associates such as Śrīvāsa Paṇḍita, Śrī Svarūpa Dāmodara, and Śrī Rāya Rāmānanda. Soon after they were seated, Lakṣmī arrived with all her associates and opulence, as if she was coming to attack Jagannātha. First she "attacked" Jagannātha's associates, who were actually Mahāprabhu's associates, like Śikhi Māhiti, Vakreśvara Paṇḍita, and so on, and then she tied them up and bound them like prisoners. Her associates then punished them all by striking them with "whips" made of soft cloth, and she

[1] In this Herā-pañcamī festival, a drama was enacted for the pleasure of Śrī Caitanya Mahāprabhu and His associates. In that drama, male devotees dressed themselves in *sarīs* and ornaments and portrayed Lakṣmī and her attendants.

accused them, "Oh, you should admit your guilt and pay something. You have taken my husband. Where are you keeping Him? Bring Him here right now."

Śrī Caitanya Mahāprabhu was extremely happy to see this pastime and, tasting its mellows, He said, "I have heard that when Satyabhāmā used to exhibit *māna*, She would remove all Her golden ornaments. Then she would enter a dark, private room, put on dirty garments, scratch the ground with her nails, and weep continually. But here I see another kind of *māna* in Lakṣmī. She is like a commander-in-chief going to attack with many soldiers. I have never seen anything like this, nor have I ever even heard of such a thing."

Svarūpa Dāmodara then explained that there are many kinds of *māna*, and that this *māna* of Dvārakā is very different from that of the *gopīs* in Vṛndāvana.

Mahāprabhu told Svarūpa Dāmodara:

yadyapi jagannātha karena dvārakāya vihāra
sahaja prakaṭa kare parama udāra
tathāpi vatsara-madhye haya eka-bāra
vṛndāvana dekhite tāṅra utkaṇṭhā apāra

Śrī Caitanya-caritāmṛta (*Madhya-līlā* 14.117–18)

Although Lord Jagannātha enjoys His pastimes in Dvārakā-dhāma and naturally manifests sublime liberality there, still, once a year He becomes unlimitedly eager to see Vṛndāvana.

Why did Kṛṣṇa leave Vṛndāvana? Ultimately He did so to please and pacify the *gopīs*. It is said that He leaves Vṛndāvana and comes to Mathurā and Dvārakā because He cannot forget the devotees there – or anywhere else. He must support and nourish them. The next question would then be: after leaving why did He not return, at least for a visit. One answer is that there is no fort in Vṛndāvana. If Kṛṣṇa had returned to Vṛndāvana, and

Jarāsandha had come to know that He was really the son of Nanda and Yaśodā rather than that of Vasudeva and Devakī, Jarāsandha would have attacked Vṛndāvana and it would have been ruined. Nanda Bābā was a cowherd, a *gopa*, not a warrior, and there were no soldiers in Vṛndāvana. Jarāsandha would therefore have destroyed all of Vṛndāvana and then imprisoned Yaśodā and Nanda Bābā, as Kaṁsa had imprisoned Vasudeva and Devakī.

This is a reason, but it is external. Someone may say, "At least Kṛṣṇa should go to Vṛndāvana from time to time, and then He should return quickly." But Kṛṣṇa has so many enemies, and all of them would come to know that He has many friends in Vṛndāvana. They would think, "They should be attacked, and they should be finished." This is another reason He did not return there, but it is also external.

Someone may say, "Kṛṣṇa was able to take all His associates of Mathurāpurī to Dvārakā in one night, in just a minute. He had abundant grand palaces built there, not only for each of His queens, but also for all His associates such as Akrūra and Uddhava, as well as for Vasudeva and Devakī. There were so many thousands and millions of Mathurāvāsīs. They went to sleep in Mathurā, and in the morning they saw that they were in Dvārakā. This was very wonderful, and it shows that Kṛṣṇa can do anything He likes. Similarly, in one night He can take to Dvārakā all His associates from Vṛndāvana, such as Rādhikā, Lalitā, Viśākhā, and all the other *sakhīs*, as well as all cowherd boys like Śrīdāmā, Stoka-kṛṣṇa, Lavaṅga, and Arjuna. He can take His mother and father, Yaśodā-maiyā and Nanda Bābā, and all the other Vrajavāsīs as well. Is there any harm in that? If all the Mathurāvāsīs can be there, the Vrajavāsīs can be there as well."

But how will Vṛndā-devī go there? Will Govardhana go there? This is a very confidential topic. There will be a conflict between *aiśvarya-bhāva* and *mādhurya-bhāva.* What will Kṛṣṇa say? Will He say, "I am the son of Vasudeva and Devakī," or "I am the son of Nanda and Yaśodā"? This contradiction of mellows would create a very difficult situation for Kṛṣṇa. Will He play His flute? Will He wear His peacock feather there? Will He go cowherding with His friends in Dvārakā? Can He tell others, "I am the son of Nanda Bābā and Yaśodā"?

By the constitutional nature of *aiśvarya* and *mādhurya*, they cannot exist together. If you become an actual *madhyama-adhikārī* and hear all these topics in good association, you will realize something about the meaning of *aiśvarya-bhāva*, and of the *mādhurya-bhāva* in Vṛndāvana. Then you can become one-pointed in your devotion to Vrajendra-nandana. Vṛndāvana cannot go to Dvārakā, and Dvārakā can never go to Vṛndāvana. They are opposites, and the attempt to combine them is called *rasa-ābhāsa,* contradiction of mellows.

You should know what is *aiśvarya* and what is the constitutional nature of *mādhurya-rasa.* In Dvārakā there is always opulence, and everyone there knows that Kṛṣṇa is the Supreme Personality of Godhead. Sometimes He is four-handed and He can do anything. He can bring a dead person back to life, and He Himself has no death and no birth.

In Vṛndāvana, on the other hand, there is always *mādhurya-bhāva.* Kṛṣṇa has taken birth from the womb of Mother Yaśodā, and He is quite helpless. As a baby, He cannot turn over without His mother's help. Sometimes He becomes angry, and He is always hungry. And when hungry, He steals butter from here and there.

And Kṛṣṇa may tell lies. He will say, "Mother, when have I stolen butter? I never steal. You send Me cowherding with My friends very early in the morning. I run here and there with the cows all day long, and when I return from cowherding in the evening, being very tired I take My meal and then go to sleep. So when have I stolen this butter? I have never done it." Then, when He begins to weep, Mother Yaśodā says, "Certainly You have stolen the butter." Continuing to weep, Kṛṣṇa replies, "Perhaps I am not your son, and that is why you are accusing Me of stealing butter. That is why. Maybe I should go away and live somewhere else." Yaśodā-maiyā then begins to weep and her heart melts. She takes Kṛṣṇa in her lap and says, "I know You have never stolen butter. You have never done so." Kṛṣṇa then tells her, "I have done it, Mother. I have done it." Then both of them weep. This is the mood of *mādhurya*. Mother Yaśodā ties Kṛṣṇa to a mortar. How would she be able to do this if she knew that Kṛṣṇa is the Supreme Personality of Godhead?

There is one point to note here. In Vṛndāvana, even if there is a manifestation of opulence, it does not disturb *mādhurya-bhāva*. There may be opulence, but the pastimes of Kṛṣṇa still remain *nara-vat*, like those of a human boy. His pastimes there do not go beyond the human level. For example, Pūtanā came and lifted Kṛṣṇa in her arms and said, "My dear boy, my dear boy," although she wanted to poison Him. He closed His eyes as if He were afraid of her, and did nothing more than simply suck the milk from her breast. How could He help it if she died? He never showed any large or wondrous form. He was like a child, a boy of only three months – but still she was killed. Although killing Pūtanā was an act of the utmost spiritual opulence, it still remains a human-like pastime.

Before this pastime took place, Kaṁsa was engaged in conquering the world, and at one point he engaged in a ferocious battle with Pūtanā. Pūtanā was just about to defeat him in the battle, but Kaṁsa was an expert politician, so he told her, "Now I accept you as my sister. You can help me, and I will help you." In this way they made an alliance. So Pūtanā was very, very powerful; it would be extremely difficult to kill a demon like her, since even Kaṁsa could not defeat her. That is why Kṛṣṇa's killing her is an example of His opulence.

Also, Kṛṣṇa lifted Govardhana and held him aloft for seven days on His finger, as an elephant would lift a lotus flower with its trunk. A man cannot do this, but Kṛṣṇa did it; and He was smiling and sometimes playing His flute. He was in a dancing mood, in a threefold-bending position. All the cowherd boys held up their sticks and touched Govardhana, saying, "Oh, don't fall – stay up there!" They were all thinking that they had lifted Govardhana. At the same time, Nanda Mahārāja, who was a very exalted devotee of Nārāyaṇa, prayed, "O Nārāyaṇa, please do not allow this mountain to fall down." And what can be said of the *gopīs*? They are the very potency of Kṛṣṇa Himself. Rādhikā looked strongly at Govardhana with a piercing sidelong glance and told him, "If you drop down, you will be burnt to ashes. You should remain aloft within My vision." From everyone's point of view, Kṛṣṇa was not doing anything.

In this way, although lifting Govardhana was a very great opulence, Kṛṣṇa did not assume a large or four-armed form. Whether there is opulence or no opulence, His pastimes are called *mādhurya* if they are human-like. In Vṛndāvana, Kṛṣṇa is the friend of all the *gopas*, He is the beloved of all the young *gopīs*, and He is the son of all the elder *gopīs*.

This atmosphere cannot exist in Dvārakā. There is only opulence there, and sometimes Kṛṣṇa may assume a four-handed form or a universal form. He is bound to say, "I am the son of Vasudeva and Devakī." He must. He will have to say, "I am a *kṣatriya*," whereas in Vṛndāvana He thinks, "I am a *gopa*." How would He be able to reconcile this if all the *gopīs* and *gopas* were to come to Dvārakā? The situation would be against the principle of *rasa*.

The Vṛndāvana mood will never come to Dvārakā. In Vṛndāvana, Kṛṣṇa can carry His flute and wear a peacock feather, and He can manifest His beautiful threefold-bending form as *manmatha-manmathaḥ*, the enchanter of Cupid. But He cannot do this in Dvārakā, nor can He perform *rāsa-līlā* there. What would all His queens think if He were to engage in *rāsa* with the *gopīs* on the shore of the ocean in Dvārakā? Thus, the *gopīs* will never go to Dvārakā, and Kṛṣṇa also never goes there in His original and complete feature. He goes there in another form, and that form is His manifestation. He will be Vāsudeva there, for Kṛṣṇa Himself cannot give up being Vrajendra-nandana Śyāmasundara. He cannot give up Vṛndāvana, even for a moment. *Vṛndāvanaṁ parityajya padam ekaṁ na gacchati*: Kṛṣṇa never goes even a step outside Vṛndāvana.

Śrīla Jīva Gosvāmī and Śrīla Rūpa Gosvāmī have quoted the Purāṇas to show that in Kṛṣṇa's last days, just after He defeated and killed Dantavakra, He left Dvārakā and went to Gokula, where He met all the Vrajavāsīs. Weeping bitterly, He embraced them all, and then He began playing with all the *gopīs* and *gopas*. Then, some days later, He went to Goloka Vṛndāvana and took with Him His associates such as Nanda Bābā, Yaśodā, all the mothers, all the *sakhīs*, all the *sakhās*, and also His Vṛndāvana-bhūmi. Vrajendra-nandana Śyāmasundara thus entered His *aprakaṭa-līlā* (unmanifest pastimes), while He simultaneously returned to Dvārakā in His form as Vāsudeva-Kṛṣṇa. These are very secret truths.

Similarly, Jagannātha-deva comes to Vṛndāvana once a year. His queen, Vimalā-devī (i.e. Lakṣmī-devī), represents Satyabhāmā, Rukmiṇī, and all the other queens in Dvārakā. Jagannātha lives in Dvārakā for the entire year, but once a year He wants to go to Vṛndāvana, and He plays a trick in order to go there.

During the Herā-pañcamī Festival, Caitanya Mahāprabhu said:

vṛndāvana-sama ei upavana-gaṇa
tāhā dekhibāre utkaṇṭhita haya mana

Śrī Caitanya-caritāmṛta (*Madhya-līlā* 14.119)

Pointing out the neighboring gardens, Śrī Caitanya Mahāprabhu said, "All these gardens exactly resemble Vṛndāvana; therefore Lord Jagannātha is very eager to see them again."

bāhira ha-ite kare ratha-yātrā-chala
sundarācale yāya prabhu chāḍi' nīlācala

Śrī Caitanya-caritāmṛta (*Madhya-līlā* 14.120)

Externally, Jagannātha gives the excuse that He wants to participate in the Ratha-yātrā Festival, but actually He wants to leave Jagannātha Purī to go to Sundarācala, the Guṇḍicā Temple, a replica of Vṛndāvana.

nānā-puṣpodyāne tathā khele rātri-dine
lakṣmīdevīre saṅge nāhi laya ki kāraṇe?

Śrī Caitanya-caritāmṛta (*Madhya-līlā* 14.121)

The Lord enjoys His pastimes day and night in various flower gardens there. But why does He not take Lakṣmī-devī, the goddess of fortune, with Him?

Caitanya Mahāprabhu asked Svarūpa Dāmodara, "If Kṛṣṇa is going to Sundarācala to play, why doesn't He take Lakṣmī-devī? He may take everyone with Him to Vṛndāvana. What's the harm in taking Lakṣmī-devī?" There is a reason behind Mahāprabhu's question: if Kṛṣṇa were to take Lakṣmī, it would be against the principles of *rasa*.

Try to understand this subject, and then you will at once come to the stage of *madhyama-adhikāra*. You cannot understand these topics through deity worship alone, even if you are always absorbed in worshiping the deities day and night – to understand them you must regularly hear high-class *hari-kathā*. *Harināma* is the superior process, especially in Kali-yuga: *harer nāma, harer nāma harer nāma eva kevalam / kalāu nāsty eva nāsty eva nāsty eva gatir anyathā*. There are always difficulties in deity worship. You cannot purchase paraphernalia for worship if you have no money, and if anyone steals your deities there will be a big problem. On the other hand, chanting *harināma* does not require any paraphernalia. Deity worship is especially essential for *gṛhastha-bhaktas*, but at the same time, you should not always remain on the level of *kaniṣṭha-adhikāra*. *Bhakti* is like a current. You should gradually develop your devotion, even if you are worshiping deities, and then you may come in the proper line.

Mahāprabhu worshiped Girirāja, who was brought to Him by a devotee returning from Vṛndāvana. He worshiped both a *guñjā-mālā* and a *govardhana-śilā*, but He was bathing the *śilā* with His own tears, keeping Him sometimes on His head or heart, and sometimes on His eyes. Then, after six years, He gave them to Śrīla Raghunātha dāsa Gosvāmī and told him to perform the daily worship by offering only one earthen pot full of water and eight *mañjarīs* (*tulasī* buds) with very soft leaves. While Śrīla Raghunātha dāsa Gosvāmī was worshiping them, he was thinking that the *guñjā-mālā* is Rādhikā, and Girirāja is Nanda-nandana, Vrajendra-nandana Śyāmasundara. He was thinking that He was serving Them personally.

We should try to come to the level of *madhyama-adhikāra* and realize all these truths. A *kaniṣṭha-adhikārī* will not understand, so try to enter *madhyama-adhikāra* and keep high-class association. This is the only process. Reading books will not be sufficient. They can never help you completely because the lock and key to understanding them is in the hands of the pure, self-realized devotees. The pure devotees can open the lock, and then you can realize these topics.

yāha bhāgavata paḍa vaiṣṇavera sthāne
ekānta āśraya kara caitanya-caraṇe

Śrī Caitanya-caritāmṛta (*Antya-līlā* 5.131)

If you want to understand *Śrīmad-Bhāgavatam*, You must approach a self-realized Vaiṣṇava and hear from him. You can do this when you have completely taken shelter of the lotus feet of Śrī Caitanya Mahāprabhu.

Mahāprabhu had asked Śrī Svarūpa Dāmodara why Kṛṣṇa did not take Lakṣmī-devī with Him to Sundarācala; what harm would there be in that? Svarūpa Dāmodara replied to Mahāprabhu's inquiry:

svarūpa kahe – śuna, prabhu, kāraṇa ihāra
vṛndāvana-krīḍāte lakṣmīra nāhi adhikāra

Śrī Caitanya-caritāmṛta (*Madhya-līlā* 14.122)

Svarūpa Dāmodara replied, "My dear Lord, please hear the reason for this. Lakṣmī-devī, the goddess of fortune, does not have the proper qualifications to enter the Vṛndāvana pleasure-pastimes."

Lakṣmī-devī is not qualified to enter Vṛndāvana. There are eight prominent queens in Dvārakā, headed by Satyabhāmā and Rukmiṇī, and 16,100 others as well. These eight are special, but none of them is qualified to go to Vṛndāvana. First they will have to take birth from the wombs of *gopīs*, marry *gopas*, and then cheat their husbands and become Kṛṣṇa's paramours, as all the *gopīs* are. They will have to give up their husbands and everything else. They will be able to serve Kṛṣṇa in Vṛndāvana if they are under the guidance of the *gopīs*; otherwise such service will not be possible. Lakṣmī-devī could not enter Vṛndāvana, even though she performed severe austerities in Baelvana. She wanted to cross the River Yamunā and see the *rāsa-līlā*, but she could not.

Yogamāyā is greater than Lakṣmī, and she can control everyone. When she saw Lakṣmī's austerities, she approached her and said, "You are a chaste lady, a *brāhmaṇī*, married to Nārāyaṇa. Can you give up your husband and marry somebody else – a *gopa*?"

Lakṣmī replied, "I cannot do it. How is it possible?"

Yogamāyā said, "Can you make cow dung paddies?"

Lakṣmī replied, "Oh, I cannot do that. I don't know how."

Yogamāyā asked, "Can you milk cows?"

Lakṣmī replied, "I have never done it before."

Then Yogamāyā told her, "You cannot go to Vṛndāvana, because you are not qualified. First you would have to take birth from a *gopī's* womb, associate with the *gopīs*, and try to follow them. You would have to marry a *gopa* like Durmukha, Durmada, Abhimanyu, or Govardhana Malla. Then, when you have given up that husband, you would be able to go to Kṛṣṇa and make Him your beloved. This is the only process."

In one *kalpa* it was Yogamāyā who questioned Lakṣmī-devī, and in another it was Kṛṣṇa Himself, but both of them had to tell her the same conclusion: she is unfit for this *rasa*.

Svarūpa Dāmodara continued:

vṛndāvana-līlāya kṛṣṇera sahāya gopī-gaṇa
gopī-gaṇa vinā kṛṣṇera harite nāre mana

Śrī Caitanya-caritāmṛta (*Madhya-līlā* 14.123)

In the pastimes of Vṛndāvana, the only assistants are the *gopīs*. But for the *gopīs*, no one can attract the mind of Kṛṣṇa.

Was Svarūpa Dāmodara telling a lie? The *gopas* are also there in Vṛndāvana, but he did not mention them. Rather, he said that no one but the *gopīs* can control and steal away Kṛṣṇa's heart, and Kṛṣṇa Himself has confirmed this by His statement in *Śrīmad-Bhāgavatam* (10.32.22):

na pāraye 'haṁ niravadya-saṁyujāṁ
sva-sādhu-kṛtyaṁ vibudhāyuṣāpi vaḥ
yā mābhajan durjaya-geha-śṛṅkhalāḥ
saṁvṛścya tad vaḥ pratiyātu sādhunā

[When the *gopīs* were overwhelmed with dissatisfaction due to Lord Kṛṣṇa's absence from the *rāsa-līlā*, Kṛṣṇa returned to them and told them:] My dear *gopīs*, our meeting is certainly free of all material contamination. I must admit that in many lives it would be impossible for Me to repay My debt to you because you have cut off the bondage of family life just to search for Me. Consequently I am unable to repay you. Therefore please be satisfied with your honest activities in this regard.

Kṛṣṇa has said this only to the *gopīs*; He has not said it to anyone else. It is stated in *Śrīmad-Bhāgavatam* (10.14.32):

aho bhāgyam aho bhāgyaṁ
nanda-gopa-vrajaukasām
yan-mitraṁ paramānandaṁ
pūrṇaṁ brahma sanātanam

How greatly fortunate are Nanda Mahārāja, the cowherd men, and all the other inhabitants of Vraja-bhūmi! There is no limit to their good fortune because the Absolute Truth, the source of transcendental bliss, the eternal Supreme Brahman, has become their friend.

One can serve Kṛṣṇa in a male form, as a *gopa*. Nanda Bābā can serve Kṛṣṇa as His father, and Gargācārya, Bhāguri Muni, or

Śāṇḍilya Ṛṣi can come to Him as *guru* and offer Him blessings. Others, such as Sudāmā, Subala, Madhumaṅgala, and of course Baladeva Prabhu, can also serve Kṛṣṇa in a male form. However, no one in a male form can serve Śrīmatī Rādhikā. Especially, no male can go to that place where Kṛṣṇa is engaged in pastimes with Rādhikā and the *gopīs*. Some friends, such as Subala Sakhā, Madhumaṅgala, Kokila, Bhṛṅga, and other *priya-narma-sakhās* who have some mood of *mahābhāva*, can approach and help somewhat from a little distance, but they cannot enter the *kuñjas*. On the other hand, all the *gopīs* can go there.

It is for this reason that Svarūpa Dāmodara especially mentioned the *gopīs*. He said that no one but the *gopīs* can go there. Even Mother Yaśodā cannot go there. She has some idea what Kṛṣṇa is doing there,[2] but she cannot go. Mother Rohiṇī also knows somewhat, but she cannot go there either. She will remain very far away and, like Mother Yaśodā, pretend not to know anything. Mother Yaśodā does not know that Kṛṣṇa meets with the *gopīs* and engages in amorous pastimes throughout the night. In the morning, when she sees Kṛṣṇa with many marks on His body, she thinks, "Oh, all these naughty boys were playing with Kṛṣṇa, and they have made scratch marks on Him."

If you want to serve Kṛṣṇa fully, you must follow the process given by Śrīla Rūpa Gosvāmī and Śrīla Raghunātha dāsa Gosvāmī. You should hear and learn all the topics discussed in *Rūpa-śikṣā*,[3] *Sanātana-śikṣā*,[3] especially in *Rāmānanda-saṁvāda*, and still more than that, here in *Ratha-yātrā-prasaṅga*, the topics of Ratha-yātrā. Everything is very clear here. The

[2] Actually, both Yaśodā-maiyā and Rohiṇī-maiyā know that Kṛṣṇa meets with the *gopīs* and that they play together like friends. They do not think anything bad about this because they consider that both Kṛṣṇa and the *gopīs* are very young. They have been playing together since their early ages and there is no concern within the minds of Yaśodā and Rohiṇī. What they do not know is that Kṛṣṇa

essence of the teachings that Mahāprabhu gave to Rūpa Gosvāmī in Prayāga, the essence of what Rūpa Gosvāmī wrote in *Ujjvala-nīlamaṇi* – the essence of everything – is all here.

This subject matter is like very sweet honey in a bottle, but the cork is very tight. Bees can fly around the bottle, and they can lick the glass, but they cannot taste the honey. If you follow the process, the seed of pure *bhakti* can be placed in your heart properly, and you will enter the line of Rūpa and Raghunātha and realize something. This is our objective. Otherwise, if you do not follow the process, your chanting and remembering and your performance of the other types of the ninefold *bhakti* process will not take you to Vṛndāvana.

If you are serving Jagannātha in the mood of the residents of Dvārakā, and not following the *gopīs*, do not be disturbed by what I am saying. First become *madhyama-adhikārī*, otherwise you will give up the worship of Jagannātha, Baladeva, Subhadrā, and Gaura-Nityānanda prematurely. Don't do anything rashly. First try to know all these truths, come to the stage of a *madhyama-adhikārī*, and then you can be one-pointed in your devotion to Kṛṣṇa. You cannot be one-pointed at your present stage. However, if you hear continually in good association, you will quickly realize what is helpful and what is not. At present you are not able to discriminate.

We should know what is *bhāvamayi*, *bhāva-sambandhī*, *bhāva-anukūla*, *bhāva-aviruddha*, and *bhāva-pratikūla*.[4] You

goes out at night and meets with the *gopīs*, but they are aware that Kṛṣṇa and the *gopīs* meet and play in the daytime. In Vedic culture it is not acceptable that boys and girls meet in the middle of the night.

[3] This refers to Śrī Caitanya Mahāprabhu's instructions to Rūpa Gosvāmī and Sanātana Gosvāmī, which are found in Chapters 19–23 of *Madhya-līlā* of *Śrī Caitanya-caritāmṛta*.

[4] Please refer to the Glossary for explanations of these terms.

will not be able to understand this in a day, but this is our aim and objective. If you are in the line of Mahāprabhu, you should be in the line of Rūpa and Raghunātha. Try to know all these established truths, and follow in their line. On the other hand, if you are not of this inclination, you can join the Rāmānuja or Madhvācārya *sampradāyas*, and chant and perform *kīrtana* in their mood of opulence.

Again, Mahāprabhu is telling Svarūpa Dāmodara:

prabhu kahe – yātrā-chale kṛṣṇera gamana
subhadrā āra baladeva, saṅge dui jana

Śrī Caitanya-caritāmṛta (*Madhya-līlā* 14.125)

The Lord said, "Using the Chariot Festival as an excuse, Kṛṣṇa goes there with Subhadrā and Baladeva."

Kṛṣṇa lives with His thousands of queens in Dvārakā, but sometimes His remembrance of Vṛndāvana is so strong that He cannot control Himself. At that time He tells his queens, represented by Lakṣmī-devī, "Now I am feeling sick. I want to go somewhere for a change of climate." Jagannātha is pretending. He is actually going to Vṛndāvana, but He does not tell His wife, Lakṣmī-devī. Lakṣmī replies, "You can go, but return very soon, and don't go alone," and Jagannātha agrees, "I will not go alone."

Baladeva is Jagannātha's brother, and Subhadrā has great affection for the *gopīs*; so He took them with Him in the chariot and went to the Guṇḍicā Mandira, which represents Vṛndāvana. He went to meet the *gopas* and *gopīs*, Nanda Bābā, and all His other associates of Vraja. He first went to Nanda-bhavana, and after meeting with His parents He left Baladeva and Subhadrā there in Nandagaon and went alone to Vṛndāvana to play with the *gopīs*.

Mahāprabhu said:

gopī-saṅge yata līlā haya upavane
nigūḍha kṛṣṇera bhāva keha nāhi jāne

Śrī Caitanya-caritāmṛta (*Madhya-līlā* 14.125)

All the pastimes with the *gopīs* that take place in the gardens are very confidential ecstasies of Lord Kṛṣṇa. No one knows them.

Why does Kṛṣṇa take Baladeva and Subhadrā with Him? There is a deep meaning behind this. Baladeva and Subhadrā would be staying with Yaśodā-maiyā. They do not understand Kṛṣṇa's confidential pastimes with the *gopīs*, and they do not know where He goes alone at night. They do not know that He is sometimes at Vaṁśīvaṭa, sometimes at Sevā-kuñja, and sometimes at Rādhā-kuṇḍa. Kṛṣṇa also goes to these places in the daytime, and He meets the *gopīs* there. He is alone with the *gopīs* there, sometimes playing on swings, and sometimes gambling with them, sometimes being defeated by them, and sometimes having His flute forcibly taken by them. And sometimes they play in Rādhā-kuṇḍa or Śyāma-kuṇḍa, throwing water on each other.

Even Yaśodā-maiyā does not actually know what goes on in these confidential pastime-places. Only Yogamāyā Paurṇamāsī, Vṛndā, Dhaniṣṭhā, and Kundalātā know. Sometimes Subala and Madhumaṅgala know, but even when they know, they do not go there. So Subhadrā and Baladeva do not know for what purpose Kṛṣṇa has gone to Vṛndāvana.

Only Kṛṣṇa knows, and He has brought Baladeva and Subhadrā only so that Lakṣmī-devī will not mistrust Him. She will not wonder, "Why has He gone away? Has He run away to Vṛndāvana?" She will believe, "If Baladeva and Subhadrā are there, they will soon tell Kṛṣṇa, 'We should now return to Dvārakā.'"

ataeva kṛṣṇera prākaṭye nāhi kichu doṣa
tabe kene lakṣmīdevī kare eta roṣa?

Śrī Caitanya-caritāmṛta (*Madhya-līlā* 14.126)

[Caitanya Mahāprabhu now asked the question:] Since there is no fault in Kṛṣṇa's pastimes, why does the goddess of fortune become angry with Him?

What is the deep meaning behind this question? Why is Mahāprabhu asking it? Kṛṣṇa is going with Baladeva and Subhadrā-devī, but they do not know why He is going, and they do not know that He will play with the *gopīs* here and there in the *nikuñjas*. Since no one knows, who has told Lakṣmī that Kṛṣṇa is going to play with the *gopīs*? No one told her. Also, Kṛṣṇa's elder brother, Baladeva, is there with Kṛṣṇa. Kṛṣṇa cannot do anything wrong in the presence of His elder brother. Subhadrā, His younger sister, is also there with Him. In their presence He cannot meet the *gopīs*. Why, then, is Lakṣmī so angry?

Svarūpa Dāmodara replied:

svarūpa kahe, – prema-vatīra ei ta' svabhāva
kāntera audāsya-leśe haya krodha-bhāva

Śrī Caitanya-caritāmṛta (*Madhya-līlā* 14.127)

It is the nature of a girl afflicted by love to become immediately angry upon finding any neglect on the part of her lover.

Because of Kṛṣṇa's delay in returning, Lakṣmī considers that He is ignoring her. She thinks, "Oh, He has not returned. He is neglecting me. He is not actually sick, as He told me; He was pretending. Now He must be playing with the *gopas* and *gopīs* there

– and He must be very happy!" This is the reason for her anger.

If a woman loves her husband, and her husband has a new lover, what will happen? An Indian lady will take a bottle of kerosene oil or petrol, pour it on her body, and set fire to herself; and only her ashes will remain. In the West there is no such problem. If one's husband keeps three, four, five, or more new lovers, no harm; the wife will also get new boyfriends. In India, however, this would create a great problem. The wife will become very angry, even if she feels a very slight neglect.

In Vṛndāvana there is not only one kind of *māna*; there are thousands. Some are without reason, some with reason, and there are so many kinds of reasons. *Māna* is an advanced stage of *prema*, and manifests when there is *sthāyibhāva*. Upon that *sthāyibhāva*, *uddīpana* and *ālambana* manifest, and then all the *sāttvika-bhāvas* and thirty-three kinds of *vyabhicārī* moods become manifest. *Vibhāva*, *anubhāva*, *sāttvika*, and *vyabhicārī*[5] all mix together on the platform of *sthāyibhāva*, of which there are five kinds, and they never change. Before *sthāyibhāva* comes *rati*, and then, after some time, *sthāyibhāva* descends from a *rāgātmikā-bhakta* of Goloka Vṛndāvana, and that *sthāyibhāva* is the permanent platform of *prema*.

What is the nature of *prema*? Even when there are many strong and compelling reasons to break one's love and affection, it will increase hundreds of thousands of times instead. That is *prema*. There is no self-interest there. The *gopīs* only want to please Kṛṣṇa, and Kṛṣṇa wants to please the *gopīs*. It is not like the so-called love of this world, which ends in quarrel and divorce.

After *prema* comes *sneha*, the stage in which one's heart will melt if one sees Kṛṣṇa, and one's eyes will be always full of tears. There are two kinds of *sneha*: *ghṛta-sneha* and *madhu-sneha*.

[5] Please refer to the Glossary for explanations of these terms.

Śrīmatī Rādhikā has *madhu-sneha*, and Candrāvalī and others like her have *ghṛta-sneha*. *Madhu-sneha* occurs when a *gopī* thinks, "Kṛṣṇa is mine," whereas the mood, "I am Kṛṣṇa's" is the *ghṛta-sneha* of Candrāvalī.

After *sneha* comes *praṇaya*, which can be understood by the following example. We can take massage and bathe in front of our shadows, or in front of a mirror, without feeling any shame. We can be naked in front of the mirror because only our reflection is with us, but we will be ashamed if another person is present. Similarly, *praṇaya* is the stage at which *sneha* increases to such an extent that one thinks she and Kṛṣṇa are one soul in two bodies – like a person and his reflection in a mirror.

After *praṇaya* comes *māna*. Sometimes *māna* arises before *praṇaya*, but the general process is that intense *praṇaya* comes first, and *māna* comes after that. *Māna* appears when one thinks, "Kṛṣṇa will surely come and pacify me. He is bound to come." If this strong faith is there, that is *māna*. There are many kinds of *māna*, as mentioned earlier, some without reason, and some with reason – and there are many kinds of reasons.

Rādhikā has unlimited moods. The prominent ones number 360, and therefore there are 360 kinds of *gopīs*. All the *gopīs* have separate individual moods, and all these moods are found in Śrīmatī Rādhikā. In other words, all the *gopīs* are manifestations of Śrīmatī Rādhikā. All the *gopīs* and their different moods have manifested by Her desire, and She is a combination of them all. All moods reside in Rādhikā, and Her various moods are manifest in different *gopīs*. Lalitā is *prakharā* (outspoken), some *gopīs* are *dhirā* (sober), some *adhirā* (restless), and so on. Svarūpa Dāmodara was explaining this, and Mahāprabhu replied, "More, more, more – I want to hear more."

When those who have the mood "I am Kṛṣṇa's" are in *māna*, they will weep. They will not protest or call Kṛṣṇa ill names, and they cannot speak any harsh words to Him; they will only weep. However, those with the mood that "Kṛṣṇa is mine" become very angry, and in their anger they will shoot Kṛṣṇa with the arrows of their harsh words. When Kṛṣṇa comes to those whose mood is in between the two aforementioned moods, they will not say very much. They may say, "You can come. Oh, now You are very tired." They will give Him a seat, and sometimes they will speak harsh, taunting words like, "Oh, You look so beautiful. You now look like Śaṅkara Mahādeva – Nīla-rohita Rudra."[6]

While Caitanya Mahāprabhu was tasting all this *kathā*, He said, "I have never heard anything like this before – that Lakṣmī has come with her whole party as a commander-in-chief, as if to attack." Lakṣmī began to beat Kṛṣṇa's chariot, and Śrīvāsa Paṇḍita began clapping. He was very happy that the associates of Lakṣmī were chastising the associates of Vṛndāvana, imprisoning them, "beating" them, taking a fine from them, taking their garlands and ornaments, and punishing them.

śrīvāsa hāsiyā kahe, – śuna, dāmodara
āmāra lakṣmīra dekha sampatti vistara

Śrī Caitanya-caritāmṛta (*Madhya-līlā* 14.203)

At this time, Śrīvāsa Ṭhākura smiled and told Svarūpa Dāmodara, "My dear sir, please hear! Just see how opulent my goddess of fortune is!"

vṛndāvanera sampad dekha, – puṣpa-kisalaya
giridhātu-śikhipiccha-guñjāphala-maya

Śrī Caitanya-caritāmṛta (*Madhya-līlā* 14.204)

[6] Śaṅkara's complexion is a mixture of blue, black, and red. This comparison is made when Kṛṣṇa comes to Rādhikā with blackish and reddish spots on His face and limbs, and She thinks the spots are a result of His sporting with other *gopīs*.

"As far as Vṛndāvana's opulence is concerned, it consists of a few flowers and twigs, some minerals from the hills, a few peacock feathers, and the plant known as *guñjā.*"

Śrīvāsa Paṇḍita smiled and said, "There are no golden crowns in Vṛndāvana. There are only flutes made of dry bamboo, and some peacock feathers, and Kṛṣṇa only wears a *pītāmbara* and flower garlands. There is nothing of any value there."

eta sampatti chāḍi' kene gelā vṛndāvana
tāṅre hāsya karite lakṣmī karilā sājana

Śrī Caitanya-caritāmṛta (*Madhya-līlā* 14.206)

Lakṣmī wondered, "Why did Lord Jagannātha give up so much opulence and go to Vṛndāvana?" To make Him a laughing-stock, the goddess of fortune made arrangements for much decoration.

People in the mood of opulence may think like this. They are all on the side of Lakṣmī-devī. Svarūpa Dāmodara, however, being Lalitā in *kṛṣṇa-līlā,* is of her mood and therefore a pure Vrajavāsī.

tomāra ṭhākura, dekha eta sampatti chāḍi'
patra-phala-phula-lobhe gelā puṣpa-bāḍī

Śrī Caitanya-caritāmṛta (*Madhya-līlā* 14.207)

[Then the maidservants of the goddess of fortune said to the servants of Lord Jagannātha:] Why did your Lord Jagannātha abandon the great opulence of the goddess of fortune and, for the sake of a few leaves, fruits, and flowers, go see the flower garden of Śrīmatī Rādhārāṇī?

Śrīla Bhaktivedānta Swāmī Mahārāja wrote these translations; I am not saying all this. He has translated the verses, and I am only reading them, so I am not "guilty." If anyone says, "Nārāyaṇa

Mahārāja is a *sahajiyā* and that is why he is saying all these things," then my *śikṣā-guru*, Śrīla Swāmī Mahārāja, must be a greater *sahajiyā* than me. He will be the *guru* of the *sahajiyās*, and Śrīla Kṛṣṇadāsa Kavirāja Gosvāmī, who has written *Śrī Caitanya-caritāmṛta*, will be the *mahā-guru* of all *sahajiyās*. If that is the case, there is no harm in being "*sahajiyā*." If all my *gurus* are "*sahajiyā*," I will also want to be "*sahajiyā*." Actually, those who criticize may claim to be in the line of Mahāprabhu, but they are not in the line of our *guru-paramparā*, of Rūpa-Raghunātha, or of Svarūpa Dāmodara. Others may say whatever they like, but we will remain very securely in the line of Svarūpa Dāmodara. We follow Śrīla Bhaktivedānta Swāmī Mahārāja, and we follow his translations:

> "Your master is so expert at everything. Why does He do such things? Please bring your master before the goddess of fortune." In this way, all the maidservants of the goddess of fortune arrested the servants of Jagannātha, bound them around the waist, and brought them before the goddess of fortune. When all the maidservants brought Lord Jagannātha's servants before the lotus feet of the goddess of fortune, the Lord's servants were fined and forced to submit. All the maidservants began to beat the *ratha* with sticks, and they treated the servants of Lord Jagannātha almost like thieves. (*Śrī Caitanya-caritāmṛta* (*Madhya-līlā* 14.208–11))

Here, Jagannātha's servants were the associates of Mahāprabhu, and those who were with Lakṣmī-devī were also the servants of Jagannātha.

saba bhṛtya-gana kahe – yoḍa kari' hāta
'kāli āni diba tomāra āge jagannātha'

Śrī Caitanya-caritāmṛta (*Madhya-līlā* 14.212)

Finally all of Lord Jagannātha's servants submitted to the goddess of fortune with folded hands, assuring her that they would bring Lord Jagannātha before her the very next day.

Jagannātha's servants made this promise, and then Lakṣmī fined and punished them and returned to her abode. Now Śrīvāsa Paṇḍita asked Svarūpa Dāmodara the following question: "Do you know that all the *gopas* and *gopīs* in Vṛndāvana are very poor? They have no golden ornaments. They only milk cows and make butter, ghee, and similar things, and then they use it all themselves. Vṛndāvana is not like Mathurā and Dvārakā; there are no palaces there, and the residents have only carts and *kuñjas*. All the garlands there are made of flowers, whereas the garlands in Dvārakā are made of pearls, diamonds, and other jewels. So why does Kṛṣṇa go to Vṛndāvana?"

Kṛṣṇa goes to Vṛndāvana because the natural love and affection there is not found in Dvārakā, or anywhere else. In Dvārakā, love and affection is controlled by rules and regulations, just as the Vedas control by rules and regulations. In Vṛndāvana there is no control, for the *gopīs* serve Kṛṣṇa by their *parakīya* mood. This is possible only in Vṛndāvana, not in Mathurā and Dvārakā.

svarūpa kahe, – śrīvāsa, śuna sāvadhāne
vṛndāvana-sampad tomāra nāhi paḍe mane?

Śrī Caitanya-caritāmṛta (*Madhya-līlā* 14.218)

Svarūpa Dāmodara then retorted, "My dear Śrīvāsa, please hear me with attention. You have forgotten the transcendental opulence of Vṛndāvana."

vṛndāvane sāhajika ye sampat-sindhu
dvārakā-vaikuṇṭha-sampat – tāra eka bindu

Śrī Caitanya-caritāmṛta (*Madhya-līlā* 14.219)

"The natural opulence of Vṛndāvana is just like an ocean. The opulence of Dvārakā and Vaikuntha is not even to be compared to a drop."

One flower of Vṛndāvana can give millions of diamonds and other opulences, though Kṛṣṇa's associates do not want that. They only make garlands for decoration, and their ankle bells are made of desire stones (*cintāmaṇi*) although they have no need of them. They only use them when they are dancing.

Suppose you are very wealthy and have many millions of dollars, but you are not getting any love and affection; and suppose that somewhere else there is no wealth, but there is love and affection. Where would you prefer to be? As long as there is love and affection, there is no loss in being poor. Similarly, there is no deficiency in Vṛndāvana because there is only love and affection. Vṛndāvana is the place of the most elevated love and affection.

Kṛṣṇa is the Supreme Personality, and therefore He wants to taste supreme love and affection. He is not satisfied with any second-class love. Svarūpa Dāmodara was explaining this, and Mahāprabhu responded, "More, more! I want to hear more!" The topics presented at the Herā-pañcamī Festival are all very secret topics from *Ujjvala-nīlamaṇi*. Mahāprabhu questioned, and Svarūpa Dāmodara replied with many *ślokas* regarding all the moods of *madhyā*, *pragalbhā*, *dhīrā*, *adhīrā*, *mugdhā*,[7] and so on. Try to be at least in *madhyama-adhikāra*, and then try to understand all these topics. This is the aim and object of everyone in Caitanya Mahāprabhu's line.

[7] Please refer to the Glossary for an explanation of these terms.

Why Kṛṣṇa did not take Lakṣmī

For advanced devotees, who are conversant with the truths concerning this *līlā*, the Herā-pañcamī Festival is superior even to that of Jagannātha's riding to Sundarācala. Such devotees know why Caitanya Mahāprabhu descended to this world. If you are not reading and hearing the Tenth Canto of *Śrīmad-Bhāgavatam*, you can never know why He came, and you will be cheated. Try to hear *Śrīmad-Bhāgavatam* from elevated Vaiṣṇavas, and do not listen to those who say, "Oh, we should not read the Tenth Canto of *Śrīmad-Bhāgavatam.*"

Actually, there are three reasons one may say this. The first is that one has no knowledge, and the second is that one is following the order of the good devotees who know everything. These devotees are actually telling us, "You should begin from the First Canto, proceed to the Ninth Canto, and then you can finally come to the Tenth Canto." The third reason is to create an interest. For example, one may close his fist and ask, "What is in my hand? Can you tell what is in my hand?" If someone else hears this, he may become curious to know. Similarly, if anyone says, "Don't read the Tenth Canto of *Śrīmad-Bhāgavatam*," an aspiring devotee will automatically become curious and ask, "What is there? I should know."

In my village there was a devotee who used to bathe in the Gaṅgā every day. If anyone said to him, "Rāma! Rāma!" he would appear very furious and hold his stick up as though he wanted to beat that person. The boys of all the nearby villages used to come to him and say, "Rāma! Rāma!" and he used to run after them. Why did he do this? It was just to enthuse them to say, "Rāma! Rāma!" It was like a game. Similarly, if anyone tells you not to read *Śrīmad-Bhāgavatam*, you should be curious to know, "What is inside? There must be some jewel there."

If you do not read and hear the Tenth Canto, you will never be able to decide the aim and object of your life and devotion. For example, if you hear about Mother Yaśodā, a greed for motherly love may arise. You may begin to think about how she loves Kṛṣṇa, the Supreme Personality of Godhead, and how she bound Him with her love and affection. A greed for friendship may arise when you hear that the cowherd boys sometimes play with Kṛṣṇa, and when you hear that Kṛṣṇa is their life and soul, and that they cannot remain alive unless they are playing with Kṛṣṇa; they will die. If Kṛṣṇa hides behind a tree for a moment, all the cowherd boys wonder anxiously, "Where is Kṛṣṇa? Where is Kṛṣṇa?" And, if you hear the most elevated topic in *Śrīmad-Bhāgavatam*, the service of the *gopīs* to Kṛṣṇa – and especially what is told in *Gopī-gīta*, *Veṇu-gīta*, *Bhramara-gīta*, and other such chapters – you may develop a greed for this service. This is the aim and objective of the most exalted and pure devotees, and it is not possible to develop greed without reading and knowing *Śrīmad-Bhāgavatam*.

The first nine cantos create a platform for the Tenth Canto by removing all your unwanted desires, offenses, and worldly requirements and attachments. After that you should read the Tenth Canto, then you should decide how to attain the goal of life, and then you should read the Eleventh Canto.

An even easier process is to follow the essence of *Śrīmad-Bhāgavatam*, and that essence is *Śrī Caitanya-caritāmṛta*. You will have to read *Caitanya-caritāmṛta* and the books of Rūpa Gosvāmī, Sanātana Gosvāmī, Jīva Gosvāmī, Raghunātha dāsa Gosvāmī, Kṛṣṇadāsa Kavirāja Gosvāmī, Narottama dāsa Ṭhākura, Viśvanātha Cakravartī Ṭhākura, and Śrīla Bhaktivinoda Ṭhākura. In particular, Narottama dāsa Ṭhākura and Bhaktivinoda Ṭhākura have explained the essence of *Caitanya-caritāmṛta* in language that can be understood easily. If you want to be pure and high-class devotees, you must know all the truths presented in their literature.

Book distribution will not suffice by itself, and neither will *nagara-saṅkīrtana*. Why did Śrī Caitanya Mahāprabhu bring *nagara-saṅkīrtana* to this world? You will have to know the real reason. He did so only to give *gopī-prema*. And why did our *ācāryas* bring the process of book distribution? It is so that you will discover the nectar in those books. You must first read the books yourself, have faith and realize something, and then your life will be successful. Śrīla Bhaktivedānta Swāmī Mahārāja has written about all these truths in his books, and he himself has said that book distribution alone will not do; you will have to go deep and realize the nectar within. He has produced the *Kṛṣṇa* book, which is a summary of the Tenth Canto of *Śrīmad-Bhāgavatam*, and everything is there, completely. There he has instructed us to learn about the *gopīs'* pure service to Kṛṣṇa.

You should know all these facts; otherwise you will always be lusty. You must read the Tenth Canto in order to avoid lust. Śrīla Swāmī Mahārāja has vividly clarified this point in his books, and I have quoted many of his statements in this regard. You should have strong faith in this. Once he wrote a letter to a disciple who was very lusty. The disciple had asked, "I am very lusty. What should I do?" He replied, "You should read the Tenth Canto of *Śrīmad-Bhāgavatam*, especially the chapters describing the *rāsa-līlā*. Then this lust will go, and real transcendental lust for Kṛṣṇa will come." Actually, that transcendental lust is not lust; it is *prema*. Unless you read and hear, you cannot realize all these truths.

Now we are coming again to our subject: Herā-pañcamī. Jagannātha was not alone when He departed on His chariot. He was with Subhadrā and Baladeva. But why did Lakṣmī become furious? Jagannātha had become indifferent to her and was meeting with others. She felt neglected and became angry over this.

You should know the significance of these three places: Jagannātha Purī, Vṛndāvana, and Kurukṣetra. First you should know the significance of Jagannātha Purī. Kṛṣṇa is the son of Vasudeva and Devakī there. He never has a flute in His hand, He does not wear a peacock feather, and He cannot address Nanda Bābā as "Father" or Yaśodā-maiyā as "Mother." He will have to forget the *gopīs* while He is there. He can think about them in His heart, but He will not tell any of His queens, like Satyabhāmā, Rukmiṇī, and others, "I love the *gopīs* more than you." He can never say this.

Jagannātha Purī is Dvārakā. All the Yādavas are there, and Kṛṣṇa sports with all His queens there. Do you know Vimalā-devī in the Jagannātha Temple? Rukmiṇī is like Vimalā-devī. Lakṣmī-devī is also there, and she represents all the queens, especially Rukmiṇī and Satyabhāmā. There are no *gopīs* in the Jagannātha Temple or Jagannātha Purī. They can never be there, and that is why it is Dvārakā Purī.

What is Kurukṣetra? Kṛṣṇa has come from Dvārakā to Kurukṣetra, and therefore it is part of His *dvārakā-līlā*. There is a speciality there, though, in that Nanda Bābā, Yaśodā-maiyā, all the *gopīs* like Rādhā, Lalitā, Viśākhā, and most of the other Vrajavāsīs went there to meet with Kṛṣṇa. Still, there is immense opulence there, whereas in Vṛndāvana the *gopīs* freely play with Kṛṣṇa.

Lakṣmī-devī thinks, "There is so much opulence here. Why should Dvārakādhīśa-Kṛṣṇa go to any impoverished place?" Kṛṣṇa never told her, "I am going to Vṛndāvana." He cheated Her by saying, "I have caught a cold. Now I want to go somewhere to get some fresh air. I want to go to a forest, to get a breath of fresh air and feel rejuvenated." He played a trick so that Lakṣmī would not think He was going to run off to Vṛndāvana. To cheat Her, He took along His brother Baladeva Prabhu and His sister Subhadrā. He was thinking, "Yaśodā-maiyā knows them, and Rohiṇī also knows them. I will leave them with Yaśodā-maiyā and then I will stealthily go to Rādhā-kuṇḍa, Śyāma-kuṇḍa, and Girirāja-Govardhana, where all the beautiful *kuñjas* are situated. I will play with all the *gopīs* there. Baladeva Prabhu and Subhadrā will take their meals with Mother Yaśodā and be very happy there, and I will go and play. No one will know." He did not tell anyone where He was going, and He ran at once to Vṛndāvana – Sundarācala. Mahāprabhu's mood has revealed that the Guṇḍicā Mandira in Sundarācala is Vṛndāvana. Before Mahāprabhu, no one knew all these high truths, but now everyone can know.

kṛṣṇo 'nyo yadu-sambhūto
yaḥ pūrṇaḥ so 'sty ataḥ paraḥ
vṛndāvanaṁ parityajya
sa kvacin naiva gacchati

Śrī Caitanya-caritāmṛta (*Antya-līlā* 1.67)

The Kṛṣṇa known as Yadu-kumāra is Vāsudeva-Kṛṣṇa. He is different from the Kṛṣṇa who is the son of Nanda Mahārāja. Yadu-kumāra Kṛṣṇa manifests His pastimes in the cities of Mathurā and Dvārakā, but Kṛṣṇa the son of Nanda Mahārāja never at any time leaves Vṛndāvana.

vṛndāvanaṁ parityajya padam ekaṁ na gacchati

Kṛṣṇa never goes even a step from Vṛndāvana.

It is because of Rādhikā that Kṛṣṇa never leaves Vṛndāvana. He stays there only for Her, and both of Them do not go anywhere else. Then who went to Kurukṣetra? Rādhikā will never go there. It was Saṁyoginī-Rādhikā, who is Vṛṣabhānu-nandinī Rādhikā's manifestation, and not directly Rādhikā Herself, who went to Kurukṣetra. Vṛṣabhānu-nandinī Rādhikā will always remain at Rādhā-kuṇḍa and Śyāma-kuṇḍa in Vṛndāvana. If Rādhā and Kṛṣṇa are always together in Vṛndāvana, why does Rādhikā feel so much separation from Kṛṣṇa, and why does She always weep for Him? Sometimes She becomes so absorbed in love and affection in separation from Kṛṣṇa that even when She sees a *tamāla* tree, She thinks, "O Kṛṣṇa! O Kṛṣṇa! Oh, now You are here." She quarrels with "Him," becomes angry with Him, and sometimes She embraces that *tamāla* tree as if it were Him. How can there be a separation mood there in Vṛndāvana?

There is no actual separation in Vṛndāvana, but there is some separation mood. In Vṛndāvana there is the *rāsa-līlā*, and Prema-sarovara as well, and Rādhā and Kṛṣṇa feel great ecstasy in meeting there. Who experiences the separation mood in Nandagaon? Who met with Uddhava? To whom did Uddhava offer his prayers?

vande nanda-vraja-strīṇāṁ
pāda-reṇum abhīkṣṇaśaḥ
yāsāṁ hari-kathodgītaṁ
punāti bhuvana-trayam

Śrīmad-Bhāgavatam (10.47.63)

[Uddhava prayed:] I forever pray to the dust of the lotus feet of the *gopīs* in Nandagaon. The *hari-kathā* emanating from their lotus mouths in their separation mood purifies the entire universe.

āsām aho caraṇa-reṇu-juṣām ahaṁ syāṁ
vṛndāvane kim api gulma-latauṣadhīnām
yā dustyajaṁ sva-janam ārya-pathaṁ ca hitvā
bhejur mukunda-padavīṁ śrutibhir vimṛgyām

Śrīmad-Bhāgavatam (10.47.61)

> The *gopīs* of Vṛndāvana have given up the association of their husbands, sons, and other family members, who are very difficult to give up, and they have forsaken the path of chastity to take shelter of the lotus feet of Mukunda, Kṛṣṇa, which one should search for by Vedic knowledge. Oh, let me be fortunate enough to be one of the bushes, creepers, or herbs in Vṛndāvana, because the *gopīs* trample them and bless them with the dust of their lotus feet.

In Nandagaon, Rādhikā is Viyoginī-Rādhikā, another manifestation of Vṛṣabhānu-nandinī Rādhikā. Vṛṣabhānu-nandinī Rādhikā has practically no separation mood at all, for She and Kṛṣṇa always meet together and embrace. Her manifestation, Viyoginī-Rādhikā, is present in Nandagaon, and She appears as Saṁyoginī in Kurukṣetra. You cannot deeply understand these truths without being constantly in the association of pure Vaiṣṇavas.

At the Ratha-yātrā Festival, Mahāprabhu experiences the moods of Saṁyoginī-Rādhikā in Kurukṣetra, not those of Vṛṣabhānu-nandinī. Vṛṣabhānu-nandinī Rādhikā will never leave Vṛndāvana and go to Mathurā or Dvārakā, even if Kṛṣṇa weeps bitterly for Her there. Viyoginī-Rādhikā will also not give up Vṛndāvana to go to Kurukṣetra; only Saṁyoginī-Rādhikā will go there. So at the Ratha-yātrā Festival, Mahāprabhu is absorbed in the mood of Saṁyoginī-Rādhikā, pulling Kṛṣṇa on the chariot from the Jagannātha Temple – that is, from Dvārakā Purī – to Vṛndāvana. What can I say more than this? No one can say anything more.

Lakṣmī came with her associates, riding on a golden palanquin and profusely decorated with golden ornaments. She arrived at the Siṁha-dvāra along with musicians beating drums, and dancing girls who were Jagannātha's *devā-dāsīs.* Caitanya Mahāprabhu was sitting very comfortably there, and He listened to the dialogue that ensued.

Why did Kṛṣṇa not take Lakṣmī-devī to Vṛndāvana? She could not go, because she was not qualified. Even Satyabhāmā and Rukmiṇī were not qualified to go to Vṛndāvana, and that is why they never went. One may ask, "What harm would there be if Rādhikā and all the *gopīs* went to Dvārakā?" There would be so much harm; they would not be satisfied there. They would see Rukmiṇī, Satyabhāmā, and all Kṛṣṇa's queens with Him, and He would not be able to leave their company. Sometimes Kṛṣṇa's sons would come to sit on His lap, and Śrīmatī Rādhikā would not be able to do anything about it. So She will never go there – never.

If Rādhikā does not go to Dvārakā, how can Lakṣmī go to Vṛndāvana? She cannot go. After she performed austerities in Baelvana for thousands and thousands of years, Kṛṣṇa came and asked her, "Why are you doing this?" She replied, "I desire a benediction from You. I want to join the *rāsa-līlā.*" Kṛṣṇa said, "That is absurd – you cannot." "Why not?" she asked. "I'll tell you why," Kṛṣṇa replied. "After this birth, you will have to take birth in the womb of a *gopī* in Vṛndāvana, and then you will have to marry a *gopa.* After that you will have to associate with *nitya-siddha-gopīs,* and only then you can join the *rāsa-līlā,* when you are sufficiently purified." Even a *gopī* who has come from the womb of a *gopī* is unqualified if she has any children by her husband. None of the *gopīs* in the *rāsa-līlā* have had any children, and they have nothing to do with their husbands.

Kṛṣṇa continued, "So how can you go? You will have to give up your *brāhmaṇī* body and your chastity to Nārāyaṇa. You will have to cheat your *gopa* husband and absorb yourself in *parakīya-bhāva.* Then, in the form of a *gopī,* you can join the *rāsa-līlā.*" Lakṣmī objected, "How can I give up my husband Nārāyaṇa? I cannot give Him up, I cannot give up my chastity, and I cannot marry a *gopa.*" Then Kṛṣṇa said, "Then wait, wait.

You will obtain this boon from Me when you are able to do all these things." Even now Lakṣmī is performing austerities, but she is still not qualified.

You may want this *gopī-prema*, but it is so very high. Caitanya Mahāprabhu was very merciful, and He descended to the material world to give it. It is very precious – more so than anything. It is very difficult to attain even for Nārada, Lakṣmī, Śaṅkara, and all the other great personalities, so what to speak of lesser personalities? However, if someone has pure greed to serve Rādhā-Kṛṣṇa Yugala, and to serve in the *rāsa-līlā*, he is very fortunate.

Let us say someone has become greedy for a *rasagullā*, and there is no money in his pocket. Then by grabbing it, stealing it, or by any means he will get it. In the same way, if you have that kind of high-class greed for *gopī-prema*, an opportunity will come to attain it. Where there is a will, there is a way; the way must come.

Kṛṣṇa Himself gave the way in His form as Caitanya Mahāprabhu. He also sent His devotees like Svarūpa Dāmodara, Rāya Rāmānanda, Rūpa Gosvāmī, Raghunātha dāsa Gosvāmī, Kṛṣṇadāsa Kavirāja Gosvāmī, Śrīla Bhaktivinoda Ṭhākura, Śrīla Prabhupāda, our *gurudeva*, and Śrīla Bhaktivedānta Swāmī Mahārāja. I have also come, and I want to give you a little greed for this *gopī-prema*, which is the aim and object of our lives. I have not come to give *vaidhī-bhakti*, because so many people coming from India are giving that. They will tell you to serve Jagannātha, Baladeva, and Subhadrā, and they will tell you not to read the Tenth Canto of *Śrīmad-Bhāgavatam*. I have not come for this. I have come in the line of Śrīla Rūpa Gosvāmī, and in the line of Śrīla Prabhupāda, my *gurudeva*, and my *śikṣā-guru*, Śrīla Swāmī Mahārāja.

A person will not hear if he has no greed for the goal of life. He is sleeping now, and he will continue to sleep. If he has no greed or interest, he must sleep like the camels, dogs, hogs, pigs, and especially like the donkeys. I have only come for those who have some taste and greed for this, and I have come to give this greed to those who want it, so that they can advance in the line of Mahāprabhu.

When Śrīvāsa Paṇḍita heard these topics from Śrī Svarūpa Dāmodara, he began to laugh very loudly, "Hee, hee! Ho, ho!" Caitanya Mahāprabhu was deeply absorbed in the moods of the festival, and He watched silently as Śrīvāsa Paṇḍita continued to laugh and tell Svarūpa Dāmodara, "You don't know anything. Don't you see the opulence of my *ārādhya-devī* (worshipable deity) Lakṣmī-devī? She is decorated with golden ornaments, and she sits on a golden palanquin like a commander-in-chief with all her associates. But in Vṛndāvana, there is nothing. The *gopīs* there can make some garlands, but only from flowers; there is no abundance of diamonds or gold – nothing of the kind. There are no golden palanquins. There are only bullock-carts made of wood and bamboo. There is nothing there; only flowers. There are some cows there, giving milk, and there is forest. Kṛṣṇa can only graze His cows there. He has no throne to sit on, and He doesn't even have shoes or an umbrella. He goes cowherding barefoot, and if He doesn't do this, His father may chastise Him."

Śrīvāsa Paṇḍita continued:

vṛndāvana dekhibāre gelā jagannātha
śuni' lakṣmī-devīra mane haila āsoyātha

Śrī Caitanya-caritāmṛta (*Madhya-līlā* 14.205)

When Jagannātha decided to see Vṛndāvana, He went there, and upon hearing this, the goddess of fortune experienced restlessness and jealousy.

Lakṣmī, who represents Satyabhāmā and the other queens, thought angrily, "Here in Dvārakā, my husband is always sitting on a golden throne, and He has so many military commanders-in-chief, and so many beautiful queens, and each queen has ten sons and a daughter. Why did Kṛṣṇa go to Vṛndāvana?"

I have seen something like this in my boyhood. My mother would give me a slap if she was giving me something sweet and I wanted something else instead. So Lakṣmī was very unhappy and angry, and she tried to attack her husband to force Him to come under her control. She wanted to defeat Him and bring Him back to Dvārakā by quarreling and attacking Him.

Mahāprabhu smiled somewhat and said, "Oh, Śrīvāsa Paṇḍita has the nature of Nārada. He always glorifies Lakṣmī and Nārāyaṇa, and Dvārakādhīśa. Svarūpa Dāmodara is a pure Vrajavāsī, and that is why he glorifies the *gopīs*. Śrīvāsa cannot do so."

Almost everyone in this world and universe glorifies Lakṣmī. Very, very few and rare people glorify the *gopīs* and Kṛṣṇa. This is true even in India. There are some groups that put forward the view that *Śrīmad-Bhāgavatam* is not authentic evidence. They say that someone other than Vyāsadeva compiled it; so it is bogus, and therefore the love and affection of the *gopīs* is also bogus. There are many who reject all these topics, and only high-class devotees have a taste for them.

Svarūpa Dāmodara then said, "O Śrīvāsa, don't you remember that the trees in Vṛndāvana are *kalpa-vṛkṣa* (desire trees)? They can give millions of tons of gold, and everything else. Anyone can have whatever he desires from those trees, but the *gopīs* have no personal desires. They simply decorate their hair with the flowers of those trees.

"The ankle-bells of the *gopīs* are made of *cintāmaṇi*, but the *gopīs* never use them for fulfilling their desires; they only wear them to make sweet sounds while they dance with Kṛṣṇa. The cows are *kāma-dhenu*. What does that mean? They not only give milk, but they give the "milk" of the fulfillment of all desires. They can give anything a person wants, but the *gopas* and *gopīs* don't want anything from them. They only want milk and butter. You don't know all these truths because you have not gone to Vṛndāvana. You don't know even the A-B-C's of Vṛndāvana. The flowers there are more valuable than the *pārijāta* flowers of the heavenly planets. They are always fragrant, and they never become stale. They can give anything, but you don't remember this."

He then quoted *Brahma-saṁhitā* (5.56): "*śrīyaḥ kāntā-kāntaḥ parama-puruṣaḥ* – in the spiritual world, all the female lovers are goddesses of fortune and the male lover is the Supreme Personality." After Śrīvāsa Ṭhākura heard all this from Svarūpa Dāmodara, his mood changed. He entered the mood of Madhumaṅgala,[8] Kṛṣṇa's intimate *sakhā* in Vraja, and then he began to dance, remembering the glories of Vraja.

After Mahāprabhu heard Svarūpa Dāmodara's *kathā*, He went to a flower garden and along with the devotees took rest there. Then, after He awoke and bathed, He began singing and dancing with His devotees, absorbed in *kṛṣṇa-prema*. Then, when they had performed *kīrtana* throughout the day, Svarūpa Dāmodara tricked Mahāprabhu by telling Him, "Now we are all tired, so please stop Your dancing. Jagannātha-deva has sent very beautiful and sweet *prasāda*, like rice, dahl, *purī*, *kacaurī*, *chenā* (curd), *paida* (coconut), *pāna* (fruit juice), *sara-purī* (a kind of *purī* made with cream), and many other varieties of preparations." Mahāprabhu began to distribute the *prasāda* Himself, but Svarūpa Dāmodara said, "Everyone is waiting for You. No one

[8] Śrīvāsa Paṇḍita is Nārada Muni, and Nārada Muni is a partial manifestation of Madhumaṅgala in Vraja.

will take *prasāda* if You don't take." Then Mahāprabhu sat down and began to taste the *prasāda*, and everyone called out, "Hari bol!"

You can read this discussion between Śrīvāsa Paṇḍita and Svarūpa Dāmodara in its entirety in *Śrī Caitanya-caritāmṛta* [*Madhya-līlā*, Chapter 14].

CHAPTER EIGHT

THE THIRD HISTORY

We have discussed many topics regarding the Festival of the Chariots, and about the deities of Jagannātha, Baladeva, and Subhadrā, but I do not think that we have touched even a small fraction of their glory. Even if Anantadeva would come with his thousands and thousands of hoods to glorify Lord Jagannātha, and Jagannātha Himself appeared before him, Anantadeva would still not be able to glorify Him properly.

We have already related two histories explaining Jagannātha's appearance, and there is one more, a third history, which came from the heart of a very advanced devotee. This history has extraordinarily deep and secret *rasa*, transcendental flavor. I used to relate it in Mathurā and Vṛndāvana, and in Jagannātha Purī as well. When I told it, everyone listened silently, and they were moved, for they had never heard such secrets before. They wondered, "Where has he discovered this?"

A few years later I saw a magazine article by Śrīla Gour Govinda Mahārāja, a prominent disciple of Śrīla Bhaktivedānta Swāmī Mahārāja. As I began to read it, I thought, "Oh, he has written the same thing here with a few small changes. How has he taken this from my heart?" I became happy and thought, "This person, Gour Govinda Mahārāja, is one of the rare people in this world who are genuinely in the line of Caitanya Mahāprabhu and the Gosvāmīs. Only a real devotee can know all these truths."

A few years ago, while I was translating some books in Jagannātha Purī, Gour Govinda Mahārāja came with only one disciple to meet me. He heard my *hari-kathā* very patiently, and he was charmed. We became friends, and he told me, "I saw you in Vṛndāvana at the time of Śrīla Prabhupāda's disappearance, when you placed him in *samādhi*. I was there, but at that time I was quite insignificant. You moved me very much, and I wanted to meet you and hear your classes, but I could not do so at that time. Now I have come."

He continued, "There are some problems. I cannot speak the glories of Caitanya Mahāprabhu and Rādhā-Kṛṣṇa. I am controlled by some people who don't want to hear them. They are creating problems, and even stopping me from going to Australia, Germany, and other countries. I cannot open my heart and tell these glories," and he began to weep. I embraced him and said, "Don't worry – be strong like me. If problems come, jump over them like a lion. Be like Śrīla Bhaktivedānta Swāmī Mahārāja and my *gurudeva*." I consoled him so much, and then he went away. The next year he went to Māyāpura, and there he departed from this world while relating this very history. Many of his disciples came to me weeping, and I told them, "I will help you. Don't worry." His ideas were very similar to my own, and this story is therefore also related to him.

What I explained there in Jagannātha Purī and during our grand Navadvīpa Chariot Festival has also been published in our monthly magazine, *Bhāgavata Patrikā*. I also searched for the scripture in which this pastime was originally written, but no one could tell me where it was. I asked many learned *paṇḍās* in

Jagannātha Purī, and they could only tell me, "We've read it, and we'll have to search for the original book," but they could not produce it.

Kṛṣṇa returns to Vṛndāvana

All the Vrajavāsīs feel great separation when Kṛṣṇa goes to Mathurā and Dvārakā, especially Mother Yaśodā and Nanda Bābā, and above all, Kṛṣṇa's beloved *gopīs*. Sometimes they faint and lose consciousness, appearing as if dead, and one may even think, "Oh, they have died!" Kṛṣṇa also feels separation from the *gopīs*, and especially from Rādhikā. Sometimes He also loses external consciousness, and He remains in that state for many days.

As we hear and discuss these elevated topics, we feel proud and think, "My *gurudeva* and I are in the line of Śrīla Rūpa Gosvāmī as *rūpānuga* Vaiṣṇavas." The senior devotees are especially aware that our *guru-varga*, the *gurus* in our disciplic succession, are all *rūpānuga* Vaiṣṇavas. We should therefore understand Śrīla Rūpa Gosvāmī's mood at this Festival of the Chariots.

As discussed previously, Śrī Caitanya Mahāprabhu was reciting a verse of *Sāhitya-darpaṇa* over and over again, even though it was originally written in the base mood of mundane lovers and is thus against moral etiquette:

yaḥ kaumāra-haraḥ sa eva hi varas tā eva caitra-kṣapās
te conmīlita-mālatī-surabhayaḥ prauḍhāḥ kadambānilāḥ
sā caivāsmi tathāpi tatra surata-vyāpāra-līlā-vidhau
revā-rodhasi vetasī-taru-tale cetaḥ samutkaṇṭhate

Śrī Caitanya-caritāmṛta (*Antya-līlā* 1.78)

That very personality who stole my heart during my youth is now again my master. These are the same moonlit nights of the month of Caitra. The same fragrance of *mālatī* flowers is there, and the same sweet breezes are blowing from the *kadamba* forest. In our intimate relationship, I am also the same lover, yet still my mind is not happy here. I am eager to go back to that place on the bank of the Revā under the Vetasī tree. That is my desire.

One person, Svarūpa Dāmodara, understood Caitanya Mahāprabhu's inner meaning, and there was a second person who did as well – a very young man who later became Śrīla Rūpa Gosvāmī. No one other than them understood Mahāprabhu's deep meaning. Mahāprabhu had empowered Rūpa Gosvāmī at Prayāga, and given him His full mercy, so that now he was able to write the meaning in his own *śloka*:

priyaḥ so 'yaṁ kṛṣṇaḥ sahacari kuru-kṣetra-militas
tathāhaṁ sā rādhā tad idam ubhayoḥ saṅgama-sukham
tathāpy antaḥ-khelan-madhura-muralī-pañcama-juṣe
mano me kālindī-pulina-vipināya spṛhayati

Śrī Caitanya-caritāmṛta (*Antya-līlā* 1.79)

Now I have met My very old and dear friend Kṛṣṇa on this field of Kurukṣetra. I am the same Rādhārāṇī, and now we are meeting together. It is very pleasant, but still I would like to go to the bank of the Yamunā beneath the trees of the forest there. I wish to hear the vibration of His sweet flute playing the fifth note within that forest of Vṛndāvana.

The verses from *Śrī Caitanya-caritāmṛta* (*Madhya-līlā* 13.126–31) that follow this one further explain its meaning:

avaśeṣe rādhā kṛṣṇe kare nivedana
sei tumi, sei āmi, sei nava saṅgama

[In the mood of Śrīmatī Rādhikā, Śrī Caitanya Mahāprabhu spoke thus to Lord Jagannātha:] You are the same Kṛṣṇa, and I am the same Rādhārāṇī. We are meeting again in the same way that we met in the beginning of our lives.

tathāpi āmāra mana hare vṛndāvana
vṛndāvane udaya karāo āpana-caraṇa

Although we are both the same, My mind is still attracted to Vṛndāvana-dhāma. I wish that You will please again appear with Your lotus feet in Vṛndāvana.

ihāṅ lokāraṇya, hātī, ghoḍā, ratha-dhvani
tāhāṅ puṣpāraṇya, bhṛṅga-pika-nāda śuni

In Kurukṣetra there are crowds of people, elephants, and horses, and also the rattling of chariots. But in Vṛndāvana there are flower gardens, and the humming of bees and chirping of birds can be heard.

ihāṅ rāja-veśa, saṅge saba kṣatriya-gaṇa
tāhāṅ gopa-veśa, saṅge muralī-vādana

Here at Kurukṣetra You are dressed like a royal prince, and You are accompanied by great warriors, but in Vṛndāvana You appeared just like an ordinary cowherd boy, accompanied only by Your beautiful flute.

vraje tomāra saṅge yei sukha-āsvādana
sei sukha-samudrera ihāṅ nāhi eka kaṇa

Here there is not even a drop of the ocean of transcendental happiness that I enjoyed with You in Vṛndāvana.

āmā lañā punaḥ līlā karaha vṛndāvane
tabe āmāra mano-vāñchā haya ta' pūraṇe

I therefore request You to come to Vṛndāvana and enjoy pastimes with Me. If You do so, My ambition will be fulfilled.

Śrīmatī Rādhikā is saying, "I am the same, My beloved Kṛṣṇa is the same, and we are meeting now after a long time; but I am not happy here. I want to be in Vṛndāvana, under the shade of the very fragrant *kadamba* trees, where the Yamunā is flowing. We were not married at that time, and we met freely there without any messenger. Our love increased simply by our glancing at each other, and that love reached an extreme height. Now we are meeting again, here in Kurukṣetra, but I am not satisfied. I want You to come to My heart, that is, Vṛndāvana. I want to meet You there again."

Śrīla Rūpa Gosvāmī has made the meaning clear in his *śloka*. If one remembers and follows these ideas, he is actually a *rūpānuga* Vaiṣṇava, and if not, he is outside the disciplic line. Those who forbid others to think about these things are not *rūpānuga* Vaiṣṇavas in the line of Rūpa Gosvāmī. Try to understand this. It is egoistic to think, "My *gurudeva*, Śrīla Bhaktivedānta Swāmī Prabhupāda, has not encouraged us to understand this." Your *gurudeva* has explained this thousands of times, but you have no eyes to see, or ears to hear. He was a *rūpānuga*, as were all our past *ācāryas*, down to Śrīla Bhaktisiddhānta Sarasvatī Ṭhākura and my *gurudeva*.

When my *gurudeva* remembered these topics, his complexion used to become reddish, yellowish, and whitish, and then he used to become faint. And when I would tell him these pastimes, he would weep continuously. All bona fide *gurus* are in one line, and if you are not in this line, you are derailed. Granted, we should not explain this subject matter to unqualified people, but if we do not explain it at all, then all these ideas will be gone – washed away from this world forever. Śrīla Kṛṣṇadāsa Kavirāja

Gosvāmī has replied to all doubts in this regard.[1] Try to realize this reply.

Śrīmad-Bhāgavatam (7.5.23) states:

śravaṇaṁ kīrtanaṁ viṣṇoḥ
smaraṇaṁ pāda-sevanam
arcanaṁ vandanaṁ dāsyaṁ
sakhyam ātma-nivedanam

Hearing and chanting about the transcendental holy name, form, qualities, paraphernalia, and pastimes of Lord Viṣṇu, remembering them, serving the lotus feet of the Lord, offering the Lord respectful worship with sixteen types of paraphernalia, offering prayers to the Lord, becoming His servant, considering the Lord one's best friend, and surrendering everything unto Him (in other words, serving Him with the body, mind, and words) – these nine processes are accepted as pure devotional service.

Those who tell us only the general or external meaning of this *śloka* should go to the Rāmānuja or Madhvācārya *sampradāyas*, for they only know general principles. We should add the mood of Śrī Caitanya Mahāprabhu to these principles. For example, in the first line of this *śloka*, "Viṣṇu" means Kṛṣṇa with Rādhikā and the *gopīs*. This is the understanding of those in the line of Śrīla Rūpa Gosvāmī. Try to understand this. If you never remember, realize, and explain this to those who are qualified, you are derailed from our *guru-paramparā*. You must come in the proper line.

[1] "All these conclusions are unfit to disclose in public. But if they are not disclosed, no one will understand them. Therefore I shall mention them, revealing only their essence, so that loving devotees will understand them but fools will not. Anyone who has captured Lord Caitanya Mahāprabhu and Lord Nityānanda Prabhu in his heart will become blissful by hearing all these transcendental conclusions." (*Śrī Caitanya-caritāmṛta* (*Ādi-līlā* 4.231–3))

Śrīmad-Bhāgavatam (10.33.39, 36) also states:

vikrīḍitaṁ vraja-vadhūbhir idaṁ ca viṣṇoḥ
śraddhānvito 'nuśṛṇuyād atha varṇayed yaḥ
bhaktiṁ parāṁ bhagavati pratilabhya kāmaṁ
hṛd-rogam āśv apahinoty acireṇa dhīraḥ

A sober person who faithfully hears or describes the Lord's playful affairs with the young *gopīs* of Vṛndāvana will attain the Lord's pure devotional service. Thus he will quickly conquer lust, the disease of the heart.

anugrahāya bhaktānāṁ
mānuṣaṁ deham āsthitaḥ
bhajate tādṛśīḥ krīḍā
yāḥ śrutvā tat-paro bhavet

When the Lord assumes a human-like body to show mercy to His devotees, He engages in such pastimes as will attract those who hear about them to become dedicated to Him.

Tat-paro bhavet means, "You must do this; otherwise you are derailed." You should not do *anukaraṇa*; that is, you should not imitate Kṛṣṇa's pastimes. However, those of you who are coming gradually to the stage of *madhyama-adhikāra* must try to hear these pastimes; otherwise you are derailed. It is essential to follow the statements of Śrī Rūpa Gosvāmī at the Chariot Festival.

Don't be confused. Have no doubt at all. You can think in this way: "The whole world may criticize and be against me – I don't care. I care for my *gurudeva*, for Śrīla Rūpa Gosvāmī, and for our *ācārya-varga*." Kṛṣṇa has given you good intelligence. Use your own intelligence and don't run after others'. Try to judge, and see, and read the authorized *śāstras*. If you say, "We are *rūpānuga-varga*," you must follow Rūpa Gosvāmī, not conceal him. Use your intelligence and see for yourself, and then you will realize what is correct and what is incorrect. If I conceal my father's name, is it right? Is it correct to conceal the name of my father?

You can read the translation of this *śloka*, and after that you can read the explanation of Śrīla Bhaktivedānta Swāmī Mahārāja[2] and especially that of Śrīla Viśvanātha Cakravartī Ṭhākura.[2]

Now I am coming again to the point – the third history. When the *gopīs* became unconscious because of being absorbed in feelings of separation from Kṛṣṇa, He also became unconscious in Dvārakā, thinking, "Rādhikā, Rādhikā!" This had become a very big problem, and Nārada, Uddhava, Baladeva Prabhu, and others began discussing how to bring Him back to consciousness. At first, they suggested that Nārada should play on his *vīṇā* and glorify Vraja, Mother Yaśodā, the *gopīs*, and all other Vrajavāsīs, but Nārada objected: "Do you know what will happen when Kṛṣṇa awakens? He will go to Vṛndāvana at once, and no one will be able to stop Him. He will stay there with the *gopīs* and never return. You should consider this when you are deciding what to do."

Now they were in a dilemma. They thought again, and decided, "Uddhava should go to Vraja and tell Mother Yaśodā, Nanda Mahārāja, and the *gopas* and *gopīs* that Kṛṣṇa is coming. He will tell them, 'Now you can welcome Him.' No one can know what state the Vrajavāsīs are in now. Some are even lying here and there unconscious. When they hear that Kṛṣṇa is coming, they will return to consciousness and make arrangements to welcome Him. Then Uddhava will somehow bring Kṛṣṇa to Dvārakā again by a trick. There will be no problem. Uddhava must go there. Kṛṣṇa sent him previously, and therefore he should go now and tell them that Kṛṣṇa is coming."

Uddhava was very unhappy when he heard this proposal.

[2] These can be found in the Appendix.

"Listen to me," he told them. "If I go to Vṛndāvana and say that Kṛṣṇa is coming, they will not believe me because I bluffed them before. I told them, 'I am going, and very soon I will bring Kṛṣṇa here. I will definitely bring Him.' After that I requested Kṛṣṇa many times, but He gave all kinds of excuses, so what could I do? It's useless for me to go, because they will not believe me. They will say, 'Oh, the liar has come. The cheater has come!' Especially Mother Yaśodā will say this."

Nārada Muni said, "Then Baladeva Prabhu can go. He can pacify all the *gopīs* and *gopas.*" But Baladeva Prabhu replied in the same way: "I told Kṛṣṇa so many times to go there, and He always answered, 'Yes, I will go,' but He never went. Finally I went alone and I pacified them by saying, 'I promise that I will go to Dvārakā and bring Kṛṣṇa.'

"I don't know why this cruel Kṛṣṇa never wants to go there. He used to be very soft and sweet, but now His heart has turned to stone. What can I say? If I go, the Vrajavāsīs will also say about me, 'Oh, this cheater and liar has come!' There is no use in my going because they will not believe me, either. They cannot be consoled without Kṛṣṇa's direct presence. Kṛṣṇa should go Himself."

While they were discussing what to do, Kṛṣṇa's sister Subhadrā came in and heard everything. "Don't worry," she said, "I'm going. I will go to Vṛndāvana and take *darśana* of Mother Yaśodā. First I will sit on her lap, and then I will caress her and tell her, 'Mother, Kṛṣṇa is coming. He was traveling with me, but on the way many kings surrounded Him and began performing *arcana* to Him, praying to Him, and offering Him many presentations. That is why I have arrived here first. Kṛṣṇa will be a bit late, but He's on His way. It may be some hours, or one or two days, but He is coming.' I will go door-to-door to the *gopīs'* homes. I will console them and tell them, 'Oh, now be happy.

Don't feel separation. Kṛṣṇa is coming!' They will become happy, and then I will tell them, 'You should all be ready to welcome Kṛṣṇa.' Later, I will play a trick and tell My brother, 'Oh, You are sitting here, while Your mother Devakī, Your father Vasudeva, and all Your queens are living there in Dvārakā?' I will bring Him back to Dvārakā by some trick, so don't worry. Let me first bring a good chariot. After that Nārada should sing the glory of Vraja accompanied by his *vīṇā*, then Kṛṣṇa will return to consciousness, and after that He will come to Vṛndāvana, where everything will be ready."

A chariot was brought and Subhadrā was ready to go. Then Baladeva said, "If my brother and sister are going, I must go. I want to meet with my mother and father, Yaśodā-maiyā and Nanda Bābā, and I want to meet all my friends and the *gopīs*. I cannot remain here. I must go." Subhadrā said, "Yes, we will go together. Baladeva Prabhu will go first, and I will follow Him." So another chariot was brought, and Baladeva's *ratha* was placed in front of Subhadrā's. As they were about to leave, Baladeva Prabhu told Dāruka, Kṛṣṇa's chariot driver, "Bring your chariot here and be ready. When Kṛṣṇa returns to consciousness, take the chariot and fly to Vṛndāvana."

Nārada Muni was then requested to glorify Vraja and, accompanied by his *vīṇā*, he began to sing very beautifully. As Nārada's sweet glorification of Vraja entered Kṛṣṇa's ears, He regained consciousness and thought, "It is morning, and I am in Vraja. Where is My sweet *vaṁśī*?" He asked. "Where, where? Oh, I know. The *gopīs* are very tricky. They have stolen it. I'll give them a good lesson." Then He stood in a beautiful threefold-bending form, as He had previously done in Vraja, and He appeared in a way that no one in Dvārakā had ever seen before.

As He began searching, He said, "Oh, Lalitā has taken it! If not Lalitā, then Rādhikā Herself has stolen it with Viśākhā's help." He acted as though He was searching them to see where they had kept His flute. In the meantime, He saw Uddhava and asked, "Uddhava, why are you in Vṛndāvana?" Then He saw Nārada and asked, "Oh, you are also in Vṛndāvana? From where have you come?" Nārada replied, "Oh my Lord, You are not in Vṛndāvana. You are in Dvārakā. This is not the Yamunā; it is the ocean in Dvārakā Purī. Please remember where You are."

Kṛṣṇa was so absorbed that He forgot Uddhava and Nārada and everyone else, and He was ready to run away to Vṛndāvana to quickly meet the *gopas* and *gopīs*. Uddhava told Him, "Prabhu, Your chariot is ready, because we knew that You would do this. You can mount Your chariot and go to Vṛndāvana immediately."

Kṛṣṇa wanted to ascend His chariot, but He was so mad in *rādhā-prema* that He could not walk alone. Many people began to assist Him as He walked by, holding Him and helping Him from the front and back, and from both sides. He was like a mad person, lost in Rādhā's love and affection. Somehow He was taken to the chariot and raised upon it, and Dāruka at once drove off with great speed toward Vṛndāvana. Balarāma and Subhadrā were ahead, and Kṛṣṇa followed behind.

In the meantime, in Vṛndāvana, Rādhikā was in the last stage of Her life, feeling unbearable separation. She was just about to die, not breathing in or out, and all the Vrajavāsīs were very worried, thinking, "She is going to leave Her body!" Everyone had lost hope that She would remain alive, and they were totally grief-stricken. They all thought, "We cannot save Her! She will certainly die!" Lalitā and Viśākhā were trying hard to revive Her, but there were no signs of revival.

While this was going on, all the other *sakhīs* also assembled there, and they were also extremely upset – and even Candrāvalī came to show her sympathy. Somehow Rādhikā said in a very low voice, "If I die, My dead body should be placed around a *tamāla* tree. Let the air in My body be mixed with the air of Nandagaon where Kṛṣṇa takes His breaths. Let the fire in My body mix with the sun-rays at Nanda Bābā's house so that it will shine there and I will touch Kṛṣṇa. May the earth of My body mix with the courtyard of Nanda-bhavana, so that Kṛṣṇa can walk on Me and I can touch Him." As She lamented in this way, She again became unconscious.

In the meantime, three chariots arrived in Vraja – Subhadrā's and Baladeva's in front, and Kṛṣṇa's following. As soon as Kṛṣṇa reached there, He heard, "Rādhikā is going to die, and She will not remain alive for even one more moment." He ran very quickly to the spot where She was giving up Her body, and when He saw Her, He began to cry bitterly. Becoming more and more absorbed in *rādhā-prema*, His hands began melting. The lower part of His body also melted, then His face as well; and only two large round eyes remained. Just then, Baladeva Prabhu and Subhadrā arrived, and when they saw this scene, they could not control themselves and they also became like Kṛṣṇa.

In the meantime, Lalitā spoke repeatedly in the ear of Rādhikā, "Rādhā, Rādhā! Kṛṣṇa has come. Kṛṣṇa has come to meet You! Don't die." Viśākhā said in the other ear, "Kṛṣṇa has come to meet You!" Gradually Rādhikā regained Her external consciousness, opened Her eyes, and thought, "Oh, beautiful Kṛṣṇa has come!" She became further absorbed in the ecstasy of love and affection. Seeing Her, Kṛṣṇa's love also increased, and He lost external consciousness. In that same state He began rolling on the earth.

Rādhikā told Viśākhā, "Please help Kṛṣṇa; otherwise He may die. You know the *mantra* to revive Him. Say in His ear, 'Rādhā, Rādhā!'" When Kṛṣṇa heard this sweet injection of the powerful *mantra* from the lips of Viśākhā, "Rādhā, Rādhā, Rādhā, Rādhā!" He opened His eyes and became so happy again. Gradually He revived, and They met together and everyone became happy.

Nārada also arrived, and he requested Kṛṣṇa, "Prabhu, please manifest these three forms that You revealed when You were absorbed and melted. In that way everyone will see and realize these truths about You. Please manifest these forms somewhere in this world." Kṛṣṇa replied, "*Tathā 'stu, tathā 'stu evam bhavatu*! So be it. I will always remain in this shape in Nilācala, which will be like Dvārakā, and everyone will be able to come and see Me there."

I have told this very beautiful pastime in brief. This *līlā* is in the hearts of pure devotees, and Śrīla Gour Govinda Mahārāja has also touched it. I have also reconciled some points to clarify any doubts or misunderstandings about this *līlā*.

You should know that there are four groups of *gopīs* in Vraja: *svapakṣā* (belonging to Rādhikā's own group), *vipakṣā* (belonging to the group of Her rivals), *taṭastha-pakṣā* (belonging to the group that is neutral to Her), and *suhṛt-pakṣā* (belonging to the group that is friendly to Her), and Kṛṣṇa's pastimes cannot take place without them. However, there are no parties when Kṛṣṇa disappears, or when He goes to Mathurā or Dvārakā and a separation mood manifests in the *gopīs'* hearts. At that time, all the parties become one for Kṛṣṇa, and they help each other. Candrāvalī, or Bhadrā, or any of the others may come and pacify Śrīmatī Rādhikā, because Her separation is the highest. They are very sympathetic towards Her, because their separation mood is not as high in comparison. They tell Her, "O Rādhikā, You should not weep. Kṛṣṇa will come." Even Candrāvalī, who has a deep separation mood of her own, will also come and speak like this.

The interactions here are very mysterious, and I want to give you realization and entrance into these very extraordinary pastimes, but you have to become qualified first. Try to follow regulated *bhakti* – *śravaṇaṁ kīrtanaṁ viṣṇoḥ smaraṇam* – otherwise you will not be able to maintain your spiritual life. You will become lusty, and after some time you will think that Kṛṣṇa's pastimes are the same as your pastimes of getting divorced. I have not read scriptures like *Govinda-līlāmṛta*, but I know that most of you have copies of all these books. Many of those who read these have fallen down, so you should not read them at this time, nor should you give classes on these topics. Be very, very careful. Our aim and object is to realize Kṛṣṇa's pastimes, but you cannot jump to this. If you want to be situated on a tree, you must first try to climb up from the root, and from there you can go to the highest places. If you try to jump, you will fall down.

I request you to read *Upadeśāmṛta*, *Manaḥ-śikṣā*, and books like them. Try to chant more. Chanting only sixteen rounds will not suffice. Your *gurudeva* has given sixteen and then one, sixteen and then one, sixteen and then one; there are four sets of sixteen.[3] Has he given this without a purpose? A man may be very expert in speaking *hari-kathā* and performing related services, but if he does not chant because he has no taste, he is a very weak devotee, and after some time he may fall down.

tan-nāma-rūpa-caritādi-sukīrtanānu-
smṛtyoḥ krameṇa rasanā-manasī niyojya
tiṣṭhan vraje tad-anurāgi-janānugāmī
kālaṁ nayed akhilam ity upadeśa-sāram

Upadeśāmṛta (8)

The essence of all advice is that one should utilize his full time – twenty-four hours a day – in nicely chanting and remembering the Lord's divine name, transcendental form, qualities, and eternal pastimes, thereby gradually engaging his tongue and mind. In this

[3] There are twenty counter beads attached to the bead-bag, and they are divided into two sections: sixteen and four. Whenever the devotee completes a set of sixteen rounds, he moves one of the four. This arrangement enables him to count sixty-four rounds.

way one should reside in Vraja and serve Kṛṣṇa under the guidance of devotees. One should follow in the footsteps of the Lord's beloved devotees, who are deeply attached to His devotional service.

Be in Vṛndāvana, under the guidance of a *rasika-tattvajña* Vaiṣṇava *guru*, and always chant the names with their meaning, knowing and remembering Śrī Rādhā-Kṛṣṇa's pastimes. Then you will become fully qualified for this highest object of life.

CHAPTER NINE

JUST AFTER THE FESTIVAL

Who is a Vaiṣṇava?

The first Chariot Festival has now been completed, and the chariot has returned to Nīlācala. On the return journey, Mahāprabhu and all His associates continued to think they were going to Vraja from Kurukṣetra, and they performed the same pastimes as on their journey to Guṇḍicā. Śrīla Kṛṣṇadāsa Kavirāja Gosvāmī explained that they did not think, "Kṛṣṇa is returning to Dvārakā." Even at the time of returning, they always maintained the idea, "We are taking Kṛṣṇa to Vṛndāvana."

One day, after the Chariot Festival was over, Nityānanda Prabhu sat with Mahāprabhu discussing something confidentially. After that, Mahāprabhu called all His Gauḍīya *bhaktas* and one by one glorified them all to each other. For example He said, "Do you know this devotee? This is Rāghava Paṇḍita. Throughout the year, he and his sister Damayantī cook many delicious dry preparations and bring them here to Me. I keep them with Me and eat them, little by little, throughout the next year."

Then He said, "You know this Vāsudeva Datta? He is a very high-class devotee. I cannot repay him. Every day he spends whatever money he receives for Hari, Guru, and Vaiṣṇavas; he does not keep a single *paisā* for himself. O Śivānanda Sena, you should be his accountant and try to keep his accounts. A householder should have some balance to maintain his family; he should not be penniless. Try to keep some of his money aside so that he can maintain his family; otherwise he will spend everything on Me."

In this way, Mahāprabhu called the devotees one by one. He called Satyarāja Khān, a devotee of Kulīna-grāma, and said, "Guṇarāja Khān, the father of Satyarāja Khān, has written in his book *The Glory of Kṛṣṇa* (*Śrī Kṛṣṇa-vijaya*), 'Kṛṣṇa is my *prāṇanātha*, my beloved. He is the only Lord of my life breath.' For this reason I have sold myself to his dynasty forever. What to speak of his family, I honor a dog of their village – all the dogs – because they take only *prasāda* and observe Ekādaśī. I must honor them. If they come to me, I must pacify and caress them. They are devotees."

Mahāprabhu blessed Satyarāja Khān and told him, "Every year you should bring a very thick, strong rope from your village. You are extremely wealthy, like a king, so bring it somehow." Each year Satyarāja Khān would bring new rope, because the rope by which the chariots are pulled breaks every year during the festival.

Caitanya Mahāprabhu glorified many devotees in this meeting, and He also requested Nityānanda Prabhu, "O Nityānanda, return to Bengal and preach there. Advaita Ācārya, you should also go there and preach everywhere. Go to those who are neglected by society. Preach to them and inspire them to chant the holy name. I will be very happy if you do this, and I will also be happy if Nityānanda Prabhu does not come here each year. He should spend most of his time preaching there."

I am explaining this same mission to you. You should all try to preach, distribute books, and help other devotees; and when I come next year, each of you should bring at least ten sweet flowers (people) and help them to become devotees. Nityānanda Prabhu tried to do this, and he especially embraced those who were neglected, like the *śūdras*, *kāyasthas*, and *suvarṇa-vaṇiks*. *Suvarṇa-vaṇik* means "gold jewelers." They are neglected in India because they charge money even when making an ornament for their mothers. They will not give any concession even to their fathers and mothers, and because of their greediness they are hated by society. No *brāhmaṇa* or *kṣatriya* will take even water from their homes, but Nityānanda Prabhu mercifully went to them, embraced them, and told them, "Can you chant 'Hare Kṛṣṇa'? Please say it just once." In this way, he preached all over Bengal. I am also going everywhere in a similar mood, and you should also follow these principles.

Satyarāja Khān and the residents of Kulīna-grāma then approached Mahāprabhu and asked some questions. In *Śrī Caitanya-caritāmṛta* (*Madhya-līlā* 15.102–3) it is stated:

tabe rāmānanda, āra satyarāja khāṅna
prabhura caraṇe kichu kaila nivedana

After this, Rāmānanda Vasu and Satyarāja Khān both submitted questions at Śrī Caitanya Mahāprabhu's lotus feet.

gṛhastha viṣayī āmi, ki mora sādhane
śrī-mukhe ājñā kara prabhu – nivedi caraṇe

[Satyarāja Khān said:] My dear Lord, I am a householder and a materialistic man, and I do not know the process of advancing in spiritual life. I therefore submit myself unto Your lotus feet and request You to instruct me."

This question was not for Satyarāja Khān; it was for all householders. Try to hear this instruction of Mahāprabhu and obey it. We have also completed our own Chariot Festival, so Caitanya Mahāprabhu is speaking to all of you:

prabhu kahena, – 'kṛṣṇa-sevā', 'vaiṣṇava-sevana'
'nirantara kara kṛṣṇa-nāma-saṅkīrtana'

Śrī Caitanya-caritāmṛta (*Madhya-līlā* 15.104)

Śrī Caitanya Mahāprabhu replied, "Continue to chant the holy name of Lord Kṛṣṇa without cessation. Whenever possible, serve Him and His devotees, the Vaiṣṇavas."

Yes, this is the main thing – always serving Vaiṣṇavas, and always engaging in Kṛṣṇa's service. Śrī Satyarāja Khān then asked another question for clarification. He said, "I know how to chant Kṛṣṇa's name. What you have explained is clear. One pair of *karatālas* and two, three, four, five, or more devotees chanting together: 'Hare Kṛṣṇa, Hare Kṛṣṇa, Kṛṣṇa Kṛṣṇa, Hare Hare, Hare Rāma, Hare Rāma, Rāma Rāma, Hare Hare.' This is *saṅkīrtana*." *Kīrtana* is performed when one chants alone, and *saṅkīrtana* is performed when many assemble together under the guidance of a self-realized devotee. At that time it will be *saṅkīrtana*; otherwise, without such guidance, it is like the barking of dogs. Try to know these truths.

"So it is clear," Satyarāja and Rāmānanda Vasu told Mahāprabhu, "and we also know how to serve Kṛṣṇa by performing *arcana* from the beginning of the day, from morning to evening: offering *ārati*, bathing the deities, offering them *rāja-bhoga* at midday, and at three o'clock offering more *bhoga*, and then again at night, *rāja-bhoga*, *kīrtana*, and *ārati*. This is *kṛṣṇa-sevā*. In addition, those who are qualified should remember the pastimes of Kṛṣṇa throughout the eight divisions of the day and night. This is *kṛṣṇa-sevā*.

"But what is *vaiṣṇava-sevā*? How can we recognize a Vaiṣṇava? Please let us know who is a Vaiṣṇava, and what are his common symptoms?" Śrī Caitanya Mahāprabhu replied in the following verses (*Śrī Caitanya-caritāmṛta* (*Madhya-līlā* 15.106–8)):

prabhu kahe, yāṅra mukhe śuni eka-bāra
kṛṣṇa-nāma, sei pūjya, śreṣṭha sabākāra

Whoever chants the holy name of Kṛṣṇa just once is worshipable and is the topmost human being.

eka kṛṣṇa-nāme kare sarva-pāpa kṣaya
nava-vidhā bhakti pūrṇa nāma haite haya

Simply by chanting the holy name of Kṛṣṇa, one is relieved from all the reactions of a sinful life. One can complete the nine processes of devotional service simply by chanting the holy name.

dīkṣā-puraścaryā-vidhi apekṣā nā kare
jihvā-sparśe ā-caṇḍāle sabāre uddhāre

One does not have to undergo initiation or execute the activities required before initiation. One simply has to vibrate the holy name with his lips. Thus even a man in the lowest class (*caṇḍāla*) can be delivered.

Caitanya Mahāprabhu then quoted a *śloka* from the Purāṇas to support this:

ākṛṣṭiḥ kṛta-cetasāṁ sumanasām uccāṭanaṁ cāṁhasām
ācaṇḍālam amūka-loka-sulabho vaśyaś ca mukti-śriyaḥ
no dīkṣāṁ na ca sat-kriyāṁ na ca puraścaryāṁ manāg īkṣate
mantro 'yaṁ rasanā-spṛg eva phalati śrī-kṛṣṇa-nāmātmakaḥ

Padyāvalī (29); *Śrī Caitanya-caritāmṛta* (*Madhya-līlā* 15.110)

The holy name of Lord Kṛṣṇa is an attractive feature for many saintly, liberal people. It is the annihilator of all sinful reactions and is so powerful that, except for the dumb who cannot chant, it is readily available to everyone, including the lowest type of man, the *caṇḍāla*. The holy name of Kṛṣṇa controls the opulence of liberation and it is identical with Kṛṣṇa. Immediate effects are produced when one simply touches the holy name with one's tongue. Chanting the holy name does not depend on initiation, pious activities, or the *puraścaryā* (regulative principles generally observed before initiation). The holy name does not wait for all these activities. It is self-sufficient.

ataeva yāṅra mukhe eka kṛṣṇa-nāma
sei ta' vaiṣṇava, kariha tāṅhāra sammāna

Śrī Caitanya-caritāmṛta (*Madhya-līlā* 15.111)

[Śrī Caitanya Mahāprabhu then finally advised:] One who is chanting the Hare Kṛṣṇa *mantra* is understood to be a Vaiṣṇava; therefore you should offer all respects to him.

This reply was given in the first year. Śrī Satyarāja Khān asked his question again the next year, and Caitanya Mahāprabhu replied with deep meaning, "You should honor one who chants with some honor for *harināma*, whether he is initiated or not, if he does not commit any offense and he follows the basic principles regarding gambling, smoking, meat-eating, and other sins. He should be honored because he can be freed from past offenses and he may become liberated."

On the third year the question was asked again. This time Mahāprabhu explained something more, and His explanation became complete. Through the Kulīna-grāma residents He is gradually teaching the general public, saying in effect that if you want to advance, you will have to take initiation. Śrī Caitanya Mahāprabhu Himself took initiation. All these descriptions of the good effects of chanting will not apply to you if you neglect the teachings of Śrīla Rūpa Gosvāmī, Śrīla Sanātana Gosvāmī, and Mahāprabhu by not taking initiation.

Śrī Caitanya Mahāprabhu's replies in the first and second years were meant to encourage those who do not know that we must accept initiation. Those who want to be pure devotees and have heard *hari-kathā* from such pure devotees must accept initiation, give up all their offenses, become advanced, and realize their relationship with Kṛṣṇa.

Narahari Sarakāra, Mukunda dāsa, and Raghu-nandana were Śrī Caitanya Mahāprabhu's intimate associates from the village of Śrīkhaṇḍa, near Navadvīpa-dhāma. They were also present there in that first year, and Mahāprabhu glorified them, too. He called Mukunda dāsa and asked him in front of all the devotees, "Mukunda dāsa, are you Raghu-nandana's father, or is Raghu-nandana your father?" Mukunda and Vasu Ghoṣa were both very good *kīrtanīyās* and very near and dear associates of Caitanya Mahāprabhu, and Raghu-nandana was Mukunda's son. Still, Mahāprabhu asked Mukunda, "Are you Raghu-nandana's father, or is Raghu-nandana your father? I have some doubt." He knew that Raghu-nandana was Mukunda's son, but He still asked, "Who is the son and who is the father? Tell me your decision."

Mukunda smiled as he replied, "Raghu-nandana is my father, and I'm his son. A 'father' is actually he who gives *kṛṣṇa-bhakti*. Our whole family has received *kṛṣṇa-bhakti* from Raghu-nandana, so he is not my son; I am his son." One may be considered someone's father in a worldly sense, but the real father is he who can give *kṛṣṇa-bhakti*.

Mahāprabhu became extremely happy and said, "Oh, My doubt has been dispelled. One who awakens *kṛṣṇa-bhakti* is the real spiritual master. You are truly a very advanced devotee."

A devotee may have received *dīkṣā*[1] (initiation) from someone

[1] *Hari-bhakti-vilāsa* (2.9) states, "That religious undertaking which bestows *divya-jñāna*, transcendental knowledge, and destroys *pāpa* (sin), *pāpa-bīja* (the seed of sin), and *avidyā* (ignorance) to the root is called *dīkṣā* by learned authorities in the absolute truth." *Dī* means transcendental realization of one's relationship with Kṛṣṇa, and *kṣā* means destruction of the above-mentioned obstacles. Therefore, unless one gets initiated by a *mahā-bhāgavata* devotee, he has not received *dīkṣā* in the real sense.

who is not actually qualified to give *kṛṣṇa-bhakti*. For example, the devotee may have followed others who inspired him to take *dīkṣā*. It may be that he did not know the meaning of *dīkṣā* when he took initiation, but that upon receiving the good association of a pure devotee afterwards, he came to understand, "I am receiving *bhakti* from this pure devotee." Who, then, is his *guru*? *Yāṅhā haite kṛṣṇa-bhakti sei guru haya*. The person from whom one receives pure *bhakti* is actually *guru*, and he should be honored as such. This is called *bhāgavata-paramparā*.[2]

The *kṛṣṇa-bhakti* referred to by Caitanya Mahāprabhu is the goal of life (*prayojana*) of all those in the line of Śrīla Rūpa Gosvāmī, the goal He had explained to Rūpa Gosvāmī himself. Madana-mohana establishes our *sambandha* (relation) with Him, Govinda gives *abhidheya* (the process to realize that relationship), and Gopīnātha is the presiding deity of *prayojana*. However, Gopīnātha Himself is not our *prayojana*; our *prayojana* is the love and affection that Rādhikā has for Gopīnātha.

Our *prayojana* is not the *prema* that Kṛṣṇa has for Rādhikā and others. Kṛṣṇa is undoubtedly the ocean of *rasa*, but He is not our *prayojana*. The topmost *prayojana* is the *gopīs'* love for Kṛṣṇa, and amongst all the *gopīs*, Śrīmatī Rādhikā's love and affection, Her *adhirūḍha-mahābhāva* for Kṛṣṇa – not for Kṛṣṇa, but for Gopīnātha. This understanding is not for everyone; it is for rare devotees.

The process to achieve this *prayojana* is stated in *Śrī Caitanya-caritāmṛta* (*Madhya-līlā* 8.229): "*gopī-ānugatya vinā aiśvarya-jñāne bhajileha nāhi pāya vrajendra-nandane* – no one can attain realization of this love of Rādhikā for Gopīnātha unless he follows in the footsteps of the *gopīs*." But this is not achieved by following all the *gopīs*. We can never achieve it by

[2] Please refer to the Glossary for an explanation of this term.

following Yaśodā, and we cannot attain it if we follow other *gopīs*. Candrāvalī has *mahābhāva*, but there is something lacking in her. This highest love is only possible by following the special mood of Rādhikā, and it is achieved if we will practice under guidance (*ānugatya*). However, we cannot serve under the guidance of Rādhika, nor can we follow Her dear *sakhīs* Lalitā and Viśākhā. We can only perform *ānugatya* to Śrī Rūpa Mañjarī, Rati Mañjarī, and *sakhīs* like them.

We must especially follow Rūpa Mañjarī, who is always serving Śrīmatī Rādhikā. Rūpa Mañjarī becomes happy when Rādhikā is happy, and she feels separation when Rādhikā feels separation. Sometimes she is so absorbed in the same mood as Rādhikā that she cannot pacify Her, whereas Lalitā and Viśākhā can do so. This is because Lalitā and Viśākhā are not as absorbed as Rūpa Mañjarī and Rati Mañjarī. The highest class of love that a *jīva* can achieve is *kṛṣṇa-prema*, namely Rādhikā's *prema* for Gopīnātha, attained under the guidance of the *mañjarīs*. There is no other process, and there will never be another process; Caitanya Mahāprabhu Himself has said this.

Here, Mahāprabhu is speaking about the person who can give *kṛṣṇa-bhakti*, and the *kṛṣṇa-bhakti* to which He refers is this *prayojana*. One who gives this is actually *guru*. If the *śikṣā-guru* is giving this whereas the *dīkṣā-guru* is not, then the *śikṣā-guru* is in *bhāgavata-paramparā* and he should be given preference. He is more authentic and he should be honored more. Because you are performing regulative *bhakti* at present, you cannot understand this or follow it fully. Only those who are engaging in spontaneous devotion, *rāgānuga-bhakti*, will understand. Śrīla Bhaktivinoda Ṭhākura could realize this, and therefore he gave more preference to Śrīla Jagannātha dāsa Bābājī Mahārāja than to his *dīkṣā-guru* Vipina-bihārī Gosvāmī. Śyāmānanda Prabhu, Narottama dāsa Ṭhākura, and Śrīnivāsa Ācārya gave more preference to Śrīla Jīva Gosvāmī than to their own *dīkṣā-gurus*. Śrīla Kṛṣṇadāsa Kavirāja Gosvāmī gave more preference to Śrīla Rūpa Gosvāmī and Śrīla Raghunātha dāsa Gosvāmī than to his *dīkṣā-guru*, and he writes at the end of every chapter of his *Śrī Caitanya-caritāmṛta*: "*śrī-rūpa-raghunātha-pade yāra āśa caitanya-caritāmṛta kahe kṛṣṇadāsa* – praying at the lotus feet of Śrī Rūpa and Śrī Raghunātha, always desiring their mercy, I, Kṛṣṇadāsa, narrate *Śrī Caitanya-caritāmṛta*, following in their footsteps." This is *bhāgavata-paramparā*, and it is very good if the *dīkṣā-guru* is also in this *bhāgavata-paramparā*. Try to know these very secret truths.

Totally absorbed in glorifying all His devotees, one by one, Śrī Caitanya Mahāprabhu then said, "Just hear the glory of Mukunda. By occupation he is an Ayurvedic doctor, a *rāja-vaidya* (royal physician), and he only treats kings and other royalty. He is not available for ordinary people. Externally, he appears to be a royal physician engaged in governmental service, but internally he has deep love for Kṛṣṇa. Who can understand his love?"

One day the royal physician Mukunda dāsa was seated on a high platform with the Muslim King and was telling the King about medical treatment. While the King and Mukunda dāsa were conversing, a servant brought a fan made of peacock feathers, which he held above the King's head to shade him from the sun. When Mukunda dāsa saw the fan of peacock feathers, he became absorbed in ecstatic love of Godhead, and fell from the high platform onto the ground. The King was afraid that the royal physician had been killed, so he descended and personally brought him to consciousness. When the King asked Mukunda, "Where are you in pain?" Mukunda replied, "I am not very much in pain." The King then inquired, "Mukunda, why did you fall down?" Mukunda replied, "My dear King, I have a disease like epilepsy." The King was extraordinarily intelligent, however, so he could understand the whole affair. In his estimation, Mukunda was a most uncommon, exalted, liberated personality.

Mahāprabhu then glorified the devotion of His associate Raghu-nandana:

raghu-nandana sevā kare kṛṣṇera mandire
dvāre puṣkariṇī, tara ghāṭera upare

kadambera eka vṛkṣe phuṭe bāra-māse
nitya dui phula haya kṛṣṇa-avataṁse

Śrī Caitanya-caritāmṛta (*Madhya-līlā* 15.128–9)

Raghu-nandana is constantly engaged in serving Lord Kṛṣṇa in the temple. On the bank of a lake beside the entrance of the temple is a *kadamba* tree, which daily delivers two flowers to be used for Kṛṣṇa's service.

It was because of Raghu-nandana's love and elevated *bhakti* that the *kadamba* tree used to give two flowers every day, even in the winter, whether or not it was the season for them to bloom. Mahāprabhu said that his *bhakti* was so high that the tree was always controlled by his love and gave two flowers to him only because he wished it to do so.

Mahāprabhu then gave three different instructions to three different devotees. He again spoke to Mukunda with sweet words: "Your duty is to earn both material and spiritual wealth. Furthermore, it is Raghu-nandana's duty to always engage in Lord Kṛṣṇa's service. He has no other intention but the service of Lord Kṛṣṇa." He then ordered Narahari: "I wish you to remain here with My devotees. In this way the three of you should always execute these three duties for the service of the Lord."

Rāghava Paṇḍita is another intimate associate of Mahāprabhu. He used to collect very sweet coconuts from different places to offer to Kṛṣṇa. One day he had some coconuts brought from very far away. He had them cut and prepared, and he was going to offer them to the deity. However, as his servant was carrying the basket of coconuts on his head, he put his hands on the ceiling and then touched the coconuts again. Rāghava Paṇḍita told his servant, "Take the coconuts out and throw them into the river or anywhere else; they cannot be offered to the deity. The dust from peoples' feet has risen onto the ceiling, and you touched the ceiling and then touched the basket of coconuts; so the basket and everything in it is impure."

Just see how strict these Vaiṣṇavas were!

The next year

As mentioned previously, in the second year Mahāprabhu again glorified all the devotees after the Ratha-yātrā Festival. You should also try to glorify devotees, and do not criticize them. If you want *bhakti*, never commit any offense. Try to honor others, even if they are not initiated, as long as they are not offensive and as long as they do not criticize anyone. Otherwise, do *praṇāma* to them from very far away – in other words, avoid their association.

One of the Kulīna-grāma-vāsīs again asked, "Now we are returning home; so what is our duty? What should we do?"

Listen very carefully and try to understand this. The Lord replied, "You should engage yourself in the service of Kṛṣṇa's servants, and always chant Kṛṣṇa's holy name. If you do these two things, you will very soon attain shelter at Kṛṣṇa's lotus feet."

The inhabitant of Kulīna-grāma asked, "Please let me know who is actually a Vaiṣṇava, and what his symptoms are."

Understanding his mind, Śrī Caitanya Mahāprabhu smiled and explained two principles: *vaiṣṇava-sevā* and *nāma-saṅkīrtana.*

kṛṣṇa-nāma nirantara yāṅhāra vadane
sei vaiṣṇava-śreṣṭha, bhaja taṅhāra caraṇe

Śrī Caitanya-caritāmṛta (*Madhya-līlā* 16.72)

A person who is always chanting the holy name of the Lord is to be considered the best Vaiṣṇava, and your duty is to serve his lotus feet.

In the first year Mahāprabhu had given a general answer, but now He is replying more specifically. Actually, to chant means to chant the pure name. Those who are not initiated can never chant the pure name; rather, they always chant with offenses. In this verse, the word *śreṣṭha*, meaning "best," does not refer to the *uttama-adhikārī* devotee. In this specific connection it refers to those who are initiated and who are *madhyama-madhyama-adhikārī* or *uttama-madhyama-adhikārī*; that is, it refers to the intermediate and topmost *madhyama-adhikārīs*. They have given up all varieties of offenses and they always chant and remember Kṛṣṇa's holy name in their specific relationship with Him.

The first year, Caitanya Mahāprabhu had told the inhabitants of Kulīna-grāma that one should give respect to Vaiṣṇavas, and the second year He told His followers to serve them. *Bhaja* means "to serve." There are some differences between those Vaiṣṇavas who should be only honored and those who should be served, but those who do not have high-class association cannot understand these differences. On the one hand, they seem very subtle, but on the other hand they are like the difference between the earth and sky.

A *nirantara* devotee is one who can continuously chant and remember Kṛṣṇa twenty-four hours a day. The word *nirantara* means "without any interruption," and it applies to one who is like Śrīla Haridāsa Ṭhākura, who was a disciple of Caitanya

Mahāprabhu Himself. Haridāsa Ṭhākura chanted without offense, and he even transformed a prostitute into a *śuddha-bhakta* by his association.

What do you think about the *bhajana* of Srila Raghunātha dāsa Gosvāmī and Srila Rūpa Gosvāmī? Were they always chanting Kṛṣṇa's names twenty-four hours a day? They were writing books like *Ujjvala-nīlamaṇi* throughout the day and night, so how could they chant all the time? In fact, sometimes they did not chant for two, three, four, or five days, because they were not in external consciousness. Tears would flow from their eyes and they would begin to faint when they tried to chant. Does this verse apply to Śrīla Rūpa Gosvāmī and Śrīla Raghunātha dāsa Gosvāmī? Certainly it does. Theirs was real chanting of Kṛṣṇa's names. Their cooking was chanting, and everything else they did was chanting. They were totally absorbed in chanting.

Similarly, Śrīla Śukadeva Gosvāmī was the best *kīrtanīyā*, even though he was not playing on harmonium or *kartālas*. His *kīrtana* took the form of always glorifying Kṛṣṇa and His holy name, remembering Him, and being absorbed in Him. Such devotees are more than *nirantara*. Haridāsa Ṭhākura and many others can be accepted in the category of *nirantara*, but Rūpa Gosvāmī, Raghunātha dāsa Gosvāmī, and Śukadeva Gosvāmī are more than this.

The inhabitants of Kulīna-grāma had asked this question in the previous year. Why are they asking again? This was the same question. First, "Who is a Vaiṣṇava?" and then again, "Who is a Vaiṣṇava?" It is not that the Kulīna-grāma-vāsīs were foolish for asking the same question each year. They were exalted Vaiṣṇavas, *uttama-adhikārīs*, and that is why they were asking – for the benefit of all ordinary devotees.

Mahāprabhu first explained about general Vaiṣṇavas, then about the "best" (second-class) Vaiṣṇavas, and after that in the third He told about the first-class Vaiṣṇavas. What he had said in the previous year concerned the second-class devotees, and what He had said in the first year was about the third-class (*kaniṣṭha*) devotees. Third-class, second-class – and now He is speaking about the *uttama-mahā-bhāgavatas*, who are all more than liberated.

yāṅhāra darśane mukhe āise kṛṣṇa-nāma
tāṅhāre jāniha tumi 'vaiṣṇava-pradhāna'

Śrī Caitanya-caritāmṛta (*Madhya-līlā* 16.74)

[Śrī Caitanya Mahāprabhu said:] A first-class Vaiṣṇava is he whose very presence makes others chant the holy name of Kṛṣṇa.

krama kari' kahe prabhu 'vaiṣṇava'-lakṣaṇa
'vaiṣṇava', 'vaiṣṇavatara', āra 'vaiṣṇavatama'

Śrī Caitanya-caritāmṛta (*Madhya-līlā* 16.75)

In this way, Śrī Caitanya Mahāprabhu taught the distinctions between different types of Vaiṣṇavas: the Vaiṣṇava, Vaiṣṇavatara, and Vaiṣṇavatama. Thus He successively explained all the symptoms of a Vaiṣṇava to the inhabitants of Kulīna-grāma.

All devotees are Vaiṣṇavas, but some are third-class, some are second-class, and others are first-class. We are all Vaiṣṇavas, but the degrees of our *vaiṣṇavatā* (qualification as Vaiṣṇava) are not the same. In fact, there may be thousands of degrees. A *kaniṣṭha-adhikārī* can never discriminate between one degree and another. He has no intelligence to think about the differences. The *kaniṣṭha-madhyama* (lower level *madhyama*) is also not very qualified, but the *madhyama-madhyama* (intermediate *madhyama*) is somewhat more qualified, and the *uttama-madhyama* (topmost *madhyama*) can behave towards all Vaiṣṇavas according to their quality and stage.

Śrī Caitanya Mahāprabhu said that there are three divisions – Vaiṣṇava, Vaiṣṇavatara, and Vaiṣṇavatama – but there are not only three divisions. Śrī Rūpa Gosvāmī explained the many thousands of stages of Vaiṣṇavas, but who will recognize all these different stages? Śrīla Bhaktivinoda Ṭhākura has said: *"ye yena vaiṣṇava ciniyā laiyā ādara koribe yabe* – if you know an advanced Vaiṣṇava's category of qualification and you show him respect according to that category or ability, you can get his mercy and achieve the ultimate goal of life very quickly. Otherwise, it is not possible to achieve your ultimate goal in spiritual life."

If you cannot recognize what Vaiṣṇava is in what class, you will wrongly judge, "Oh, he is like me," or "He is a *mahā-mahā-bhāgavata* and everyone else is junior to him. Śrīla Rūpa Gosvāmī is also junior to my *mahā-mahā-bhāgavata.*" You are helpless in this regard, so how can you decide? If you have the causeless mercy of Rūpa Gosvāmī and his associates, you can be qualified to recognize Vaiṣṇavas and honor them accordingly; otherwise not. For example, it may be that when you consider the respective qualities of Rūpa Gosvāmī and Haridāsa Ṭhākura, you will respect Haridāsa Ṭhākura and not Rūpa Gosvāmī. You may think that Rūpa Gosvāmī is just a young boy, a mere neophyte who knows nothing. But Svarūpa Dāmodara will embrace that same Rūpa Gosvāmī to his chest, and Mahāprabhu will affectionately pat him on the back and tell him, "Oh, good boy! Good boy! How did you know My heart?" Try to understand and absorb all these high-class teachings of Mahāprabhu, and don't criticize any Vaiṣṇava.

In regard to the first-class devotee who is always established in his relationship with Kṛṣṇa, why does he sometimes want another relationship? For example, Nārada is an *uttama-mahā-bhāgavata* in the mood of servitude (*dāsya-rasa*), but he also wants to be a *gopī*. Such devotees are very "tricky." They want to taste everything from top to bottom. They are like Kṛṣṇa. Kṛṣṇa is also tricky, for He plays with Rādhikā and He plays with Kubjā. Why did He go to Kubjā? He is fully satisfied with Rādhikā, but still He wants to taste everything, from top to bottom.

A *kaniṣṭha-adhikārī* cannot know his own level of advancement, nor can he know how to properly respect devotees according to their respective quality of *bhakti*. He must be in the association of a *madhyama-adhikārī*. One can know who is *madhyama-adhikārī* by association and by hearing *hari-kathā*. The *madhyama-adhikārī* will know some *hari-kathā*, and especially he will be serving the Vaiṣṇavas more than the deities. He has great respect for Vaiṣṇavas, and that is not possible for a *kaniṣṭha-adhikārī*. A *kaniṣṭha-adhikārī* cannot give up serving the deity to respect any devotee, whereas a *madhyama-adhikārī* can do so.

A *kaniṣṭha-adhikārī* will consider whether or not something has been offered to Kṛṣṇa, and then he will give it to that pure devotee as Ṭhākurajī's *prasāda*. The *madhyama-adhikārī* will not see in this way. When he sees an *uttama-adhikārī* taking *prasāda*, the *madhyama-adhikārī* will understand that his offering was millions of times greater than the *kaniṣṭha-adhikārī's* formal offering, even though the *uttama-adhikārī* may not have offered the *bhoga* to Kṛṣṇa outwardly at all. The *uttama-adhikārī* has offered the *bhoga* by his eyes and by his heart, and that offering is much more acceptable than a formal offering by a less advanced devotee. Actually, he has offered himself, so there is nothing left to offer. This is very hard for a *kaniṣṭha-adhikārī* – or even a beginning-level *madhyama-adhikārī* – to understand, because it is a highly elevated stage.

CHAPTER TEN

THE RELATIONSHIP BETWEEN JAGANNĀTHA PURĪ AND NAVADVĪPA

Kṛṣṇa is the Supreme Personality of Godhead. He is *sarva-śaktimān*, almighty, and He is extremely merciful. He is also very *rasika*. He is the ocean of *rasa*, and therefore He is our worshipable deity. If you go deeply into *bhajana*, you will understand many truths in this regard. Because Kṛṣṇa is *rasika-śekhara* (the topmost enjoyer of mellows) and causelessly merciful, He considers, "How can I show kindness to all the souls who, having deviated from Me, are suffering so grievously? How can I attract them?" Thinking in this way, He wanted to personally descend to this world to bestow His mercy.

Kṛṣṇa is the ocean of *rasa*, but this ocean is divided into two. The first is Kṛṣṇa as the taster and relisher of *rasa*, and the second is the container of the ocean of *rasa*. Kṛṣṇa is the object of love and the ocean of *rasa*, but He is not the container. This *rasa* is situated in the heart of Rādhikā. If Rādhikā were not present, there would be no *rasa* and Kṛṣṇa would be *nirviśeṣa-brahma*.

Kṛṣṇa wants to give to the world this ocean of *rasa* found in Rādhikā's heart, which is called *mahābhāva*. He wants to donate it to this world, but He cannot. He is the object of love, and therefore He can only sprinkle upon the world an idea of what it is like to be the object. He cannot give the love of those who serve Him. He cannot give love for Himself because He does not have it. In order to have that love, therefore, He "stole" the beauty and intrinsic mood of Rādhikā.

Actually, Kṛṣṇa cannot steal the mood of Rādhikā because She is always very alert. She is more clever and intelligent than Kṛṣṇa, because She is His power. Kṛṣṇa's intelligence is also Rādhikā. His everything is Rādhikā. He can only wish, and therefore He discovered another way to get Her mood: He begged it. Because She and all Her *sakhīs* are always so alert, if His plan was to cheat Her and steal away Her love, He would not have been able to do so. He was not able to independently enter that realm of love, and therefore He prayed to Her, "Oh, I beg Your mercy. Please give Me Your beauty and Your *mahābhāva* – that love which no one else possesses."

Even Lalitā and Viśākhā don't have that kind of love, and Kṛṣṇa also does not have it. His love reaches up to *mahābhāva*, but the highest feature of *mahābhāva*, called *mādana*, is not found in Him. Kṛṣṇa wanted to take Śrīmatī Rādhikā's *mādanākhya-mahābhāva* – in order to fully relish His own beauty and His sweetness, and in order to relish the happiness of such taste.

Rādhikā replied to His prayer, "Yes, I will donate this to You for some time – as You wish. But You will have to be admitted into the school of My *sakhīs*, and You will have to attend their classes. They can then bestow that mood upon you, and I will also be there to help You."

In this way Kṛṣṇa begged, and He thus became Śacīnandana Gaurahari.

anarpita-carīṁ cirāt karuṇayāvatīrṇaḥ kalau
samarpayitum unnatojjvala-rasāṁ sva-bhakti-śriyam
hariḥ puraṭa-sundara-dyuti-kadamba-sandīpitaḥ
sadā hṛdaya-kandare sphuratu vaḥ śacī-nandanaḥ

Śrī Caitanya-caritāmṛta (*Ādi-līlā* 1.4)

May the Supreme Lord who is known as the son of Śrīmatī Śacī-devī be transcendentally situated in the innermost chambers of your heart. Resplendent with the radiance of molten gold, He has appeared in the age of Kali by His causeless mercy to bestow what no incarnation has ever offered before: the most sublime and radiant mellow of devotional service, the mellow of amorous love.

Who is Śacīnandana, the son of Mother Śacī? He is *gopī-bhartuḥ*, Kṛṣṇa Himself – *avatīrṇaḥ kalau*. Why did He descend to this world? *Karuṇayā* – He descended by His causeless mercy. Nṛsiṁhadeva and Vāmanadeva came here, and Kūrma, Varāha, and Rāmacandra also came; and they all gave something to the world. Rāmacandra taught so many things, especially *maryādā* – etiquette and worship in majesty and awe and reverence. Also, many *ācāryas* came to this world, like Śrī Madhvācārya, Śrī Rāmānujācārya, Śrī Viṣṇusvāmī, and Śrī Nimbāditya, but they gave only regulative *bhakti*. They taught, "Kṛṣṇa is worshipable" – not anything else. Similarly, Śrī Prahlāda Mahārāja explained in *Śrīmad-Bhāgavatam* (7.5.23–4):

śravaṇaṁ kīrtanaṁ viṣṇoḥ
smaraṇaṁ pāda-sevanam
arcanaṁ vandanam dāsyaṁ
sakhyam ātma-nivedanam

iti puṁsārpitā viṣṇau
bhaktiś cen nava-lakṣaṇā
kriyeta bhagavaty addhā
tan manye 'dhītam uttamam

> The following nine processes are accepted as pure devotional service: hearing and chanting about the transcendental holy name, form, qualities, paraphernalia, and pastimes of Lord Viṣṇu; remembering them; serving the lotus feet of the Lord; offering the Lord respectful worship with sixteen types of paraphernalia; offering prayers to the Lord; becoming His servant; considering the Lord to be one's best friend; and surrendering everything unto Him (in other words, serving Him with the body, mind, and words). One who has dedicated his life to the service of Kṛṣṇa through these nine methods should be understood to be the most learned person, for he has acquired complete knowledge.

You must surrender to the lotus feet of the Lord, but you will have to surrender first to *dāsa-bhagavān*, the *guru*, and then ultimately you can perform *ātma-nivedanam*, full surrender, to Kṛṣṇa. Moreover, this is *vaidhī-bhakti*, and it can only lead us to Vaikuṇṭha – never to Vṛndāvana. It is not so powerful.

Śrī Caitanya Mahāprabhu descended to this world mainly to give *rāgānuga-bhakti*, and therefore He is *karuṇayā*, the most merciful incarnation. *Samarpayitum* means to give. To give what? To give *unnata-ujjvala-rasa*. *Unnata-ujjvala* is not *vaidhī-bhakti*. *Unnata-ujjvala-rasa* is only the love of the *gopīs* of Vṛndāvana. This love is not found even in Mother Yaśodā, Rohiṇī, and others like them. They know something about this *rasa*, but it is not found in them.

Mahāprabhu especially descended to give *sva-bhakti-śriyam*. *Sva* means "own." Who is the "own" of Kṛṣṇa? Only Śrīmatī Rādhikā is Kṛṣṇa's own. Her love, Her *bhakti*, is *prema*, *sneha*, *māna*, *rāga*, *anurāga*, *bhāva*, *mahābhāva*, and even more than this – *modana* and *mādana*. Everything is included in *mādana*. Separation and meeting are both included – to the highest point.

Mahāprabhu came to sprinkle this mercy of *sva-bhakti-śriyam* upon the *jīvas*. *Śriyam* means beauty. It is the beauty of *unnata-ujjvala-rasa*, but not *unnata-ujjvala-rasa* itself. Śrīmatī Rādhikā

Herself is the embodiment of *unnata-ujjvala-rasa*, and Lalitā, Viśākhā, and all the other *sakhīs* are also participants in that *rasa*. *Śriyam* is the mood of Rūpa Mañjarī, Rati Mañjarī, and others including Kamala Mañjarī and her followers. This is the mood of service to Śrīmatī Rādhikā.

Mahāprabhu came to sprinkle the mercy of *rāga-mārga*, the path by which we can attain the service of Rādhā-Kṛṣṇa Yugala. This path is called *rāgānuga-bhakti*, and it will take you to the stage of *rāga*. In this connection, *rāga* is the *gopīs'* moods to please Kṛṣṇa.

Mahāprabhu mercifully came to give this mood, but He Himself was not trained. He was like a person who wants to become a lawyer, but who must first go to law school and pass the exams. Still, even after that he cannot enter the court right away. He must become an apprentice and practice under the guidance of a qualified and senior lawyer. After two or three years, when he has completed his training, he can then enter the court and plead – not otherwise.

Mahāprabhu descended to this world in Navadvīpa, and there He appeared from the womb of Śrīmatī Śacī-devī. Navadvīpa is Vṛndāvana. Navadvīpa and Vṛndāvana are the same, but in Navadvīpa everything is hidden – as Kṛṣṇa is hidden in the shape of Śrī Caitanya Mahāprabhu. As Śacīnandana does not look like Kṛṣṇa, similarly Vṛndāvana, the abode of Kṛṣṇa, is covered in Navadvīpa. Yet, it is Vṛndāvana. All the twelve forests of Vṛndāvana exist here and there in Navadvīpa, but in a covered way.

You should know that there are no Vṛndāvana forests in Jagannātha Purī. Therefore, Jagannātha Purī can never be equal to Navadvīpa. A very high class of separation is tasted by Mahāprabhu in the Gambhīrā, but at the same time Navadvīpa is Vṛndāvana and Purī is not. Purī is like Dvārakā. In Dvārakā,

Kṛṣṇa laments for the *gopīs*. He cannot wear His peacock feather or carry His sweet *vaṁśī*, and He cannot declare, "My father and mother are Nanda and Yaśodā. These are not My real queens – the *gopīs* are My dearmost beloveds."

Do you know the meaning of the word Navadvīpa? *Nava* refers to *nitya-nava-navāyamāna*, which means "always ever-fresh." *Nava* also means nine. Navadvīpa consists of nine islands, and they denote the nine processes of *bhakti* headed by *śravaṇam* and *kīrtanam*. The Vedas, Upaniṣads, and many other Vaiṣṇava literatures have referred to Navadvīpa in the following way (*Brahma-saṁhitā* (5.56)):

śriyaḥ kāntāḥ kāntaḥ parama-puruṣaḥ kalpa-taravo
drumā bhūmiś cintāmaṇi-gaṇa-mayi toyam amṛtam
kathā gānaṁ nāṭyaṁ gamanam api vaṁśī priya-sakhī
cid-ānandaṁ jyotiḥ param api tad āsvādyam api ca

sa yatra kṣīrābdhiḥ sravati surabhībhyaś ca su-mahān
nimeṣārddhākhyo vā vrajati na hi yatrāpi samayaḥ
bhaje śvetadvīpaṁ tam aham iha golokam iti yaṁ
vidantas te santaḥ kṣiti-virala-cārāḥ katipaye

I worship that supreme abode of Śvetadvīpa, where the beloved heroines are a host of transcendental goddesses of fortune, and the Supreme Personality Śrī Kṛṣṇa is the only lover; where all the trees are spiritual desire-trees, and the earth is made of transcendental wish-fulfilling *cintāmaṇi* jewels; where the water is nectar, natural speaking is a melodious song, and walking to and fro is an artful dance; where the flute is the dearmost friend; where light is full of knowledge and bliss, and the supreme spiritual substance that comprises all things is relishable; where a vast transcendental ocean of milk is always flowing from millions upon millions of *surabhī* cows; and where time is not subject to passing away, even for half the blink of an eye, because it is not divided into past and future, but remains in the undivided eternal present. That divine abode, which is practically unknown in this world, is known by the name of Goloka to only a few, rare *sādhus*.

In his writings, Śrīla Rūpa Gosvāmī has quoted this verse, and Śrīla Bhaktivinoda Ṭhākura also quoted it, along with many similar verses. Navadvīpa is Śvetadvīpa. In transcendental Goloka Vṛndāvana there are two parts: Vṛndāvana and Śvetadvīpa. Vṛndāvana and Navadvīpa are complementary – without Navadvīpa, Vṛndāvana is incomplete, and without Vṛndāvana, Navadvīpa is incomplete. Together they are complete, as when separation and meeting mix together, the resulting situation is complete. Where there is no separation mood, *saṁyoga* (meeting) is incomplete.

The twelve *vanas* (forests) and *upavanas* (sub-forests) of Vṛndāvana are in Navadvīpa, within the nine islands: Madhuvana, Tālavana, Kumudavana, Bahulāvana, Kāmyavana, Khadiravana, Bhadravana, Bhāṇḍīravana, Bilvavana, Mahāvana, Vṛndāvana, and Lauhavana. All of these forests, in some way, are in Navadvīpa.

Do not think that Jagannātha Purī is superior to Navadvīpa. Do not think that the bank of the River Godāvarī where Mahāprabhu revealed His *mahābhāva-rasarāja* mood to Rāya Rāmānanda is superior to Navadvīpa. Navadvīpa is far superior to both these places. On one hand, Śrī Caitanya Mahāprabhu revealed His transcendental form of *rasarāja-mahābhāva* at Godāvarī, and that very high class of *hari-kathā*, *Rāmānanda-saṁvāda*, took place there. Also, Caitanya Mahāprabhu showed His extreme moods of separation in the Gambhīrā. He jumped in the ocean near there, and He relished Śrīmatī Rādhikā's moods of separation with Svarūpa Dāmodara and Rāya Rāmānanda there. These may be said, therefore, to be the deepest and highest *hari-kathās*, but there are so many reasons why they are not.

Jagannātha Purī is a very elevated pastime place, especially regarding the *gambhīrā-līlā* of Śrī Caitanya Mahāprabhu, but still it is like Dvārakā. There is no forest or sub-forest of Vṛndāvana there. Neither Gokula, Bhāṇḍīravana, Nandagaon, nor Varṣāṇā are there. They are not on the bank of the Godāvarī, nor are they found in Kurukṣetra or Jagannātha Purī. Therefore, Navadvīpa must be superior to these places.

Because so many places exist in Navadvīpa in a hidden way, Navadvīpa is known as *gupta-vṛndāvana*. One of the nine islands of Navadvīpa is Godrumadvīpa, which is described by Śrīla Bhaktivinoda Ṭhākura in his *Jaiva-dharma*. Godrumadvīpa is Nandagaon, nearby Varṣāṇā. The birthplace of Caitanya Mahāprabhu in Māyāpura is Mathurā and Gokula combined. Caitanya Mahāprabhu is Kṛṣṇa, with the internal mood and complexion of Śrīmatī Rādhikā. Kṛṣṇa took birth in Vṛndāvana; partly in Mathurā, but fully in Gokula, and both places are combined there in Māyāpura Yogapīṭha.

Then, crossing the Gaṅgā from there to Koladvīpa where our Devānanda Gauḍīya Maṭha is situated, we find Girirāja-Govardhana. There, all the *kuñjas* and caves where Kṛṣṇa played with the *sakhās* and *sakhīs* are situated. Nearby there is Rasauli, or *rāsa-sthalī*, where Candra-sarovara is located at the foot of Girirāja-Govardhana, and nearby there is Ṛtudvīpa, where Rādhā-kuṇḍa and Śyāma-kuṇḍa are situated. The Gaṅgā and Yamunā rivers meet together at Prayaga and continue to flow side-by-side to Navadvīpa and all around its nine islands. Our Devānanda Gauḍīya Maṭha was constructed by our *gurudeva* on the west bank of the Gaṅgā, the bank where the Yamunā flows; and Māyāpura is on the east bank of the Gaṅgā, the bank where the Gaṅgā flows. Lord Brahmā performed thousands of austerities on that east bank.

In Navadvīpa there is Pañcaveṇī, the meeting place of the

Gaṅgā, Yamunā, Sarasvatī, Alakanandā, and Mandākinī. Mānasī-gaṅgā is there, Rādhā-kuṇḍa and Śyāma-kuṇḍa are there, and this is all very wonderful. In Māmagāchi (Modadrumadvīpa) Bahulāvana is present, and in the north of Māyāpura is Bhadravana. Jahnudvīpa is Bhāṇḍīravana, and Sīmantadvīpa is Mathurā. All these truths have been explained by Śrīla Bhaktivinoda Ṭhākura in his *Śrī Navadvīpa-dhāma-māhātmya*. Vṛndāvana is in Navadvīpa, not in Jagannātha Purī or Godāvarī.

There is one very important thing to know, and you should know it very deeply. With regards to Navadvīpa being Vṛndāvana, there are two *aṣṭa-kālīya-līlās*, eternal pastimes performed during the eight periods of the day. One is Śrī Caitanya Mahāprabhu's *aṣṭa-kālīya-līlā* and one is Rādhā and Kṛṣṇa's *aṣṭa-kālīya-līlā*. Mahāprabhu's *aṣṭa-kālīya-līlā* took place in Navadvīpa, and it is that *aṣṭa-kālīya-līlā* upon which devotees meditate. There is no such *aṣṭa-kālīya-līlā* on which to meditate in Jagannātha Purī.

In their *gaura-gāyatrī-mantra*, the *brāhmaṇas* chant, "*viśvambharāya dhīmahi*" and "*gaurāya*." Why do they utter "*gaurāya*?" Who is Gaura? Gaura, or Gaurāṅga, is Kṛṣṇa, with the intrinsic mood, beauty, and golden complexion of Rādhikā. He is actually Kṛṣṇa, but now He is fully absorbed in the mood of Rādhikā. He feels as though He has become Rādhikā, but there are three Rādhikās: Vṛṣabhānu-nandinī Rādhikā, Viyoginī-Rādhikā, and Saṁyoginī-Rādhikā.

Like Kṛṣṇa, Vṛṣabhānu-nandinī Rādhikā never goes out of Vṛndāvana. Kṛṣṇa and Rohiṇī-nandana Balarāma also cannot go out of Vṛndāvana, because Balarāma always remains with Kṛṣṇa. Only Their manifestations, Vasudeva-nandana Kṛṣṇa and Vasudeva-nandana Baladeva, will go to Mathurā and Dvārakā. The pastimes of Kṛṣṇa in Mathurā and Dvārakā are transcendental and everlasting, as are the pastimes of Vrajendra-nandana Kṛṣṇa in Vṛndāvana. Vāsudeva-Kṛṣṇa eternally sports in Mathurā, and in Vṛndāvana, Vrajendra-nandana Kṛṣṇa is eternally playing.

Similarly, there are three Rādhikās. Actually there is only one Rādhikā, but She has three moods or features. Kṛṣṇa will not change when He goes to Mathurā, but He will not use His flute and peacock feather. He will change His father and mother, but not His form. Only His mood will be changed, and mood is the predominant factor of determination. If He takes His flute and peacock feather and tells everyone, "I am the son of Nanda and Yaśodā," then He is Vrajendra-nandana Kṛṣṇa. On the other hand, if He has no peacock feather and flute and He tells everyone, "I am the son of Vasudeva and Devakī," then He is present by His *prakāśa* (manifestation). His manifestation is not fully Kṛṣṇa Himself, the Supreme.

In the same way, Vṛṣabhānu-nandinī Rādhikā is always with Kṛṣṇa in Vṛndāvana. In Nandagaon, where Rādhikā felt great separation and spoke *Bhramara-gīta*, She is Viyoginī-Rādhikā. Actually, She is never in *viyoga* (separation), in the sense that she is never separated from Kṛṣṇa. Śrīla Rūpa Gosvāmī has explained this truth in his *Lalita-mādhava* and also in *Ujjvala-nīlamaṇi*. This is why Kavi Karṇapūra has not discussed the *līlā* of Mathurā and Dvārakā. He completes his *Ānanda-vṛndāvana-campū* just after the *rāsa-līlā*. Our *ācāryas* can never tolerate the idea that Rādhikā should be separated from Kṛṣṇa. In Her original and complete feature She is called Vṛṣabhānu-nandinī. She is always with Nanda-nandana Kṛṣṇa, and the Rādhikā who feels separation in Nandagaon is Her manifestation, Viyoginī-Rādhikā. She is the same Rādhikā, but She is feeling separation. Then, in Kurukṣetra, She is Saṁyoginī-Rādhikā. She goes there for a moment, for one or two days and, keeping Kṛṣṇa on the chariot of Her mind, She brings Him back to Vṛndāvana. *Saṁyoga* means "always meeting."

In the *mantra* "*gaurāya svāhā*" or "*tan no gauraḥ pracodayāt,*" the name Viśvambhara is uttered. Viśvambhara never lived in the cave (the Gambhīrā) in Jagannātha Purī, for He is Śacīnandana Gaurahari in Navadvīpa. From there He gives so much knowledge, so much love and affection, and a very high-class *prema* to the *jīvas.* He even gave *prema* to Jagāi and Mādhāi. *Viśvambharāya dhīmahi* – we meditate on Him in Navadvīpa.

In the cave of the Gambhīrā, Mahāprabhu played a role of great opulence. At that time, in the night, no one but Rāya Rāmānanda and Svarūpa Dāmodara – that is, Viśākhā and Lalitā – were able to witness His pastimes. At that time, although he was intimately familiar with all of Mahāprabhu's pastimes, even Śrīla Rūpa Gosvāmī could not go there. In Godāvarī, Mahāprabhu manifested His form as *rasarāja-mahābhāva* – this is opulence. At that time even Rāmānanda Rāya began to pray like Devakī or Arjuna, "Oh, You are that same Supreme Personality of Godhead!"

In Navadvīpa there is no opulence. In Navadvīpa, Śacīnandana played as Kṛṣṇa played with the girls in Vṛndāvana. While bathing in the Gaṅgā He would say to the little girls, "Will you marry Me? I want to marry you; if you will not marry Me then you will not be happy. Give your offerings of *sandeśa* and bananas to Me rather than to Śiva." This comes in the category of the *aṣṭa-kālīya-līlā* of Caitanya Mahāprabhu, and it is therefore far superior to any *līlā* in Jagannātha Purī. In Navadvīpa there is *svārasikī-upāsanā*, meditational worship on the continual flow of unlimited *līlās* taking place throughout the various periods of each day, whereas in Purī there is *mantramayī-upāsanā*, meditational worship of a specific *līlā*, in this case Śrīmatī Rādhikā's feelings of separation for Kṛṣṇa. In Navadvīpa, Mahāprabhu performed His *mādhurya-līlā*, whereas in Jagannātha Purī the *līlā* is full of *aiśvarya.* In Navadvīpa, Śacīnandana's school friends could quarrel with Him. Gadādhara Paṇḍita and Jagadānanda Paṇḍita always used to quarrel with Him as young schoolboys, and Śacī Mātā used to chastise her son. In Jagannātha Purī, however, even the King, although wanting to keep his head at Mahāprabhu's lotus feet, could not approach Him. Rāya Rāmānanda and all others always prayed to Mahāprabhu. He was not considered their friend, but rather He was considered much greater than them. In this way, *navadvīpa-līlā* is sweeter than the *līlā* of Jagannātha Purī, and there are many deep truths hidden there.

If you take bath in Navadvīpa at Bārakoṇa-ghāṭa, you will emerge at Keśī-ghāṭa, Vṛndāvana, where the *rāsa-līlā* is taking place. However, if you bathe in the ocean at Jagannātha Purī at Svarga-dvāra, you will not emerge in Vṛndāvana. Only if you are in the Gambhīrā can you know something of the glory of Vṛndāvana, and only then if you have intense greed to go there. Navadvīpa is therefore more glorious than Jagannātha Purī and it is even more glorious than the bank of the Godāvarī.

Although Caitanya Mahāprabhu enacted plentiful pastimes in Navadvīpa, He still felt the necessity to accept *sannyāsa*. He did not only want to taste *rasa*, He also wanted to sprinkle mercy. In Navadvīpa He was both tasting and giving something, but in order to give even more, He accepted the renounced life of a *sannyāsī*. He quickly left Śacī Mātā and Viṣṇupriyā, and these were very sorrowful scenes. Kṛṣṇa abandoned the *gopīs* in Vṛndāvana, went to Mathurā, and after that to Dvārakā. Similarly, Mahāprabhu left Viṣṇupriyā-devī just as Rāmacandra left Sītā forever, and this was particularly heart-rending.

After taking *sannyāsa*, Mahāprabhu went to Purī. After that He was admitted into the school of Rāya Rāmānanda and then into the school of Svarūpa Dāmodara, and after that He preached His mission of *rāga-mārga*; that is, *rāgānuga-bhakti*.

Śrī Caitanya Mahāprabhu at Ṭoṭā-gopīnātha in Purī

On the occasions that Mahāprabhu saw Subhadrā and Baladeva, He did not experience much pleasure. Rather, in front of Baladeva and His sister Subhadrā, He felt shy and thought, "I have come to Kurukṣetra." He was in the mood of Śrīmatī Rādhikā at Kurukṣetra where, in great separation, She tried to bring Kṛṣṇa (Jagannātha) to Vṛndāvana. In the mood of Śrīmatī Rādhikā, Mahāprabhu did not like to see Kṛṣṇa at Kurukṣetra because all His associates, along with all His queens of Dvārakā, were present, and there were many horses and elephants.

There was no chance for Rādhikā to be with Kṛṣṇa in private at Kurukṣetra, and this is why Mahāprabhu felt unbearable separation during the Ratha-yātrā Festival. He also felt unbearable separation in the Gambhīrā. There, His mood was like that of Rādhikā's in Vṛndāvana as She felt separation from Kṛṣṇa when He was in Dvārakā. The mood of separation was always present in Mahāprabhu when He was in Purī. When Rādhikā went to Kurukṣetra, She could not take rest with Kṛṣṇa. Instead, She was given separate accommodation in a tent, and Kṛṣṇa lived with the Yādavas and His queens. When He went to His own accommodation, She felt great separation from Him.

In Purī, Śrī Caitanya Mahāprabhu sometimes saw the sea as the Yamunā and jumped in it, but once there He wept still more because Kṛṣṇa would disappear. Sometimes He became like a tortoise, His limbs drawn into His body, and sometimes the joints of His hands and legs would become separated by as much as eight inches and remain connected only by skin. At that time He sometimes appeared like a ghost, and when the devotees would see Him in that condition, they would become fearful and begin to weep for Him. All this was due to His separation from Kṛṣṇa.

Therefore, to get some relief, He would go to take *darśana* of the deity of Ṭoṭā-gopīnātha. Seeing Ṭoṭā-gopīnātha, He thought, "Oh, I have come to Vṛndāvana. My *prāṇanātha* is here." In this way His tears of separation would subside.

On the left side of Ṭoṭā-gopīnātha is Rādhikā, on the right side Lalitā, and both are black like Kṛṣṇa. Rādhā becomes black by seeing Her *prāṇanātha* and becoming deeply absorbed in Him. She sometimes takes Kṛṣṇa's flute and begins to play it, and in this way also, being fully absorbed in Him, She becomes black. This is also true of Lalitā. Thinking of black Kṛṣṇa, she also becomes black. This is the mood of Ṭoṭā-gopīnātha accompanied by Rādhikā and Lalitā. Likewise, in the mood of Śrīmatī Rādhikā, Kṛṣṇa becomes Mahāprabhu, and at that time Lalitā becomes Śrī Svarūpa Dāmodara.

Although you will not see any other *vigraha* sitting, He sits. Some say that when Śrīla Gadādhara Paṇḍita became old, he could no longer offer garlands to Ṭoṭā-gopīnātha, and therefore Ṭoṭā-gopīnātha sat down. But this is not actually true. Caitanya Mahāprabhu disappeared at the age of 48, and Gadādhara Paṇḍita was only one year younger. He left this world a year after Mahāprabhu disappeared, and thus there was no chance for him to become old. The actual history is that when Mahāprabhu disappeared, following Mahāprabhu's order, Gadādhara Paṇḍita did not leave the worship of Ṭoṭā-gopīnātha. Always feeling separation from Mahāprabhu, he quickly became lean and thin, and it was for this reason that he could not stand up to give Ṭoṭā-gopīnātha a garland. Seeing Gadādhara Paṇḍita in such a state, Ṭoṭā-gopīnātha sat down for him, and Gadādhara Paṇḍita continued to offer garlands along with his tears.

There was a devotee of Śrī Caitanya Mahāprabhu named Māmu Ṭhākura who used to render various services to Him. Soon after Mahāprabhu disappeared, Gadādhara Paṇḍita also disappeared, and at that time his disciple Māmu Ṭhākura was appointed by the government of Purī to serve Ṭoṭā-gopīnātha. He was old – about 84 years – and he could not properly offer garlands to Ṭoṭā-gopīnātha. Some say that perhaps because Māmu Ṭhākura could not give garlands to Ṭoṭā-gopīnātha in his old age, Ṭoṭā-gopīnātha sat down for him. Actually, however, Ṭoṭā-gopīnātha sat only for Śrīmatī Rādhikā (who appeared as Gadādhara Paṇḍita). It is a common thing for Kṛṣṇa to stand up and sit down for Śrīmatī Rādhikā.

At first Mahāprabhu resided in Navadvīpa, from childhood up to *kiśora-līlā*, reading and writing. When He was 24 years old He left His home and came to Jagannātha Purī, where He bestowed His mercy upon Sārvabhauma Bhaṭṭācārya. After that He went to South India, and there He met Śrī Rāya Rāmānanda at Godāvarī. First Rāya Rāmānanda saw Him as *rasika-śekhara* (Kṛṣṇa). Then He saw *rasarāja-mahābhāva*, Śrīmatī Rādhikā and Kṛṣṇa combined, and he fainted. After that Mahāprabhu returned to Purī and fully relished the *vipralambha-bhāva* of Śrīmatī Rādhikā.

Caitanya Mahāprabhu performed His *kiśora-līlā* in Navadvīpa, and therefore Navadvīpa is none other than Vṛndāvana. Śrīla Narottama dāsa Ṭhākura and others have explained that it is actually non-different from Vṛndāvana, but they never said that Jagannātha-kṣetra is Vṛndāvana. Rather, Jagannātha-kṣetra represents Dvārakā or Kurukṣetra.

Those who follow Śrī Caitanya Mahāprabhu and perform *bhajana* in Navadvīpa will emerge in Vṛndāvana on the bank of the Yamunā at Vaṁśīvaṭa. Our *ācāryas* have revealed this in their writings, but they have never said that Jagannātha Purī is the same as Vṛndāvana. Śrī Kṣetra means Lakṣmī-kṣetra, where Satyabhāmā and Rukmiṇī, or Mahā-Lakṣmī, reside. If someone leaves his body in Jagannātha Purī, he assumes a four-handed form (in Vaikuṇṭha), but this is not so in Vṛndāvana and

Navadvīpa. There, one will become two handed like the associates of Rādhā and Kṛṣṇa. Therefore, Navadvīpa is superior to Jagannātha Purī.

The four places of Mahāprabhu are Navadvīpa, Purī, Godāvarī, and Vṛndāvana. Vṛndāvana and Navadvīpa are the same, but they are seen as two. At the time of *sādhana*, Navadvīpa is seen as Navadvīpa, and when the devotee has reached perfection, it is seen as Vṛndāvana. In *sādhanāvastha* (the stage of performing *sādhana*) we will see Śrī Caitanya Mahāprabhu in the form of Śrī Caitanya Mahāprabhu, but when we become perfected, we will exclaim, "Oh, Rādhā and Kṛṣṇa have together become Śrī Caitanya Mahāprabhu." So both are one.

In the intense separation of *divyonmāda*, Śrī Caitanya Mahāprabhu used to see Purī as Kurukṣetra and Dvārakā. As far as Godāvarī is concerned, it is Mahāprabhu's "school." There He learned from His *śikṣā-guru*, Viśākhā-devī, in the school of Rāya Rāmānanda, and after that He returned to Purī. And in Purī, He was always absorbed in thoughts of Vṛndāvana.

Some people say that the part of Purī in which Ṭoṭā-gopīnātha resides is *gupta-vṛndāvana*. It is true that Mahāprabhu used to see Ṭoṭā-gopīnātha's dwelling as Vṛndāvana, but it is not Vṛndāvana. It is part of Dvārakā and Kurukṣetra, and Śrī Caitanya Mahāprabhu used to feel separation there in Purī throughout the entire day and night. He would only lament in the mood of separation.

The *ācāryas* in our disciplic line are associates of Śrīmatī Rādhikā, *pālyadāsīs*. They want Śrīmatī Rādhikā to be always cheerful, and She is cheerful when She is with Kṛṣṇa. We are pleased when Rādhikā is hidden in a *kuñja* and Kṛṣṇa is searching for Her, calling, "Where is Rādhā? Where are Rādhā, Lalitā, Viśākhā, and the others?" At that time the *gopīs* are most pleased, thinking, "Oh, today He is searching." We should come to the stage in which we can also be pleased in that way.

In Purī, Rādhikā (Caitanya Mahāprabhu) is always calling, "O Kṛṣṇa! O Kṛṣṇa!" We do not desire that. We select as the best place, that place where Kṛṣṇa will search – a place like Rādhā-kuṇḍa. There Kṛṣṇa approaches Rādhikā and serves Her lotus feet, and at that time Rādhikā feels proud and happy. In Purī there is no *rāsa-līlā*. Yet Jagannātha Purī is extremely important. For us, at our stage, the mood of separation is more helpful than meeting. But ultimately we want Śrīmatī Rādhikā to be always pleased. In Purī She is always weeping and we don't want to see that. We consider Vṛndāvana the best place, because Vṛndāvana is where Rādhikā will place Her feet in Kṛṣṇa's lap, and He will paint His name on them. Kṛṣṇa will then keep Her feet on His head and heart, and the fresh color on Her feet will make stamp-like prints on His body. Kṛṣṇa always serves Her in Vṛndāvana, where She will say, "Oh, He loves Me best." This is what we desire. For *sādhana*, on the other hand, separation is helpful. Without developing feelings of separation, we cannot advance an inch.

Ratha-yātrā in Śrīdhāma Navadvīpa – is it contradictory to the conception of rūpānuga-bhakti?

[*In the following article originally printed in the December 1969 issue of Śrī Bhāgavata Patrikā, Śrīla Nārāyaṇa Mahārāja replies to some doubts regarding the present-day performance of Śrī Ratha-yātrā in Navadvīpa by the Gauḍīya Vedānta Samiti, as established by Śrīla Bhakti Prajñāna Keśava Gosvāmī Mahārāja.*]

Doubt 1: Ratha-yātrā is not performed in Śrī Vṛndāvana. Therefore, in Śrī Navadvīpa-dhāma, which is *abhinna-vraja-*

maṇḍala (non-different from Vraja), why should this *līlā* be exhibited?

Reply 1: The three worshipable deities of the Gauḍīya Vaiṣṇavas, namely Śrī Madana-mohana, Śrī Govinda, and Śrī Gopīnātha, have Their respective temples in Vṛndāvana. The festival of *ratha-yātrā-līlā* has been held in these temples with great pomp and splendor for hundreds of years. At the same time as the Śrī Ratha-yātrā procession is held in Purī, the same festival is also held in the temples established by the Gosvāmīs, such as the Śrī Rādhā-Dāmodara Mandira, and also in the Śrī Rādhā-Śyāmasundara Mandira, the Śrī Rādhā-Gokulānanda Mandira, and others. In addition, it is also held in almost all the prominent temples of the other *sampradāyas* such as the Śrī Raṅganātha Temple and the Śrī Śaha-bihārī Mandira. This annual *ratha-yātrā-līlā* is also a common sight in the homes of thousands of Vrajavāsīs. This procession takes place not only in Vṛndāvana but also in Mathurā, Nandagaon, Varṣāṇā, and even at Rādhā-kuṇḍa. Moreover, there are also ancient temples of Śrī Jagannātha-deva in Vṛndāvana and at Rādhā-kuṇḍa. Therefore, the statement that the *ratha-yātrā-līlā* is not performed in Vṛndāvana or Vraja-maṇḍala is completely false.

There are *rūpānuga* Vaiṣṇavas throughout the world. They have performed the procession of *śrī-ratha-yātrā-līlā* in the past, and they are still performing it, in order to nourish their *bhajana*. An associate of Śrī Gaurasundara, Śrī Kamalākara Pippalāi, is a friend of Kṛṣṇa named Mahābala Sakhā among the *dvādaśa-gopālas* (twelve prominent cowherd boys) in *kṛṣṇa-līlā*. He manifested the service and pastimes of *ratha-yātrā-līlā* of Śrī Jagannātha-deva in Bengal, in the district known as Maheśa. Even today, this Ratha-yātrā Festival is observed annually with magnificent pageantry. In the nearby district of Śrī Rāma-pura, the service of Śrī Jagannātha-deva is conducted both in Vallabhapura and Chatra, where Ratha-yātrā has been observed for hundreds of years. In the village of Dhāma-rāi (in the district of Ḍhākā), Ratha-yātrā is also very famous.

The Vyāsadeva of *śrī-gaura-līlā*, Śrī Vṛndāvana dāsa Ṭhākura, has also established a deity of Śrī Jagannātha-deva in his own village of Śrīpāṭa, Śrī Māmagāchi in Śrī Modadrumadvīpa in Śrī Navadvīpa-dhāma. The service of Śrī Jagannātha-deva is still going on there even today. The Ratha-yātrā of Mahīṣadala, in the district of Medinīpura, is also very famous. These days, even in large cities of America such as San Francisco, Śrī Ratha-yātrā is celebrated in a grand style, in accordance with the mood of Śrī Caitanya Mahāprabhu.

Śrīman Mahāprabhu expressed a particular mood in regard to Ratha-yātrā. He always considered that Śrī Kṛṣṇa, being mounted upon His chariot, is returning to Vṛndāvana to meet with all the *gopīs*, especially Śrīmatī Rādhikā, who had been afflicted by the severe pains of separation from Kṛṣṇa for a very long time. We should always remember that the *rūpānuga-ācāryas* who had the necessary facilities manifested this pastime of the Ratha-yātrā Festival on the earthly plane in order to stimulate the aforementioned mood of Śrī Caitanya Mahāprabhu within their hearts and to nourish their *bhajana*. Some *niṣkiñcana-rūpānuga* Vaiṣṇavas, being bereft of the necessary facilities for observing this festival, have stimulated this mood within their hearts by *mānasī-sevā*, service performed within the mind. Alternatively, they nourish their *bhāva* by taking *darśana* of *śrī-ratha-yātrā-līlā* in various places such as Purī-dhāma. The purpose of both approaches is fundamentally one; there is no difference between them.

Doubt 2: Seeing the *ratha* would stimulate a terribly undesirable apprehension in the hearts of the *vraja-gopīs*. Therefore, how can the *rūpānuga* Vaiṣṇavas, who are following the moods of the *gopīs*, join in the Ratha-yātrā procession?

Reply 2: This concept is also completely wrong in all respects. Adorned with the sentiment and complexion of Śrī Rādhā, Śrī Gaurasundara is directly Śrī Kṛṣṇa Himself. Śrī Gadādhara Gosvāmī (Śrīmatī Rādhikā), Śrī Svarūpa Dāmodara (Śrī Lalitā), Śrī Rāya Rāmānanda (Śrī Viśākhā), Śrīla Rūpa Gosvāmī (Śrī Rūpa Mañjarī), Śrī Sanātana Gosvāmī (Śrī Lavaṅga Mañjarī), Śrī Raghunātha dāsa Gosvāmī (Śrī Rati Mañjarī), and all of the associates of Śrī Gaurasundara, who were all mainly *sakhīs* or *sakhās* in Vraja, assembled together for Ratha-yātrā. They all danced and chanted before the chariot, deeply immersed in the mood: "*kṛṣṇa lañā vraje yāi e-bhāva antara* – let us take Kṛṣṇa and go back to Vṛndāvana." Did the associates of Mahāprabhu feel any distress or anguish upon seeing the chariot? Definitely not. Then why will their followers, the *rūpānuga* Vaiṣṇavas, feel any anguish or undesirable apprehension?

The internal moods of Ratha-yātrā as promoted by Śrī Gaurasundara are as follows: after a long period of separation, on the occasion of the solar eclipse at Kurukṣetra, Śrīmatī Rādhikā and the *gopīs* met with Śrī Kṛṣṇa. But Śrīmatī Rādhikā was not satisfied because Śrī Kṛṣṇa was dressed as a king and surrounded by immense opulence, elephants, horses, military generals, and His associates of Dvārakā. She wanted to see Kṛṣṇa dressed as a cowherd boy in Vṛndāvana, the place of His sweet, human-like pastimes. Therefore She wanted to bring Kṛṣṇa back to Vraja. It is evident from the *Padma Purāṇa* that *śrī-ratha-yātrā-līlā*, the pastime of Kṛṣṇa's returning again to Vṛndāvana on a chariot, is exhibited in Śrī Jagannātha Purī and other places. Therefore, what is there to impede the manifestation of Ratha-yātrā in Śrī Vṛndāvana or Śrī Navadvīpa-dhāma? In order to stimulate this profound mood that was established by Śrīman

Mahāprabhu, His devout followers can perform Ratha-yātrā everywhere, and have indeed done so. The mood of Śrīman Mahāprabhu has been revealed in this verse:

yaḥ kaumāra-haraḥ sa eva hi varas tā eva caitra-kṣapās
te conmīlita-mālatī-surabhayaḥ prauḍhāḥ kadambānilāḥ
sā caivāsmi tathāpi tatra surata-vyāpāra-līlā-vidhau
revā-rodhasi vetasī-taru-tale cetaḥ samutkaṇṭhate

Śrī Caitanya-caritāmṛta (*Madhya-līlā* 13.121)

That very personality who stole away my heart during my youth is now again my master. These are the same moonlit nights of the month of Caitra. The same fragrance of *mālatī* flowers is there, and the same sweet breezes are blowing from the *kadamba* forest. In our intimate relationship I am also the same lover, yet still my mind is not happy here. I am eager to go back to that place on the bank of the Revā under the Vetasī tree. That is my desire.

And also:

ei dhuyā-gāne nācena dvitīya prahara
kṛṣṇa lañā vraje yāi e-bhāva antara

Śrī Caitanya-caritāmṛta (*Madhya-līlā* 1.56)

Śrī Caitanya Mahāprabhu used to sing this song [*sei ta parāṇa-nātha*] especially during the latter part of the day, and He would think, "Let Me take Kṛṣṇa back to Vṛndāvana." This ecstasy was always filling His heart.

Yes, it is true that when the *gopīs*, or the Vaiṣṇavas who have taken shelter of *gopī-bhāva*, see the chariot which takes Kṛṣṇa out of Vraja and far away from them, they feel anguish and the apprehension that Kṛṣṇa will not return. However, when they see the chariot on which Kṛṣṇa sat and returned to Vṛndāvana, they become overjoyed – not sorrowful.

After taking permission from the *gopas* and *gopīs* of Vṛndāvana, Uddhava sat upon his chariot and was about to return to Mathurā to meet with Kṛṣṇa. At that time the *vraja-gopas* and *gopīs*, overwhelmed with *prema*, adorned the chariot with various gifts for Kṛṣṇa and bade Uddhava farewell with great respect.

atha gopīr anujñāpya
yaśodāṁ nandam eva ca
gopān āmantrya dāśārho
yāsyann āruruhe ratham

Śrīmad-Bhāgavatam (10.47.64)

[Śukadeva Gosvāmī said:] Uddhava, the descendant of Daśārha, then took permission to leave from the *gopīs* and from Mother Yaśodā and Nanda Mahārāja. He bade farewell to all the cowherd men and, about to depart, mounted his chariot.

Furthermore, after some time, Śrī Baladeva came to Nanda-Gokula on a chariot. When he arrived, all the *gopas* and *gopīs* welcomed Him with great affection.

balabhadraḥ kuru-śreṣṭha
bhagavān ratham āsthitaḥ
suhṛd-didṛkṣur utkaṇṭhaḥ
prayayau nanda-gokulam

Śrīmad-Bhāgavatam (10.65.1)

[Śukadeva Gosvāmī said:] O best of the Kurus, once Lord Balarāma, eager to visit his well-wishing friends, mounted his chariot and traveled to Nanda-Gokula.

pariṣvaktaś cirotkaṇṭhair
gopair gopībhir eva ca
rāmo 'bhivādya pitarāv
āśīrbhir abhinanditaḥ

Śrīmad-Bhāgavatam (10.65.2)

Having long suffered the anxiety of separation, the cowherd men and their wives embraced Lord Balarāma. The Lord then offered respects to his parents, and they joyfully greeted him with blessings.

Śrīla Jīva Gosvāmī, on the basis of the verses of the *Padma Purāṇa*, has described that Kṛṣṇa, after killing Dantavakra, indeed returned to Vraja upon a chariot. Upon hearing the sound of Kṛṣṇa's conch and the rumbling of His chariot, all the *gopas* and *gopīs* of Vraja surmised that Kṛṣṇa was returning. Driven by excessive eagerness to see Him, even feeble old women ran with great haste from wherever they were in the direction of the sound of Kṛṣṇa's conch and chariot. When they drew nearer and saw that Garuḍa was sitting on the flag of the chariot, they became sure that Kṛṣṇa was definitely returning to Vraja. Being overwhelmed with joy, they became motionless like statues and were unable to go any further. Only their gaze advanced in the direction of the approaching chariot. This is described in the following verse from *Śrī Gopāla-campū* (30.34):

strī-bāla-vṛddha-valitā vraja-vāsinās te
kṛṣṇāgatiṁ yadu-purād anumāya-śaṅkhāt
evaṁ dravanti capalaṁ sma yathā vidur na
svātmānam apy ahaha kiṁ punar agra-paścāt

Therefore, the idea that the *vraja-gopīs* become distressed and apprehensive upon seeing a chariot in all circumstances is incorrect.

In the pastime of Śrī Ratha-yātrā, and also on the path of *śrī-rūpānuga-bhajana*, the importance of the internal mood is predominant. Externally perceived substances or places are not more important than the internal mood. In Ratha-yātrā, the internal mood that Kṛṣṇa is returning to Vraja is stimulated and inspired, not the pastimes of Dvārakā or Mathurā. Kṛṣṇa returned to Vraja after being absent for a very long time, and it is in this mood that Śrī Jagannātha-deva travels from the Jagannātha Mandira in Purī to the Śrī Guṇḍicā Mandira. During this journey Śrī Gaurasundara and His confidential associates experienced the utmost jubilation, being deeply absorbed in the moods of Śrī Rādhā and the *vraja-gopīs*, respectively. Moreover, they all assembled together before the chariot, singing and dancing in great joy, fully absorbed in exactly the same *bhāva*, during the *ulta-ratha-yātrā* (the festival of Jagannātha-deva's return to Śrī Mandira from Śrī Guṇḍicā).

Did they think that by observing Ratha-yātrā as it proceeded in the opposite direction that Śrī Kṛṣṇa was leaving Vṛndāvana and returning to Mathurā or Dvārakā? Never. Such an understanding must be mistaken. It has been mentioned in *Śrī Caitanya-caritāmṛta* how Śrī Caitanya Mahāprabhu and His associates assembled together, danced, and performed *kīrtana* at the *ulta-ratha-yātrā*:

āra dine jagannāthera bhitara-vijaya
rathe caḍi' jagannātha cale nijālaya

Śrī Caitanya-caritāmṛta (*Madhya-līlā* 14. 244)

The next day Lord Jagānnātha came out from the temple and, riding on the car, returned to His own abode.

pūrvavat kaila prabhu lañā bhakta-gaṇa
parama ānande karena nartana-kīrtana

Śrī Caitanya-caritāmṛta (*Madhya-līlā* 14. 245)

As previously, Śrī Caitanya Mahāprabhu and His devotees chanted and danced with great pleasure.

Although the *vraja-gopīs*, especially Śrīmatī Rādhikā, were extremely anxious to see Śrī Kṛṣṇa, they would not leave Vṛndāvana even to go the very short distance to where Kṛṣṇa was staying in Mathurā. Then how can Śrī Gaurasundara, who is adorned with the sentiments of Śrīmatī Rādhikā, along with His associates, stay at the Purī Mandira or Śrī Gambhīrā? The Purī Mandira and Śrī Gambhīrā are the embodiment of Dvārakā because the Ratha-yātrā sets off from there. Alternatively, Śrī Gaurasundara used to see the gardens of Purī as Vṛndāvana, the ocean as Yamunā, and Caṭaka-parvata as Govardhana. In such a Vṛndāvana, what aspect of the Ratha-yātrā Festival would be contrary to the principles of *rāgānuga-* or *rūpānuga-bhakti*?

Why did the Vrajavāsī Gosvāmīs, Śrīla Ṭhākura Bhaktivinoda, Śrīla Bhaktisiddhānta Sarasvatī Ṭhākura Prabhupāda, Śrīla Śrīdhara Mahārāja, and all the prominent *rūpānuga-ācāryas* go to Śrī Purī-dhāma to have *darśana* of Ratha-yātrā, if Ratha-yātrā *darśana* would be the cause of any type of disturbance or apprehension that something undesirable was about to happen? It appears that *darśana* of Ratha-yātrā simply stimulates *vraja-gopī-prema.*

Doubt 3: From ancient times up until the present day, no great personality who was expert in the performance of *bhajana* has ever performed the procession of *ratha-yātrā-līlā* in Śrī Navadvīpa-dhāma, which is *abhinna-vraja*, non-different from Vraja-maṇḍala.

Reply 3: This statement is meaningless and incoherent in all respects for the following reason. From the time of Śrīman Mahāprabhu until the present day, almost all Gauḍīya *ācāryas* and *bhaktas* have made a pilgrimage to Purī-dhāma at the time of Ratha-yātrā to have *darśana* of the festival. In this way, the divinely inspired vision of the moods exhibited by Śrī Gaurasundara is stimulated within their hearts and thus their *bhajana* is nourished. Until now, there had been no impetus to manifest Ratha-yātrā in Śrī Navadvīpa-dhāma and our previous *ācāryas* had not considered it necessary to do so. However, whenever the inspiration came in the hearts of great personalities, they manifested this *līlā* in various places in Gauḍa-maṇḍala, such as in the district of Maheśa. Thus if a great personality is also inspired to manifest this *līlā* in Śrī Navadvīpa-dhāma, then it is in no way contrary to the path of *śrī-rūpānuga-bhajana*.

For example, in the Gauḍīya Vaiṣṇava *sampradāya*, from the time of Śrīman Mahāprabhu, *Śrīmad-Bhāgavatam* has been considered the natural commentary on *Śrī Brahma-sūtra*. However, when the necessity arose, Śrī Gauḍīya Vedāntācārya Baladeva Vidyābhūṣaṇa Prabhu manifested a separate commentary, namely *Śrī Govinda-bhāṣya*. Is this activity contrary to *siddhānta*, or is it the embodiment of prestige for our Gauḍīya *sampradāya*?

Doubt 4: Śrīla Bhaktisiddhānta Sarasvatī Ṭhākura did not perform *ratha-yātrā-līlā* in Śrī Gaura-dhāma.

Reply 4: Śrīla Bhaktisiddhānta Sarasvatī Ṭhākura manifested Śrī Rādhā-kuṇḍa and Śrī Śyāma-kuṇḍa in Vrajapattana (at Śrī Caitanya Maṭha) within Śrīdhāma Māyāpura. He preached *daiva-varṇāśrama-dharma*, re-established the use of saffron cloth and *tridaṇḍi-sannyāsa* in the Gauḍīya Vaiṣṇava *sampradāya*, and flew the victory flag of Gauḍīya Vaiṣṇava *dharma* throughout the world. Prior to the appearance of this crown jewel in the dynasty of *ācāryas*, no other *ācārya* ever inaugurated the aforementioned activities. Yet, can any of these projects of Śrīla Bhaktisiddhānta Prabhupāda be considered contrary to the principles of *rūpānuga-bhakti*? Never. Anyone who says such a thing is utterly ignorant of *bhakti-tattva*. [The point here being that, just as Śrīla Bhaktisiddhānta Sarasvatī Ṭhākura set precedents in certain areas, so his disciple, Śrīla Bhakti Prajñāna Keśava Gosvāmī Mahārāja, can also set precedents when there is a need to do so.]

Doubt 5: In Śrī Navadvīpa-dhāma, how is the *darśana* of Dvārakā possible or appropriate?

Reply 5: We have already explained that the predominant *bhāva* in *śrī-ratha-yātrā-līlā* is "*kṛṣṇa lañā vraje yāi* – let us take Kṛṣṇa to Vraja." There is not even the slightest scent of a *sphūrti* (momentary vision) or *darśana* of Dvārakā in this *bhāva*. Therefore, even the question of any kind of *dvārakā-darśana* arising from the performance of *ratha-yātrā-līlā* in Śrī Navadvīpa-dhāma is irrelevant. On the other hand, Śrī Navadvīpa-maṇḍala, which is non-different from Vṛndāvana, is *aṁśi-dhāma*, i.e. the root *dhāma* in which all other *dhāmas* exist. Mathurā, Dvārakā, Ayodhyā, and Paravyoma are all eternally existing in Śrī Navadvīpa-dhāma, just as all the plenary portions of *aṁśī* Kṛṣṇa, such as Nārāyaṇa and Viṣṇu, exist eternally within Him.

At Candraśekhara-bhavana (Vrajapattana) in Māyāpura-dhāma, Śrī Gaurasundara personally used to dance in the mood of Śrī Rukmiṇī, yet it is well known that Śrī Rukmiṇī-devī is an associate of *dvārakā-līlā*. Therefore, if this *līlā* is possible in Vrajapattana, which is non-different from Vraja or Śrī Rādhā-kuṇḍa, then how can *dvārakā-darśana* be impossible in Śrīdhāma Navadvīpa? Thus on what grounds can it be said that the manifestation of *ratha-yātrā-līlā* is not possible?

Hence, the conclusion is that there is an inseparable relationship between *ratha-yātrā-līlā* and *rūpānuga-ānugatya*, the pursuance of the pure path established by Śrīla Rūpa Gosvāmī. *Śrī-rūpānuga* Vaiṣṇavas manifest this *līlā* throughout Navadvīpa-dhāma and thus, according to the path founded by Śrīman Mahāprabhu, they inspire the internal mood expressed in the following verse written by Śrīla Rūpa Gosvāmī:

priyaḥ so 'yaṁ kṛṣṇaḥ sahacari kuru-kṣetra-militas
tathāhaṁ sā rādhā tad idam ubhayoḥ saṅgama-sukham
tathāpy antaḥ-khelan-madhura-muralī-pañcama-juṣe
mano me kālindī-pulina-vipināya spṛhayati

Śrī Caitanya-caritāmṛta (*Madhya-līlā* 1.76)

[Śrīmatī Rādhārāṇī said:] My dear friend, now I have met My very old and dear friend Kṛṣṇa on this field of Kurukṣetra. I am the same Rādhārāṇī, and now we are meeting together. It is very pleasant, but still I would like to go to the bank of the Yamunā beneath the trees of the forest there. I wish to hear the vibration of His sweet flute playing the fifth note within that forest of Vṛndāvana.

This mood thoroughly nourishes the *bhajana* of the genuine *śrī-rūpānuga* Vaiṣṇavas.

CHAPTER ELEVEN

CLOSING WORDS

Sending the deity back

Toward the end of His *līlā*, Śrī Caitanya Mahāprabhu read a sonnet written by Śrī Advaita Ācārya:

bāulake kahiha, loka ha-ila bāula
bāulake kahiha, hāṭe nā vikāya cāula

Śrī Caitanya-caritāmṛta (*Antya-līlā* 19.20)

Please inform Śrī Caitanya Mahāprabhu, who is acting like a madman, that everyone here has become mad like Him. Inform Him also that rice is no longer in demand in the marketplace. It is fully available in the market, but no one is purchasing.

What does this mean? Caitanya Mahāprabhu had been called by Śrī Advaita Ācārya when there was no "rice" anywhere, when there was only emptiness everywhere. Mahāprabhu and His associates then brought "rice," which was the love and affection for Kṛṣṇa that is attained through chanting His name. Now, everyone everywhere had become satisfied and wealthy. No one needed to buy rice any more, so there was no more need for shops and shopkeepers. Advaita Ācārya had called the deity, and now he was sending Him back to His abode.

Practically no one could understand the letter. Only one person, Śrī Svarūpa Dāmodara, understood, and that is why he questioned Caitanya Mahāprabhu:

jāniyā svarūpa gosāñi prabhure puchila
'ei tarajāra artha bujhite nārila'

Śrī Caitanya-caritāmṛta (*Antya-līlā* 19.25)

Although he knew the secret, Svarūpa Dāmodara Gosvāmī inquired from the Lord, "What is the meaning of this sonnet? I could not understand it."

Caitanya Mahāprabhu replied:

upāsanā lāgi' devera karena āvāhana
pūjā lāgi' kata kāla karena nirodhana

Śrī Caitanya-caritāmṛta (*Antya-līlā* 19.26)

Advaita Ācārya invites the Lord to come and be worshiped, and he keeps the deity for some time to perform the worship.

Svarūpa Dāmodara wanted to hear from Śrī Caitanya Mahāprabhu's own mouth, and Mahāprabhu explained everything: "He called Me, and now he is praying, 'Please return to Goloka Vṛndāvana.'" Śrīla Haridāsa Ṭhākura was one of the few people who knew that the Lord would soon depart, and that is why he left the world before Mahāprabhu. He was very intelligent.

Then, one day, Caitanya Mahāprabhu went to the temple of Ṭoṭā-gopīnātha to listen to Śrī Gadādhara Paṇḍita reciting *Bhāgavatam*. Gadādhara Paṇḍita was weeping while explaining the verses, especially this one:

barhāpīḍaṁ naṭa-vara-vapuḥ karṇayoḥ karṇikāraṁ
bibhrad vāsaḥ kanaka-kapiśaṁ vaijayantīṁ ca mālām
randhrān veṇor adhara-sudhayāpūrayan gopa-vṛndair
vṛndāraṇyaṁ sva-pada-ramaṇaṁ prāviśad gīta-kīrtiḥ

Śrīmad-Bhāgavatam (10.21.5)

Śyāmasundara entered the forest of Vṛndā-devī, accompanied by His cowherd boyfriends. His head was decorated with a peacock feather, He wore yellow *karṇikāra* flowers over His ears, and a dazzling golden-yellow garment on His body. A fragrant *vaijayantī* garland made of five kinds of flowers hung around His neck, and extended down to His knees. He was splendidly attired as a beautiful *naṭavara*, a most expert dancer, and He appeared just like a very fine actor on stage. He poured the nectar of His lips through the holes of His flute, and the cowherd boys followed behind Him, singing His glories. Śrī Kṛṣṇa made the land of Vṛndāvana even more charming than Vaikuṇṭha, for He beautified it with prints of His lotus feet, which were marked with the conch, disk, and other symbols.

Mahāprabhu became very absorbed and cried out in separation, "Where is My beloved Vrajendra-nandana Śyāmasundara?" Then He entered the altar of Ṭoṭā-gopīnātha, although the curtains of the altar were closed, and He never returned from there. Hardly anyone knew what became of Him. He finished His worldly pastimes, and merged into Ṭoṭā-gopīnātha forever.

Mahāprabhu's final teaching

Caitanya Mahāprabhu was thinking, "I am Rādhā, and I am taking Kṛṣṇa to Vṛndāvana." This is the essence of the entire Chariot Festival. Your *prayojana* (goal) is that *prema.*

We also go to Jagannātha Purī with that objective. Because Jagannātha Purī is Dvārakā or Kurukṣetra, I would not be in the mood to go there if it were not for Śrī Caitanya Mahāprabhu. I go because of Caitanya Mahāprabhu's dancing, and because of the way He saw that unusual figure with round eyes. Caitanya Mahāprabhu never thought, "Here are Jagannātha, Baladeva, and Subhadrā." He saw Vrajendra-nandana Śyāmasundara. At present, we cannot see Jagannātha like that. We only go there to obtain that mood of Caitanya Mahāprabhu – to take all His moods within us. That is why Śrīla Rūpa Gosvāmī used to go, and that is why Śrīla Sanātana Gosvāmī and all the other Gosvāmīs were there, as well as Śrī Svarūpa Dāmodara, Śrī Rāya Rāmānanda, and all their associates. It was only for this.

You should try to remember all these histories properly. Then you will have a taste for them, and you will forget all worldly attachments. You will forget where you are, and that is the symptom that your *bhakti* is developing. It is for this reason that Kṛṣṇa came, Mahāprabhu came, Nityānanda Prabhu came, Rūpa Gosvāmī and all other *gurus* came: only to give these mellows. If you receive even one drop of them, or even a tiny fraction of a drop, your life will be successful.

First we should decide on our objective, and that objective is *kṛṣṇa-prema-prayojana*. What is *kṛṣṇa-prema*? Hanumān's love for Rāma is *prema*, and Rukmiṇī and Satyabhāmā also serve Kṛṣṇa with *prema*. Subala Sakhā and Madhumaṅgala also have *prema*, and so do Pradyumna and Aniruddha. Uddhava is a high-class *premātura-bhakta* (a devotee imbued with overwhelming love); Mother Yaśodā and Nanda Bābā love Kṛṣṇa still more than Uddhava; and the *gopīs* have still greater affection for Kṛṣṇa. Among these various kinds of *prema*, which *kṛṣṇa-prema* is the highest and most superior?

Caitanya Mahāprabhu did not come to this world to sprinkle all types of *prema*, nor did He come only to give regulated *bhakti*:

anarpita-carīṁ cirāt karuṇayāvatīrṇaḥ kalau
samarpayitum unnatojjvala-rasāṁ sva-bhakti-śriyam
hariḥ puraṭa-sundara-dyuti-kadamba-sandīpitaḥ
sadā hṛdaya-kandare sphuratu vaḥ śacī-nandanaḥ

Śrī Caitanya-caritāmṛta (*Ādi-līlā* 1.4)

May the Supreme Lord who is known as the son of Śrīmatī Śacī-devī be transcendentally situated in the innermost chambers of your heart. Resplendent with the radiance of molten gold, He has appeared in the age of Kali by His causeless mercy to bestow what no incarnation has ever offered before: the most sublime and radiant mellow of devotional service, the mellow of amorous love.

What is *unnatojjvala-prema*? Is it the mood of Subala? Can we call his love *unnatojjvala-prema*? We cannot attain that type of *prema* if we do not know this *siddhānta*. We can only know these truths if we have high-class association, because those who have no *gopī-prema* cannot explain them. We should therefore go to *rasika* Vaiṣṇavas, and they will explain the meaning of *unnatojjvala-bhakti-rasa* and *kṛṣṇa-prema*. *Unnatojjvala* or *upapati-bhāva* refers only to the moods of the *gopīs*. *Upapati-bhāva* means paramour love. Subala does not have this type of love. He has a high class of love, and the love of Nanda and Yaśodā is also greatly elevated. They can control and bind Kṛṣṇa, but not fully. The love of the queens of Dvārakā is also very exalted, but it still cannot be called *unnatojjvala-prema*, because they do not think, "Kṛṣṇa is my beloved." Consequently, they can never actually control Him.

Only the *kṛṣṇa-prema* of the *gopīs* can be called *unnatojjvala-rasa*, and it can never be given to anyone else. However, the "beauty" (*śrī*) of this *prema* can be sprinkled upon the *jīva*, and it is for this purpose that Kṛṣṇa came to this world in the form of Caitanya Mahāprabhu. The beauty of this *prema* is Śrī Rūpa

Mañjarī's love and affection for Kṛṣṇa and Rādhikā; it is Rūpa Mañjarī's service to Rādhā-Kṛṣṇa Yugala, with an inclination toward Rādhikā. If Rādhikā is happy, she is happy. If Rādhikā is unhappy and in a mood of separation, she will also be in that mood. If Kṛṣṇa comes to meet Rādhikā, and Rādhikā tells Rūpa Mañjarī, "Oh, you should stop Kṛṣṇa there at the door," she will at once go and say to Him, "You cannot enter Rādhikā's *kuñja*. You must remain here. You are a cheater, and Rādhikā is not pleased with You." Kṛṣṇa will then fall down at Rūpa Mañjarī's lotus feet and pray, "Please permit Me to enter."

yat kiṅkarīṣu bahuśaḥ khalu kāku-vāṇī
nityaṁ parasya puruṣasya śikhaṇḍa-mauleḥ
tasyāḥ kadā rasa-nidher vṛṣabhānu-jāyās
tat-keli-kuñja-bhavanāṅgana-mārjanī syām

Śrī Rādhā-rasa-sudhā-nidhi (8)

O daughter of Vṛṣabhānu Mahārāja, O ocean of *rasa*! The Supreme Bhagavān, who wears a peacock feather in His hair, falls at the feet of Your maidservants and propitiates them with many humble and grief-stricken words to be allowed entrance into Your *kuñja*, where You engage in playful, amorous pastimes. If only I could become one stick in the broom used by Your *sakhīs* to clean Your delightful grove, I would consider my life a success.

Śrī Prabodhānanda Sarasvatī prays to Śrīmatī Rādhikā, "Kṛṣṇa folds His palms and prays to the lotus feet of Rūpa Mañjarī and Rati Mañjarī, 'Please let Me enter. I want to take *darśana* of Rādhā.' They reply, 'Never. You cannot go in.' I therefore want to be one of the sticks in the broom that is used for sweeping those *kuñjas* of Rādhikā. I just want to be one stick of that broom, and then I will think myself fortunate."

This is the greatest *prema-prayojana* – the moods of the *mañjarīs* who are always serving Śrīmatī Rādhikā.

āśā-bharair amṛta-sindhu-mayaiḥ kathañcit
kālo mayāti-gamitaḥ kila sāmprataṁ hi
tvaṁ cet kṛpāṁ mayi vidhāsyasi naiva kiṁ me
prāṇair vrajena ca varoru bakāriṇāpi

Vilāpa-kusumāñjali (102)

Śrīla Raghunātha dāsa Gosvāmī prays, "O Rādhikā! O Radhikā! Where are You? If You are not merciful to me, I will give up my body. I will die, I will die, I will die. I don't want to live in Vṛndāvana or at Rādhā-kuṇḍa. I don't want to live at Govardhana, I don't want to worship Kṛṣṇa, and I don't even want to see Him if You are not merciful to me. I am only waiting for You, waiting for You. I will die if You are not merciful to me."

This is the highest class of *prema-prayojana*. We must know that this rare *prema* is the object of life, and then we must enter the process to achieve it. This is the pinnacle of *vraja-prema*, and you cannot know this truth if you are not in the association of pure *rasika* Vaiṣṇavas. You will not be able to differentiate between the many grades of *prema*, and you will be cheated. You will think "Hanumān's *prema* is the highest," or "Uddhava's *prema* is the highest." You will not be able to differentiate between the *prema* of Dvārakā and the *prema* of Vraja.

Caitanya Mahāprabhu came especially to give this rare mood, and we should try to understand it. But you cannot achieve this goal if you are not in good association, and you are only hearing this verse: *śravaṇaṁ kīrtanaṁ viṣṇoḥ smaraṇaṁ pāda-sevanam* – that is in relation to regulated *bhakti*. Caitanya Mahāprabhu did not come for that at all; Śrī Rāmānujācārya and Madhvācārya had already given it. They gave *bhakti* – but not *bhakti-rasa*. Therefore, you cannot have it if you do not read the books of Śrīla Rūpa Gosvāmī and Śrīla Raghunātha dāsa Gosvāmī, and if you have no greed to attain this elevated *unnatojjvala* mood. You should follow only the regulative principles of *this* type of *bhakti* – life after life, after life, after life.

I have only come to remind you of this, and to give you some understanding and taste. Never be weak. Do not think about girlfriends and boyfriends. Be situated in your current position. If you are a family man, remain in that position. If you are a *brahmacārī*, remain there. If you are in the renounced order, remain there. Don't deviate from that position. If you are a *brahmacārī* or *brahmacāriṇī*, your love and affection for Kṛṣṇa should develop. How can you decide to marry if you have taste for chanting, remembering, and hearing these sweet pastimes? How can you decide to be attached to any girl or boy? Material attachment cannot touch those who have some taste. Such devotees cannot deviate.

Mahāprabhu explained the process for chanting and remembering *harināma*, and it is written in *Śrī Caitanya-caritāmṛta*. Mahāprabhu prayed, "I do not want wealth, reputation, position, a beautiful wife, or advanced education. I want nothing material. I only want to serve Kṛṣṇa in all of My lives – birth after birth." Mahāprabhu instructed:

tṛṇād api sunīcena
taror api sahiṣṇunā
amāninā mānadena
kīrtanīyaḥ sadā hariḥ

Śikṣāṣṭaka (3)

Thinking oneself to be even lower and more worthless than insignificant grass which is trampled beneath everyone's feet, being more tolerant than a tree, being prideless, and offering respect to all others according to their respective positions, one should continuously chant the holy name of Śrī Hari.

Do not desire praise for yourself, but try to honor everyone else according to their qualities. If you have no taste – if you are chanting, but tears do not come and your heart does not melt – you should think, "Surely this is due to my past activities, especially my offenses to Vaiṣṇavas." Repent for this, and chant and remember the pastimes of Kṛṣṇa always. Chant twenty-four hours a day, as Haridāsa Ṭhākura did.

Chant His name thinking, "I am in Vṛndāvana under the guidance of a qualified and *rasika* Vaiṣṇava." This is the process. You should think, "I am like a particle of dust at the feet of Kṛṣṇa. This is my constitutional position; I am part and parcel of Kṛṣṇa. I don't want to be separated from Him, but because of my own fault I am separated. O Vaiṣṇavas! O Gurudeva! Please be merciful to me so that I can be a dust particle at your lotus feet forever. I want the same mood felt by the *gopīs*."

yugāyitaṁ nimeṣeṇa
cakṣuṣā prāvṛṣāyitam
śūnyāyitaṁ jagat sarvaṁ
govinda-viraheṇa me

Śikṣāṣṭaka (7)

O *sakhī*, in separation from Govinda, even a moment seems like a millennium to Me. Tears begin to shower from My eyes like rain from the clouds, and this entire world seems void to Me.

The highest aspiration is to serve Śrīmatī Rādhikā, whose love is very elevated: "Kṛṣṇa is still My beloved, whether He crushes My heart by separation, or gives Me great happiness by meeting with Me. I want to serve Him with love. If He gives intense separation and crushes Me, He will still be My beloved. I cannot live without Him in any way." This was the final teaching of Śrīman Mahāprabhu.

Jagannātha-deva is Patita-pāvana, the savoir of the fallen

Now I will tell a recent story about Jagannātha. There was a *brāhmaṇa* from Orissa who was very old and could not walk well. He vowed, "I will go to Jagannātha Purī and see Jagannātha." Although it was four hundred miles to Purī, he began to walk, and he arrived in Bhuvanesvara at about midnight one night. By that time his feet and legs were so swollen that he could not walk another inch, and he sat down under a tree on the side of the road. Having had nothing to eat or drink for some time, he was practically starving to death. He had vowed, "I will not eat until I have taken *darśana* of Jagannātha," but he could not move, and the night was terribly dark. He had also vowed, "If I don't get *darśana* by this coming morning, I will leave my body." Consequently, he simply sat under the tree praying, "O Jagannātha, I am hopeless. I cannot go on. I will die right here."

Just then a car was driving by; something went wrong with it and it stopped just at the spot where the old *bābā* was sitting. The people in the car tried to make it start, without success. They thought that something might have dropped into the oil tank and they began to search for an object with which to take it out, but they could not find anything. When they saw the old man sitting there, they wanted to use his stick to remove whatever had fallen into the oil tank. "O Bābā, where are you coming from?" they asked. "Why are you sitting here?" "I was on my way to take *darśana* of Jagannātha, but I can't walk any further," he replied. "I simply can't go on. I will die right here." He let them take his stick, and with its help they were able to easily start their car. "Come with us in our car," they told that *bābā*, and they helped him into their car and drove off.

They all reached the Jagannātha Temple at exactly four in the morning. After taking *darśana* of Jagannātha, the *bābā* felt completely better and thought, "My swelling has gone. All my problems have gone away. Now everything is fine." He began to pray to Jagannātha, "Oh, You are so kind. I could not walk any further, so You sent a car for me. That car stopped there only for me. They brought me, and now I am here." At that moment, someone approached him and said, "Do you want to take *prasāda*? Please, come and take Jagannātha *prasāda*."

This is not just a story; it is factual, a true history that I have heard from a very realized source. You can believe in Jagannātha. We should pray to Jagannātha, "We don't want to go to Vaikuṇṭha to become four-handed. If You are pleased with us, please be merciful and grant us the service of Your most beloved Śrīmatī Rādhikā in Vṛndāvana and Rādhā-kuṇḍa.

śyāmasundara śikhaṇḍa-śekhara
smera-hāsa muralī-manohara
rādhikā-rasika māṁ kṛpa-nidhe
sva-priyā-caraṇa kiṅkarīṁ kuru

Śrī Rādhā-prārthanā (2)

O Śyāmasundara! O You who have a crown of peacock feathers! Your face is always graced with a playful smile, Your flute playing is enchanting, and You are so expert in relishing *rasa* with Śrīmatī Rādhikā. Because You are an ocean of mercy, I am appealing to You to please make me a *kiṅkarī* (maidservant) at the feet of Your beloved.

Śrī Viṭṭhalācārya prays here, "O Śyāmasundara, if You are pleased with me, if You want to be merciful to me, then be so kind as to write my name in the register of Śrīmatī Rādhikā's *dāsīs*. I request that my name be written there. I just want to be

Her *dāsī*; I do not want anything else." If we sincerely pray in this way, Kṛṣṇa will reply, "Yes, I am satisfied. I agree." We are chanting and remembering, "Hare Kṛṣṇa, Hare Kṛṣṇa," the names which are the direct embodiment of Kṛṣṇa and Śrīmatī Rādhikā. We pray that They may be pleased to give us this benediction.

Mercy upon the Muslim

Kṛṣṇa is very merciful, especially in His form of Jagannātha, who is called Patita-pāvana, the savior of the fallen. The priests and worshipers of Jagannātha only allow Hindus to have His *darśana*. Hindus can come to Purī from anywhere in the world and take *darśana*. An Indian Hindu will be allowed inside even if he drinks great quantities of wine and has a very bad character with many impure habits, but pure-hearted Western devotees are not allowed inside the temple, even if they have given up wine, wealth, reputation, and all material entanglements. We oppose this policy.

What to speak of others, even India's late Prime Minister Indira Gandhi was not allowed to enter the Jagannātha Temple. They thought that she was not a pure Hindu, but rather a Parsee or some other religion. They also doubted whether I am Indian, and they asked me, "Where are you from?" I told them, "I have come from Bengal." "But you don't have the eyes of an Indian," they objected. Then I told them, "Bring my *paṇḍā* of Jagannātha. He is an elevated devotee, and one of the most important men in Jagannātha Purī." When my *paṇḍā* came, he said, "He is my client," and then they were satisfied.

Once a devotee from China came to Purī and wanted to see Jagannātha. I told her, "You should tell them that you are from Maṇipura." She told this to the guards and they let her in, but after a while, they became suspicious and began to follow her. I then told her, "Go at once. Take *darśana* and then fly away from here." They followed me, and that devotee as well, but they could not find out where she had gone, and she was able to take *darśana.*

Once there was a pure-hearted devotee, who was a Muslim by birth, so he was not allowed to enter the temple even though he was always chanting Hare Kṛṣṇa. At last he stopped taking food and water, and he went on a hunger strike outside the temple in front of the gate known as Siṁha-dvāra, the lion gate on the east side. He danced and remembered Jagannātha, and after two or three days he became very weak. He then sat down and continually called out, "Patita-pāvana Prabhu Jagannātha! Alas Jagannātha! I have heard that You are very merciful, but You are not giving me *darśana.* They are preventing me from entering the temple."

Then, at eleven or twelve o'clock at night, out of His great compassion, Jagannātha opened the main door to the temple. He came out alone, without Baladeva and Subhadrā, passed through the doors, and arrived at Siṁha-dvāra where the devotee was sitting. When the devotee saw Jagannātha, he became very happy and began to dance and sing. Later, when the priests opened the door of the altar at four in the morning to perform *ārati,* they saw that Jagannātha had disappeared. They began to search here and there, and at last they came to the Siṁha-dvāra and saw Him sitting there alone. "Jagannātha is sitting here!" they exclaimed. "What is He doing here?" They saw that the Muslim devotee was chanting, singing, and weeping, and Jagannātha was also weeping. The devotee then went away, and Jagannātha was taken back inside the temple. Jagannātha is truly Patita-pāvana.

Concluding words

Those who do not chant the names of the Supreme Personality of Godhead and remember Him can never be happy. We are all eternal servants of Kṛṣṇa. This includes those who are chanting and remembering, and those who are not, those who accept Kṛṣṇa, and those who do not. All the creepers, trees, worms, insects, animals, birds, and humans are eternal servants of Kṛṣṇa. They are His parts and parcels.

Even if you are healthy and wealthy now, and even if you have all the paraphernalia to be happy, still you will become old after some time. Your beauty will be transformed into ugliness, and no one will be able to help you. Your teeth will fall out, your cheeks will cave in, your hair will turn gray, and you will be so weak that you will not be able to walk by yourself; you will have to take the help of a stick. Then, at the time of death, you will not be able to take even a hair with you, no matter what you are collecting now. You will pass stool and urine, weeping bitterly, and then you will enter a coma and have to give up your body. Then, the very dangerous and powerful messengers of death will come and beat you. They will throw you into a fire, or they will force you to embrace a red-hot iron pillar. They will say, "Why were you embracing ladies? Why were you lusty? Now you should be lusty with this hot iron pillar." Remember this. At that time neither your father, mother, and uncle, nor your wealth, reputation, and position, will be able to help you.

Śrīla Bhaktivedānta Swāmī Mahārāja was sent to this world by the mercy of his holy master Śrīla Bhaktisiddhānta Sarasvatī Ṭhākura, and that of Kṛṣṇa Himself, Lord Caitanya Mahāprabhu. He was very powerful – a very powerful *ācārya*. He went everywhere, establishing centers and inspiring everyone.

Previously I used to think, "In Śrīla Swāmī Mahārāja's last days, when he was returning to Kṛṣṇa, why did he tell me, 'You should help my devotees. I have brought so many monkeys – so many disciples'?" I used to think, "They are so good. Why did he say that to me?" At that time his disciples served him with their wealth, and by distributing his books everywhere, by establishing centers like New Māyāpura, by training hundreds of students in various *gurukulas*, by keeping so many cows, and by preaching extensively. But now I realize why he gave me that instruction. He had told me, "You should help my devotees, because after my departure they will be neglected by superiors and become weak. They may give up their *tulasī* neck beads and chanting beads, and even their chanting. They do not know what is real *bhakti*. They do not know what is transcendental devotional service." He therefore requested me to come to Western countries. I came, and now I see that so many senior devotees are very weak.

I have come here to beg something to put in my *jholī* (a *sannyāsī's* begging cloth), just as Haridāsa Ṭhākura and Nityānanda begged, "Please give me a donation." I do not want wealth. I do not want any worldly attainments. I just want you to be bold and strong again. Take *tulasī* beads and begin to chant again. If you cannot chant very much, you can do even two rounds, four rounds, or sixteen rounds. *Harināma* is so powerful that it will very soon attract you, and you will begin to do more than sixteen – even sixty-four. Some devotees who are now with me chant sixty-four rounds daily.

We should preach everywhere again, with inspiration. Many devotees now lack spiritual energy, so I have come to re-inspire them. Please give me that donation: to chant again, and to be strong devotees again. Also, try to help others. Books should be distributed again. Do some service and always chant Kṛṣṇa's names and remember Him.

You can also maintain your life; there is no harm in that. *Sannyāsīs* should be *sannyāsīs*, and *brahmacārīs* should be as strong as they were during the time of Śrīla Bhaktivedānta Swāmī Mahārāja. They should have no girlfriend, and if the lady devotees are very strong, they should be like the *brahmacārīs* and thus preach everywhere. Chanting and remembering is the only way to be happy. There is no other way.

Guru-niṣṭhā, honor for the powerful and bona fide spiritual master, is the backbone of *bhajana*. If you do not have a pure *guru*, whom will you worship first, before you worship Kṛṣṇa and Mahāprabhu? Kṛṣṇa will not accept your worship if you have no *guru*, or if your *guru* is fallen. Try to realize all these truths.

The main purpose of the Jagannātha Chariot Festival is this: Jagannātha is Kṛṣṇa Himself. Kṛṣṇa is so merciful that He has manifested as Jagannātha, Baladeva, and Subhadrā from Nīlamādhava, as "melted" forms. Why "melted?" This was due to Kṛṣṇa's love and affection for the *gopīs*. All the ancient scriptures say that we are searching for Kṛṣṇa, but this is not true. *Śrīmad-Bhāgavatam* tells us something else: "Kṛṣṇa is searching for us." He is playing on His flute as if to say, "Come on! Come on!" He is always searching for His friends, thinking, "Where are My friends? Where are My cows? Where are My calves?" He is actually worried for us, searching and thinking, "They are My eternal servants, and they are unhappy in this world."

We have so many problems every day. We are all in a well where poisonous snakes are hissing, and we cannot know when they will bite. Tigers, which represent death, are at the top of the well, and we cannot know when death will come. Parīkṣit Mahārāja had seven days left to live, but we may not have even a single moment.

Kṛṣṇa has come, and He has sent Śrīla Bhaktivedānta Swāmī Mahārāja for you all. All the Western devotees were previously like hippies: dancing, drinking wine, smoking, and eating meat, eggs, and many other abominable things. No one ever called for Śrīla Swāmī Mahārāja, but by His mercy Kṛṣṇa sent him: "Go to all these unhappy people, and try to give them a process by which they will chant and become happy."

Kṛṣṇa is sending all this help, and He has also sent me. I never thought, even in my dreams, that I would leave Vṛndāvana and come to these Western countries. He forcibly took my *śikhā* and dragged me here. He told me, "You should go and help them. Your *guru* has helped you, so why should you not help others? You should go."

This is Kṛṣṇa's causeless mercy. He is telling you, "Somehow chant once in your life, 'Kṛṣṇa, Rādhā, Rādhā, Kṛṣṇa, Rāma.' If you chant, 'Hare Kṛṣṇa, Hare Kṛṣṇa, Kṛṣṇa Kṛṣṇa, Hare Hare, Hare Rāma, Hare Rāma, Rāma Rāma, Hare Hare' with your heart and soul even once in your life, I will take you to Goloka Vṛndāvana."

Don't commit *nāma-aparādha*, offenses to the lotus feet of the holy name. The holy name is Kṛṣṇa Himself, the Supreme Personality of Godhead. He is so powerful, and so merciful. Don't offend any devotees, whether they are initiated or not. If they are initiated, very good; honor them with *daṇḍavat-praṇāma*. If they are not initiated, then you should think in your mind and your heart as well, "They are part of Caitanya Mahāprabhu's family. Our family is so large." Try to follow these principles. If you chant in this way even once in your whole life, Kṛṣṇa will quickly liberate you.

Do not believe in wealth and do not believe in your job. A job cannot give you happiness. Your job will not save you, and it cannot give you pleasure for even a moment. You can collect wealth, but that cannot save you either. If you sometimes become so absorbed in Kṛṣṇa that you forget your job or some other important duty for which you are responsible, Kṛṣṇa will save you. If you are so absorbed in chanting Kṛṣṇa's name that you neglect your job as a government servant, the government could punish you. Instead, however, Kṛṣṇa will assume your form and He will surely do the job for you. Have strong faith in this.

Available in this world is an especially valuable thing, something which is very rare – very rare. What is that rare thing?

sādhu-saṅga, sādhu-saṅga sarva-śāstre kaya
lava-mātra sādhu-saṅge sarva-siddhi haya

Śrī Caitanya-caritāmṛta (*Madhya-līlā* 22.54)

The verdict of all revealed scriptures is that one can attain all success by even a moment's association with a pure devotee.

APPENDIX

Further material related to Chapter 7 in question and answer format

[Question:] During the Herā-pañcamī Festival, in order to prove the superiority of Vṛndāvana, Śrī Svarūpa Dāmodara and Lord Caitanya quoted from *Ujjvala-nīlamaṇi*. How was it possible to quote from a book that Śrīla Rūpa Gosvāmī wrote later on?

[Śrīla Nārāyaṇa Mahārāja:] Kṛṣṇadāsa Kavirāja Gosvāmī has explained that actually this came from Svarūpa Dāmodara. Śrīla Rūpa Gosvāmī was a disciple and follower of Svarūpa Dāmodara, and Svarūpa Dāmodara sprinkled his mercy on him. These *ślokas* of *Ujjvala-nīlamaṇi* were actually in the heart of Svarūpa Dāmodara, and then they arose in the heart of Rūpa Gosvāmī. We can reconcile it in this way.

[Question:] Generally we think of Lakṣmī in Vaikuṇṭha, but Jagannātha Purī is Dvārakā; so why is Jagannātha's consort called Lakṣmī?

[Śrīla Nārāyaṇa Mahārāja:] All of Kṛṣṇa's queens, like Rukmiṇī, Satyabhāmā, and so on, are more than Lakṣmī. Here, Kṛṣṇadāsa Kavirāja Gosvāmī is taking only one Lakṣmī from Dvārakā. Lakṣmī, or Vimalā-devī, represents all the queens of Dvārakā.

[Question:] This Lakṣmī, who became more angry than Satyabhāmā, who has more *māna* than Satyabhāmā – that is Vimalā-devī?

[Śrīla Nārāyaṇa Mahārāja:] Yes, Satyabhāmā was sometimes like this, but not as much. Satyabhāmā does not have so much honor for such opulence, because she is very near and dear to Kṛṣṇa. She was a manifestation of Rādhikā, as Rukmiṇī is a manifestation of Candrāvalī.

[Question:] You said that when Jagannātha is going to the Guṇḍicā Temple, He brings Baladeva and Subhadrā, because in this way Lakṣmī-devī will not suspect Him of enjoying with the *gopīs*. But Balarāma also performs *rāsa-līlā* in Vṛndāvana.

[Śrīla Nārāyaṇa Mahārāja:] But Kṛṣṇa never took him to any of the *kuñjas* where He sported with Rādhikā and the *gopīs*. Balarāma may go there in the form of Anaṅga Mañjarī, but he cannot go in the direct way. Nityānanda Prabhu cannot touch Mahāprabhu when He is in the mood of Rādhikā, even if Mahāprabhu falls over. Nityānanda Prabhu will watch from a distance. So Baladeva Prabhu will never go to the *kuñjas*. He can go cowherding with Kṛṣṇa, and Kṛṣṇa will stealthily take Madhumaṅgala or Subala to Rādhā-kuṇḍa. He will not take Baladeva Prabhu there, nor will He take Rādhikā's brother, Śrīdāmā. He will not take any *sakhā*, *priya-sakhā*, or even *prāṇa-sakhā*; He will only take a *priya-narma-sakhā*, and then only as a messenger.

[Question:] Since all female expansions of Kṛṣṇa manifest from Rādhikā, what kind of expansion is Subhadrā?

[Śrīla Nārāyaṇa Mahārāja:] She is Lakṣmī, an expansion of Śrīmatī Rādhikā. She plays the role of a sister, but actually she is Mahā-Mahā-Lakṣmī and she serves Kṛṣṇa in great opulence. She came from Devakī's womb after Kṛṣṇa.

[Question:] When Kṛṣṇa, Baladeva, and Subhadrā were listening to the Vṛndāvana pastimes and their arms began to melt, Sudarśana *cakra* was not present at that time. Yet, he is also worshiped in a form similar to theirs.

[Śrīla Nārāyaṇa Mahārāja:] Sudarśana is the vision of Kṛṣṇa, and therefore he is always with Kṛṣṇa. If Sudarśana will be merciful and give us the vision of Kṛṣṇa, then you will see Kṛṣṇa as He is; otherwise you will see Him as an ordinary boy.

Explanations of Śrīmad-Bhāgavatam (10.33.39) from p. 233

In the Second Canto of *Śrīmad-Bhāgavatam*, Mahārāja Parīkṣit also explains that the pastimes and activities of Lord Kṛṣṇa are medicine for the conditioned souls. If they simply hear about Kṛṣṇa they become relieved from the material disease. They are addicted to material enjoyment and are accustomed to reading sex literature, but by hearing these transcendental pastimes of Kṛṣṇa with the *gopīs*, they will be relieved from material contamination. The conditioned soul should hear the *rāsa-līlā* dance from an authorized spiritual master and be trained by him so that he can understand the whole situation; thus one can be elevated to the highest standard of spiritual life. Otherwise, one will be implicated. Material lust is a kind of heart disease of the conditioned soul. It is recommended that one should hear, but not from impersonalist rascals. If one hears from the right sources with right understanding, then his situation will be different. (*Kṛṣṇa* book, Chapter 32)

Śrīla Viśvanātha Cakravartī Ṭhākura states as follows in his *Sārārtha-darśinī* commentary on this verse:

The prefix *anu* (repeatedly or methodically) when applied to *sṛṇuyāt* (to hear) indicates constant hearing. By continuously hearing from the lips of the *śravaṇa-guru* and Vaiṣṇavas and thereafter reciting, narrating, or describing (those pastimes) in poetry of one's own composition, one attains *parā-bhakti*, or in other words *bhakti* that is of the nature of *prema* (*prema-lakṣaṇa-bhakti*).

The suffix *ktvā* has been used in the formation of the verb *pratilabhya* (obtained) as follows: *prati* + *labh* + *ktvā*. According to the rules of Sanskrit grammar, when the suffix *ktvā* is applied to a verbal root with a prefix, it is replaced by *yap*. Then letter *p* is dropped and thus the final form of the word *pratilabhya* is obtained. The suffix *ktvā* is applied to the first of two verbs performed by the same agent to show successive action (i.e. having attained *prema*, he relinquishes all lusty desires of the heart). In this case, the first action is *pratilabhya* (the attainment of *prema*) and the second action is *apahinoti* (renunciation of the lusty desires of the heart).

Therefore, the suffix *ktvā* in the verb *pratilabhya* indicates that although lust and other evils still remain within the heart, *prema-bhakti* first enters the heart and by its extraordinary influence destroys all vices to the root. In other words, hearing and reciting *rāsa-līlā* possesses such astonishing power that the lust in the heart of the faithful *sādhaka* is destroyed and he attains *prema*. Though these two take place simultaneously, the influence of *prema* manifests first and through its effect, all lusty desires of the heart are dissipated.

Thus, as a result of hearing and chanting the narrations of the Lord's pastimes, one first attains *prema* for the Lord's lotus feet and thereafter one's heart is liberated from lusty desires and all other contamination. In other words, he becomes perfectly pure because *prema* is not feeble like the processes of *jñāna* and *yoga*. *Bhakti* is omnipotent and supremely independent.

The words *hṛd-roga kāma* indicate the difference between lusty desires of the heart and the *kāma* in relationship to the Supreme Lord. *Kāma* which is in relationship to the Supreme Lord is of the very nature of the nectar of *prema* (*premāmṛta-svarūpa*), whereas the lusty desires of the heart are exactly the opposite. Therefore, these two items are distinct from each other. This is substantiated by use of the words *hṛd-roga kāma*.

The word *dhīra* means a *paṇḍita*, or one who is learned in the *śāstra*. One who refuses to accept the claim of this verse and thinks, "As long as the disease of lust remains in the heart, *prema* cannot be obtained," is said to possess an atheistic temperament. One who is free from such a foolish, atheistic demeanor is known as a *paṇḍita* or sober person (*dhīra*). Consequently, only those who have firm faith in the *śāstra* are known as *dhīra*. Those who have no faith in the statements of the *śāstras* are atheists and offenders to the holy name. Such persons can never attain *prema*.

Consequently, in the heart of the *sādhakas* who firmly believe in the statements of the *śāstra*, faith arises by hearing *rāsa-līlā* and other narrations. Only in the hearts of such faithful devotees does *prema* manifest its influence as a result of hearing *līlā-kathā*. Thereafter, lust and all evils present within the heart of the devotees are destroyed to the root.

Śrīla Viśvanātha Cakravartī Ṭhākura's commentary on *Śrīmad-Bhāgavatam* (10.47.59) is also relevant to the discussion. There it is stated that *bhakti* is the only cause of superior qualities being found in any individual. Austerities, learning, knowledge, and so on are not the cause of superior qualities. Although *bhakti* is itself of the highest excellence, it does not appear only in the most exceptional individuals endowed with all good qualities. On the contrary, it may manifest or remain even in the most condemned and vile persons. Furthermore, it causes thoroughly wretched and fallen persons to attain all good qualities, to become worthy of the respect of all, and to attain the highest and most rare association.

For this reason, the opinion that Bhakti-devī enters the heart only after all *anarthas*, *aparādhas*, lust, and other diseases of the heart have been eradicated, is not appropriate. On the contrary, by the mercy of the Supreme Lord or the devotees, or by faithfully executing *sādhana* and *bhajana*, this rare *bhakti* enters the heart first and then all *anarthas* are automatically dissipated – this conclusion is thoroughly agreeable.

Therefore, only faithful *sādhakas* with firm belief in the statements of *śāstra*, *guru* and Vaiṣṇavas are eligible to hear the *līlā-kathā* of *Śrīmad-Bhāgavatam* that are saturated with *rasa*. And conversely, those who believe that only *sādhakas* who are completely free from all *anarthas* are eligible to hear the above-mentioned pastimes, will neither become free from *anarthas* nor obtain eligibility to hear, even after millions of births.

Excerpts from Śrīla Prabhupāda's Rātha-yātra lecture in London, on July 13, 1972:

Ladies and gentlemen, I thank you very much for your kindly participating in this Ratha-yātrā Festival. This festival is coming down from five thousand years ago, when Lord Kṛṣṇa, along with His elder brother Balarāma and His younger sister Subhadrā, came together on a chariot from Dvārakā to Kurukṣetra. Kurukṣetra still exists, and the city of Dvārakā also still exists.

According to Vedic culture, when there is a lunar eclipse people take bath in sacred rivers. They especially go to the pilgrimage place of Kurukṣetra. At that time Kṛṣṇa, along with His brother and sister and other family members, came to Kurukṣetra; and, receiving this news, the *gopīs* and inhabitants of Vṛndāvana, where Lord Kṛṣṇa lived in His childhood, came to see Him there. Among the *gopīs*, Śrīmatī Rādhārāṇī was the chief, and when she saw Kṛṣṇa in Kurukṣetra full with opulence, She said, "My dear Kṛṣṇa, You are also here; I am also here. But we are missing Vṛndāvana. So I wish that You come along with Me again to Vṛndāvana and we enjoy in the forest of Vṛndāvana."

This feeling of separation was preached by Lord Caitanya, and this Ratha-yātrā Festival is still observed in Jagannātha Purī in India. Lord Caitanya participated in this festival five hundred years ago, and at that time He was in Rādhārāṇī's mood of separation when She was taking Kṛṣṇa back to Vṛndāvana. So this Ratha-yātrā Festival is a festival of sentiments for the Vaiṣṇavas. Lord Caitanya taught us how to feel separation from God. He never taught us that He had seen God, but He felt the separation of God very severely. Similarly, His direct disciples, the Six Gosvāmīs, also prosecuted their devotional service by feelings of separation.

he rādhe vraja-devīke ca lalite he nanda-suno kutaḥ
śrī-govardhana-kalpa-pādapa-tale kālindī-vane kutaḥ
ghoṣantāv iti sarvato vraja-pure khedair mahā-vihvalau
vande rūpa-sanātanau raghu-yugau śrī-jīva-gopālakau

Ṣaḍ-gosvāmy-aṣṭaka (8)

I offer my respectful obeisances to the Six Gosvāmīs, namely Śrī Rūpa Gosvāmī, Śrī Sanātana Gosvāmī, Śrī Raghunātha Bhaṭṭa Gosvāmī, Śrī Raghunātha dāsa Gosvāmī, Śrī Jīva Gosvāmī, and Śrī Gopāla Bhaṭṭa Gosvāmī, who were chanting very loudly everywhere in Vṛndāvana, shouting, "Queen of Vṛndāvana, Rādhārāṇī! O Lalitā! O son of Nanda Mahārāja! Where are you all now? Are you just on the hill of Govardhana, or are you under the trees on the bank of the Yamunā? Where are you?" These were their moods in executing Kṛṣṇa consciousness.

So this Ratha-yātrā Festival is very nice – a "feelings festival" for the Vaiṣṇava – and anyone who participates in this festival will gradually develop his dormant love for Kṛṣṇa. Thank you very much for your kindness.

It doesn't matter in whatever condition you may be. Our only request is that you please try to chant these sixteen words, if it is possible, whenever you have got time. You have got enough time. You can chant the Hare Kṛṣṇa *mantra* when you are walking on the street, when you are traveling in the bus, or when you are sitting alone. There is no loss, but the gain is very great. Therefore our only request is that you take this *mahā-mantra*:

hare kṛṣṇa, hare kṛṣṇa, kṛṣṇa kṛṣṇa, hare hare
hare rāma, hare rāma, rāma rāma, hare hare

And we shall periodically remind you by such functions as we are holding today – the Ratha-yātrā Festival. This Ratha-yātrā

Festival is very old; at least 5000 years old. Lord Kṛṣṇa, along with His elder brother Balabhadra, or Balarāma, and His sister Subhadrā, came in a chariot from Dvārakā to Kurukṣetra. We are commemorating this arrival of Lord Kṛṣṇa with His family on their chariot.

This function is held in Jagannātha Purī. In India it is a great festival, and we are introducing this Ratha-yātrā Festival in Western countries, along with the Hare Kṛṣṇa movement. The original progenitor of this Hare Kṛṣṇa movement, namely Lord Caitanya, took a very active part in this festival, and therefore, following in His footsteps, we are also introducing it in Western countries. As it is being observed in London, it is simultaneously being held in San Francisco, Buffalo, Melbourne, Tokyo, and many other places. It is also being held in India, in Calcutta. Taking part in these festivals means a step forward for our self-realization. *Rathe ca vāmanaṁ dṛṣṭvā punar janma na vidyate* – simply by seeing the Lord on the chariot, one makes advancement for stopping the repetition of birth and death.

GLOSSARY

A

Abhiṣeka – bathing of a deity in milk, yogurt, water, and other ingredients.

Ācārya – spiritual preceptor; one who teaches by example.

Adhīrā – a *gopī* who is restless in jealous anger.

Adirūḍha-mahābhāva – the highest state of *mahābhāva*, found only in the *gopīs* of Vraja. The mood in which all the *anubhāvas* that are manifested in resolute *mahābhāva* attain special characteristics that are even more astonishing than those *anubhāvas* in their normal forms. There are two types of *adhirūḍha-bhāva*: (1) *modana* and (2) *mādana*. (1) The *adhirūḍha* in which all the *sāttvika-bhāvas* of the *nāyaka* and *nāyikā* are aroused to a much greater extent than in the brightly burning (*uddīpta*) condition is called *modana*. *Modana* does not occur anywhere other than in Śrī Rādhā's group. In some special conditions of separation *modana* becomes *mohana*, and as an effect of this helpless condition of separation, all the *sāttvika-bhāvas* manifest in the blazing (*sūddīpta*) condition. (2) When *mahābhāva* increases even further it attains an extremely advanced condition. The paramount emotion in which it becomes jubilant due to the simultaneous manifestation of all types of transcendental emotions is called *mādana*. This *mādana-bhāva* is eternally and splendidly manifest only in Śrī Rādhā, and occurs only at the time of meeting. It is also referred to as *mādanākhya-mahābhāva*.

Aiśvarya – opulence, splendor, magnificence, majesty, supremacy; in regard to *bhakti* this refers to devotion which is inspired by the opulence of the Lord's majesty, especially in His feature as Lord Nārāyaṇa. This type of devotion restricts the intimacy of exchange between Śrī Bhagavān and His devotees.

Ālambana – an aspect of *vibhāva*; "the support". It is divided into *viṣayālambana*, the object of *rati* – that is, he for whom *rati* is aroused – and *āśrayālambana*, the receptacle of *rati*; that is, the one in whom *rati* is aroused.

Anartha – (*an-artha* meaning "non-value") unwanted desires, activities or habits that impede one's advancement in *bhakti*; in other words, everything that is against *bhakti*.

Anubhāvas – one of the five essential ingredients of *rasa*. The actions which display or reveal the spiritual emotions situated within the heart are called *anubhāvas*. They are thirteen in number: dancing (*nṛtya*), rolling on the ground (*viluṭhita*), singing (*gīta*), loud crying (*krośana*), writhing of the body (*tanu-moṭana*), roaring (*huṅkāra*), yawning (*jṛmbhaṇa*), breathing heavily (*śvāsa-bhūmā*), neglecting others (*lokānapekṣitā*), drooling (*lālāsrāva*), loud laughter (*aṭṭahāsa*), staggering about (*ghūrṇā*), and hiccups (*hikkā*).

Anurāga – (1) attachment, affection, or love; (2) an intensified stage of *prema* which comes just prior to *mahābhāva*. In *Ujjvala-nīlamaṇi* (14.146) *anurāga* has been defined as follows: "Although one regularly meets with the beloved and is well-acquainted with the beloved, the ever-fresh sentiment of intense attachment causes the beloved to be newly experienced at every moment, as if one has never before had any experience of such a person. The attachment which inspires such a feeling is known as *anurāga*."

Aparādha – (*apa* = against, taking away; *rādha* = flow of affection) an offense committed against the holy name, Vaiṣṇavas, the spiritual master, the scriptures, holy places, or the deity.

Aprākṛta – transcendental, beyond the influence of material nature, beyond the perception of mind and senses, not created by any human, beyond the material world, situated in Kṛṣṇa's transcendental abode, extraordinary, divine, pure, or consisting of spiritual consciousness and bliss.

Ārati – the ceremony of offering a deity articles of worship, such as incense, lamp, flowers, and fan, accompanied by chanting and bell-ringing.

Arcana – deity worship; one of the nine primary processes of devotional service.

Āsakti – attachment; this especially refers to attachment for the Lord and His eternal associates. *Āsakti* occurs when one's liking for *bhajana* leads to a direct and deep attachment for the personality who is the object of that *bhajana*. This is the sixth stage in the development of the creeper of devotion, and is awakened upon the maturing of one's taste for *bhajana*.

Aṣṭa-sakhīs – Śrīmatī Rādhikā's eight principal *gopīs*: Lalitā, Viśakhā, Citrā, Indulekha, Campakalatā, Raṅgadevī, Sudevī, and Tuṅgavidyā.

Aṣṭa-sāttvika-bhāvas – see **Sāttvika-bhāvas**.

Ātma-nivedanam – to offer one's very self to Kṛṣṇa. When one offers oneself to the Lord, he no longer acts for his independent pleasure. One engages body, mind, life, and everything in the service of Śrī Bhagavān. This is one of the nine primary limbs of *bhakti*.

B

Bhāgavata-paramparā – there are two disciplic lines: the *pañcarātrika-guru-paramparā* and the *bhāgavata-guru-paramparā*. The *bhāgavata-guru-paramparā* is the disciplic succession of self-realized souls who may be acting as either *śikṣā-gurus* or *dīkṣā-gurus*. *Pañcarātrika-guru-paramparā* is the disciplic succession consisting of *dīkṣā-gurus* who may or may not be self-realized souls and who perform the formal procedures of initiation as delineated in *śāstra*. The *pañcarātrika-guru-paramparā* will be included in the *bhāgavata-paramparā* if the *dīkṣā-guru* is a self-realized soul who can bring his disciple to the ultimate goal of life. Śrīla Prabhupāda Bhaktisiddhānta Sarasvatī Ṭhākura, Śrīla Bhaktivinoda Ṭhākura, and Śrīla Rūpa Gosvāmī have all accepted this *bhāgavata-guru-paramparā*.

Sometimes, when the *dīkṣā-guru* is a conditioned soul, the *pañcarātrika-guru-paramparā* may be illegal and against *bhakti*. In this case it stands alone and is not included in the *bhāgavata-paramparā*. The *bhāgavata-paramparā*, however, under the guidance of *śikṣā-gurus* like Śrīla Rūpa Gosvāmī, Śrīla Sanātana Gosvāmī, Śrī Svarūpa Dāmodara, and Śrī Rāya Rāmānanda, is always authentic.

If a *pañcarātrika-dīkṣā-guru*, in his constitutional spiritual form, is situated in a *rasa* which is lower than that of his disciple, the disciple must ultimately go elsewhere and take shelter of a Vaiṣṇava who is qualified to give the appropriate superior guidance. It may happen that the *guru* and disciple in *pañcarātrika-guru-paramparā* are in the same *rasa*, but that the *guru* is not very highly qualified. Under such circumstances, the disciple must take shelter of an *uttama* Vaiṣṇava for higher *bhajana-śikṣā*, and this Vaiṣṇava will be called his *guru* in *bhāgavata-paramparā*. We can see from these two considerations that the *pañcarātrika* process has some inherent defects, whereas the *bhāgavata-paramparā* is completely free from these defects, and is flawless in all respects.

Bhajana – (1) activities performed with the consciousness of being a servant of Śrī Kṛṣṇa. The *Garuḍa Purāṇa* (*Pūrva-khaṇḍa* 231.3) explains that the verbal root *bhaj* is used specifically in the sense of *sevā*, service; (2) in a general sense *bhajana* refers to the performance of spiritual practices, especially hearing, chanting, and meditating upon Śrī Kṛṣṇa's name, form, qualities, and pastimes.

Bhajana-kuṭīra – a small hut or cottage where a Vaiṣṇava or saintly person performs his *bhajana*, personal meditation.

Bhakta – a devotee.

Bhakti – loving devotional service to Śrī Kṛṣṇa. The word *bhakti* comes from the root *bhaj*, which means to serve; thererfore the primary meaning of the word *bhakti* is to render service.

Bhakti-rasa – the mellow derived from devotional service.

Bhāva – (1) spiritual emotions, love, or sentiments; (2) the initial stage of perfection in devotion (*bhāva-bhakti*). A stage of *bhakti* in which *śuddha-sattva*, the essence of the Lord's internal potency consisting of spiritual knowledge and bliss, is transmitted into the heart of the practicing devotee from the heart of the Lord's eternal associates and softens the heart by different kinds of taste. It is the sprout of *prema*, and it is also known as *rati*. This is the seventh stage of the creeper of devotion.

Bhāva-śābalya – overcoming; the clashing and jostling of many *vyabhicāri-bhāvas*, in which one *bhāva* suppresses another and becomes predominant.

Bhāva-sandhi – union; when two *vyabhicāri-bhāvas*, either of the same type or of different types, meet together.

Bhāva-śānti – pacification; when an extremely powerful *vyabhicāri-bhāva* becomes pacified.

Bhāva-udaya – the awakening or generation of a *vyabhicāri-bhāva*.

Bhāva-anukūla – (favorable to one's desired mood); wearing neck-beads made of *tulasī*, applying *tilaka*, adopting the outward signs of a Vaiṣṇava, rendering *tulasī-sevā*, performing *parikramā*, offering *praṇāma*, and so forth are *bhāva-anukūla*. One of the five kinds of *sādhana* in *rāgānuga-bhakti*.

Bhāva-aviruddha – (neither opposed to nor incompatible with one's desired mood); respecting cows, the banyan tree, the myrobalan tree and *brāhmaṇas* are conducive activities and therefore called *bhāva-aviruddha*. One of the five kinds of *sādhana* in *rāgānuga-bhakti*.

Bhāvamayi – (composed of one's desired mood); when *śravaṇa*, *kīrtana*, and other such limbs of *bhakti* are saturated with one of the primary *bhāvas* (*dāsya*, *sakhya*, *vatsālya*, or *mādhurya*), they nourish the tree of the *sādhaka's* future *prema*. At that time they are called *bhāvamaya-sādhana*. When *prema* manifests, they are called *bhāvamaya-sādhya.* One of the five kinds of *sādhana* in *rāgānuga-bhakti.*

Bhāva-pratikūla – (that which is opposed to one's desired mood) one of the five kinds of *sādhana* in *rāgānuga-bhakti.*

Bhāva-sambandhī – (related to one's desired mood); the limbs of *bhakti,* including *śrī-guru-padāśraya, mantra-japa, smaraṇa, dhyāna,* and so on, are known as *bhāva-sambandhī-sādhana.* Because the following of vows on holy days such as Ekādaśī and Janmāṣṭamī assists the limb of *smaraṇa,* it is considered partial *bhāva-sambandhī.* One of the five kinds of *sādhana* in *rāgānuga-bhakti.*

Bhoga – food before it has been offered to the deity.

Brahmacārī – a member of the first *āśrama* (stage of life) in the *varṇāśrama* system; a celibate, unmarried student.

Brāhmaṇa – the highest of the four *varṇas* (castes) in the *varṇāśrama* system; a priest or teacher. A *brāhmaṇī* is a wife of a *brāhmaṇa.*

C

Cakra – disc.

Candana – sandalwood paste, used in deity worship.

Cintāmaṇi – a spiritual, potent gemstone ("desire-stone"), found in the transcendental realm. It fulfills all the desires of one who possesses it.

Citra-jalpa – variegated speech; an ecstatic symptom appearing in *mohana-mahābhāva. Ujjvala-nīlamaṇi* (14.174, 178–80) explains it as follows: "It is virtually only within Śrīmatī Rādhārāṇī that the ecstasy of bewilderment arises. She has attained to a special stage of this bewilderment, a wonderful state that resembles delusion, and is known as *divyonmāda.* It has many aspects, which come and go unsteadily, and one of these manifestations is *citra-jalpa.* This talk, induced by Her seeing Her beloved's friend, is filled with covered anger and comprises many different ecstasies. It culminates in Her intense, anxious eagerness. *Citra-jalpa* has ten divisions: *prajalpa*, *parijalpa*, *vijalpa*, *ujjalpa*, *sañjalpa*, *avajalpa*, *abhijalpa*, *ājalpa*, *pratijalpa*, and *sujalpa*."

D

Daṇḍavat-praṇāma – *daṇḍa* = stick, *praṇāma* = obeisances; thus, *daṇḍavat-praṇāma* means obeisances by falling like a stick; prostrated obeisances.

Darśana – seeing, meeting, visiting or beholding (especially in regard to the deity, a sacred place, or an exalted Vaiṣṇava).

Dharma – (from the verbal root *dhṛ* = to sustain; thus, *dharma* means that which sustains). (1) religion in general; (2) the socio-religious duties prescribed in the scriptures for different classes of persons in the *varṇāśrama* system that are meant to liberate one to the platform of *bhakti*.

Dhīrā – a *gopī* who is gentle, sober, or supressed in jealous anger.

Dīkṣā-guru – the initiating spiritual master.

Divyonmāda – a wonderful divine state that resembles a state of utter confusion. It occurs in the stage of *mohana-mahābhāva* and it has many different features, such as *udghūrṇā* and *citra-jalpa*. It is found virtually only in Śrīmatī Rādhikā.

Dvārakāvāsīs – residents of Dvārakā

G

Gadā – club.

Ghṛta-sneha – a manifestation of *sneha* (the stage coming after *prema*). *Ghṛta* means ghee, which is not independently sweet like honey, and only delicious when mixed with sugar and other ingredients. Similarly, *ghṛta-sneha* is not independently sweet like *madhu-sneha* (see **Madhu-sneha**); it only become palatable when mixed with other *bhāvas*. It is found in Candrāvalī and her group.

Gokula-Vṛndāvana – the highest realm of the spiritual world. This is the abode of Śrī Kṛṣṇa where He is manifest in His original and topmost features as a cowherd boy, surrounded by His intimate and loving servitors, the *gopas* and *gopīs* of Vraja.

Gopa – (1) a cowherd boy who serves Kṛṣṇa in a mood of intimate friendship; (2) an elderly associate of Nanda Mahārāja who serves Kṛṣṇa in a mood of parental affection.

Gopī – (1) one of the young cowherd maidens of Vraja headed by Śrīmatī Rādhikā who serve Kṛṣṇa in a mood of amorous love; (2) an elderly associate of Mother Yaśodā who serves Kṛṣṇa in a mood of parental affection.

Gośālā – cowshed; a shelter for the cows.

Gṛhastha – a member of the second *āśrama* (stage of life) in the *varṇāśrama* system; a householder.

Guñjā – a small, bright red seed with a black patch on the top. This seed is said to represent Śrīmatī Rādhikā.

Gurukula – a school of Vedic learning. Boys begin at five years old and live as celibate students, guided by a spiritual master.

Guru-paramparā – the disciplic succession through which spiritual knowledge is transmitted by bona fide spiritual masters.

H

Hari-kathā – narrations of the holy name, form, qualities, and pastimes of the Lord.

Harināma – the chanting of Śrī Kṛṣṇa's holy names. Unless accompanied by the word *saṅkīrtana*, it usually refers to the practice of chanting the Hare Kṛṣṇa *mahā-mantra* softly to oneself on a strand of *tulasī* beads.

Hlādinī – this refers to the *svarūpa-śakti* that is predominated by *hlādinī. Hlādinī* is the potency which relates to the bliss aspect (*ānanda*) of the Supreme Lord. Although the Supreme Lord is the embodiment of all pleasure, *hlādinī* is that potency by which He relishes transcendental bliss and causes others to taste bliss.

I

Iṣṭadeva – one's worshipable deity; the particular form of Kṛṣṇa toward whom one is attracted, and who is the object of one's love and service.

J

Jīva – the eternal individual living entity who, in the conditioned state of material existence, assumes a material body in any of the innumerable species of life.

Jñāna – (1) knowledge; (2) knowledge leading to impersonal liberation.

Jñānī – one who pursues the path of *jñāna*, knowledge directed towards impersonal liberation.

Jñānī-bhakta – a devotee who worships Bhagavān in the mood of opulence, and due to that sense of the Lord's all-pervasiveness and completeness, does not render personal services.

K

Kajjala – an ointment used to darken the edges of the eyelids.

Kali-yuga – the present age of quarrel and hypocrisy that began five thousand years ago.

Kalpa – the four *yugas* are calculated in terms of the heavenly calendars and accordingly are twelve thousand years in terms of the heavenly planets. This is called a *divya-yuga*, and one thousand *divya-yugas* make one day of Brahmā. The creation during the day of Brahmā is called *kalpa*, and the creation of Brahmā is called *vikalpa*. When *vikalpas* are made possible by the breathing of Mahā-Viṣṇu, this is called a *mahā-kalpa*. There are regular and systematic cycles of these *mahā-kalpas*, *vikalpas* and *kalpas*.

Kaniṣṭha-adhikāra – the neophyte stage of *bhakti*. A *kaniṣṭha-adhikārī* or *kaniṣṭha-bhakta* is a devotee on this neophyte stage.

Karatālas – small brass hand cymbals used for devotional songs.

Karma – (1) any activity performed in the course of material existence; (2) reward-seeking activities; pious activities leading to material gain in this world or in the heavenly planets after death; (3) fate; previous actions that yield inevitable reactions.

Kavi – poet.

Kīrtana – one of the nine most important limbs of *bhakti*, consisting of either: (1) congregational singing of Śrī Kṛṣṇa's holy names, sometimes accompanied by music; (2) loud individual chanting of the holy name; or (3) oral descriptions of the glories of Śrī Kṛṣṇa's names, forms, qualities, associates, and pastimes.

Kīrtanīyā – a performer of *kīrtana*.

Kiśorī, Kiśora – a girl or boy, respectively, in the prime of youth.

Kṣatriya – the second of the four *varṇas* (castes) in the *varṇāśrama* system; an administrator or warrior.

Kuñja – a grove or bower; a natural shady retreat with a roof and walls formed by trees, vines, creepers, and other climbing plants.

Kuṭīnāṭī – duplicity or fault-finding.

L

Līlā – the divine and astonishing pastimes of Śrī Bhagavān and His eternal associates, which grant all auspiciousness for the living entity, which have no connection with this mundane world, and which lie beyond the grasp of the material senses and mind.

M

Mādana – highly advanced ecstasy is divided into two categories: *mādana* and *mohana*. Meeting together is called *mādana*, and separation is called *mohana*. On the *mādana* platform there are kissing and many other symptoms, which are unlimited. In the *mohana* stage, there are two divisions: *udghūrṇā* (unsteadiness) and *citra-jalpa* (varieties of mad emotional talks). *Citra-jalpa* has ten divisions, called *prajalpa* and so on. An example of this is the ten verses from *Śrīmad-Bhāgavatam* spoken by Śrīmatī Rādhārāṇī entitled "The Song to the Bumblebee."

Mādhurya – sweetness or beauty. In regard to *bhakti* this refers to devotion which is inspired by attraction to Kṛṣṇa's sweet and intimate feature as a beautiful young cowherd boy. This type of devotion allows for the greatest exchange of love between the Lord and His devotees.

Madhu-sneha – a manifestation of *sneha* (the stage coming after *prema*). This is the affection that is imbued with excessive possessiveness ("Kṛṣṇa is mine"). *Madhu* means honey and it is itself sweet, so this affection manifests its own sweetness without depending on any other *bhāvas*. It is found in Śrīmatī Rādhikā and Her group.

Madhyā – a *gopī* whose qualities place her midway between a *prakhara* (a *gopī* who is harsh) and a *mṛdvi* (a *gopī* of a sweet and gentle disposition).

Madhyama-adhikāra – the intermediate stage of *bhakti*. *Madhyama-adhikārī* or *madhyama-bhakta* is a devotee on this stage.

Mahā-bhāgavata – a pure devotee of Bhagavān in the hightest stage of devotional life, who is expert in Vedic literature, who has full faith in Śrī Kṛṣṇa, and who can deliver the whole world.

Mahābhāva – the highest stage of *prema*, divine love. In *Ujjvala-nīlamaṇi* (14.154) *mahābhāva* is defined thus: "When *anurāga* reaches a special state of intensity, it is known as *bhāva* or *mahābhāva*. This stage of intensity has three characteristics: (1) *anurāga* reaches the state of *sva-samvedya*, which means that it becomes the object of its own experience; (2) it becomes *prakāśita*, radiantly manifest, which means that all eight *sātvika-bhāvas* become prominently displayed; and (3) it attains the state of *yāvad-āśraya-vṛtti*, which means that the active ingredient of the intensified state of *anurāga* transmits the experience of Rādhā and Kṛṣṇa's *bhāva* to whomever may be present and qualified to receive it."

Mahājana – a great personality who teaches the highest ideal and who by his conduct sets an example for others to follow.

Mahāmāyā – the illusion-generating potency that is responsible for the manifestation of the material world, time, and material activities. (Also see **Māyā**.)

Maharṣi – a great sage.

Māna – (1) jealous anger; (2) an intensified stage of *prema*; a stage in the development from *prema* up to *mahābhāva*. It is described as follows in *Ujjvala-nīlamaṇi* (14.96): "When *sneha* reaches exultation, thus causing one to experience the sweetness of the beloved in ever new varieties, yet externally takes on a crooked feature, it is known as *māna*."

Mandira – temple.

Mañjarī – a maidservant of Śrīmatī Rādhikā in the category of *nitya-sakhī* or *prāṇa-sakhī*.

Mantra – (*man* = mind; *tra* = deliverance) a spiritual sound vibration that delivers the mind from its material conditioning and illusion when repeated over and over; a Vedic hymn, prayer or chant.

Mathurāvāsīs – residents of Mathurā.

Māyā – illusion; that which is not; Śrī Bhagavān's external potency which influences the living entities to accept the false egoism of being independent enjoyers of this material world. (Also see **Mahāmāyā**.)

Māyāvāda – the doctrine of impersonalism.

Māyāvādī – one who advocates the doctrine of impersonalism.

Mṛdaṅga – a two-headed clay drum used for *kīrtana* performances and congregational chanting.

Mugdhā – this heroine is young, charming, and innocent.

Muralīdhara – a title of Kṛṣṇa meaning "holder of the flute."

N

Nagara-saṅkīrtana – act of singing religious songs in procession through a city or village.

Nāma-ābhāsa – a semblance of the holy name. The stage of chanting in which one is becoming cleared of sins and offenses but has not yet attained pure chanting.

Nāma-aparādha – offensive chanting of the holy name.

Naṭavara – a title of Śrī Kṛṣṇa meaning "the expert dancer."

Navakiśora – a title of Śrī Kṛṣṇa meaning "everfresh youth."

Nikuñja – (also *kuñja*) bower, grove; a solitary place for the meeting and enjoyment of Rādhā and Kṛṣṇa.

Niśānta-līlā – Śrī Kṛṣṇa's daily, eternal pastimes that takes place at the end of the night, just prior to dawn.

Niṣkiñcana – free from all material possessions, entirely destitute; a renunciant.

Niṣṭhā – firm faith; established devotional practice that does not waver at any time. The fourth stage in the development of the creeper of devotion.

P

Padma – lotus flower.

Paṇḍā – a *brahmāṇa* guide at temples and holy places.

Parakīya – the relationship between a married woman and her paramour; particularly the relationship between the *gopīs* of Vṛndāvana and Kṛṣṇa.

Paramātmā – the Supersoul situated in the hearts of all living entities as a witness and source of remembrance, knowledge, and forgetfulness.

Paramparā – see **Guru-paramparā**.

Patita-pāvana – a title of the Lord meaning "the deliverer of the fallen souls."

Pragalbhā – this *nāyikā* (heroine) is a mature, clever, outspoken *gopī* expert at controlling her lover.

Praṇāma – respectful obeisances.

Praṇāmī – donation given to the deity.

Prāṇanātha – literally means "the lord of one's life," but it carries the sense of one who is infinitely more dear to one than one's life.

Praṇaya – an intensified stage of *prema*; a stage in the development from *prema* up to *mahābhāva*. It is described in *Ujjvala-nīlamaṇi* (14.108): "When *māna* assumes a feature of unrestrained intimacy known as *viśrambha*, learned authorities refer to it as *praṇaya*." The word *viśrambha* used in this verse means complete confidence devoid of any restraint or formality. This confidence causes one to consider one's life, mind, intelligence, body, and possessions to be one in all respects with the life, mind, intelligence, and body of the beloved.

Prasādam – (literally means "mercy") especially refers to the remnants of food offered to the deity; may also refer to the remnants of other articles offered to the deity, such as incense, flowers, garlands, and clothing.

Pratiṣṭhā – desire for name and fame or high position.

Prema – (1) love for Kṛṣṇa which is extremely concentrated, which completely melts the heart, and which gives rise to a deep sense of *mamatā*, possessiveness, in relation to Śrī Kṛṣṇa. (2) When *bhāva* becomes firmly rooted and unchecked by any obstacle it is known as *prema*. When some cause arises that could conceivably ruin the relationship between the lover and beloved and yet their bond remains completely unaffected, such an intimate loving relationship is known as *prema*. When *prema* is augmented it is gradually transformed into *sneha*, *praṇaya*, *rāga*, *anurāga*, and *mahābhāva*.

Prema-bhakti – a stage of *bhakti* which is characterised by the appearance of *prema*; the perfectional stage of devotion; the eighth and fully blossomed state of the creeper of devotion.

Priya-narmā-sakhās – the most intimate friends of Kṛṣṇa.

Pūjā – offering of worship.

Pūjārī – priest, one who offers *pūjā* or worships the deity in a temple.

Purāṇa – the eighteen historical supplements to the Vedas.

R

Rāga – a deep attachment which is permeated by spontaneous and intense absorption in the object of one's affection. The primary characteristic of *rāga* is a deep and overpowering thirst for that object of affection. The desire for water is called thirst. When the body is deprived of water, thirst arises. The greater the thirst the greater the longing for water. When this thirst reaches the point that without water one can no longer maintain the body, it is known as overpowering thirst. Similarly, when the loving thirst to please the object of one's affection becomes so intense that in the absence of such service one is on the verge of giving up his life, it is known as *rāga*.

Rāga-mārga – the path of *rāga*, spontaneous attachment (see **Rāgānuga-bhakti**).

Rāgānuga-bhakti – devotion that follows in the wake of Śrī Kṛṣṇa's eternal associates in Vraja, the *rāgātmikā-janas*, whose hearts are permeated with *rāga*, an unquenchable loving thirst for Kṛṣṇa that gives rise to spontaneous and intense absorption.

Rāgātmikā-bhakta – one in whose heart there naturally and eternally exists a deep spontaneous desire to love and serve Śrī Kṛṣṇa. This specifically refers to the eternal residents of Vraja.

Rasa – (1) the spiritual transformation of the heart that takes place when the perfectional state of love for Śrī Kṛṣṇa, known as *rati*, is converted into "liquid" emotions by combining with various types of transcendental ecstasies; (2) taste, flavor.

Rāsa-līlā – Śrī Kṛṣṇa's dance with His most confidential servitors, the *vraja-gopīs*, which is a pure exchange of spiritual love between them.

Rasika – one who is expert at relishing *rasa*; a connoisseur of *rasa*.

Ratha – cart, chariot.

Ṛṣi – a great sage learned in the Vedas.

Ruci – taste; *ruci* develops after one has acquired steadiness in *bhajana*. At this stage, with the awakening of actual taste, one's attraction to spiritual matters, such as hearing, chanting, and other devotional practices, exceeds one's attraction to any type of material activity; this is the fifth stage in the development of the creeper of devotion.

Rūpānuga – a devotee who follows Śrī Rūpa Gosvāmī on the path of spontaneous devotion.

S

Sac-cid-ānanda – (*sat* = eternal existence; *cit* = spiritual consciousness; *ānanda* = spiritual bliss) that which is eternal, composed of spiritual consciousness, and full of transcendental bliss; often refers to the transcendental form of Śrī Kṛṣṇa.

Sādhana – the method one adopts in order to obtain one's specific goal, *sādhya*.

Sādhu – (1) (in a general sense) a saintly person or devotee; (2) a highly realised soul who knows life's aim (*sādhya*), who is himself practicing *sādhana*, and who can engage others in *sādhana*.

Sahajiyās – a class of so-called devotees who, considering the Lord cheap, ignore the scriptural injunctions and try to imitate His pastimes.

Sakhā – a male friend, companion, or attendant.

Sakhī – a female friend, companion, or attendant.

Samādhi – (1) meditation or deep trance upon either the Supersoul or upon Kṛṣṇa's sweet pastimes; (2) the tomb in which a pure Vaiṣṇava's body is laid after his departure from this material world.

Samartha-rati – the love of the *vraja-gopīs*, which can control Kṛṣṇa.

Sampradāya – a line of disciplic succession.

Saṁvit – the knowledge portion, cognizant aspect, of the Lord's spiritual potency. Although Bhagavān is the embodiment of knowledge, *saṁvit* is the potency by which He knows Himself and causes others to know Him.

Saṅga – association.

Śaṅkha – conch.

Saṅkīrtana – congregational chanting of the names of Kṛṣṇa.

Sannyāsa – the fourth *āśrama* (stage of life) in the *varṇāśrama* system; renounced, ascetic life.

Śāstra – the Vedic scriptures.

Sāttvika-bhāvas – one of the five essential ingredients of *rasa* (see **Rasa**); eight symptoms of spiritual ecstasy arising exclusively from *viśuddha-sattva*, or in other words, when the heart is overwhelmed by emotions in connection with the five primary moods of affection for Kṛṣṇa or the seven secondary emotions. The eight (*aṣṭa*) *sāttvika-bhāvas* are: (1) becoming stunned, *stambha*; (2) perspiration, *sveda*; (3) standing of the hairs on end, *romāñca*; (4) faltering of the voice, *svarabheda*; (5) trembling, *kampa*; (6) loss of colour, *vaivarṇya*; (7) tears, *aśru*; and (8) loss of consciousness or fainting, *pralaya*.

Satya-yuga – the first of the four cyclic ages of a *mahā-yuga* in the progression of universal time. Satya-yuga is characterized by virtue, wisdom, and religion. It is known as the golden age, when people lived as long as one hundred thousand years. It lasts 1,728,000 solar years.

Sevā – service, attendance on, reverence, devotion to.

Siddha – (1) realized or perfected; (2) liberated souls who reside in the spiritual world; (3) a liberated soul who accompanies Bhagavān to the material world to assist in His pastimes, or one who has attained the perfectional stage of *bhakti* (*prema*), whose symptoms are described in *Bhakti-rasāmṛta-sindhu* (2.1.180): "One who is always fully immersed in activities related to Śrī Kṛṣṇa, who is completely unacquainted with impediments or material distress, and who incessantly tastes the bliss of *prema*, is called a *siddha-bhakta*."

Siddhānta – philosophical truth or precept, demonstrated conclusion, established end; admitted truth.

Śikhā – a lock of unshaved hair on the upper, back part of the head.

Śikṣā-guru – the person from whom one receives instructions on how to progress on the path of *bhajana*; the instructing spiritual master.

Siṁhāsana – throne.

Śloka – a Sanskrit verse.

Sneha – an intensified stage of *prema*; a stage in the development from *prema* up to *mahābhāva*. It is described as follows in *Ujjvala-nīlamaṇi* (14.79): "When *prema* ascends to its ultimate limit, intensifies one's perception of the object of love, and melts the heart, it is known as *sneha*."

Śraddhā – faith in the statements of the *śāstras* that is awakened after accumulating pious devotional activities over many births. Such faith is aroused in the association of devotees.

Sthāyibhāva – the permanent sentiment of love for Śrī Kṛṣṇa in one of five primary relationships of tranquility (*śānta*), servitude (*dāsya*), friendship (*sakhya*), parental affection (*vātsalya*), or amorous love (*mādhurya*). This also refers to the dominant sentiment in the seven secondary mellows of laughter, wonder, heroism, compassion, anger, fear, and disgust.

Sudarśana cakra – the disc weapon of the Supreme Lord.

Śuddha-bhakta – a pure devotee; one who performs *śuddha-bhakti*.

Śuddha-bhakti – pure devotion; defined in *Bhakti-rasāmṛta-sindhu* (1.1.11) as the uninterrupted flow of service to Śrī Kṛṣṇa, performed through all endeavors of the body, mind, and speech, and through the expression of various spiritual sentiments, which is not covered by *jñāna* (knowledge aimed at impersonal liberation) and *karma* (reward-seeking activity), and which is devoid of all desires other than the aspiration to bring happiness to Śrī Kṛṣṇa.

Svarūpa – constitutional nature, inherent identity; the eternal constitutional nature and identity of the self which is realized at the stage of *bhāva*.

Svayam Bhagavān – the original feature of the Supreme Personality of Godhead.

T

Tattva – truth.

Ṭhākura – a term addressing Śrī Bhagavān, the deity or an elevated devotee.

Tilaka – clay markings worn on the forehead or other parts of the body by Vaiṣṇavas, signifying their devotion to Śrī Kṛṣṇa or Viṣṇu, and consecrating the body as the Lord's temple.

Tīrtha – holy place, place of pilgrimage.

Tulasī – a sacred plant whose leaves and blossoms are used by Vaiṣṇavas in the worship of Śrī Kṛṣṇa; the wood is also used for chanting beads and neck beads.

U

Uddīpana – an aspect of *vibhāva*; it refers to all those things which stimulate remembrance of Śrī Kṛṣṇa such as His dress and ornaments, the spring season, the bank of the Yamunā, peacocks, and so forth.

Upaniṣads – 108 principal philosophical treatises that appear within the Vedas.

Uttama-adhikārī – the topmost devotee, who has either attained perfection in his devotion unto Śrī Kṛṣṇa, or who is naturally perfect.

V

Vaidhī-bhakti – devotion prompted by the regulations of the scriptures. When *sādhana-bhakti* is not inspired by intense longing, but is instigated instead by the discipline of the scriptures, it is called *vaidhī-bhakti.*

Vaiṣṇava – literally means one whose nature is "of Viṣṇu", in other words, one in whose heart and mind only Viṣṇu or Kṛṣṇa resides. A devotee of Śrī Kṛṣṇa or Viṣṇu.

Veda – the four primary books of knowledge compiled by Śrīla Vyāsadeva, namely, the *Ṛg Veda*, *Sāma Veda*, *Atharva Veda*, and *Yajur Veda*.

Vibhāva – this is defined in *Bhakti-rasāmṛta-sindhu* (2.1.15) as follows: "That in which *rati* is tasted (*ālambana*) and that cause by which *rati* is tasted (*uddīpana*) is called *vibhāva.*"

Vigraha – (1) individual form, shape, or embodiment; (2) the deity form of Kṛṣṇa.

Vraja-prema – the love of the residents of Vṛndāvana, particularly the love of the *gopīs.*

Vrajavāsīs – the residents of Vṛndāvana.

Vyabhicāri-bhāvas – same as *sañcāri-bhāvas*; thirty-three internal emotions which emerge from the nectarean ocean of *sthāyibhāva*, cause it to swell, and then merge back into it. These include emotions such as despondency, jubilation, fear, anxiety, and concealment of emotions.

Y

Yoga – (1) union, meeting, connection or combination; (2) spiritual discipline to link one with the Supreme; to stabilize the mind so that it is not disturbed by sense objects. There are many different branches of *yoga* such as *karma-yoga*, *jñāna-yoga*, and *bhakti-yoga*. Unless specified as such, the word *yoga* usually refers to the *aṣṭāṅga-yoga* system of Patañjali.

Yogamāyā – the internal potency of Bhagavān that engages in arranging and enhancing all His pastimes. Paurṇamāsī is the personification of this potency.

Yogī – one who practices the *yoga* system with the goal of realization of the Supersoul or of merging into the Lord's personal body.

VERSE INDEX

A

āge pāche, dui pārśve 80
ahaṁ hi sarva-bhūtānām 131
aho bhāgyam aho bhāgyaṁ 199
āhuś ca te nalina- 133, 148
ākṛṣṭiḥ kṛta-cetasāṁ 245
amānī mānada hañā 60
āmā lañā punaḥ līlā 229
anarpita-carīṁ cirāt 110, 261, 291
anugrahāya bhaktānāṁ 232
anyābhilāṣitā-śūnyaṁ 64
anyera hṛdaya mana, 135, 149
āra dine jagannāthera 282
āśā-bharair amṛta-sindhu- 193
āsām aho caraṇa-reṇu 113, 217
asat-saṅga-tyāga, 55
ataeva kṛṣṇera prākaṭye 204
ataeva yāṅra mukhe 246
ataḥ śrī-kṛṣṇa-nāmādi 50
atha gopīr anujñāpya 280
atha punaḥ paryagin- 281
atyāhāraḥ prayāsaś ca ix, 58
avaśeṣe rādhā kṛṣṇe 228

B

bāhira ha-ite kare 195
balabhadraḥ kuru-śreṣṭha 280
barhāpīḍaṁ naṭa-vara- 289
bāulake kahiha, loka 287
bhogera samaya lokera 80

C

caitanya-gosāñira līlā 172

D

deha-smṛti nāhi yāra, 158
dhanyāḥ sma mūḍha- 30
dīkṣā-puraścaryā-vidhi 245

E

ei dhuyā-gāne nācena 279

ei-mata mahāprabhu 154
eka kṛṣṇa-nāme kare 245
eta sampatti chāḍi' 208
eta tāṅre kahi kṛṣṇa, 183

G

gaura yadi pāche 128
gopī-saṅge yata 203
gopyaś ca kṛṣṇam 130
grāmya-kathā nā 60
gṛhastha viṣayī āmi, 243

H

he nātha he ramā- 105
he rādhe vraja- 313

I

ihāṅ lokāraṇya, hātī, 229
ihāṅ rāja-veśa, saṅge 229
iti puṁsārpitā viṣṇau 177, 261

J

jagannāthe āni' dila 96
jagannāthera choṭa-baḍa 80
jāniyāo svarūpa gosāñi 288
jayati jana-nivāso 99
jayati te 'dhikaṁ 78, 82

K

kadambera eka vṛkṣe 251
krama kari' kahe prabhu 255
kṛṣṇa-nāma nirantara 253
kṛṣṇo 'nyo yadu- 216

M

mac-cittā mad-gata- 105
mayi bhaktir hi 138, 183
mora bhāgya mo-viṣaye, 181
mṛgayur iva kapīndraṁ 89

N

nāhaṁ tiṣṭhāmi vaikuṇṭhe 21
nāhaṁ vipro na ca 102
nahe gopī yogeśvara, 157
nānā-puṣpodyāne 195
na pāraye 'haṁ niravadya- 199
na prema-gandho 'sti 62
naumīḍya te 'bhra- 169
nija-vastre kaila 49
niṣiddhācāra kuṭīnāṭī 54
nivṛtta-tarṣair upagīyamānād 84

P

pariṣvaktaś cirotkaṇṭhair 281
prabhu kahe, yāṅra 245
prabhu kahe – yātrā- 202
prabhu kahena, – 'kṛṣṇa- 244
prāṇa-priye, śuna, 173
priyā priya-saṅga-hīnā, 175
priyaḥ so 'yaṁ kṛṣṇaḥ xii, 228, 286
puruṣottama-deva sei 95
pūrvavat kaila prabhu 283

R

raghu-nandana sevā 251
rākhite tomāra jīvana, 179
rathera upare kare 37

S

saba bhṛtya-gaṇa 37, 209
sādhu-saṅga, sādhu-saṅga 304
satāṁ prasaṅgān mama 68
sarva-dharmān parityajya 139
sei rājā jini' nila 95
sei satī premavatī, 175
sei śatru-gaṇa haite, 182
sei ta parāṇa-nātha vii, xi, 37, 104, 128, 129
śravaṇaṁ kīrtanaṁ 177, 231, 261
śrī-caitanya-mano-'bhīṣṭaṁ 178
śrī-guṇḍicā-mandiram 49
śrī-haste kareṇa 49
śrī-rūpa-raghunātha- 172
śrīvāsa hāsiyā kahe, 207
śriyaḥ kāntāḥ kāntaḥ 264
śṛṇvatāṁ sva-kathāḥ 83
strī-bāla-vṛddha-vanitā- 281
sukhera lāgiyā, 165
śuniyā rādhikā-vāṇī, 173
svarūpa kahe, – prema- 204
svarūpa kahe, – śrīvāsa, 210
svarūpa kahe – śuna, 197
śyāmasundara śikhaṇḍa-śekhara 297

T

tabe rāmānanda, āra 243
tabe śānta hañā 37
tan-nāma-rūpa-caritādi- 239
tāṅra bhakti-vaśe 95
tathāpi āmāra mana 229
tava kathāmṛtaṁ 78, 82
tomāra caraṇa mora 153
tomāra ṭhākura, dekha 208
tomāra ye prema-guṇa, 183
tomā-sabāra prema- 174
tri-bhaṅga-sundara 154
tṛṇād api sunīcena 46, 50, 54, 294
tuhuṅ se rahila madhupura 163

U

upāsanā lāgi' devera 288
utkalera rājā puruṣottama- 95

V

vāco vegaṁ manasaḥ ix, 57
vande nanda-vraja- 107, 112, 171, 217
veṇu-karān nipatitaḥ 29
vidagdha, mṛdu, sad-guṇa, 159
vikrīḍitaṁ vraja-vadhūbhir 232
vraje tomāra saṅge 229
vraja-vāsī yata jana, 174
vṛndāvana dekhibāre 221
vṛndāvana, govardhana, 159
vṛndāvana-līlāya kṛṣṇera 198
vṛndāvanaṁ parityajya 216
vṛndāvana-sama ei 195
vṛndāvane sāhajika 210
vṛndāvanera sampad dekha, 207

Y

yā te līlā-rasa- 154
yādavera vipakṣa, yata 181
yadyapi jagannātha 189
yaḥ kaumāra-haraḥ xi, 123, 227, 279

yāha bhāgavata paḍa 197
yāṅhāra darśane mukhe 255
yasya prasādād bhagavat- 180
yat karoṣi yad aśnāsi 65
yata bhakta kīrtanīyā 81
yat-kiṅkarīṣu bahuśaḥ 152, 292
ye yathā māṁ prapadyante 143
yo brahma-rudra-śuka- 168
yugāyitaṁ nimeṣeṇa 295

BOOK CATALOG 2003

Gauḍīya Vedānta Publications

Śrī Śrīmad Bhaktivedānta Nārāyaṇa Mahārāja

— and —

Śrī Śrīmad A.C. Bhaktivedānta Swami Prabhupāda

Jaiva-Dharma

The groundbreaking spiritual novel by Śrīla Bhaktivinoda Ṭhākura

Jaiva-dharma reveals the ultimate development of the path of pure devotion to the English-speaking world.

Hardbound, 5 x 7.5", 1077 pages, Bible paper, 8 color plates, glossaries of terms, indexes of quoted verses and general index. Code JDC $15.00

Śrīmad Bhagavad-Gītā

With extensive commentaries

This edition of *Bhagavad-gītā* contains two commentaries: the *Sārārtha-varṣiṇī Ṭīkā* by Śrīla Viśvanātha Cakravartī Ṭhākura and the *Sārārtha-varṣiṇī Prakāśikā-vṛtti* by Śrīla Bhaktivedānta Nārāyaṇa Mahārāja.

Hardbound, 5.5 x 8.5", 1120 pages, 12 color plates. Code SBG $15.00

Śrī Śrīmad Bhakti Prajñāna Keśava Gosvāmī

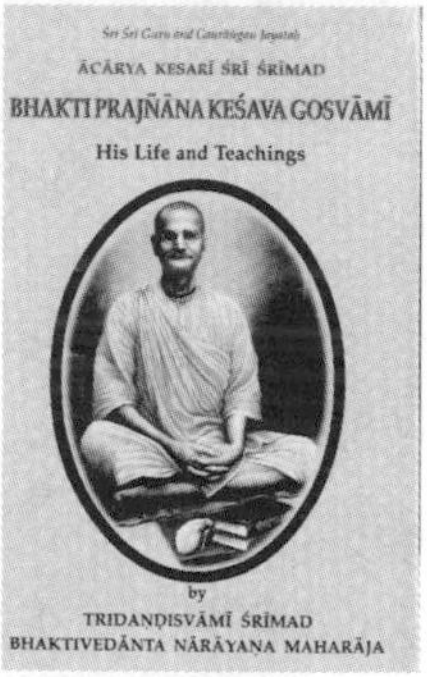

His Life and Teachings

A unique biography of a contemporary saint, the spiritual master of Śrīla Bhaktivedānta Nārāyaṇa Mahārāja and the *sannyāsa-guru* of Śrīla A.C. Bhaktivedānta Swami Prabhupāda.

Softbound, 5.5 x 8.5", 580 pages, 22 color illustrations. Code PKGB $15.00

Pinnacle of Devotion

An introduction to the most powerful yoga system

We all have a tendency to love, and no one can live without loving someone. The problem is, however, where to place our love.

Hardbound, 5.5 x 8.5", 200 pages. Code POD $10.00

Veṇu-Gīta

Tenth Canto, Chapter 21 of Śrīmad-Bhāgavatam

"By just hearing that flute-song that attracts the hearts of the whole universe, Sanaka and Sanandana and other *ātmārāma munis* became overwhelmed with joy and lost consciousness."

Softbound, 5.5 x 8.5", 188 pages, 8 color illustrations. Code VG $10.00

Bhakti-rasāmṛta-sindhu-bindu

A drop of the nectarean ocean of bhakti-rasa

This book is Viśvanātha Cakravartī Ṭhākura's summary of Śrīla Rūpa Gosvāmī's classic *Bhakti-rasāmṛta-sindhu* (*Nectar of Devotion*).

Softbound, 6 x 9", 305 pages, numerous diagrams. Code BRSB $8.00

Śrī Bhajana-rahasya

Deep analysis of the Hare Kṛṣṇa mahā-mantra

This revolutionary work by Śrīla Bhaktivinoda Ṭhākura presents an astounding analysis of the Hare Kṛṣṇa *mantra*, based on the eight verses of *Śrī Śikṣāṣṭakam*, covering all stages of *bhakti*.

Softbound, 5.5 x 8.5", 497 pages, 4 color plates. Code SBR $10.00

The Origin of Ratha-yātrā

The world's most ancient religious festival

Lectures by Śrīla Bhaktivedānta Nārāyaṇa Mahārāja on the Ratha-yātrā, or the Cart Festival of Lord Jagannātha.

Softbound, 5.5 x 8.5", 372 pages, 8 color plates. Code ORY $10.00

Śrī Brahma-saṁhitā

Lord Brahmā's prayers of devotion to Kṛṣṇa

These prayers offered at the dawn of creation by Brahmā, the secondary creator of the universe, contain all the essential truths of Vaiṣṇava philosophy.

Softbound, 5.5 x 8.5", 452 pages. Code SBS $10.00

Śrī Gauḍīya Gīti-guccha

An unprecedented collection of devotional songs

Sanskrit, Bengali and Hindi devotional poems, prayers, songs and *bhajanas* written by the Gauḍīya Vaiṣṇava *ācāryas* and compiled for the practicing devotee.

Spiral bound, 6 x 9", 224 pages.
Code GGG $10.00

Śrī Manaḥ-śikṣā

Instructions to the mind by
Śrīla Raghunātha dāsa Gosvāmī

Śrī Manaḥ-śikṣā consists of twelve verses composed by Raghunātha dāsa Gosvāmī that instruct the mind on how to make progress on the path of *bhajana*.

Softbound, 5.5 x 8.5", 153 pages. Code SMS $5.00

Jaiva-dharma, Part One

Part one of a spiritual novel by
Śrīla Bhaktivinoda Ṭhākura

"Out of all the books of Śrīla Ṭhākura Bhaktivinoda, *Jaiva-dharma* is considered to be the quintessence by religious thinkers of different countries."
– Śrīla Nārāyaṇa Mahārāja

Softbound, 5.5 x 8.5", 288 pages, 10 color illustrations.
Code JD1 $5.00

Secret Truths of the Bhāgavatam

Discourses on Śrīmad-Bhāgavatam

A series of lectures by Śrīla Nārāyaṇa Mahārāja at the New Vraja community in Badger, California, in June 1999.

Softbound, 5.5 x 8.5", 192 pages, 16 color illustrations. Code STB $5.00

Bhakti-tattva-viveka

The true nature of devotion

Śrīla Bhaktivinoda Ṭhākura has presented the grave and deep conclusions of devotional service, pure *bhakti*, in simple language that is accessible to any sincere reader.

Softbound, 5.5 x 8.5", 112 pages. Code BTV $4.00

Rays of Hope

A compilation of divine discourses, 1996–99

"The real connection with *guru* is through *bhāgavata-paramparā*. Even if one is not initiated by him in *guru-paramparā*, such a qualified disciple has understood his *guru's* mood."
– Śrīla Nārāyaṇa Mahārāja

Softbound, 5.5 x 8.5", 192 pages, 18 color photos and numerous illustrations. Code ROH $5.00

My Śikṣā-guru & Priya-bandhu

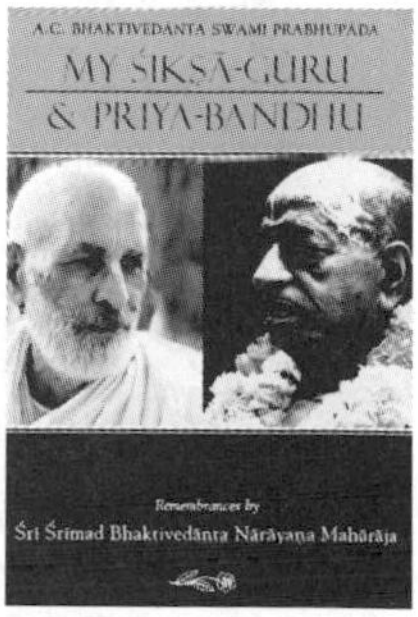

Remembrances by Śrīla Bhaktivedānta Nārāyaṇa Mahārāja

A deep and revealing account of the intimate relationship between Śrīla Bhaktivedānta Nārāyaṇa Mahārāja and his instructing spiritual master and dear friend, Śrīla A.C. Bhaktivedānta Swami Prabhupāda, from 1947 up until final instructions given in 1977.

Softbound, 5.5 x 8.5", 49 pages. Code SGPB $2.00

Their Lasting Relation

An Historical Account

A detailed and nectarean account of Śrīla A.C. Bhaktivedānta Swami Prabhupāda's long-standing relationship with both his *sannyāsa-guru*, Śrīla Bhakti Prajñāna Keśava Gosvāmī, and Śrīla Bhaktivedānta Nārāyaṇa Mahārāja.

Softbound, 5.5 x 8.5", 49 pages. Code TLR $2.00

Guru-Devatātmā

Accepting Śrī Guru as One's Life and Soul

Śrīla Bhaktivedānta Nārāyaṇa Mahārāja speaks on the importance of accepting a bona fide *guru*, who is more dear than life itself, the absolute necessity of second initiation, and other topics of *guru-tattva*.

Softbound, 5.5 x 8.5", 52 pages. Code GD $2.00

Our Gurus: One in Siddhānta, One in Heart

Clearing up the confusion

Nowadays some persons claim there are differences in the conclusions taught by Śrīla Bhaktivedānta Nārāyaṇa Mahārāja and Śrīla A.C. Bhaktivedānta Swami Prabhupāda. These authoritative responses to many of the objections will help the reader understand things as they are, without any politically motivated interpretation.

Softbound, 5.5 x 8.5", 61 pages. Code OIS $2.00

Śrī Hari-Nāma Mahā-Mantra

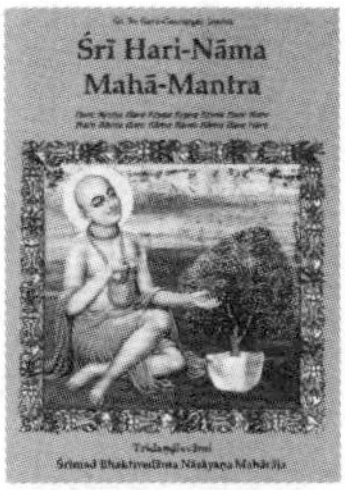

The transcendental holy name of the Lord

"When a qualified person chants *harināma*, this light diffuses, thus keeping the darkness of illusion away from the soul."

Softbound, 5.5 x 8.5", 64 pages. Code SHN $2.00

Happiness in a Fool's Paradise

The futility of material enjoyment

"Everyone wants to be happy, but generally we can find only a little happiness and affection in this world."

Softbound, 5.5 x 8.5", 32 pages, 6 color illustrations.
Code HFP $2.00

To Be Controlled By Love

The guru–disciple relationship

"Even Kṛṣṇa, the Supreme Personality of Godhead, wants to be controlled by love and affection."
– Śrīla Nārāyaṇa Mahārāja

Softbound, 5.5 x 8.5", 32 pages. Code CBL $2.00

The Butter Thief

The true nature of devotion

This book describes Kṛṣṇa's sweet childhood pastimes, in which He plays with Mother Yaśodā as an ordinary child.

Softbound, 5.5 x 8.5", 64 pages, 8 color illustrations.
Code TBT $2.00

The Essence of Bhagavad-gītā

Absorbing the mind in Śrī Kṛṣṇa

"Absorb your mind and heart in Me, become My devotee, worship Me, offer your obeisances to Me, and certainly you will come to Me."

Softbound, 5.5 x 8.5", 32 pages, 4 color illustrations.
Code EBG $2.00

Books by Śrīla A.C. Bhaktivedānta Swami Prabhupāda

These special editions are the authorized and approved versions, with the artwork and format specially designed by Śrīla Prabhupāda for introducing the Western world to Kṛṣṇa consciousness. Not one word or picture has been changed from Śrīla Prabhupāda's original version.

Kṛṣṇa: The Supreme Personality of Godhead

Who is Kṛṣṇa?

Śrīla Prabhupāda's summary of the entire Tenth Canto of *Śrīmad-Bhāgavatam*

Volume 1: hardbound, 7.5 x 10.5", 425 pages, 84 plates. Code KB1 $15.00
Volume 2: hardbound, 7.5 x 10.5", 400 pages, 24 plates. Code KB2 $15.00

Bhagavad-gītā As It Is

The most beloved of all Vedic literatures

Reprint of the historic original, authorized and approved 1972 Macmillan Complete Edition, with the original Sanskrit text, Roman transliteration, English synonyms, translation and elaborate purports.

Hardbound, 6.25 x 9.25", 1000 pages, 40 color illustrations. Code BG $15.00

Teachings of Lord Caitanya

The Golden Avatar

Lord Caitanya Mahāprabhu appeared in Bengal, India, in 1486, and began a revolution in spiritual consciousness that has profoundly affected the lives of millions.

Hardbound, 440 pages, many original color illustrations. Code TLC $15.00

Kṛṣṇa, the Reservoir of Pleasure

Eternal enjoyment through transcendental sound

"Kṛṣṇa – this sound is transcendental. Kṛṣṇa means the highest pleasure. All of us, every living being, seeks pleasure. But we do not know how to seek pleasure perfectly." – Śrīla Prabhupāda

Softbound, 5.5 x 8.5", 32 pages. Code ROP $1.00

The Perfection of Yoga

"There have been many *yoga* systems popularized in the Western world, especially in this century, but none of them have actually taught the perfection of *yoga*." The original, authorized and approved version.

Softbound, 4 x 7", 56 pages, 8 color plates.
Code POY $2.00

U.S. Regional Book Distributors

Northwest (Seattle)

Mark Haines
11321 74th Ave. E
Puyallup, WA 98373
Attn: Maitreya Muni Prabhu
Phone: (866) HARIBOL (427-4265)
Email: maitreyamuni@yahoo.com

California Northern (Berkeley)

Westside & Company
5659 Telegraph Ave. #D
Berkeley, CA 94609
Attn: Kavidatta & Kṛtakarma Prabhus
Phone: (510) 655-5018, 883-0736
Email: kavidatta2000@yahoo.com

California Central (Badger)

Mt. Kailāsa Foundation
PO Box 99
Badger, CA 93603
Attn: Nanda-gopāla Prabhu
Phone: (559) 337-2448
Email: nandagopal@gaudiya.net

California Southern (Los Angeles)

IGVS
111 Dudley Ave
Venice, CA 90291
Attn: Jaga-mohana Prabhu
Phone: (310) 450-5371
Email: purebhakti@hotmail.com

California Southern (San Diego)

Padayatra America
PO Box 2179
La Jolla, CA 92038
Attn: Jayanta Prabhu
Phone: (858) 518-5209
Email: jayantadasa@yahoo.com

South (Houston)

IGVS - Houston
16119 Abergreen Trail
Houston, TX 77095
Attn: Kṛṣṇa dāsa Prabhu
Phone: (281) 550-2940
Email: kris4basics@hotmail.com

Eastern (Washington DC)

Rupa Raghunath Gaudiya Math
6925 Willow St. NW
Washington, DC 20012
Attn: Vamsivadana & Mukunda
Phone: (301) 864-3354
Email: ruparaghunatha@hotmail.com

Southeast (North Carolina)

Maria Christopher
4619 Timberwood Terr.
Efland, NC 27243
Attn: Rāma dāsa Prabhu
Phone: (919) 563-9464
Email: ramdas@mebtel.net

South (Florida)

Acolapissa Foundation
PO Box 1689
Alachua, FL 32616-1689
Attn: Bhāgavata Prabhu
(386) 418-2046 (800) 814-7316 Ext. 00
Email: Bhagavatdasa@msn.com

International Book Distributors

Canada - Western (Vancouver)

Stanley A. Gill
#25 - 15030 58th Ave.
Surrey, B.C. CANADA V3S 9G3
Attn: Prasasya Prabhu
Phone: (866) 575-9438
Email: stannshel@shaw.ca

Europe - UK (England)

Gour Govinda Gaudiya Math
32 Handsworth Wood Rd.
Birmingham B20 2DS, UK
Attn: Jīva-pāvana Prabhu
Phone: (44) 121 682 9159
Email: gourgovinda@hotmail.com

International Spanish Distributors

Vedic Cultural Association
1002 S. Austin St.
Santa Ana, CA 92704 USA
Attn: Haridāsa Prabhu
Phone: (714) 775-8760
Email: hsalas1@prodigy.net

For information on becoming a distributor in your area: e-mail vd@regalgift.com or isani@mail.com, or call Niścintya at 310-837-3518

Book Order Form

Book Code	Price each	Copies	Subtotal
	$		$
	$		$
	$		$
	$		$
	$		$
	$		$
	$		$
	$		$
	$		$
	$		$

Books Total $ ____________

Add 10% Shipping + $3 Handling $ ____________

Ship to:

Grand Total: $ ____________

Name ____

Address ____

____

Telephone____

Email ____

Instructions: Fill in the book codes of the books you want to order, the price each, and the total number of copies you want. **Calculate the Grand Total and mail this form and a check or money order to the Regional Distributor nearest to you (listed on the previous page). Make your check or money order payable to the name listed in bold type.** Please allow two weeks for delivery—more for international orders.

CENTERS AROUND THE WORLD

AUSTRALIA • **Murwillumbah** • Sri Giriraja Govardhan Gaudiya Matha • 56 Brisbane Street • Murwillumbah N.S.W 2482 ☎ +61 66-728499 ✉ lilasuka@bigpond.com •
GERMANY • **Berlin** • Gaudiya Vedanta Samiti Berlin • Emserstrasse 70 • 12051 Berlin ☎ +49 30 62 00 87 47 ✉ gvsberlin@yahoo.com •
INDIA • **Mathura** • Sri Keshavaji Gaudiya Matha • Opp. Dist. Hospital • Jawahar Hata • Mathura (U.P.) 281001 ☎ +91 565 250-2334 ✉ mathuramath@gaudiya.net ♦ **Navadwipa** • Sri Devananda Gaudiya Matha • Tegharipada, PO Navadwipa, D/O Nadiya, West Bengal ☎ +91 343 240-068 ♦ **New Delhi** • Sri Ramanvihari Gaudiya Math • OCF pocket, Block B-3, near musical fountain park • Janakpuri, New Delhi ☎ +91 11 2553-3568 ☎ +91 11 3230-2159 ♦ **Vrindavan** • Sri Rupa-Sanatana Gaudiya Matha • Danagali, Vrindavana U.P. ☎ +91 565 244-3270 •
INDONESIA • **Bali** • Ananta Gaudiya Math • Br. Juntal, Desa Kaba-Kaba • Kediri, Tabanan • Bali, Indonesia ☎ +62 361 830986 ☎ +62 361 830987 •
NETHERLANDS • **Rotterdam** • Preaching Center Rotterdam • 1e Pijnackerstraat 98 • 3035GV Rotterdam ☎ +31 010-2650405 ✉ sanga@worldmail.nl •
NEW ZEALAND • **Auckland** • Hare Krishna Vegetarian Restaurant • 214 Karangahape Road • Auckland ☎ +64 9 303-1560 ♦ **Wellington** • IGVS Wellington • 22 Wrights Hill Road • Karori, Wellington ☎ +64 4 476-6784 ✉ benhc@hotmail.com ♦ **Kati Kati & Whangamata** • IGVS Bay of Plenty • Kati Kati & Whangamata ☎ +64 7 552-0073 ✉ bhadradasi@hotmail.com •
PHILIPPINES • **Manila** • International Gaudiya Vedanta Society of the Philippines • Radha Krsna Gopala Mandir • 96 ROTC Hunters Clusters 23 Tatalon • Quezon City, Metro Manila 1113 ☎ +63 2783 0267 ☎ +63 91873-32659 ✉ jaipur_art@mailcity.com •
UNITED KINGDOM • **Birmingham** • Sri Gour Govinda Gaudiya Matha • 32 Handsworth Wood Road • Birmingham, B20 2DS ☎ +44 121 682 9159 ✉ gourgovinda@hotmail.com •
USA • **Los Angeles** • Sri Sri Radha-Govinda Gaudiya Math • 111 Dudley Ave. • Venice, CA 90291 ☎ +1 310-450-5371 ✉ purebhakti@hotmail.com ♦ **Miami** • Institute for Gaudiya Vaishnavism • 934 N. University Drive, #102 • Coral Springs, FL 33071 ☎ +1 754-245-2345 ✉ Mbuddhi@cs.com ♦ Sri Gaudiya Vedanta Samiti of South Florida • 701 N.W. 16th Ave. • Pompano Beach, FL 33069 ☎ +1 954-344-5404 ✉ alankar@adelphia.net ♦ **New York** • The Bhaktivedanta Gaudiya Matha • 134-06 95th Ave. • South Richmond Hill, NY 11419 ☎ +1 718-526-9835 ✉ unclepuru108@yahoo.com ♦ **Washington, DC** • Rupa Raghunath Gaudiya Math • 6925 Willow Ave. NW • Washington, DC 20012 ☎ +1 301-864-3354 ✉ ruparaghunatha@hotmail.com •
VENEZUELA • Sri Venezuela Kesavaji Gaudiya Math and Gaudiya Vedanta Publications (spanish) • Carrera 17, entre calles 50-51 • #50-47, Barquisimeto • Edo. Lara ☎ +58 51-452574 ✉ janardana@postmark.net

For more information please visit the following web sites: **www.gaudiya.net** and **www.purebhakti.com**